PREVIOUS The magic of the still: producing great whisky for hundreds of years (here at Glenfiddich).
THIS PAGE Across the world hundreds of thousands of casks are being filled with whisky spirit (here at Glenmorangie).
OVERLEAF Nature and whisky making are ideal partners in regions such as Scotland's Speyside (here at Balblair).

THE WORLD'S BEST WHISKIES

750 UNMISSABLE DRAMS FROM TAIN TO TOKYO

DOMINIC ROSKROW

jacqui small

First published in 2018 by
Jacqui Small for White Lion Publishing
An imprint of the Quarto Group
The Old Brewery, 6 Blundell Street
London, N7 9BH, United Kingdom

T (0)20 7700 6700 F (0)20 7700 8066

*This book is dedicated to friends, family
and whisky drinkers everywhere.*

Publisher Jacqui Small

Editorial Direction Joanna Copestick

Editor Hilary Lumsden

Designer Robin Rout

Project Editor & Picture Editor Joe Hallsworth

Production Maeve Healy

British Library Cataloguing-in-Publication Data
A catalogue record for this book is available from the British Library.

ISBN 978-1-911127-60-4

Printed and bound in China.

2020 2019 2018

10 9 8 7 6 5 4 3 2 1

CONTENTS

6   Introduction
8   Adventures with whisky
10   The story of whisky
12   Making whisky
14   The role of peat and oak
16   How to make single-malt whisky
18   How to make blended whisky
20   How to make bourbon

22   WHISKY BASICS
24   Tasting whisky
26   Flavour categories
28   The art of drinking whisky
30   Whisky styles
32   Whisky cocktails
34   Classic whisky cocktails
36   Modern whisky cocktails

38   A WORLD OF WHISKY
40   A world of whisky
42   Making the selection
43   Tasting symbols
44   The face of modern whisky

46   SCOTLAND
48   Introduction
50   Single malt
52   Distillery profile: Aberlour
56   Distillery profile: Ardbeg
70   Distillery profile: Bruichladdich
82   Distillery profile: Glenfarclas
86   Distillery profile: Glenfiddich
90   Distillery profile: Glen Garioch
94   Distillery profile: The Glenlivet
98   Distillery profile: Glenmorangie
104 Distillery profile: Highland Park
108 Distillery profile: Lagavulin
112 Distillery profile: Laphroaig
124 Distillery profile: Talisker
126 Distiller profile: Rachel Barrie
130 Blended whisky
142 Distiller profile: Ronnie Cox
144 Blended malt
148 Distiller profile: John Glaser
151 Grain whisky

152 USA & CANADA
154 USA introduction
157 Bourbon
158 Distillery profile: Balcones
162 Distillery profile: Buffalo Trace

168 Distillery profile: Heaven Hill
170 Distillery profile: Jim Beam
174 Distillery profile: Maker's Mark
180 Distillery profile: Wild Turkey
182 Distiller profile: Allison Parc
184 Tennessee whiskey
186 Distillery profile: Woodford Reserve
188 Rye whiskey
190 Distillery profile: Corsair
194 Corn whiskey
195 Wheat whiskey
196 American single malt
198 Other American whiskey
200 Canada introduction
201 Canadian single malt
202 Canadian blended whisky

204 IRELAND
206 Introduction
208 Irish single malt
210 Distillery profile: Bushmills
212 Irish blended whiskey
216 Distillery profile: Teeling
220 Distillery profile: Walsh

222 JAPAN
224 Introduction
225 Japanese single malt
226 Distillery profile: Chichibu
230 Distillery profile: Nikka
233 Japanese blended whisky
234 Distillery profile: Suntory
237 Japanese blended malt

238 NEW WORLD
240 Introduction
242 Profile: Australian distilleries
248 Profile: Alpine distilleries
254 Distillery profile: Stauning *Denmark*
258 Distillery profile: Warenghem *France*
262 Distillery profile: John Distilleries *India*
266 Profile: The rise and rise of Swedish whisky
272 Distillery profile: Mackmyra *Sweden*
276 Distillery profile: Kavalan *Taiwan*

278 Independent bottlers

280 Whisky directory
282 Whisky index
287 General index
288 Acknowledgements

ADVENTURES WITH WHISKY

It's nearly impossible to over-estimate how much the world of whisky has changed since 2010. It has grown immeasurably. and continues to evolve on a weekly basis.

Most of what made the world of whisky what it was in 2010 is still there; all the traditional distilleries are still working, and in most cases, thriving. The classic whiskies are still to be found on the shop shelves. Whisky enthusiasts still flock to auctions or specialist online sites in order to find rare whiskies on the secondary market. But, today everything feels different, and that's because it is.

Turn the clock back and the world of whisky was effectively an elitist club, one dominated by ageing men. In the main it was consumed after dinner, after a round of golf, or, in some markets, as a chaser after a nice beer. Drinking whisky wasn't exactly frowned upon, but nor was it feted.

In just one decade whisky has grown and evolved. Men still drink whisky after dinner, but today younger trendsetters partake, too. You'll still see men at the 19th hole sipping whisky, but an increasing number of women choose it as well. Scotland and Ireland remain important, but an increasing number of people are dabbling with whiskies from India, and also Taiwan. The Jims and Jacks remain huge, but a new wave of craft distillers are spreading out across the world. So how has this happened?

Firstly, whisky got fashionable. It not only came in from the cold but it headed straight for the centre of the bar and it hasn't moved since. Whisky started to chime with the times. Drinking less but better became a thing, consumers looking for provenance and heritage found it aplenty on whisky shelves, and a new generation of whisky drinkers discovered it – and each other – through social media. Twenty-something-year-old bloggers turned the world of whisky on its head.

But, if consumer attitudes changed, then the physical world of whisky changed even more. Across the world, new craft distilleries have been built and are making whisky. The first wave of new distillers are now bottling expressions with ages in double digits, many many more have only bottled their first spirit in the last four or five years, and yet more are just beginning out on their journey.

Updating this book for a second edition has been fascinating. Some of the great characters have retired, sold up and moved on, or died. Distilleries have been expanded or have changed hands, and whisky companies have grown bigger or merged. New whisky styles have appeared on the market, and whisky now attracts a younger clientele, and many more women.

There has been a more profound shift since 2010, too. Where once there were perhaps 150 distilleries of any note across the world, with 100 of them in Scotland, now that figure is closer to 1000, with up to 150 of them in Scotland. Countries such as Sweden and Australia have grown from fledgling whisky-producing countries to countries with a wide range of excellent whiskies, countries as diverse as England, the Netherlands, Taiwan and India are capable of matching many of the malts from the traditional whisky nations. While in the United States, the likes of Balcones, Corsair and Westland are offering strong and tasty alternatives to the Jim Beams and Jack Daniel's.

That has presented its own set of problems. This book celebrates the best 750 whiskies widely available. To include any of the new whiskies has meant having to remove whiskies that once made the cut. In some cases there has been a natural cull, as rarer whiskies in the first edition have all but disappeared now. However, that left some tough decisions.

Many of the new whiskies such as those from Kavalan and Spirit of Hven, are featured here. Many others – and there are scores of them – narrowly missed out, even though they are very good and will only get better.

In the end, the winner is you. There is more great whisky out there than ever. It's been some ride since 2010, and it ain't over yet. Hopefully, though, this new edition of *The World's Best Whiskies* has captured some of the excitement that is modern whisky. Strap yourself in and enjoy the ride.

THE STORY OF WHISKY

Pinpointing when whisky distilling began is like trying to spot shining pebbles in the murky depths of Scotland's Loch Lomond.

History points us to the Far East, Middle East and Northern Africa. The earliest stills were found in Taxila in Pakistan and in Cyprus, while there is some evidence that distillation was used in these regions for medicine and perfume. We know, too, that a heavy form of beer was fermented in Mesopotamia, in the region now covered by Iran and Iraq. Quite when grain-distilled drink was first consumed for pleasure is lost in time. I like to think, though, that an Irish priest stumbled upon it and, being Irish, didn't bother waiting to be ill to start to appreciate its redemptive qualities.

Clues to whisky's origins are all here, though. Much of the language of drink is derived from Arabic, for instance, including the word 'alcohol'. The link between distilled drink and distilled medicine is borne out by the large number of drinking toasts that refer to good health and happiness.

And, of course, the church has had a long and fruitful relationship with alcoholic beverages. It is highly likely that priests brought the techniques of brewing and distilling back first to Ireland and then to the west of Scotland. The monasteries became thriving centres for beer and spirits production. Monks and priests were among the few sectors of society able to flee from the ravages of the Black Death, taking their distilling skills with them further afield. When Henry VIII consigned many of them to the dole queue by decommissioning their places of worship, many of them changed careers and became brewers and distillers instead. So thanks Henry – not great on the women front, but on the plus side a big help for the British drinks trade.

The Irish make many claims when it comes to whisk(e)y, but claiming to have brought grain spirit to Scotland is probably among the more credible ones. Ireland can also boast the world's oldest licensed distillery in Bushmills, which was registered in 1608, and Irish whiskey, the choice tipple of the nobility, was established on the high table of gentry long before its Scottish counterpart. Scotch whisky, meanwhile, rapidly gained a foothold among the tenant farmers and landed masses of Scotland as both a libation and a currency, with communities

trading it for clothes and shoes with travelling salesmen. That in turn attracted the attention of the authorities, who quickly saw a chance to make money through taxation, and so began a cat-and-mouse game of tax avoidance between the governments in Edinburgh and London and local Scottish communities who saw it as a patriotic duty to avoid paying the tax.

One of the driving forces behind the Jacobite uprisings of the seventeenth and eighteenth centuries was a campaign against malt tax. When those uprisings finally ended in defeat for the Jacobites and the brutal slaughter of Culloden in 1746 and in the ensuing Highland Clearances that drove crofters from their lands, many Scots took their distilling skills to the furthest corners of the world. In the United States, they were joined by Europeans such as Johannes 'Jacob' Beam, by Irishmen, and by Welshmen forced from their homeland by the Temperance Movement. Among them were Kentucky's Evan Williams and the Scottish and Welsh grandparents of Jack Daniel of Tennessee whiskey fame.

Scotch whisky's journey to the drinks cabinets of first England, then the Empire and finally the world was to be defined by a remarkable 50-year period between 1825 and 1875. The basic foundations had already been laid in the decades beforehand, with the start of the Industrial Revolution and the technological advances that came with it. The Industrial Revolution brought railways to Scotland, and with them the means and fuels for greater and better quality production. Highland whiskies began to be smuggled to the pubs and drinking houses of Edinburgh and Glasgow, and their reputation rapidly spread well beyond these environs.

Three events would promote Scotland to the position of world leader in whisky. First, whisky makers in Scotland and the authorities called a truce in their taxes battle, reaching a compromise. From 1823, distillers began to turn their trade in to a legal one, providing quality malt.

Secondly, Scotsman Robert Stein developed a completely new way of distilling grain in a continuous process. The system would be improved

upon by Irishman Aeneas Coffey, but the new column-still process was eschewed by the Irish while being gleefully seized upon by the Scots, who found that when coupled with their rough malts it made for a smoother, easier-to-drink style of whisky.

Finally, Scotland's whiskies were to benefit massively from a disaster that struck across Europe in 1860. A destructive aphid by the name of *Phylloxera vastatrix* began a 15-year feeding frenzy that was to wipe out the vineyards of France and beyond, destroying the wine and brandy industry in the process. Scotch was ready and willing to take brandy's place.

It has never looked back. Scotch whisky reinforced its new status in the twentieth century, finding its way to the Prohibition-era speakeasies of the United States and into the affections of American servicemen stationed in Great Britain during World War II.

Irish whiskey, on the other hand, went through a rapid decline in the second half of the twentieth century, but is now enjoying a remarkable

resurrection as emerging craft distillers bring new whiskeys to the market.

In fact, this is now a worldwide trend and America in particular is in the middle of a craft-distilling revolution, as hundreds of new micro-distillers bring innovation to the world of whisky. Japanese whisky is much in demand and enjoys iconic status, and Canada has emerged from years of slumber with some world-class whisky releases. And across the world, from Iceland to Australia, and Taiwan to Argentina, new distillers are contributing to a dynamic and rapidly evolving whisky world. Best of all, blue-sky thinking is helping to evolve the category and bring new drinkers to it.

Whisky already has a proud and glorious history to point to, but it's clear that the story has only just begun. The history of this great drink is being written by the day.

ABOVE The introduction of the steamer opened up northern markets to bourbon producers.

MAKING WHISKY

Water, malted barley and yeast are the holy trinity of whisky – three ingredients that are bland individuals, yet their whole is very much greater than the sum of their parts. They are to the world of drinks what certain household items are to homemade explosives: innocuous until combined by an expert into a combustible mix. So what role do they play?

WATER

If you have visited a distillery pretty much anywhere in the world, you have undoubtedly sat through one of those cutesy documentaries where clichéd local folk music accompanies pictures of gurgling brooks and vast waterways, and a portentous über-voice melodramatically explains how centuries of evolution and geology have combined to provide the perfect water for producing the distillery's liquid gold.

These movies can be unintentionally hilarious. In one, made by a Scottish island distillery, the celebrity actor hired to narrate the distillery's story looked positively ill as he concluded his dramatic speech and sipped at his dram. It turned out that midway through filming he had suddenly discovered he had an allergy to malt whisky and was violently ill on set. Rather than dispense with his services, the film-makers carried on, replacing his dram with a glass of cold tea. It didn't stop him looking dreadful though.

But we digress. These movies, as well as occasionally being awful, may also be guilty of being economical with the truth. Much store is put on the importance of water. Distillery owners sometimes go to extreme lengths to protect their sources by buying up neighbouring land, and undoubtedly the bond between pure, clean water and the resulting malt spirit is an important one. The source of water has long been held in reverence and many claims have been made for it. And to some extent the facts support the romance: soft water, with low mineral content, may help the malting process and make for better absorption of water by the grain and therefore result in higher-yielding barley. Undoubtedly the peaty journey experienced by water on Islay, in particular, influences the island's malt.

But the science works against the argument, too. Many would maintain that the nature of distillation is such that the influences of the water are all but removed. And, if they aren't, then how is it that some

distillers – although they don't like to shout about it – have used treated and chlorinated water in their production process on occasion, and yet have continued to make great whisky?

Most of Scotland's water is soft, and the country's distillers understandably argue that this is a key factor in the excellence of Scottish single malt. But there is an argument, too, that nutrients and minerals feed yeast and therefore aid fermentation. Single malt whisky is successfully made in other countries, including Wales and England, where the water is hard. Also, when it comes to brewing, the best British source is considered to be around Burton-on-Trent, in Staffordshire, where the water is rich in minerals.

The waters of Kentucky in the United States are deemed essential to the bourbon-making process because they contain calcium – the same reason that the state produces strong-limbed thoroughbred racehorses. And while it is true that you can count on one hand the distilleries in Scotland that use hard water, on that shortlist are true heavyweights Highland Park and Glenmorangie. How does that work?

Moreover, water can be, and is, treated these days to be whatever it needs to be. Some argue that mashing, fermenting and finally distilling mean that the difference between soft and hard water in the end flavour is negligible.

That's not to say water is not important, of course it is. Pure water – water free of micro-organisms – is crucial to ensuring that the rest of the process passes off correctly.

But today, in the twenty-first century, the most important factor governing water source isn't whether it is hard or soft, or whether it contains certain minerals or not, or even whether it passes through flavour-imparting peat beds. No, the most important factors governing water are that there is plenty of it and that it is of sufficiently cool temperature.

In recent years, climate change certainly seems to have made its mark on whisky production. In Scotland, for instance, there have been an alarming number of instances where water shortages have forced distilleries to stop production. The picture is far from predictable, however. After a series of mild winters in Scotland that saw water levels as low in April as they would usually be in September, the winters of 2007–2010 were all exceptional for their long and deep snowfalls.

A further problem stems from the generally warmer climate. If water isn't cool enough for condensing, it means either longer closed seasons for distilleries or an investment in expensive cooling equipment.

BARLEY

Barley is nature's answer to Doctor Who's Tardis – a simple telephone box on the outside, a complex giant engine room within. It has been part of brewing and distilling history for centuries, a durable grain capable of growing on harsh, infertile terrain, seemingly the simplest of grains, loved and cherished by generations of folk living off the land since medieval times. But science has caught up with barley, and on a regular basis laboratories create a new strain that moves the goal posts when it comes to yield. Some argue that higher-yielding barley produces barley that results in a sacrifice of flavour and some distillers stay loyal to particular barley strains, but attempts to stem the tide of commercialism will ultimately prove fruitless. Macallan and Glengoyne, for instance, both extolled the qualities of Golden Promise and chose it despite its relatively low yields. In 2009, Golden Promise ceased to exist.

Some argue that, as long as barley meets certain production criteria, it does not matter where it comes from. Others contend fiercely that provenance of the barley is of crucial importance. Some take the default position that while Scottish barley is ideally best for making Scottish whisky, the practical realities are that there is not enough of it. Certainly a fair proportion of barley used in Scotch whisky production is imported, particularly from the east of England.

And nothing makes a distiller pale quicker than when a Scottish National Party (SNP) politician calls for Scotch whisky to be made with only home-produced ingredients.

YEAST

Yeast is the great unknown in whisky, rarely talked or written about, or fully understood. A living micro-organism, yeast can lay for years in a dormant state, but in the right wet and warm conditions and with the right food – sugar – it will multiply rapidly, feed ravenously and produce carbon dioxide and alcohol. This fermentation process can be an impressively aggressive and violent one, and can make a huge and sturdy washback (fermentation vessel) rock with the force.

Thousands of yeasts occur naturally, which is why some fermentation can take place without any yeast being added, and when a successful strain is created artificially it must be stored carefully to avoid contamination. Exactly what effect yeast has on flavour is the subject of fierce debate and the degree of attention given to yeast production varies from one distiller to another. Most yeasts used in whisky production are a combination of brewers' yeasts and yeasts created in the lab, and in some cases – particularly in the United States – brewers and distillers fiercely guard details about the exact nature of their yeasts.

ABOVE Barley being turned in a traditional floor maltings. Barley malted in this way, on a wooden floor, is said to provide better flavour for whisky.

THE ROLE OF PEAT AND OAK

Single-malt whisky may be made only with malted barley, yeast and water. Apart from supposedly flavourless caramel for colouring, nothing else may be added. That said, though, there are two other major influences on the flavour of a single malt – peat and oak – and for a full appreciation of single malt it is essential to understand their role in the overall flavour of the finished whisky.

PEAT

Peat is made up of decaying vegetation and grasses that has formed over centuries in boggy and wet marshland areas. It has been used as a burning fuel in communities across the world for centuries. In Scotland, in particular, peat has played a central role in the drying of barley for Scotch whisky making. When the Industrial Revolution brought trains and they in turn carried coal across the country, many distilleries abandoned peat as a fuel, but it remained in use in the islands – and it is on the islands that it is still most widely used today.

Most of the big phenolic, smoky-flavoured whiskies derive their taste from this process, and not from the water that has travelled through peat bogs. Peat in Scotland is graded into three categories. The deepest layer looks like dark-chocolate fudge cake when it is wet, and dries in to a hard fuel that resembles coal and burns slowly. The top layer, made up of the least decayed or suppressed vegetation, crumbles in the hand when dry and burns rapidly, but produces high quantities of peat smoke. The three layers are cut from the ground in spring and dried naturally during the summer, before being collected in the autumn; Highland Park on Orkney will cut just enough peat to see it through the ensuing year.

Peat differs from place to place because it is made up of vegetation. This is significant because the vegetation in a country such as Australia will be vastly different than that found in Scotland, so while the raw ingredients would seem to be the same they have different effects on the whisky. In Sweden, some of the peat was submerged under the Baltic Sea at one time, and is therefore very salty. Furthermore, the rules governing malt whisky production do not dictate what exactly barley should be dried over, so in Sweden Mackmyra has incorporated the traditional drying method of using juniper twigs in the drying of malted barley. This process makes a further distinction from the usual whiskies produced in Scotland.

OAK

If geographical differences affect the flavours that peat gives to malt, then oak from different parts of the world results in even greater variations. The differences between oak from Europe and its cousin in America is so pronounced that you can see it with the naked eye. Even within Europe there is variance, with Swedish and Spanish oak imparting different flavours to spirit.

It takes 100 years or more to grow an oak big enough to turn in to a cask and, while some environmentalists are critical of an industry that fells trees for whisky making, more oak is being planted in the second decade of the new millennium than at any time in the last 1000 years, and most distillers are keenly aware of their environmental responsibilities and the need for sustainability. Certainly few countries face the acute shortages of oak that resulted in the Middle Ages after the great warring nations had felled the trees for ships, fortifications and weapons in the desire to build empires.

Oak is in such demand because it is very strong but still malleable, waterproof yet porous and able to let oxygen (and indeed water and alcohol) molecules pass through it. It is also rich in flavour compounds that are easily accessible by charring or toasting the wood. On its own in a brand new cask, the spirit contained within would be quickly dominated by the spiciness of the wood, the maturing process is therefore improved by using a cask that has been used previously for maturing a different liquid. Most malt spirit is matured in casks already used for the production of sherry in Europe or bourbon in the United States. While all bourbon casks will be made of American wood (even though there is no law saying they have to be), it does not follow that all sherry produced in Spain is matured in European oak. Sherry styles such as oloroso are matured in American oak, so there are on the whole three main types of casks for whisky making: bourbon cask, European oak sherry and American oak sherry.

SPECIAL FINISHES

The rules governing the production of single-malt whisky do not stipulate what the cask has to have contained before, and considerable experimentation has taken place in recent years. It is not unusual to find whiskies that have been matured in part in wine casks, port pipes or casks used for the production of madeira or rum. Although the rules forbid the addition of anything to a single-malt whisky, some do take on distinctly ruddy and pink hues from their contact with the spirit- or fortified-wine-soaked wood, and such casks can have a major impact on flavour.

ABOVE Coopering skills are much in demand again now that barrels are such a valuable commodity. This craftsman makes ready with tools in hand at William Grant's own cooperage on the site of Glenfiddich and Balvenie in Scotland.

HOW TO MAKE SINGLE-MALT WHISKY

The magic of single-malt whisky lies in the fact that it contains just three simple ingredients: malted barley, yeast and water. The process of making single malt and the equipment needed to make it are pretty much the same throughout the world. And yet such a simple and uniform production process produces a vast array of different flavours and aromas.

Whisky is like a collection of seemingly identical landscape paintings; each picture looks the same from a distance, but study them closely and there are countless differences between each one. The first step in whisky making is to turn barley into malted barley by tricking it into growing, which is done by soaking the barley in water. The grains will start to produce shoots, breaking down the grain husk, and this in turn gives access to the enzymes and starches contained within each barley kernel.

After a few days it is necessary to halt the growing process, and this is achieved by drying out the barley over a heat source. Traditionally barley was dried over fire fuelled by peat. This process imparts the smoke and peaty flavours that produce the phenolic medicinal styles of whisky for which Scotland's west coast is famous. Nowadays, though, most barley is malted in large commercial maltings and most malt is dried in modern electricity-fuelled ovens.

Once dry, the malted barley is ground into flour, known as grist, and mixed with hot water in a vessel known as a mash tun. The water removes the starches and enzymes that are needed to produce alcohol. The process is known as mashing and is exactly the same as the one used to make a pot of tea. The spent grains are removed from the process at this point, leaving a sweet brown non-alcoholic liquid known as wort.

The wort is moved to a large vessel called a washback and yeast is now added to the mix to start the process of fermentation. Yeast feeds on the wort, converting the starches to sugars and the sugars to alcohol and carbon dioxide. After a period of two to three days the wort is converted into a beer with an alcoholic strength of about 7–9% alcohol by volume (ABV). Unlike beer produced in breweries, which is made under sterile conditions, distillery beer is sharp and sour – not unlike Belgian lambic beer. This is due to the presence of bacteria

and is crucial to the success of the whisky-making process. Distillation is the process of separating water from alcohol through the use of heat. For malt whisky, this involves boiling the beer solution in large copper kettles known as pot stills. Alcohol evaporates at a lower temperature than water and, once in vapour form, will pass up the copper still. It is condensed back into liquid by passing through a condenser cooled by cold water, lowering its temperature so that it returns to a liquid state. The copper plays a pivotal role in the process, catching fats and oils as they pass over it and reacting with the spirit to influence flavour and removing unwanted sulphur compounds from the vapour.

TWICE DISTILLED

Malt distillation is usually – but not always – carried out twice. The first process is carried out in a wash still and produces a solution known as low wine with an alcoholic strength of a little over 20% ABV. This is mixed with the rejected residue from the previous distillation, raising its alcoholic strength to the high 20s, and this is distilled in the spirit still.

This is where the first major piece of magic takes place. The spirit collected in the second distillation is the spirit that will be put into casks to make whisky, so its composition needs to be considered carefully. Unlike the first distillation, where all the condensed liquid is retained, much of the second run will be rejected. As the liquid is heated, the first alcohols to evaporate are by definition the most volatile. They have the highest alcoholic content and tend to be at worst poisonous and at best foul tasting. They are not desirable. So the first part of the run, known as heads or foreshots, is collected in a holding vessel and rejected.

Over time the strength of the alcohols in the vapour will fall and flavoursome spirit worthy of keeping will be produced. So this spirit is collected in a second vessel. This is known as the cut and is the part of the run that will be put into casks for maturation. Finally the condensed spirit will reach a point where the alcohols are weak and unpleasant to taste. This portion will also be rejected and is known as the tails or the feints. The whole process was once vividly described to me as like cutting the head and tail off a fat fish and retaining the juicy, fleshy part in the middle. Where exactly that cut is made varies from distillery to distillery, and in some cases is little more than a sliver. At the end of the run, the middle cut forms the 'new make' spirit that will be stored to make whisky. The rejected parts of the cycle are recycled and used in the next distillation, and then the whole process begins again.

To make whisky, the new spirit – which is clear, but has a distinctive and strong flavour – must be stored in oak casks and matured. In Europe, this process has to be for a minimum of three years. Malt spirit is not robust enough to fend off the dominant spicy flavours of new oak over this time, so it is matured in casks that have already been used for something else, most often bourbon or sherry.

MATURATION

Malt's greatest mystery is how it matures. No two casks will produce exactly the same whisky and, although recognizable distillery characteristics may be found in each one, there will be significant variations on the central theme. Different cask sizes will be used, and they will have previously contained different liquids. But even two identical casks with spirit from the same run, stored side by side in exactly the same conditions and for exactly the same period of time may well produce different whiskies.

So the bottle of 12-year-old single malt you eventually buy will contain a marriage of whiskies from an array of different casks, cleverly combined by a whisky maker so that, whether you taste the distillery's malt in New York today or London next year, you will not notice any great variance in

taste, even though the two bottles will have been produced from different batches. The word 'single' in single-malt whisky refers to the fact that the whisky is the product of just one distillery, rather than referring to it being from a single cask or batch.

ABOVE The size and shape of pot stills vary from distillery to distillery, and often affect the taste of the spirit made. You will find these ones at the Glendronach distillery in Speyside, Scotland.

HOW TO MAKE BLENDED WHISKY

Blends are to whisky what fast food is to catering: immensely successful across the world, popular and enjoyed by the mainstream, but rarely truly loved or cherished; often unfairly dismissed as bland and unexciting; and only occasionally garnering the positive press bestowed elsewhere.

There are two principle reasons for this. Firstly, because while the world of single malts is all about variety and new expressions are constantly being added to the menu, fuelling the enthusiasm of aficionados, blended whiskies are all about consistency and reliability, and new releases in the category are few and far between. As a result blends rarely create news. Secondly, while the rules governing the production of single malts are rigid and ensure an extremely high standard, the rules governing blends are more flexible. Poor-quality blends can be made within the rules so a vast number of ordinary or poor blends have sullied the reputation of the category as a whole. This is a shame, because blended whiskies at their best can be stunning and require a level of craftsmanship that not even the very best malts can match.

THE BLEND

Scotland actually produces four styles of whisky (see right), but it is blended whisky that has given the country its status as the world's best and leading producer of whisky. Most single-malt whisky is produced with the intention of forming part of a blend rather than for being consumed alone. Even with all the current focus on single-malt whisky, blended whisky still accounts for nine out of ten glasses of Scotch whisky consumed across the world.

Blended whisky not only constitutes an important export market for Scotland, but also for Great Britain. Not surprisingly, therefore, Scottish whisky makers take blends very seriously indeed. The biggest ones – Johnnie Walker, Chivas Regal, Bell's Famous Grouse, Teacher's – are made to exacting standards and are supported by huge marketing budgets. They might not be anywhere near as sexy as a premium single malt, but they are the industry's bread and butter and are quality products. Trouble is, there are plenty of inferior brands that cannot make the same claim.

Blended whisky's inconsistent reputation stems from the inclusion of grain whisky. Grain plays an essential role in rounding off some of the more extreme flavours of single malt, making the drink more palatable to a greater cross-section of people. Grain has a less distinctive taste than single malt and much of the flavour it does have is given to it by the cask. The rules governing blends do not dictate what proportions of grain and single malts need to be in the blend, so often a higher proportion of less tasteful grain is used. Moreover, grain is often matured in old and much-used casks, where the wood has little to offer the spirit, further making for a bland and characterless whisky. Buy a cheap bottle of Clan Bagpipe McTavish and chances are

you're going to get a low-quality grain-heavy blend coloured with caramel to make it more impressive than it actually is.

But it does not have to be that way, and the great names of blended whisky have obtained their status through generations of blending perfection and the employment of the finest malt and grain whiskies. A good blend is a lovingly constructed oil painting, balanced and in harmony, and bursting with colour and style. It may include more than 40 malts and grains, and the number might actually be considerably higher. The Scottish whisky industry has cleverly adopted an exchange system by which each whisky company swaps its malts with other producers, so that each one has the widest possible range of flavours to work with.

THE MASTER BLENDER

Master blenders understand the characteristics of different malts and know how to construct beautiful blends with them. A great blend is like an American football team; there are big-name heavy-hitting stars in the line-up but many of the most important jobs are done by lesser-known names. If they weren't there, the team would fall apart. When the whole team is firing, the result is a study in excellence. When they're not, it's one big unholy mess.

Although each brand of blended whisky is designed to be consistent time after time, different blends can be suited and tailored to satisfy the palates of different people in different countries. For this reason blends are often created for specific markets with specific tastes and are not sold elsewhere, making it a difficult, bordering on impossible, task to monitor them all.

OPPOSITE Checking on the blending process at Glendronach.

Scotland's four styles of whisky

SINGLE MALTS
Made from malted barley, yeast and water and the product of just one distillery.

BLENDED WHISKY
A combination of different malts and grain whisky usually – but not always – mixed together after the individual whiskies have been fully matured separately and brought together by the whisky maker before bottling.

BLENDED MALT WHISKY
The confusing name given to a mix of malts from different distilleries but one that contains no grain whisky. This category is different to blended whisky and its whiskies used to be known as vatted malts.

GRAIN WHISKY
Made with a variety of grains including corn, wheat, rye, malted and unmalted barley. It is normally produced in a continuous process in a different style of still to that used for malt whisky, which is known variously as a column, continuous or Coffey still.

ABOVE Glendronach (single malt), Johnnie Walker Black Label (blended whisky), Compass Box Spice Tree (blended malt) and The Snow Grouse (grain whisky) are the main types of Scottish whisky.

HOW TO MAKE BOURBON

Bourbon is whisky because it is made with grain, yeast and water. But these three ingredients vaguely connect it to single-malt whisky in the same way as a bat, ball and the participation of two teams links baseball to cricket. Beyond the basics the two have little in common, and where there is an opportunity to head off in a different direction, the Americans have tended to take it.

Although bourbon and single-malt whisky follow a template under which grain is converted to beer and the beer is distilled, the raw materials, the distillation process and the maturation of the spirit differ significantly. Single malt is made using malted barley alone. Bourbon, meanwhile, is made up with more than one grain in the mix and must include at least 51% corn, although in practice this percentage is much higher. While some malted barley will probably be included in the process, because malted barley is a good catalyst for aiding the conversion of sugars to alcohol, it is also probable that there will be some wheat, rye and/or unmalted barley in the mix, which is known as the mashbill.

As with malt whisky, American whiskey makers at different distilleries will tweak the process so that each distillery has its own whiskey DNA, but in broad strokes the process is similar across them all. As with malted barley, the aim of the American whiskey maker is to release the sugars and starches from the grains so that yeast can convert them to alcohol through fermentation and, as with malted barley, the process is known as mashing because hot water is used to flush out the sugars. The three grains are crushed into flour individually, before being added to boiling water in what is known as the three-step process. Each distillery will have its own view of what temperature the water should be when each grain is added, but generally: corn (a tough grain with a hard outer shell) will be added at the highest temperatures, while wheat, unmalted barley and rye are added at slightly lower temperatures, and malted barley (the most delicate of the grains) added last, when the water has cooled significantly. When mashing is complete, the whole solution, spent grains and all, goes forward to the fermentation stage.

THE SOUR MASH PROCESS
The sour-mash process plays a key role in the production of American whiskey, and it is a further point of difference from Scotch whisky production. At the end of each bourbon-distillation process there is stillage – a residue made up of the used grain from the process. This is known as backset, and is made up of the last of the solution left after distillation and the remnants of the grain with all its sugars removed. It has a sharp, sour taste – hence it is 'sour'. This stillage is added back to the mash before the yeast is added. Its purpose is to provide a chemical balance to the solution and control bacteria, creating a fermentation process that is conducive to distilling clean and characterful spirit. When fermentation is complete, the beer – a thick viscous solution that is completely different to the wash that is produced in Scotland – is ready for distillation. Where distiller's beer in Scotland is thin, sour and fruity, in bourbon production it is rich, creamy and sickly, more akin to warm milk on soggy cornflakes.

THE CONTINUOUS STILL
Single-malt whisky is produced in batches, with a quantity of single malt converted into beer, and the beer distilled in two stills before the process starts again. Bourbon is produced in a continuous still, where the distillery beer is passed in at one end and comes out as a spirit at the other. The continuous still is just that, allowing an ongoing distillation, and it is capable of producing larger quantities of spirit in a more efficient and commercial manner. But far less copper is involved, the separation of spirit from water is done differently, and the resulting spirit has a higher alcoholic strength, but none of the depth and variety of flavour that single-malt distillation produces. Where single-malt whisky spirit is created by boiling the beer solution in a glorified copper kettle, the continuous still works by forcing the distiller's beer down pipes containing a series of sloping plates and into a wall of pressurized and very-high-temperature steam, which converts the alcohol into vapour and drives

it out. It is recondensed and channelled out of the still at different points during its downward journey, is collected and undergoes what is effectively a second distillation process by being passed through a simple pot still known as a doubler. The resulting spirit is clear and is known as white dog.

MATURATION

Even the maturation process in the United States is different, because the spirit that continuous distillation produces is less distinctive than new-make single malt, and hence maturation is particularly important to the overall process. While American law requires that an oak barrel be used, it also dictates that a new barrel is used for each production run. When you consider the size of Jack Daniel's, the world's biggest whiskey, and Jim Beam, the world's biggest bourbon, and the huge number of barrels that they are using – which, by law, must become redundant each year – it explains why so much single malt is matured in ex-American whiskey casks.

The new barrels are charred or toasted to varying degrees on the inside before spirit is added, helping to release all the qualities in the wood that will impart flavour and character as the spirit matures. Once more, bourbon maturation is to single-malt whisky maturation what baseball is to cricket: an altogether more brash, aggressive and less time-consuming affair. Kentucky is, in every sense, a state of extremes, and the weather is no exception. It has long, extremely hot and high-humidity summers and viciously cold, sharp winters. When the sun is at its hottest, temperatures at the top of the tower block warehouses can hit the 40°C (104°F)-plus mark. In winter fierce frozen winds from the Appalachians bring sub-zero temperatures.

The effect on the spirit is to provoke rapid and dramatic distillation. As with all chemical reactions, heat makes change happen faster. The extreme changes in temperature make the spirit expand and contract faster, and to move more rapidly in the

cask, regularly bringing all the spirit into contact with wood and accelerating the transfer of flavour and colour from wood to spirit. For these reasons, bourbon reaches maturity much faster than malt whisky does in Scotland.

There is one final difference between the ways in which the two whiskies reach their destinations. In Scotland, alcohol evaporates from the maturing spirit, escaping from the cask and providing the angels with their share. This gradually reduces the alcoholic strength of the spirit in the cask. Alcohol also evaporates from the cask in Kentucky, but in the vast majority of cases, not as fast as water does. The humidity makes a crucial intervention and in most cases the alcoholic strength of the bourbon spirit gets higher during maturation. This process is not uniform and in some Kentucky distilleries there are areas where spirit in the cask remains at about the same strength throughout the process, and in some cases actually declines, as it does in Scotland. American law requires that 'straight' bourbon is matured for a minimum of two years. Unlike the case in Scotland, where colouring may be added to the finished product, nothing may be added to bourbon.

ABOVE Open-top fermentation at Maker's Mark distillery in Kentucky.

BASICS

TASTING WHISKY

Whisky suffers from an identity crisis, particularly when it comes to nosing and tasting it.

Whisky is a simple drink made of grain, yeast and water, and is effectively distilled beer. It is the drink of the tenant farmer and the common man. In its crudest form it is harsh firewater, and at its most sophisticated it is an ideal lubricant for socializing, celebrating, bonding and peace-making. It should have no airs or graces and most of the time it doesn't.

But the world of whisky is split between those who accept whisky as the drink of the people and those who would prefer it to sit on an altogether higher table. They prefer to link it not with the grain but with the grape, and they dress it in the livery of wine and of wine language. There was even a magazine that brought the two together. It failed.

And it is from this that the identity crisis stems. For while many whisky books are broadly in agreement as to how whisky should be nosed, tasted and appreciated, scratch below the surface and there is little common agreement among writers and experts on the subject. Some believe that water should be added, others not. Professional 'nosers' or tasters add lots of water. Some say that you should spit whisky, others that you cannot appreciate the full experience without swallowing it.

My view is that whisky is not wine and should not be treated as such. Whisky is three or four times as strong for a start, and the process of distillation takes spirit several steps away from the provenance of the ingredients from which it is made. While many flavours and aromas can be found in whisky, it does not command the same degree of nuance or subtlety as wine and therefore does not demand the same indulgences of language. Whisky is made all the more attractive because, on the whole, it is free of the pretentiousness that goes with wine tasting, and snobs and drinks bores would not be tolerated in the distilleries of Scotland, Kentucky, Ireland – or anywhere else for that matter. Whisky is all about independence and free spirit, and for this reason nobody should tell you how to taste it. That said, though, while how you travel down the whisky road is a matter entirely for you, it doesn't hurt to have some signposts along the route. Here are a few pointers.

TASTING SEQUENCE
First look at the whisky, note the colour and whether it has 'legs'; approach at arm's length. Breathe in the aromas through both nostrils then one at a time. Finally, taste it.

VIEW

APPROACH 1

WHAT GLASS TO USE
How you want to drink your whisky is entirely up to you. But while you often see whisky in a tumbler glass, this is not the way to go if you want to appreciate its subtle aromas. Tumblers are fine for blended whisky or bourbon, when mixers or ice might be added. They are useless for nosing single-malt whisky.

For the record, the whisky industry favours a tulip-shaped glass with a tapered neck, because this concentrates the aromas into the nose. You can buy them from most whisky shops at a modest cost. A Champagne flute, sherry glass or small red wine glass are all better than tumblers for tasting.

WATER OR NOT?

If any so-called expert says you should not add water to your whisky, tell them that the whisky industry started the practice. New spirit comes off the still with an alcoholic strength in the high 60s or early 70s. Until recently, when warehouse space and barrel shortages became an issue and casking smaller quantities of liquid at higher strength became fashionable, most distillers brought the strength at which the spirit entered into the cask down to about 63% ABV by adding water. After maturation, a Scottish single-malt whisky will have a strength of 50–65% ABV and, again, water is added to bring the strength down to the bottling strength of normally 40, 43 or 46%. In other words, more than a third of the whisky in your bottle is added water. Who's to tell you that you should not add a bit more? Blenders will take samples down to just 20% ABV and water is crucial for breaking down the whisky and releasing an array of aromas, thereby making appreciation of the drink easier. But, a few tasters dislike adding water and will only do so when tasting strong whiskies.

SPIT OR SWALLOW?

Whisky is a strong spirit, which means that the palate will tire quite rapidly when swallowing, and after three or four samples further tasting is impossible. It therefore makes sense to spit if you intend to be judging or appraising whisky for more than just fun or personal reasons. But that doesn't happen very often does it?

There are two compelling arguments for swallowing and not spitting. One is the fact that whisky is a drink. There is a clue in the title. The other is that when describing whisky we talk about the finish. How can we do this if we do not finish it? It's like watching a film then leaving 15 minutes before the end. Surely the warming feeling as the spirit passes down the throat and the taste left in your mouth afterwards are crucial to the whisky-tasting experience. For this reason it is best to sip and savour any whisky you have not tasted before, in order to fully appreciate the sight, aroma, flavours and finish of the drink. This is the way to gather a complete profile of each whisky you taste.

OPPOSITE The Glencairn whisky-glass shape is perfect for nosing whisky. Ignore anyone who says you should not add water – it is a personal choice. Drink water between whiskies to refresh the palate.

APPROACH 2

NOSE

SIP

BEWARE HIGH-VOLTAGE ALCOHOL

Approach a glass of neat whisky with caution. Whisky has a strong alcoholic content and should be respected. Nose a strong spirit too quickly and it will hurt your nostrils. Not only that, but your senses will batten down the hatches if they perceive that they are under threat, making further sensory perception redundant, at least in the short term.

Approach a new glass of whisky in the same way that you would approach an unfamiliar animal; at arm's length at first, then with caution until you are both happy in each other's company. Taste a very small amount of the spirit neat before you do anything else to it.

FLAVOUR CATEGORIES

While whisky isn't wine, identifying flavours will enhance your enjoyment of it, not least because you will be able to identify the specific flavours that most appeal to you.

THE MAIN CATEGORIES

Perhaps the easiest way to improve your tasting and nosing skills is to start with the broadest and most general of categories. When you are happy with those, introduce sub-sectors, and then sub-sectors of those, and so on. I base my sub-categories around high-street stores.

PEATY/SMOKY – OR NOT

This is the most fundamental split certainly in Scottish whisky. Drying barley over peat fires imparts smoky and peaty flavours that some people hate and some people would kill for. The characteristics are:

PEATY
TCP/medicine
Tar, coal and engine oil
Iodine and salt
Seaweed
Chilli and pepper

SMOKY
Barbecue
Grilled meat
Bonfire
Charcoal
Tobacco

SWEET OR SAVOURY?

In whisky, these two are not mutually exclusive, but at the same time there are many where these are defining characteristics. Most American and Irish whiskey, many Speyside and Lowland whiskies and some Highland whiskies fall into the sweet category, a number of Highland and Island whiskies and a proportion of Japanese whiskies could be considered to be in the savoury spectrum.

SWEET
Exotic tinned fruits in syrup
Maple syrup
Candy sticks
Banoffee pie
Vanilla ice cream
Sweet ginger barley
Christmas cake
Summer pudding

SAVOURY
Mushrooms
Meat
Earthiness
Olives
Nuts
Cheese
Stewed fruits
Forest walk, damp leaves
Autumn bonfires
Seaside and beach
Fish and seaweed

SUB-CATEGORIES

From these three broad categories I like to take a stroll down the high street:

THE SWEET SHOP (SWEET)

Candy sticks
Parma violets
Toffee
Banoffee pie
Vanilla ice cream
Maple syrup
Liquorice
Crystallized ginger

THE BAKERS
Dough
Yeastiness
Fresh bread
Toast and melted butter
Biscuits
Crème brûlée and cake

THE PET SHOP
Muskiness
Breakfast cereal
Porridge
Pencil shavings,
wood chips, sap, sawdust

THE FRUIT SHOP (FRUIT)

Green fruit:
*apple, pear, gooseberries,
grapes and unripe fruit
such as banana and melon*
Orange fruit:
*marmalade, blood oranges,
mandarins, tangerines*
Sweet yellow fruit:
*ripe melon, tinned pear,
plum, banana, pineapple*
Red and berry fruits:
*summer fruits, raisins,
currants, blackberries,
strawberries, raspberries*
Citrus and exotic fruits:
*grapefruit, lime, lemon,
kiwi, guava, lychee*
Nuts

THE FLORISTS
Scented flowers
Heather
Lavender
Powdery and sherbety, zingy
Handbag, perfume, lipstick
Grass and hay
Christmas tree, firs,
forest walk

THE FURNITURE STORES

Furniture polish
New wood
Cleaning products
Pine

THE HIPPY JEWELLERS
Sandalwood and incense stick
Nutmeg, cinnamon and
sweet spices
Spent matches
Leather

THE DIY STORE
Oil and lubricant
Rubber
Creosote
Charcoal

THE TOBACCONISTS
Tobacco and cigars
Cigar box
Leather saddle
Smoke

THE ART OF DRINKING WHISKY

It may not be politically correct to say it these days, but alcohol has played a major and positive role in society for thousands of years. It has been used for medicinal purposes and as a tonic.

It was consumed before battle to give warriors courage, taken by defeated armies to drown their sorrows or by conquering armies to celebrate victory. Former enemies coming together to make peace have blessed their deals with alcohol.

In Scotland and Ireland clans have shared whisky at the end of conflict, passing around a shared cup – a quaich – in a communal ritual that is echoed in many Christian churches to this day. But whisky stands apart from many other drinks. It takes years to make, and centuries to make well, so it deserves respect, like wine.

A culture has grown up around whisky. Today there are different glasses for different occasions but in short, if you want to appreciate whisky by nosing it, you need a narrow, relatively short glass like those illustrated here. While a tumbler is fine if you are adding ice, it is not a glass that is particularly suited to nosing.

GLENCAIRN TASTING GLASS

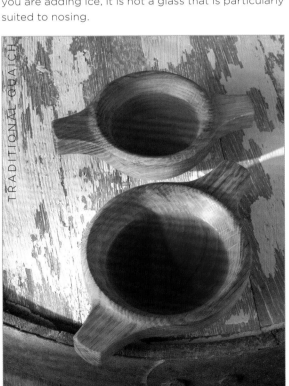

TRADITIONAL QUAICH

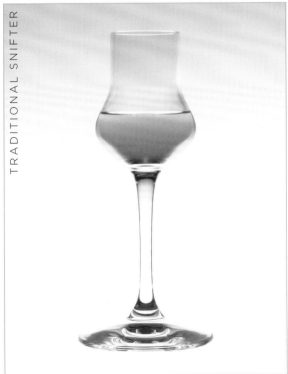

TRADITIONAL SNIFTER

MODERN TASTING GLASS

CLASSIC TUMBLER

CLASSIC TULIP TASTING GLASS

CLASSIC TASTING GLASS

WHISKY STYLES

All whisky is made with grain, yeast and water, but under that umbrella there are many variations. Here are the main ones.

Ardbeg Blasda SINGLE MALT

Compass Box Hedonism GRAIN WHISKY

Johnnie Walker Blue Label BLENDED WHISKY

Wemyss The Hive BLENDED MALT

Redbreast Lustau POT STILL WHISKEY

The Irishman IRISH BLENDED WHISKEY

SINGLE-MALT WHISKY

Whisky made only of yeast, water and malted barley and the product of one distillery only. Scotland is the leading player in this sector but single malts are made across the world, in countries including the United States, Japan, Australia, South Africa and many European countries. In Europe, malt must be matured for a minimum of three years in oak casks, and must be of at least 40% ABV.

GRAIN WHISKY

Whisky made with grain or grains other than malted barley only. Grains might include wheat, corn, unmalted barley and rye. In Europe, the minimum maturation period of three years also applies. Great Scottish examples include Cameronbrig from Fife and Imperial from Morayshire, as well as Compass Box Hedonism, produced by a young company that specializes in artisanal blends.

BLENDED WHISKY

A combination of single malts from different distilleries mixed together with grain whisky. Look out for Johnnie Walker, Chivas Regal, Grant's, Famous Grouse and Ballantine's for a taste of blended whisky that steers away from the bland and is rich in flavour.

BLENDED MALT WHISKY

Whisky made using malted whisky from a number of different distilleries. Monkey Shoulder – made from a blend of single malts from Glenfiddich, Balvenie and Kinivie – and Johnnie Walker Green Label from Scotland exemplify this particular style.

POT STILL WHISKEY

An Irish style of whiskey, which in its purest form is made using malted barley and another grain, normally unmalted barley, mixed to form the grist before mashing and then fermentation. The term has been used to describe any whiskey made in a pot still but this does not do this unique style of whiskey justice.

IRISH BLENDED WHISKEY

Most commercial Irish whiskeys are blends, and are normally made up of pot still whiskey mixed with grain whiskey, though The Irishman 70 is made up of 70% single malt and 30% Midleton pot still whiskey, a unique north-meets-south whiskey, which may be described as a blend but is in effect in a category of its own.

Buffalo Trace BOURBON

Jack Daniel's TENNESSEE WHISKEY

Sazerac Rye AMERICAN RYE WHISKEY

Bernheim Original WHEAT WHISKEY

Balcones Baby Blue CORN WHISKEY

Glen Breton CANADIAN RYE WHISKEY

BOURBON

Whiskey made in the United States using grains including at least 51% corn, although in practice the amount is normally considerably higher. Bourbon is produced under strict guidelines and must be matured in fresh oak barrels. The most celebrated bourbons include Jim Beam, Maker's Mark, Buffalo Trace and Woodford Reserve. Straight bourbon must be matured for two years.

TENNESSEE WHISKEY

Whiskey made in the state of Tennessee in a similar style to bourbon, but which differs to bourbon because it has undergone the 'Lincoln County process' – where the spirit is passed through Maplewood charcoal before it is put into the cask. Jack Daniel's is the most famous example.

RYE WHISKEY (UNITED STATES)

Whiskey made in a similar way to bourbon, but with a minimum of 51% rye in the grist. It must also be matured for more than two years. Look out for Rittenhouse Rye and Pappy Van Winkle's Family Reserve 13-year-old Rye, both produced in Louisville, as well as Sazerac Kentucky Straight Rye from Frankfort.

WHEAT WHISKEY

Whiskey made in a similar way to bourbon but including a minimum of 51% wheat. One of the best-known wheat whiskeys is Bernheim Original, a relative newcomer from the Heaven Hill distillery in Louisville, Kentucky.

CORN WHISKEY

Whiskey made up of at least 80% corn. There are no ageing requirements and, if corn whisky is aged, it is usually for no more than than six months. Heaven Hill's Mellow Corn and Georgia Moon are key examples of the style, as is Dixie Dew from the same distillery.

RYE WHISKY (CANADA)

Canadian Rye describes any whisky that has the aroma, taste and character of Canadian whisky, whether it contains rye or not. There is an irony here because rye produces aggressive and spicy whiskies and Canadian whisky can be soft, rounded and quite characterless. In practice, Canadian whisky will probably have a number of different whiskies in it, with only a small proportion of rye among them. Canadian whisky also permits a small amount of other liquid (eg. American bourbon or fruit juice). Look for Canadian Club, Glen Breton, Forty Creek.

WHISKY COCKTAILS

ABOVE Coupette, London.

These days exciting cocktails go hand-in-hand with a successful whisky bar.

Big beards, slicked hair with side partings, tattoos, braces and the term 'mixologist'... the cocktail has plenty to answer for when it comes to fashion car crashes. But, creative drinks making has revolutionized the world of spirits in general – and whisky in particular. Bar men and women, once frightened off by the price and taste challenges of good whisky and bourbon, now wear their whisky creations as badges of honour, and no self-respecting bar would dare not to offer an

innovative cocktail list. Not just new and exciting drinks either: many are discovering classic cocktails and giving them a modern twist. Some bars are putting drinks such as the Old Fashioned at the very heart of their offering.

The stellar rise of the cocktail in the last decade has been reflected in the growth of craft distilling. The two work in tandem, with many craft distilleries creating spirits almost exclusively for use in cocktails, and cocktails being served at weekends

RIGHT
Barman at
Coupette
in London
mixes an Old
Fashioned...

2 dashes Angostura bitters

7.5ml (¼oz) sugar syrup

50ml (1¾oz) Woodford Reserve

TOP TEN WHISKY BARS

and evenings to attract tourists to the distillery. New spirits styles in the United States particularly – some of them described as whiskey, even though they're strictly not – are taking cocktails in to new and exciting areas.

And cocktails have provided a fillip to bars across the world. You'd expect to find a good cocktail menu in an upmarket hotel bar, but these days the self-styled dive bar will also be offering up a cool range of mixed drinks.

Atlas Singapore
Boilermaker House Melbourne, Australia
Bourbons Bistro Louisville, Kentucky, United States
Delilah's Chicago, Illinois, United States
Dick Macks Dingle, Ireland
The Flatiron Room New York, United States
Jack Rose Dining Saloon Washington, United States
Multnomah Whiskey Library Portland, Oregon, US
The Pot Still Glasgow, Scotland
Villa Konthor Limburg, Germany

Stir with ice.

Pour over more ice.

Zest.

Garnish.

CLASSIC WHISKY COCKTAILS

Whisky traditionalists don't hold much truck with cocktails, which is a bit bizarre really.

Why? Well, the malt whisky produced in the Highlands a few hundred years ago tasted so awful that they added anything – mint, honey, heather – to hide the taste. The story goes that Bonnie Prince Charlie handed over the recipe to Drambuie to thank the people who saved him – a lot of rubbish admittedly, but the point is it is plausible that in the mid-eighteenth century whisky was served with flavourings – and that's all a cocktail is, after all. These days a good cocktail is not about concealing the taste of whisky, it's about showing it off. The classic, and longest-surviving whisky cocktails, therefore, are the simplest and the ones that add a twist to the whisky.

Mizuwari

50ml (1¾oz) Nikka from the Barrel
soda water

Take the best quality ice you can find, and fill a highball glass. Pour in whisky, then add soda carefully and slowly, to retain carbonation.

Boulevardier

25ml (0.9oz) Woodford Reserve
25ml (0.9oz) Campari
25ml (0.9oz) sweet vermouth

Add all ingredients to a mixing glass, and stir with lots of ice. Strain into a Coupette, and garnish with a twist of orange peel.

Morning Glory Fizz

40ml (1.4oz) Dewar's 12-year-old
20ml (0.7oz) lemon juice
10ml (⅓oz) sugar syrup
25ml (0.9oz) egg white
2 dashes absinthe
soda water

Add all ingredients, except soda, to a cocktail shaker. Use a hand blender to combine, then add lots of ice and shake. Pour into a fizz glass, and top with soda.

Whisky Sour

50ml (1¾oz) Aberfeldy 12-year-old
25ml (0.9oz) lemon juice
15ml (½oz) sugar syrup
25ml (0.9oz) egg white
1 dash Angostura bitters

Add all ingredients to a cocktail shaker. Use a hand blender to combine, then add lots of ice and shake. Pour into a tumbler over ice, and garnish with another drop of bitters and a wedge of lemon.

Old Fashioned

50ml (1¾oz) Woodford Reserve
7.5ml (¼oz) sugar syrup
2 dashes Angostura bitters

Add all ingredients to a mixing glass, and stir with lots of ice. Strain into a tumbler with more ice, and garnish with a trimmed orange twist.

OPPOSITE Mizuwari *top left*, Boulevardier *middle*, Morning Glory Fizz *top right*, Whisky Sour *bottom left*, Old Fashioned *bottom right*.

MODERN WHISKY COCKTAILS

Modern takes on traditional whisky cocktails deliver a new twist to hip whisky drinking.

Whisky is to bartenders – or mixologists – what Mount Everest is to the climber: the ultimate challenge. Mix a cocktail with vodka and the spirit quietly goes under without a struggle, providing an alcoholic kick but giving the mixologist free licence to paint pictures. Whisky and especially single-malt whisky doesn't do that. It's the untamed tiger of the drinks world and if you're going to work with it you're going to need a lot of patience.

In the early part of the millennium, *Whisky Magazine* held a cocktail competition that divided the room between those who made good cocktails despite having whisky in them, and those who made good cocktails because they had whisky in them. Things have moved on since then and here are five specially created whisky cocktails made by the some of the sector's hottest drinks makers.

The modern cocktails included here were crafted by renowned mixologist and owner of award-winning bar Coupette, Chris Moore. Chris had a long and prestigious tenure as the head bartender at The Savoy's Beaufort Bar, and under his guidance it won Best International Hotel Bar at Tales of the Cocktail in 2015. He opened Coupette, in London's Bethnal Green, in 2017 and the bar was promptly named 2017's Best New Bar in the CLASS Bar Awards.

The Alliance

30ml (1oz) Craigellachie 13-year-old
20ml (0.7oz) Lillet Blanc
5ml (0.2oz) Campari
2.5ml (0.8oz) Crème de Peche

Add all ingredients to a mixing glass, and stir with lots of ice. Strain into a sherry glass, twist a lemon peel over the top and discard.

First Things First

40ml (1.4oz) Woodford Rye
20ml (0.7oz) Noilly Prat dry vermouth
10ml (⅓oz) exotic cordial
Bloomsbury Pastis (spray)

For the exotic cordial: heat 500ml (17oz) sugar syrup in a pan with 30g (1oz) each of lime peel, dried mango, dried pineapple.

Add all ingredients to a mixing glass, and stir with lots of ice. Spray a tasting glass with the pastis, and then strain the drink in to this.

Ramos/Sam Ross

40ml (1.4oz) Dewar's 12-year-old
5ml (0.2oz) Laphroaig 10-year-old
25ml (0.9oz) Half & Half (cream/milk)
25ml (0.9oz) Toddy syrup
25ml (0.9oz) egg white
20ml (0.7oz) lemon juice
Carbonated lemon and ginger tea

For the syrup: add 30g (1oz) each of lemon peel and chopped ginger and a spoon of honey to 500ml (17oz) sugar syrup and cook for 10 minutes. For the tea: as above, replacing sugar with water; place in a soda siphon.

Add all ingredients, except the tea, to a cocktail shaker. Combine with a hand blender, then add lots of ice and shake. Strain into a fizz glass, and top with the carbonated tea.

In the Shadows

45ml (1½oz) Dewar's 12-year-old
20ml (0.7oz) stout reduction
15ml (½oz) Maury wine
5ml (0.2oz) Cassis
coffee beans

For the stout reduction: pour good-quality stout into a pan, and heat to reduce by half.

Place all ingredients into a re-sealable container for ten minutes. Strain, then pour over ice and serve.

Grand Master

40ml (1.4oz) Woodford Rye
15ml (½oz) Amandine Liqueur
10ml (⅓oz) oloroso sherry
10ml (⅓oz) fino sherry
5ml (0.2oz) Crème de Apricot
2 dashes Suze Blue Bitters

Add all ingredients to a mixing glass, and stir with lots of ice. Strain into a Coupette, then garnish with a twist of lemon.

BELOW *From left to right* The Alliance, First Things First, Ramos/Sam Ross, In the Shadows, Grand Master.

A WORLD OF WHISKY

A WORLD OF WHISKY

Whisky is now produced across the entire world,
ensuring an even greater range of tastes to enjoy.

The world whisky map has changed massively
since the turn of the millennium, and there are
new distilleries springing up on all five continents.
We're fast reaching the point where it would be
easier to show where it is not made. Beyond the
headlines, all sorts of weird and wonderful grain
spirits are adding diversity and excitement for
whisky lovers worldwide.

Scotland
p.46

The
Netherlands
p.261

Canada
p.200

Ireland
p.204

Wales
p.275

USA
p.152

England
p.253

Argentina
p.241

PREVIOUS Gentle as she goes: casks maturing at Balvenie in Speyside.

Denmark
p.252

Sweden
p.265

Belgium
p.252

Germany
p.257

France
p.256

Switzerland
p.271

Austria
p.252

Japan
p.222

Taiwan
p.274

Italy
p.261

India
p.257

South
Africa
p.265

Australia
p.241

New
Zealand
p.264

MAKING THE SELECTION

Keeping a tab on the number of whiskies available across the world is like counting leaves in the garden during a hurricane. The world of whisky is not only in a permanent state of evolution, but it is segregated, too, with Scottish blends, in particular, finding favour in certain territories but unavailable elsewhere.

If counting the whiskies has been extremely difficult, then picking a definitive 750 best is, if the truth be told, quite a challenge. You simply could not taste every single one, but even if you could, deciding which should and should not make the cut is an entirely subjective and deeply unscientific process.

What would be hard to do in any drinks category is made all the harder in the field of whisky because of the presence of independent bottlers. These are companies that buy up casks of whisky and then bottle them under their own labels, often in tiny quantities because they are the product of one, two or three casks. Every cask produces slightly different whisky to the next, so independent bottlers do not seek to produce uniform representative malt from the distillery in question, but rather offer the whisky lover a variation of it. If an official distillery bottling is to whisky what an official CD release is to a rock band, then the independent bottling is a live bootleg: often a rougher and rawer version, clearly by the same artist but reproduced differently; sometimes better than the original, sometimes not, but highly attractive to the true fan nonetheless.

As independent bottlers often bottle just one cask and produce only 250 or 300 bottles from it, many whiskies are literally gone before they can be written about, and are rapidly replaced by another wave of bottles. This area of the industry is an ever-changing quicksand and for this reason many great whiskies produced even a couple of years ago by independent bottlers have had to be ignored because they have gone forever, though I have touched on this area in a bid to recognize the biggest and best independent bottlers (see p.278).

The selection process can be simplified further by ignoring the scores of poor-quality drinks passing themselves off as whisky made outside the guidelines laid down by the Scottish (and therefore European) and American whisky industries. Both continents work to a code where the highest standards are maintained, and they provide a good base camp from which to work. While some rare whiskies are included, other extremely exclusive one haven't made it in.

But that doesn't mean the net has not been cast far and wide: it has, and there has been a conscious effort to include some of the most esoteric whiskies and to recognize countries where the whisky light has only just been switched on. Some of them are distinctly weird, others are a shock to the palate, which has grown used to the finest Scottish malts and the tastiest bourbons. But every whisky mentioned in this book has been well made by a master craftsman and is included on merit.

FINDING YOUR WHISKY

For ease of reference whiskies are listed by the country of origin with the biggest regions of Scotland and America to the fore. Within each country section whiskies are listed by whisky style; within these sections, brands and/or distilleries are listed in alphabetical order. The symbols are designed to help make selection and categorization of each whisky easier. Each entry includes tasting notes, but I've tried to avoid being too prescriptive. More importantly, I've attempted to capture some of the personality of the whisky, and the people or events that shaped it, to give it greater context and interest.

While everything possible has been done to ensure accuracy, the pace of evolution in the world of whisky inevitably means that some whisky distilleries and whisky brands will have changed or changed hands. Some will have been swallowed up, some closed, new ones opened. A significant number of the whiskies included here are produced by small independent distillers and might be hard to find. I have not deliberately attempted to be obscure, but on the other hand, I have had considerably more time and greater resources to seek out these whiskies, and if you struggle to find some of them, my apologies in advance.

Tasting symbols

The following symbols have been used in the whisky listings to help describe each of the 750 listings, from classic blends to special cask-aged bottlings. They correspond to the following definitions listed below.

CONNOISSEUR CLASSIC
Cult or classic whiskies that should be high up the wish list for a whisky connoisseur.

SESSION SIP
Everyday whiskies that often feature in the cupboard at home.

PREMIUM TIPPLE
Special whiskies for occasional drinking or best reserved for celebrations.

OLD AND VENERABLE
Whiskies aged 25 years or more.

SUPER STYLE
Whiskies that exemplify a particular style of whisky.

FOR PEAT'S SAKE
Whiskies whose smokiness or peaty phenolic flavour is a major component of the overall taste.

MIND HOW YOU GO
Whiskies bottled at the strength they came out of the cask or at more than 50% ABV, 100 Proof.

A LITTLE UNUSUAL
Quirky or unusual whiskies with a unique taste or featuring an unusual or unique aspect to their production.

RAREST OF THE RARE
Hard to find and very special whiskies.

GONE BUT NOT FORGOTTEN
Whiskies from a distillery that has closed.

THE FACE OF MODERN WHISKY

New distilleries, new whisky-making nations and new marketing-savvy companies are ensuring that whisky looks as exciting and varied as it tastes.

It was not so long ago, when buying a whisky either meant selecting from a weak and predictable selection of bottles and labels at the superstore or liquor store or venturing into a 'specialist' shop for something more exciting.

But whisky packaging has come on in leaps and bounds in recent years. If you like the formal, somewhat grandiose and elegant style of the traditional whisky bottle that's fine. There are plenty of them still out there. But these days a new generation of whisky producers such as Buffalo Trace and Compass Box have helped transform the way whisky is presented, and companies across the world have adopted bottles in such a range of shapes and sizes that whisky shelves are as vibrant and colourful as those of any other spirits drink. The traditional qualities are now being served up in a modern context.

THE WHISKY LABEL

There are rules as to what can be stated on whisky labels, varying by country. Generally, if there is an age on the label, that age refers to the youngest whisky in the mix. There may be many older whiskies, but one drop of 12-year-old whisky is enough to 'age' the overall bottle.

SCOT LAND

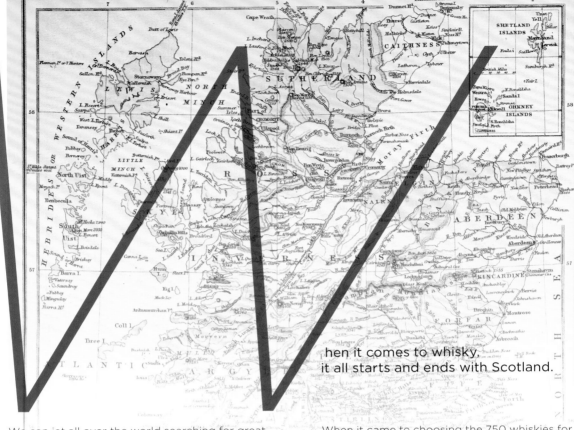

When it comes to whisky, it all starts and ends with Scotland.

We can jet all over the world searching for great whisky and in Kentucky, Ireland and Japan and increasingly lots of other places, too, we can find plenty of it – and even some that is better than a good proportion of Scotland's. We can marvel at the whiskies of distilleries such as Lark and Sullivans Cove in Australia, Amrut in India, Mackmyra, Hven and Box in Sweden, Millstone in The Netherlands, Kavalan in Taiwan and Balcones and Westland in America, but when all is said and done, we always return once more to Scotland.

Why? Because not only does Scotland produce a breathtaking quantity of stunning whiskies but it seems to be setting the pace effortlessly for whisky as we go forward, celebrating its traditions but looking towards the next goal and challenge. And because overall the standard of its whiskies – blends, blended malts and grains as well as single malts – is consistently so high.

It is true that from time to time another nation will produce a whisky that is a match for the very finest from Scotland, but it doesn't happen every day. Scotland's whiskies are like the New Zealand All Blacks – they can be beaten, but rarely, and over any era, they still dominate their field.

When it came to choosing the 750 whiskies for this book, there was no pre-planned decision over the numbers. Lists were made of all the potential candidates for inclusion, then they were tasted and chosen on their merit. The fact that around two-thirds of the final number should come from Scotland is down to quality alone. The proportion is spot-on.

There are just over 130 single-malt distilleries in Scotland, and there are hundreds of single malts. Probably thousands. For that reason single malt is the dominant style and is reflected here by the largest number of entries. But it should also be remembered that 90%-plus of all Scotch whisky sold is blended whisky, and most of it conforms to the same high standard as malts. You do not get to be a global household name such as Johnnie Walker or Chivas Regal by being average. Some blends go even further, using the finest aged malts and commanding the highest price tags as even the rarest malts.

Scotland is the home of whisky, where every whisky lover returns eventually. No matter what is happening elsewhere, that will not change any time soon. If ever.

PREVIOUS Speyside in Scotland: Balvenie is one of about 70 distilleries in the region.

ABOVE The view from Scapa distillery: Scotland's distilleries are woven into the beautiful landscape.

Single malt

Scottish single-malt whisky is the world's most exciting, dynamic and complex spirit. While wonderfully diverse concoctions of other spirits exist, no other drink style can amaze and delight so consistently and so frequently as Scottish single malt does. And no other drink exhibits its qualities quite so flamboyantly and stylishly.

Single malts are now produced in a number of countries, but none of them can hold a candle to the better Scottish malts. If you are not convinced, line up a world selection of malts alongside the best of Scotland and taste them. Even if they match up in the first instance, add a few drops of water, leave them for 20 minutes and compare again. You can almost guarantee that a proportion of the non-Scottish malts will have fallen apart.

The attention to detail in production, the involvement of copper, the craftsmanship honed over centuries, the calm and patient maturation and the loving attention to detail all combine to form what is nothing less than a fortress in a drink. To you and me, it is a glass of whisky. To a scientist it is a feat of molecular engineering, a complex unyielding liquid, so well structured it delivers on the palate every time you approach it.

There's an air of mystery and romance about Scottish single-malt whisky. Produced from the simplest of ingredients, it serves up tastes and aromas that really have no right to be there. How is this? And why is it that wine matches or outperforms beer in terms of diversity of flavour, and yet brandy comes nowhere near malt whisky when it comes to taste?

Scottish single-malt whisky as a hobby is still in its infancy. Most malt whisky is produced as a component for blended whisky, and only a handful of malts are widely recognized in their own right. But as interest grows, that may change, and there are many cases of distillery owners recasking malt in order to give it a chance to shine in the future.

Much has been made of the growth of new whisky-making nations. Indeed, this book strongly argues for a number of countries and why they deserve to be on whisky's highest tasting table. But the head of that table is Scotland. Annually this country serves up a feast of fresh single-malt whisky and it is a trend we will continue to see.

ABERFELDY
www.dewarswow.com

High up in the hills behind the Aberfeldy distillery is a group of cottages available for hire. In the morning the cloud gathers in the valley below and you can watch golden eagles dip in and out as they swoop to find breakfast. Then you can walk down to the village with the distillery below you to the right. I'm not sure there is a better way to start the day.

Aberfeldy distillery lies in the village of the same name to the north of Perth and not far from Pitlochry. It is also the home of Dewar's World of Whisky, an excellent visitor facility telling the story of the Dewar family and its famous blended whisky. The distillery itself is kept in pristine condition and is also open to the public. There are enough interactive facilities to keep the children occupied, too, though whether it's a good thing that my youngest son now knows how to blend a whisky and is, according to one machine in the centre, better at it than me, is up for debate.

The distillery – of course – also produces a great malt, too.

Aberfeldy 12-year-old 40% ABV

Rich, oily and honeyed, this malt has lots of orange and exotic fruits, some soft spices and a soft earthy peat carpet.

Aberfeldy 16-year-old Single Cask
40% ABV

Introduced in 2015 as part of the Last Great Malts series, this is an absolute stormer. It is a smooth, rich malt with honey, orange, apples, butterscotch and spices, but best of all, it has a weighty punch to it.

Aberfeldy 21-year-old 40% ABV

Rich honey is often a defining characteristic of Aberfeldy bottlings, and here it is at its most potent. There are also lovely orange notes, a little peat and just enough oak to give some gravitas. But, I wish it was bottled at a higher strength.

ABERLOUR

www.aberlour.com

Of all the tours offered by Scotland's malt distilleries, Aberlour's is among the very best. Owner Pernod Ricard has several distilleries in the Speyside region and it seems that those involved sat down way back and thought about how they could offer the visitor a different experience at each. The Glenlivet, with its smuggling past and large visitor centre, looks after itself. Strathisla is the home of Chivas and that provides an obvious angle. And Aberlour? Well there are those of us who regard the distillery as Speyside royalty. VIP tours are commonplace now, but Aberlour was offering them years back. Today your visit will be a lengthy one, with knowledgeable guides. At the end you can taste the whisky, then pour an exclusive cask-strength version from a bourbon or a sherry cask and bottle it.

Aberlour 10-year-old 43% ABV

This is classic Speyside, with an emphasis on the green fruit end of the Speyside spectrum. Crisp, fresh and distinctive, with traces of trademark mintiness and elements from both bourbon and sherry casks used for production. Creamy on the one hand, red berries on the other. World class.

Aberlour 12-year-old Double Cask Matured 40% ABV

Classic Speyside malt whisky. A mix of traditional oak and sherry casks. Delicate and flowery with sherried Christmas cake notes, and a rich fruity finish.

Aberlour 15-year-old Select Cask Reserve 43% ABV

Sherry and bourbon with butterscotch, candy, tangerine and red-berry fruits, on a gossamer-light pillow, with some trademark mint and spices late on.

Aberlour 16-year-old Double Cask Matured 43% ABV

Fluffy apples and fruit crumble on the nose; green fruits, vanilla and mint on the palate, with a refreshing, more-ish finish. Almost a palate-cleanser this one. This is arguably the best example of Aberlour's rich fruitiness and is as good a Speyside single malt as you'll find.

Aberlour 18-year-old Sherry Wood Matured 43% ABV

Most Aberlour expressions are akin to elegant ladies dressed in finery but this is altogether more fiesty. The 18 years in cask and fact that the casks in question are all sherry go a long way to explaining this one. Nutty, spicy and fruity, this is a complex malt, bright orangey amber in colour, which ebbs and flows but ultimately leaves the oak and sherry in charge.

Aberlour a'bunadh ('The Origin')

BATCH 21 NO AGE STATEMENT 59.6% ABV

In Gaelic, *a'bunadh* means 'the origin' and is the name given by Aberlour's owners to a series of malts released in batches. Each batch varies but the overall effect is the same – these probably represent the best-value-for-money malts in the market. Indeed, they seem to be well under-priced. Each batch is a vatting of sherry-cask Aberlours, with a range of whiskies aged from very young to more than 15 years old. They vary in strength but often tip over 60% ABV (1.5 bottles of standard 40% whisky). The flavours are intense: frequent whiffs of smoke and sulphur over concentrated red and blackcurrants, cherries, blood orange, nuttiness, spice and some mint. Each one is rich and elegant, almost liqueur-like and unforgettable. You might think such big flavours would appeal only to committed malt lovers but I once met a woman who hated most whiskies except this one. She drank it regularly. Can't blame her.

Key whiskies

Aberlour 12-year-old Double Cask M. 40% ABV
Aberlour 16-year-old Double Cask M. 40% ABV
Aberlour 18-year-old Sherry Wood M. 43% ABV
Aberlour a'bunadh ABV VARIES

ABOVE A warehouseman uses a traditional copper dog to test maturing whisky spirit.
BELOW Casks resting in one of Aberlour's warehouses.

ABERLOUR

Aberlour, Banffshire, AB38 9PJ
www.aberlour.com

Over the last decade whisky tourism has become big business, and a competitive one at that.

With cities such as Dublin in Ireland and Louisville in Kentucky going out of their way to give visitors an immersive whisk(e)y experience, and the likes of Macallan and Glenfiddich in Scotland offering state-of-the-art facilities, the stakes are high. Pernod Ricard's Glenlivet distillery is a player, too, and its visitor experience is impeccable, with a spacious distillery, restaurant, shop and smugglers' trails guaranteed to keep visitors happy. The more serious whisky enthusiast, however, might prefer to visit another of the French giant's distilleries.

Aberlour is nestled at one end of the street that passes through the town of the same name, and at first glance it doesn't seem to have a lot going for it. It's pretty enough, but there doesn't seem to be that much of it. The tour here, though, is not only one of the best in Scotland, it's up there with the very best in the world.

Pernod seemed to realize a long time ago that it wasn't enough to show visitors a short film with a commentary all about the pure spring water trickling down the bens, rush them around the production suite and then palm them off with a quick dram of a standard whisky expression.

Tours at Aberlour last a couple of hours and are aimed at true whisky enthusiasts rather than the casual visitor taking in a whisky distillery as part of their holiday.

At Aberlour it's all about the people. The distillery has selected a group of guides who are knowledgeable, engaging and when it's called for, opinionated. This is a good thing because whisky is a passionate drink, and it's hard to get a sense of that passion if you're not convinced your guide really enjoys a good malt, or indeed, has even tasted one.

A typical Aberlour tour is an unhurried affair with a small group, and it ends in a bar area where you can ask questions at your leisure and enjoy six whiskies while doing so. The tour itself isn't run-of-the-mill either. Aberlour was the first distillery to

RIGHT Aberlour's still room, the distillery offers great tours.

end the tour with a chocolate and whisky matching.

'It upset some of the traditionalists,' one Pernod Ricard employee said. 'But we just told them to drink the whiskies and give the chocolates away to someone else. Pretty simple really.'

If all that's not enough, you can trade up to tasting samples of expressions no longer on sale.

The definition of a good distillery tour is one where you come away learning something new, and that's what happens at Aberlour. At one time Aberlour let guests nose three still samples, the first of which was taken from the very start of the run, when the spirit is at its strongest and most dangerous. You would never have known from nosing it that it contained poison. Add water, though, and it turned in to a viper's nest. Fascinating.

Aberlour itself is a classic Speyside malt, all sweet and clean rich fruits. The key expressions are made up of spirit matured in a mix of bourbon and sherry casks. The exception to this is the wonderful Aberlour a'bunadh, a small-batch release bottled at cask strength and invariably heavily sherried, though the taste varies from batch to batch.

British drinkers may not be as familiar with the distillery as they are with other malts, but it is one of the top-ten biggest-selling malts in the world, and it has a particularly devoted following in France, where it is the country's best-selling malt and where the locals rhyme its name with *amour*.

ARDBEG
www.ardbeg.com

Could this be my nomination for the best whisky moment ever: drinking cask-strength Ardbeg at the distillery after a two-day sponsored charity event, which comprized travelling from Jura to Ardbeg by cycling 48 km (30 miles), walking the same and rowing five km (three miles) from Bruichladdich across Loch Indaal to Bowmore. The first day went fine until lunch, when we collected our bikes at Bunnahabhain and started up the long hill from the distillery. A nightmare that wasn't helped by Bunnahabhain's then distillery manager, who insisted on sharing a couple of cask-strength malts just as we were leaving. Problem was I hadn't been on a bicycle for 35 years. By the time we reached Bruichladdich for the first stop I could barely walk. So the rowing – and that's another story – and the lengthy walk from Bowmore was a blistery nightmare. Worth it though – for those Ardbeg drams. It is hard not to love Ardbeg regardless. The distillery is known for its big, peaty whiskies, it is one of the prettiest distilleries in the world, and provides some of the best food on Islay.

Ardbeg 10-year-old 46% ABV

The 'standard' bottling never disappoints. This is a humdinger of a whisky, big, oily, tarry and sweet, with wave after wave of solid peat. Awesome.

Ardbeg 17-year-old 40% ABV

You rarely see this any more but it does come up at auctions from time to time. It's included here because it has reached iconic status but it probably has more value as a collectable than a drinking whisky. A few years ago Ardbeg's owners released Blasda, which was Ardbeg without much peat. That's a bit like Metallica doing unplugged show. No thank you. This isn't that peat lite but it is less peaty that other bottlings. It's also very rare now.

Ardbeg Auriverdes 49.9% ABV

The name refers to green and gold, and is a reference to golden malt whisky in the iconic green bottle. This is an intriguing Ardbeg release, with a more sedate start than many other Ardbegs. It's also enjoyably but somewhat surprisingly fruity, with tropical fruits and a creamy texture, and the big wave of phenolic peat is accompanied by hot chocolate notes. Intriguing.

Ardbeg Blasda 40% ABV

This very nearly did not make the cut, but finally made it through after an intense second round of tasting. The problem here is that approaching it as an Ardbeg is like going to see heavy-metal band Iron Maiden and lead singer Bruce Dickenson playing along to a string quartet. You want the volume up to 11. You should bang your head to Ardbeg, not tap your feet. And this is a muted toe-tapper, with the peat turned well down and the strength at only 40%. The name means 'sweet and delicious', which says it all really. It is truly delicious – it just doesn't taste like Ardbeg, so bear this in mind.

Ardbeg Corryvreckan 57.1% ABV

Corryvreckan is one the most violent and dangerous whirlpools in the world, close to Islay and Jura. You can only safely pass over it at certain times of the day during low tide and even then it's an experience – a wide stretch of small eddying pools make a collective monster. With such a raw display of nature come countless fables and legends, but undoubtedly it has claimed many lives (see box, p.57). The whisky is like the reputation: calm and placid on the surface, while underneath it is dense and rich in plummy jam fruits wrapped in intense smoke, with citrus notes running through. Wonderful.

Ardbeg Kelpie 46% ABV

Released on Ardbeg Day at the Islay Festival in 2017, this malt twists and turns like a caught snapper. The spices come courtesy of Black Sea virgin oak casks. Barbecued meat, sharp spice, treacle toffee and dark chocolate dominate, but there's a delicious fruitiness in the mix too. Great to find Ardbeg still serving up surprises.

Ardbeg Perpetuum 47.4% ABV

This is the fourth and final whisky in the 'works in progress' and is effectively a cask-strength version of what has become the standard 10-year-old. What a great moment when this was released. Few Ardbeg fans would have tasted this and been disappointed. It is undeniably vintage Ardbeg – lots of sweet and sour, and fruit and peat notes to compare and contrast.

Ardbeg Supernova 58.9% ABV

From the faintly ridiculous to the truly sublime. If Blasda were acoustic Motorhead, then this would be Motorhead with your head stuck in the bass bin, the peat scale turned to max. The oily coal-like notes form a tsunami, crashing over the palate into the throat then refusing to budge. Liquorice and cocoa appear, too.

Ardbeg Uigeadail 54.2% ABV

Named after the source from which Ardbeg takes its water, this is almost the definitive distillery bottling. Bottled at cask strength it is a hugely flavoured whisky, with all the rich, tarry and phenolic peat tones that the distillery excels at. But behind the curtain is a malt of sublime complexity. You will find sweetness, citrus fruits, earthy and astringent notes, smoked fish, seaside flavours and dark cocoa.

ARDMORE
www.beamglobal.com

If there were any justice in the world Ardmore would be a household name. A Highland distillery situated to the south of Speyside, it makes a great deal of malt: one of the few distilleries at the time of writing that was still in full production as the rest of the industry slowed. Most of its output goes in to Teacher's, a malty, rugged blend with more character than many of its competitors. But now, under Beam Suntory, the single malt is becoming known in its own right. It will probably not become as familiar as The Glenlivet or Glenfiddich, because it is altogether more challenging. But I do not think any other distillery has staff who are more proud of their product, and rightly so, because at its best, Ardmore tastes like no other dram. It is the backbone of a great blend and it has the potential to win new admirers by the year.

Ardmore Legacy 40% ABV

Legacy replaced the traditional bottling in 2014. Lower alcohol with earthy, charred smoke and savoury, oaky notes offset by some floral and citrus notes late on.

Ardmore Traditional Cask 46% ABV

A few years ago the previous owners of this distillery, Allied, launched an experiment under the watchful eye of a skilled team of whiskymen including Robert Hicks and Michael Cockram. The idea was to put a number of malts into small quarter-sized casks, as would have been the way a couple of centuries ago. The small casks mean more interaction between spirit and wood, and a faster process of reaction and flavour absorption. Of the several malts involved, only two worked out well – Laphroaig and Ardmore. This whisky is not an easy ride. It has a rootsy, savoury, bamboo-like nose; on the palate it's the whisky equivalent of a delicatessen, with savoury flavours, olive and artichoke, waves of grungy peat – oily, full, demanding. It really grows on you, and the grungy brine and peat finish are a delight.

Key whiskies

Ardbeg 10-year-old 46% ABV
Ardbeg Auriverdes 49.9% ABV
Ardbeg Corryvreckan 57.1% ABV
Ardbeg Kelpie 46% ABV
Ardbeg Perpetuum 47.4% ABV
Ardbeg Supernova 58.9% ABV
Ardbeg Uigeadail 54.2% ABV

ABOVE Most of the buildings at Ardbeg, including the striking main building, were built in the nineteenth century, and stand at the head of a protected inlet on the southern side of beautiful Islay, an essential shelter from the North Atlantic.

ARDBEG

Port Ellen, Isle of Islay, PA42 7EA
www.ardbeg.com

As shards of sunlight pepper the broody inky-blue waters around Islay, the bows of the boat rise and dip in the swell, and the white walls of the distillery appear and disappear with each surge as seaspray cleans the pores and alerts all the senses.

It is an invigorating and exciting way to arrive on the Hebridean island of Islay and at the three great distilleries that hug its rugged southeastern shoreline. If whisky were the music industry, Ardbeg and its neighbours Laphroaig and Lagavulin would be its big industrial heavy metal bands, the Metallica, Iron Maiden and Motorhead of malts. For whisky lovers this compact three-km (two-mile) stretch of coastline is a peaty paradise, unrivalled anywhere else in the world.

Of the three, Ardbeg is easily the most cherished. While its neighbours flourished – healthily supported by the international drinks companies that owned them – Ardbeg struggled, stopped producing on a couple of occasions and was nearly lost entirely. It was eventually bought and rescued by The Glenmorangie Company. It was in a sorry state, its farmhouse-like still houses and production areas badly neglected, in need of some serious repair work. Since then the distillery has been restored to its full glory and it's not only a delight to visit, but it can now boast the best food on the whole island, produced in the delightful Old Kiln Cafe. Like the distillery, the remaining whisky wasn't in great shape either. Stocks of whisky in the warehouses were, by any standards, no more than ordinary.

For these reasons, what Glenmorangie's director of malts Bill Lumsden and his team have achieved with Ardbeg is nothing less than extraordinary. Unearthing a number of diamonds in the dust, they set about mixing old and new malts throughout the first years of the new millennium to produce malt gems such as Airigh Nam Beist and Uigeadail. But it wasn't until 2006 that the distillery properly qualified for whisky's Champions League and it hasn't looked back since. That year saw the launch of Very Young: a 6-year-old whisky made entirely with malt produced since the reopening, and the awards have been pouring in on a regular basis since then. By 2008 its flagship 10-year-old was being made with all new malt.

Ardbeg is small – making just over one million litres (0.25 million US gallons) a year on one pair of stills, a tenth of the amount that Glenfiddich is capable of, and the new owners show no signs of messing with quantities, having stuck doggedly to the traditional way whisky is made here.

This, though, comes with its own set of problems. The stills are stubborn old beasts, unpredictable and untameable, regularly throwing tantrums and sulkily refusing to play along with the stillmen. They are, literally, high maintenance, but don't dare suggest the distillery could do with a new pair.

When they do decide to work properly they produce a complex, distinct, sweet and peaty spirit. It is matured on site in warehouses just a few metres from the shoreline. The debate over whether coastal maturation influences the flavour of the whisky has been going on for as long as Scotland has been making whisky and is never likely to be resolved, but the warehouses in Ardbeg put up a great argument for those who believe it does – their walls are caked with salt and you can taste the saline in the air. It is a whisky every bit as exciting as the sea-crossing journey to Islay.

WELL, FANCY THAT...

Ardbeg Corryvreckan is named after a large and vicious whirlpool off the coast of Islay and close to the island of Jura. The third largest of its kind in the world, the Corryvreckan is actually a series of small whirlpools that form over a shelf on the seabed. During certain tides and at certain times of the year waves ten-metres (33-foot) high and travelling at high speed crash noisily through the narrow straits nearby. The whirlpool can only usually be crossed at certain low tides. It has claimed scores of lives over the years and wrecked dozens of boats. The writer George Orwell was left stranded by the whirlpool on Jura while writing the novel *1984*.

ARRAN
www.isleofarrandistillers.com

If you are an Elvis Presley fan you will know that the only time he set foot in the United Kingdom was when he landed very briefly at Prestwick Airport on Scotland's west coast. Why Prestwick? Because back in the day it served as Scotland's main international airport, the airport most likely to stay open, because of the fact that it rarely freezes there or struggles with snow.

If you want to travel to the distillery at Arran, then you can fly to Prestwick and take a train to Ardrossan for the ferry crossing. And the moderate climate that the airport and the island have in common has a great deal to do with the whisky that is produced on the Isle of Arran. There are palm trees on Arran. Really. The island sits slap bang in the middle of the Gulf Stream. The distillery itself, only built in the 1990s, sits in a suntrap, and all of this has had a profound effect on the whisky.

Every new distillery faces a dilemma. After three years you have whisky and you can sell it as such, but is it up to the job? How long can you afford to leave it? On the one hand, in the short term, the investors want some money and you have to keep shelling out for wages, fuel and so on; on the other, the short-term damage of bottling immature whisky may fatally impact your reputation in the longer term.

Some of Arran's early efforts were very poor indeed. But then something wonderful happened. Around seven years old, the malt went from ugly duck to beautiful swan, it took on a rich, creamy texture and the distillery started to bottle a wonderful malt that not only tasted different from anything else coming out of the islands, but it also tasted like nothing else on earth.

The Arran Malt 100 Proof 57% ABV

Arran in all its pomp and finery, and one of the distillery's very best bottlings. 100 Proof is the strength at which gunpowder soaked in the spirit will ignite. Expect a grapey green apple nose from this, some chewy barley and highly attractive sweet lime on the palate and a creamy finish.

The Arran Malt 8-year-old Madeira
50% ABV

Madeira finishes can go two ways – and there's a danger that the big dose of sweetness will be too much. Not here, though. This is an outstanding expression of Arran. The irresistible nose is of strawberry soda, sweet lime and exotic fruits, the palate is a refreshing mix of fruit Starburst, stewed apple and pear and a topping of vanilla ice cream. Clean, summery and guaranteed to have you reaching for another.

The Arran Malt 10-year-old 46% ABV

Full and creamy in feel, with some butterscotch and spearmint on the nose, a big chunk of chewy barley, rich melon and sweet candy on the palate and a gentle and rich, medium-long finish.

The Arran Malt 12-year-old 43% ABV

A coming-of-age for Arran, but slightly disappointing because there is less of the buttery richness and more orange and mandarin notes, some ginger, barley and spice. It has a good finish though, which is almost liqueur-like.

The Arran Malt 14-year-old 46% ABV

Introduced to replace the 12-year-old as the distillery's standard bottling, this 14-year-old brings a whole new wave of flavours to the Arran malt whisky party, thanks to two years finishing in fresh bourbon and sherry casks. The heightened fruitiness is matched by some additional oakiness, too.

The Arran Malt Fontalloro 55% ABV

Another sweet and fruity delight, this time with mandarin notes joining the parade of citrus fruits on the nose, and a full and oily mix of tinned fruits in syrup on the palate. Not too much, though. This whisky is not over-sweet and has a nice balance throughout.

The Arran Malt Moscatel
55% ABV

The nose on this one is a little odd, with roses, old lady's perfume, lavender and toffee all popping up. Taste-wise it is equally intriguing: sugared almonds, apple peel and some pepper combined with a certain oiliness make for a surprisingly agreeable overall package and a pleasant and warming peppery finish.

Isle of Arran Robert Burns 43% ABV

Floral, with Parma violets and some perfume notes on the nose, and a very sweet taste, reminiscent of squidgy melon and tinned exotic fruits. Clean and refreshing on the palate.

Machrie Moor Batch 7
46% ABV

Named after a peat bog lying close to the distillery, Machrie Moor is the taste of a distillery yielding to the demand for peated whisky, having consciously chosen to go the unpeated route when it first opened in 1993. The smoke is not immediately evident on the nose, which is a fruit bowl, though it works its way through given time. The peat is moderate, like burning hay, and there are some pleasant citrus notes in the mix, too.

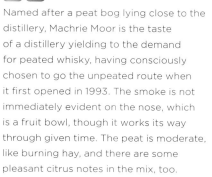

AUCHENTOSHAN
www.auchentoshan.co.uk

When the distillers at Auchentoshan started making a beer last year, it may have been that they were completing a circle, for Auchentoshan is built on the site of an old monastery where the monks were almost certainly into brewing – another link between brewing, distilling and the Church. Something of an oddball, it was once a wee rural distillery (the name means 'corner of the field') but is now part of the Glasgow urban sprawl. It can therefore lay claim to being Glasgow's distillery. It is unusual in other ways, too. It is a Lowland distillery but draws its water from Loch Katrine some ten-km (six-miles) away in the Highlands. It triple distils, too, one of the few establishments to do so in Scotland. It could be that the distillery's time has come because owner Beam Suntory has invested heavily in visitor and conference facilities, the brands got a makeover and there have been several new expressions released. This is a beautifully maintained distillery.

Auchentoshan 12-year-old 40% ABV

Replacing the standard 10-year-old two years ago, this is a big improvement, with the extra two years giving it a new dimension. Still quite light but with a nicely balanced fruit and malt taste and just enough spice to pep it up.

Auchentoshan 18-year-old 43% ABV

Not as woody as you might expect, but the sherry-cask influence gives a richness and spiciness and the slightly higher strength reflects a step up in quality.

Auchentoshan 21-year-old 43% ABV

Without a doubt the best of the range. All grapefruit, zesty citrus, hints of oak, spice. Very drinkable, utterly irresistible, right up there with the very best of the Lowlanders.

Auchentoshan Select 40% ABV

This is Auchentoshan at its fruitiest and freshest, suggesting youth. Some citrus notes, some berries and a clean refreshing barley taste all reflect its young age.

Auchentoshan Three Wood 43% ABV

A rep for Auchentoshan was sat at a bar once when the barman, a New Zealander, started explaining the background of different single malts to an American guest: 'The bar man was doing fine until he got to Auchentoshan,' he recalls. 'The guest asked him about Three Wood and he said "Oh that's a special bottling for golf clubs. Auchentoshan do a Seven Iron, too, and I think this summer they're launching a Putter." I nearly fell off my seat.' Three Wood actually refers to the oloroso, Pedro Ximénez and bourbon casks used in maturation.

AUCHROISK

The Singleton is a generic name that means different things in different countries. Buy a Singleton in Europe and the malt is Dufftown. In the Far East it's Glen Ord. In the United States it's Glendullan. But the original Singleton, and the one that commanded the most loyalty, was the Singleton of Auchroisk. When it was launched in the 1980s anybody listed in the phone book with the name Singleton received a free miniature of it. It is now bottled under its own name as a single malt but you don't see it too often because most of it goes into J&B blended whisky.

Auchroisk 10-year-old 43% ABV

Orange, lemon, a touch of smoke and a savoury under-taste makes this more than just a 'me too' Speyside malt. Light and refreshing, it makes a good summer whisky.

BALBLAIR

www.balblair.com

Balblair is a Highland distillery sited on the Dornoch Firth, very close to Glenmorangie. This is a region steeped in ancient history, stone monuments and the remains of dwellings from ancient races and tribes. Clach Biroach – the sharp stone – is not exactly Stonehenge but it proves that a race of people who predated the Picts by 2000 years understood the moon and stars, because the stone is aligned against the nearby hills and marks the summer and winter solstice, giving guidance to the people as to when to plant and harvest crops. The Picts adopted the stone, too. Four thousand years on it has been adopted as a symbol of the distillery. The whisky here is fresh, clean and sweet but relatively unknown, though owner Inver House has recently rebranded the range.

Balblair 2005 46% ABV

Balblair gains strength with simple, consistent malts. It may only be one trick, but it's a top trick, with just the right level of fresh lemon and orange, marmalade, treacle, oak-spice and milk chocolate. Bright, floral, more-ish.

Balblair 2004 46% ABV

Perfect summer malt with great music such as The Shirelles or the Mama and Papas. Sweetness and vanilla from the bourbon casks, sherbet fruits and orange Starburst on the nose, then a healthy dose of sweet barley, exotic fruits and sweet orange. An alternative dessert?

Balblair 1997 43% ABV

This is like drinking alcohol-soaked Del Monte tinned fruits. It is all kicking off here in the sweet fruit department – mouthcoating vanilla, lime cordial, kumquat and orange peel, with rich barley and a trace of sweet pepper to finish.

Balblair 1990 43% ABV

More fruit here but this time from a different bowl. The trademark vanilla is there but also pineapple and green fruits on the nose and a mix of tinned pears and icing-sugar-like spices plus an oak finish.

THE BALVENIE
www.thebalvenie.com

The Balvenie is the Jack Daniel's of Scotland – a big malt-producing distillery that has successfully managed to convince the world of whisky that it is a small, artisanal one, producing handcrafted small-batch malts. It is in fact a Speyside whisky producer owned by William Grant and occupies the same site as sister distillery Glenfiddich. And it does seem small in comparison. It has its own floor maltings that produces a fraction of the malt it requires, and it sits next to Grant's traditional labour-intensive cooperage so you get a sense that it is from a different era. Balvenie is another distillery, like Aberlour, offering outstanding VIP tours. You will be shown around in small groups, often led by someone who has 30 years' experience in the industry. The tour is as thorough as it gets.

The Balvenie DoubleWood 12-year-old 40% ABV

Matured first in American oak and then in sherry casks, this is the whisky equivalent of a show house: well presented but does not exude the warmth you get from the great Balvenies. But, there are some pleasant fruit notes and a sherry richness that make it an acceptable everyday dram.

The Balvenie DoubleWood 17-year-old 43% ABV

Exceptional: a rich velvet glove whisky, matured in two cask types. Lots of honey and vanilla, a balance of malt and oak, fluffy apple and citrus notes. A malt masterpiece, as good a malt as you'll find.

The Balvenie PortWood 21-year-old 40% ABV

An absolute masterpiece, and arguably the finest port finish available. Traces of oak reflect its age, with good nuttiness and big lashings of fruit. This is wonderful in every respect.

The Balvenie Rum Cask 17-year-old 43% ABV

Rum is influential from the off here, with dark rum and raisin notes, some oak, plus all sorts of exotic fruits, including apple and citrus. Complex and curious, another triumph from an impressive distillery.

The Balvenie Signature 12-year-old 40% ABV

The nose here is complex, dry and woody, like pencil shavings, with satsuma and orange notes. Fruitcake and orange fruits on the palate and a pleasant, fruity finish.

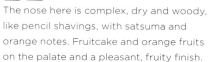

Balvenie Single Barrel 15-year-old 47.8% ABV

Up there with the very best, the intention here is to pick the sweetest, most dessert-like Balvenie. Lemon, lime, Starburst fruit with sweet barley and zingy spice. Fruit syrup dusted with icing sugar on a delicate oaky base. Enjoy.

The Balvenie Tun 1509 B4 51.7% ABV

Name refers to the marrying vat used to make this wonderful series of small-batch single malts. A hand-selected mix of sherry- and bourbon-cask whiskies are married in tun 1509. Sublime whisky: toasted oak, dark chocolate, doughnuts, ginger spice. Hefty price tag doesn't deter.

BEN NEVIS

www.bennevisdistillery.com

Fort William feels like it is the last outpost before you get to Scotland's Wild West. You can cut across country to Speyside from here, head up to the Isle of Skye and the far north, or take the scenic route along Loch Ness. But, whichever way you go, it gets pretty bleak and desolate. The Ben Nevis distillery, in the shadow of the mountain, is an odd one. Owned by Japanese company Nikka, it has a chequered stop-start history and it's not well known as a single malt. Much of the distillery's output goes into blends and it is one of the few whiskies that uses the same name for both a single malt and a blend. If you can source it though, it is a weighty, robust and complex malt.

Ben Nevis 10-year-old 46% ABV

A big and oily Highland whisky that tastes as rugged as the environment that produced it. Here you'll find attractive dark-chocolate-orange notes, chunky malt and exotic fruit.

BENRIACH

www.benriachdistillery.co.uk

It may be only a small distillery, but like Bruichladdich on Islay, BenRiach sure does make a hell of a lot of noise. BenRiach used to belong to Pernod Ricard and because the company didn't have an Islay malt it set about experimenting with peated whiskies here in the heart of Speyside. It did not release any of them, but since a consortium fronted by Billy Walker took over, bottlings have come thick and fast, and some of the peated releases have been magnificent. The distillery is something of a dream for malt fans – small and farm-like, it has its own floor maltings that Walker has started using again, and the big fires have been back in action, too, peating the barley. The whole place is in immaculate condition and all sorts of unusual casks are maturing in its warehouses, maintaining its history as a test distillery. Add to that a wide range of always interesting bottlings, and we are talking serious whisky heaven.

BenRiach 10-year-old 43% ABV

A more intense version of Heart of Speyside, this has lots of sweet fruit, honey and vanilla and a delightfully summery finale.

BenRiach 16-year-old

43% ABV

Back to classic Speyside malt, and the next step up from the 12-year-old. This offers a pretty straightforward journey from honey, vanilla and sweet fruit on the nose to a sweet and clean medium finish at the end, passing through apple crumble and vanilla ice cream. Late spices add depth, but this is about as far from the Fumosus bottlings as you can possibly get.

BenRiach 20-year-old 43% ABV

This whisky is a bit shy on the nose, and you have to work hard to find grape, apple, pear and marzipan. The palate, though, is an elegant delight – a subtle and sophisticated marriage of fresh yellow fruits, vanilla, oak and honey. A slightly higher strength and the oak influence give this whisky its shape and a sense of purpose.

BenRiach 35-year-old 42.5% ABV

The age shows through significantly with this one, where the honey and citrus of younger bottlings are joined by dusty wood so that the overall effect is like a big oak-panelled office that has recently been polished. On the palate citrus and orange fruits give way to wood and spice. The finish is quite sharp but the orange fruits just about hold their own.

BenRiach Aromaticus Fumosus
12-year-old 46% ABV

This is finished in a rum cask but of all this series it is the least affected by its finishing school. What we have here is a peaty monster, with lots of grungy smoke. The rum-cask ageing gives it a nice sweet core, but really this one is for lovers of Islay.

BenRiach Authenticus
21-year-old 46% ABV

The pick of the bunch from this great distillery, this Authenticus pulls off the rare feat of balancing rich fruit and intense peat and smoke. There is East Anglian Cromer crab and cured fried bacon on the nose, but also apples and peach. On the palate sweet tinned fruits and milk chocolate are wrapped in a wall of peat and smoke. Some astringency, an oaky influence and a spicy bite lead to an oily, charcoal finish.

BenRiach Curiositas 46% ABV

The team at BenRiach seems to have a lot of fun coming up with Latin-derived names for their peated whiskies. At 10 years old, this has been bottled at 46% and 40% (try the higher strength, a growling monster of a malt). Acrid charcoal smoke and soot mix with lemon and cocoa on the nose; on the palate is a stunning mix of melon and peach, diesel smoke and coal dust. There is a slightly acerbic wet-fire finale, but overall this is a corker.

BenRiach Dark Rum Wood
15-year-old 46% ABV

If you like your whisky sweet, this one's for you. On the nose it's all dairy chocolate, honey-and-caramel bar, on the palate it is rum-and-raisin ice cream, vanilla and exotic fruits. A touch of spice and oak come through late on. A one-trick pony.

BenRiach Heart of Speyside 40% ABV

The distillery's entry-level malt is classic Speyside – lots of sweet fruit and vanilla on the nose, pineapple barley and citrus fruits on the palate, and an agreeably sweet medium-long finish, with a touch of spice.

BenRiach Heredotus
Fumosus 12-year-old
46% ABV

You cannot accuse the whisky makers here of playing safe. One of a number of peated whiskies finished in casks used to mature other drinks. It has the potential to taste like too many paints mixed together – a browny black mess. In fact, all four bottlings in the series work. This is full, oily and peaty, with a soft yellow citrus and blackcurrant centre, like a smoky, liquid Turkish Delight. A long, smoky, fruit finish is exceptional.

BenRiach Importanticus Fumosus
12-year-old 46% ABV

Not quite reaching the dizzy heights of the last whisky, this one is still exceptional. The nose is a challenge, with brine and peat as well as vanilla, fruits and some floral notes, but the taste saves it, with port and lemon, grapefruit and smoke and a long finish.

BenRiach Maderensis
Fumosus 13-year-old 46% ABV

This one makes the claim that it is heavily peated and it is – so much so you can write your name in it, the whisky equivalent of a steam fair, but the 'spoonful of sugar helping the medicine go down' comes courtesy of soft pear and melon notes and a lemon flourish. The finish has all the classic BenRiach sootiness you could want.

BenRiach Moscatel Finish
22-year-old 46% ABV

Another dessert whisky, boasting melon, pear and vanilla on the nose. It tastes like chocolate-lime bonbons at first, with some wood influence and a touch of pepper and spice late on. All in all, though, this is sweet and lingering.

BenRiach Pedro Ximénez Finish
17-year-old 46% ABV

There is no doubt about the quality of the whisky making here. A quite restrained nose with some toffee apple and mince pie, but on the palate this is a mouthcoating and rounded malt, which elegantly unveils a procession of flavours including grapes, nuts, spice, some oak and marzipan. Sophisticated and seriously classy.

BenRiach Sauternes Wood
16-year-old 46% ABV

Another whisky with a curio for a nose, with stewed bamboo shoots, doughballs and a musty sweetness not selling the malt particularly well. But the taste is much better. It is zippy, with grape, berries and vanilla all vying for attention, some pluminess coming to the fore and distinctive sweet pepper and oakiness towards the end. It is a bit of a tangy taste sensation, this one, with its rich orange syrup colour.

BenRiach Tawny Port Wood
15-year-old 46% ABV

What a weirdo! The nose is all over the place, with rosehip syrup, chestnut and dark coffee notes. The palate is something else again, with fresh clean soft fruit and barley and a charming and clean finish.

BENROMACH
www.benromach.com

Benromach lies close to Forres, to the north and west of the Speyside region. It is a small, rustic distillery now owned by independent bottlers Gordon & MacPhail, who bought it, invested heavily in it and saved it from demolition. It was reopened in the late 1990s. Although classed as a Speyside distillery, the spirit produced here is varied but much of it has a distinctive peaty earthiness, and profile-wise it fits better with Highland distilleries such as Glen Garioch, Ardmore and Glencadam. Benromach was the first distillery to produce an organic single malt approved by the UK's Soil Association. This meant stripping down all the equipment and cleaning it to an approved standard, and using organic oak barrels.

Benromach 10-year-old 43% ABV

Malty Ovaltine, sappy damp straw and flour doughballs; a savoury wave of peat and smoke, then a delicatessen smörgåsbord, with touches of cocoa and fruit. Intriguing, challenging, different and – overall – worthwhile.

Benromach 15-year-old 43% ABV

Apple, pears and some prickly peat on the nose; lime, guava and kiwi fruits on the palate. Overall this is sweet and clean, with some vanilla and marmalade notes. Later spice arrives and stays to the conclusion.

Benromach 35-year-old 43% ABV

Lemon-and-lime jelly bonbons to the fore on the nose, backed by spice, peat and oak. The aroma suggests a treat. And it is – like a heavy-metal band with three egotistical lead guitarists trying to outperform one other. Oak, spice and peat are all to the fore here, but it is the fruity rhythm section that holds it together and prevents a random mess. 'Free Bird' in a glass.

 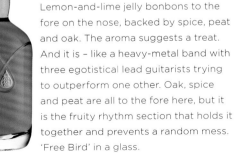 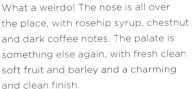

Benromach Château Cissac Wood Finish 43% ABV

The nose is a bowl of over-ripe fruit, resinous, with oak and peat vying for attention. On the palate there is chunky melon and the pleasant interplay between peat and oak remains. Yet another individual whisky from this intriguing distillery that has sailed down a little flavour creek all of its own making.

Benromach Hermitage 45% ABV

This is from Benromach's wood-finish range and was matured in a cask that had previously held French wine. It's a real cutie with lots of juicy fruits including gooseberries and orange. There is a degree of rustic earthiness underpinning the flavours and a hint of spice, but the fruit theme wins out overall. The finish is long and fresh with a hint of smoke.

Benromach Organic 43% ABV

This organic dram is softer and sweeter on the nose than the Traditional or the 10-year-old, but with oak and some toffee and mashed pear. With time, hints of raspberry and blackberry sherbet. The palate is big and bold, with oak and blackcurrant squash, followed by a wave of pepper; overall a sweet and spicy treat. A long, spicy and liqueur-like finish.

Benromach Origins 2010

(BOTTLED 2017) 46% ABV

You have to reset your radar for this one. The nose is very odd and disconcerting, with some sulphur notes and then milk chocolate. It is intriguing more than off-putting, but you do wonder what it's going to taste like. The sulphur soon gives way on the palate, and you are left with a liqueur-like treacley malt, with sweet brown sugar in the mix.

Benromach Peat Smoke 2007 46% ABV

Lemon drizzled on grilled sole and barbecue wood chips on the nose, this is a charming mix of creamy lemon and feisty peat. All in all, a big fat and fishy peaty treat.

Benromach Triple Distilled 50% ABV

This weighs in at a hefty 50%, and it needs the strength to prevent it blowing away, it's that light and flighty. The triple distillation is a nod to the whiskeys from over the Irish Sea, but here it gives Benromach some unusual notes – sweet, light, floral and citrusy aren't normal descriptors for this distillery, but they are all here with bells on. A pleasant departure.

Benromach 1976 43% ABV

The aroma of this one is reminiscent of a church sacristy with incense, fresh flowers and polished oak. Maybe a Spanish one at that, where the priest likes fruit, because there's some Seville orange marmalade in the mix, too. And it's orange marmalade that dominates the palate, as the oaky tannins give the whisky a hint of astringency.

Benromach 1955 42.4% ABV

There are few distilleries that could age a cask for more than half a century and end up with a whisky as sublime as this. It comes from a cask that was laid down and cared for by a team of people many of whom are no longer with us, from the days before pop and rock music as we now know it had yet to be invented, before Elvis and The Beatles, before computers and moon landings. Mind-blowing. The whisky is delicate and subtle, with mandarin and tangerine fruits, together with traces of peat, oak and spice.

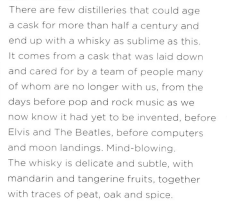

BLAIR ATHOL

www.malts.com

Blair Athol is a pristine, well-maintained Diageo distillery close to Pitlochry and this is an ideal base for a whisky lover with a less interested family. Blair Castle is only up the road, there is plenty to do and see, great walking and a handful of distilleries and whisky attractions within easy reach. This distillery is the spiritual home of Bell's and there is a small exhibition, though it pales alongside Aberfeldy (Dewar's World of Whisky) and Glenturret (The Famous Grouse Experience). All very pleasant but it is so well maintained that you can forget they make whisky here.

Blair Athol 12-year-old Flora and Fauna 43% ABV

One of those single malts that feels as though it was intended for blending. It is a surprisingly full and fruity malt, rich and thick, with some pleasant fruit notes.

BOWMORE

www.bowmore.co.uk

Bowmore lies halfway up the island of Islay on the sea loch, Loch Indaal. It faces Bruichladdich, which is about five km (three miles) away across the loch. Each summer there is a swimming event across the loch but can I suggest you do not row it unless you've taken advice on tides. This comes from bitter experience. We did it for a charity event and became a little concerned when a fishing boat came alongside and the six lads on board told us that they were escorting us for our own safety. They were bluffing though, and were in fact a bunch of distillery workers out for a laugh. We did well for three-quarters of the crossing but then realized that Bowmore wasn't getting any closer. So as we struggled to row harder the boat crew passed along a flask and tried to curb their raucous laughter. Finally they took pity on us and towed us in. They asked me to join the annual round-island row for charity after that, but I never did it, deciding I would be better off preserving what dignity I had left.

Bowmore 12-year-old 40% ABV

If Lagavulin, Ardbeg and Laphroaig are the Iron Maiden, Metallica and Motorhead of whisky, Bowmore is its Bon Jovi. The whisky from here is peated but not so fully as the southern distilleries are – altogether a more mainstream taste. Bowmore can rock when it wants to, though, and this expression might be a lightweight but it is still a classic – a sort of 'Keep The Faith' or 'Livin' On a Prayer' for malt drinkers. A peaty and seaspray nose leads to fruit and spice on the palate.

Bowmore 15-year-old Darkest 43% ABV

Combining peat and sherry is one of the most difficult tricks in the single-malt repertoire, but here Bowmore's creators pull it off with aplomb. The spirit has been matured in oloroso sherry casks and the result is a rich, seductive smoky and plumy delight, with toffee, berries and oak in the mix. Ace.

Bowmore 18-year-old 43% ABV

I believe that everybody who discovers the joys of whisky will have an enlightenment moment, when you cross the threshold from interest to passion. I remember vividly the first time I went to an English soccer match at Filbert Street, Leicester some time around 1968. I remember walking up the steps to our seats and the pitch coming into view, the sheer excitement and wonder of it illuminated by dazzling floodlights, the noise of the crowd and sense of anticipation – the beginning of a lifelong love affair. My whisky equivalent was my first taste of Bowmore 17-year-old, with its distinctive Parma-violet notes and weird fruit-and-peat mix. Sadly the 17 is long gone, and the 18 isn't a patch on it, but there are enough positives to hold the attention, even if it's all a bit too slick and clean.

Bowmore 25-year-old 43% ABV

Surprisingly clean light and delicate for a whisky of such an age, most of the distinctive flavours here are sherry-influenced, with berry fruits and some citrus in the mix. It is all rich and chewy – a very pleasant experience.

Bowmore Legend 40% ABV

Bowmore Legend had a loyal following back in the day. This version is matured in bourbon casks and is an easy-going light malt. Vanilla, sweetness and as big a wave of peat and smoke as you will get from any Bowmore. There is also some lemon and orange in the mix.

BRUICHLADDICH
www.bruichladdich.com

Reopened at the start of the millennium, Bruichladdich has proved itself a very twenty-first-century distillery ever since. Its smart packaging and distinctive sky-blue livery has made it instantly recognizable, and a large range of different and diverse bottlings – a good proportion of which are outstanding – has won it a loyal fan base across the world. The team has never been slow to exploit a marketing opportunity or to promote itself, nor has it minded being Islay's maverick distillery, and these days, under the ownership of Gruppo Campari, it is exploring the provenance of its grain.

Bruichladdich 12-year-old
46% ABV

This has a very fresh and enticing nose, with vanilla, citrus and yellow fruits. The palate is a tin of exotic fruits in syrup, with vanilla ice cream for good measure. Soft and rounded, it is a very more-ish whisky.

Bruichladdich 15-year-old Links
46% ABV

This is one of a series of releases named after classic golf courses. Not quite sure why. But this is very different from the last bottlings, with its earthy, wet grass and autumnal roots on the nose, and a challenging but not unpleasant mix of clean barley and grape on the one hand and some tannin and spice on the other. The finish is medium with wood, spice and some dryness.

Bruichladdich 16-year-old Bourbon Cask 46% ABV

Rich, sweet, honeyed and with vanilla on the nose, lots of bourbon candy and vanilla notes, masses of fruit and, again, with a touch of spice very late on.

Bruichladdich 18-year-old
46% ABV

The nose is grungy and rootsy, with stewed chestnuts reminiscent of Chinese food. The palate is savoury, with grape and clean barley, some chilli and a salt-and-pepper finale.

Bruichladdich 20-year-old
46% ABV

The nose is complex, with some mustiness and tannin kicking out at a flavour combination of date, dried apricot and tinned pear fruit compote. The palate is clean and refreshing, with some peppermint, oak and traces of peat among candied fruits and fluffy apple. All soft and subtle, with some sweet pepper and spice at the finish.

Bruichladdich 21-year-old 46% ABV

The aromas here are rich, with dried fruits and some softer citrus-candy notes. The taste is big, rich and bold, with the age of the cask adding gravitas while peach and apricot are enhanced by pepper and oaky tannins. Astringent in the finish, deep autumnal brown in colour, with a greenish hue.

Bruichladdich Black Art 5

48.4% ABV

It's called Black Art, but this just might be the most drinker-friendly version of what has become an iconic series of malt releases. Imagine Eminem donning a clown outfit and skipping out on stage for a cover of REM's 'Shiny Happy People'. This is it. All bright fruits tumbling one after another. There's still time for some rapping at the centre, in the form of some deeper, earthy notes, but overall this is a pussycat: delightful and cuddly.

Bruichladdich Blacker Still 50.7% ABV

A tidal wave of prunes, sultanas and pantry spices on the nose. The taste is heavily sherried, with great spoonfuls of over-ripe fruit, a big oak hit and an array of spice. The sort of style the Japanese make, utterly seductive – a roller coaster, but the finish delivers you gently back to earth.

Bruichladdich The Classic Laddie Scottish Barley 50% ABV

The whisky equivalent of England's Manchester City football team drawing 0–0. There is plenty good going on here, and it's all very attractive, but despite all the delightful grain notes, there's a distinct lack of finish, and it never quite manages to score.

Bruichladdich Infinity 52.5% ABV

Here you will find an Islay coastline on the nose, with brine and seaweed. Tastewise it is like eating a tin of exotic fruits while smoking. Very sweet and smoky, this is yet another Bruichladdich that is all too easy to fall in love with.

Bruichladdich Islay Barley

50% ABV

It does exactly what it says on the tin. This is young, single and free, and what it lacks in finesse it makes up on in energy and attitude. This is bouncing barley from start to finish – with a touch of ginger stem in for good measure.

Bruichladdich Octomore 63.5% ABV

This comes in stylish and very unusual packaging and is out-and-out Islay, with big waves of charry tar, barbecued bacon and grilled fish on the nose. A big oily whisky that needs water. Once unlocked it's a charmer – trout drizzled with lemon, playful phenols, a very sweet peat centre and a stunning finish.

Bruichladdich The Organic Scottish Barley 50% ABV

Bruichladdich is putting some serious effort in to its theories on terroir, and certainly it would seem differences exist. This isn't anywhere near as playful as the Islay Barley (above). It is young, a tad winey and a wee bit undercooked. But, the quality of the grain at its heart is undeniable.

Bruichladdich Port Charlotte Heavily Peated 58.7% ABV

Port Charlotte is the little town close to the distillery and the whiskies using the name have come to mean intense and highly peated wonder-beasts. Describing a Port Charlotte malt as 'heavily peated' is like describing a new Metallica track as 'heavily metal'. It doesn't disappoint though: big and peaty, with growling industrial smoke. And some bubbling fruit notes in the mix – Metallica with a bassline maybe?

Bruichladdich PC11 59.5% ABV

Not quite what you might expect, with a damp-wood and lighter peat attack, more subtle and restrained than PC6. On the palate, more tarry peat and growly smoke, but the predominant flavour is stewed tinned strawberries. As with PC6, a long and impressive finish, with fruit and smoke dancing around each other to marvellous effect.

Bruichladdich PC12 58.7% ABV

This has deep tar and strong coastal notes on the nose; oily and rich to taste, with the full range of peated flavours, from diesel engine to tarry rope, smoky barbecue and seaweed. A long, gentle fruit-and-smoke finish. Sublime.

Bruichladdich Redder Still

50.4% ABV

Remember dandelion and burdock fizzy drink? This is on the nose here, only with alcohol. Plus blackcurrant cordial and floral notes. On the palate there are lots of intense candied fruits: lemon, lime and orange. A clean intense malt stormer this.

BUNNAHABHAIN
www.bunnahabain.com

Kilchoman and Bruichladdich might be located further west, but Bunnahabhain on the island of Islay feels like Scotland's last malt outpost. To reach it you drive pretty much to the end of the island and just before Port Askaig set off down a long sloping pathway. The distillery hugs the shore under the shelter of the cliffs, and the view out across the sound of Jura and towards the Paps is breathtaking. The distillery itself is a little weatherbeaten, the offices dated, but like a loveable scruffy mongrel, the friendliness of the welcome here makes up for the tatty appearance.

Bunnahabhain promoted itself as the 'gentle taste of Islay' because its core brands have only a light peatiness. Within the distillery's warehouses, however, there are some stunning peated casks. And in recent years the distillery's owner has allowed some of the peated stock to be bottled, most notably Toiteach, meaning 'smoky'.

Bunnahabhain 12-year-old

40% ABV

Only lightly peated it may be, but this 12-year-old is a rugged, coastal malt, and there's a salt and a nutty earthiness among some solid fruit notes. Late on a rapier-sharp, barley-spice hit welcomes in a hint of sherry trifle, adding sweetness to an otherwise savoury malt.

Bunnahabhain 18-year-old

43% ABV

In some ways this is another departure for the distillery but something of a star nonetheless. Rich and full, there are some big fruity sherry notes, plenty of oak and traces of citrus.

Key whiskies

Bruichladdich 25-year-old 45% ABV
Bruichladdich Black Art 5 48.4% ABV
Bruichladdich Islay Barley 50% ABV
Bruichladdich The Classic Laddie 50% ABV
Bruichladdich Scottish Barley 50% ABV
Bruichladdich Octomore ABV VARIES
Bruichladdich Octomore Islay Barley 55–60% ABV
Bruichladdich Octomore Scot. Barley 55–60% ABV
Bruichladdich Port Charlotte Islay Barley 50% ABV
Bruichladdich Port Charlotte Scottish Barley 50% ABV

ABOVE The Bruichladdich distillery viewed from the hills behind it.
BELOW Bruichladdich is loved globally because it oozes quaint charm.

BRUICHLADDICH

Port Charlotte, Isle of Islay, PA49 7UN
www.bruichladdich.com

The most popular distilleries are a bit like soccer teams. Their loyal followers treat them like they own part of them, and see the people running them as mere custodians who will move on long before they do.

One such distillery is Bruichladdich on the island of Islay. It holds a special place in many people's hearts because in 2000 it became one of the first distilleries in Scotland to be reopened after being locked up, seemingly for good, a couple of years earlier. The small team behind the purchase nurtured strong relations with the many whisky devotees who travelled to the distillery, and made a great deal of the fact that the distillery was independently owned as opposed to the distilleries elsewhere on the island owned by international drinks companies. It didn't hurt that the distillery is a dinky and delightful one, and that the whiskies, of which there are many, were, in the main, very good indeed.

So there was considerable disquiet when a majority of the shareholders, acutely aware that the tide was in for Scotch whisky and the values of distilleries were grossly inflated, decided to sell it in 2012. There seemed to be genuine shock and anger that the people behind such a populist distillery would 'sell out' to a big purchaser for profit.

The worry was misplaced. The purchaser was Remy Cointreau, and although the company is an international one, it has proved to be remarkably sympathetic to the several businesses it has purchased, and has done nothing to change them or to interfere in the way they are run.

In the case of Bruichladdich there have been several signs that all will be well in the future. For instance, the sale allowed the distillery to close down for a few weeks to replace vital equipment, a luxury not available to the previous owners because they needed to make and sell every drop of whisky they could in order to stay afloat. The distillery says that while it respects the past, it is open to innovation and experimentation. That said, though, there are plans to reintroduce a floor malting within the distillery, reinforcing its status as a traditional hands-on operation.

Remy even took former Bruichladdich chief executive Simon Coughlin over to head a whisky division within the company. Its commitment to continuity is in evidence in just about everything Bruichladdich does, but mostly in the whiskies it has released. Former managing director Mark Reynier came from a wine background, and was very keen on the idea of terroir. To this end, whisky has been made with barley from different fields, and from barley bought from the Scottish mainland and from Islay itself. Experimentation in grains has continued and these days the distillery provides a diverse range of whiskies, including organic malts, unusual finishes and special releases.

Traditionally Bruichladdich's whiskies were peat free, but these days just under one-third of the malt spirit is peated and matured to be sold under the name Port Charlotte, and a further 10% is bottled for the very peaty and a wee bit gimmicky Octomore range, which won headlines when it was used as fuel for a sports car, and to power a rocket.

What always made Bruichladdich special is still very much in evidence – it is a small distillery with a dedicated and family-like team of people behind it. One of the most enthusiastic and friendly members of that team was the head of communications, Carl Reavey. It was a great shock to everyone who knew him, when he passed away suddenly at the start of 2018. He will be very much missed.

ABOVE Bruichladdich experiments with local barleys.

Bunnahabhain 25-year-old

46.3% ABV

The malt and salt you expect from a Bunnahabhain are in place but this is altogether a bigger, more lavish whisky than others in the portfolio. The fruits are rich and chewy, the oak influence is big and bold and the core barley is delightfully full and sweet. Very good indeed, but whether I would trade three bottles of 18-year-old for one of these is a moot point.

Bunnahabhain Ceòbanach

46.3% ABV

Anything other Islay distilleries can do... Bunnahabhain has always had heavily peated malt, and indeed, once upon a time that would have been the house style. And in recent years it has started to share them again. Ceòbanach is aged in ex-bourbon casks for more than ten years, and it has some lovely seaside notes alongside the waves of smoke.

Bunnahabhain Stiùireadair 46.3% ABV

I haven't the faintest clue how to pronounce this. What's the point of that? This whisky has a creaminess to it, some saline, salted nuts in crisp toffee and some oaky spice. It's from a sherry cask and has some rich berry and citrus notes, too. It is not typical of Bunnahabhain at all, but it does show the variety of malts on offer at the distillery – where I have tasted some wonderful whiskies and maintain that it is still underrated.

CAOL ILA

www.malts.com

Caol Ila is Islay's biggest distillery, but it's only in recent years that it has become known to the whisky public, and its widespread success is partly an accident. The distillery makes a typical Islay peated malt, but it also makes a lot of unpeated malt. Most of the output is used to make blended whisky, and its natural oiliness make it very much in demand as a binding malt. Some of it ends up in the independent bottling section but tread warily if you go down that route as there are great varieties across the distillery's output. So, how do we know it's due to an accident? Caol Ila is owned by Diageo and is one of two distilleries owned by the company on Islay. The other is Lagavulin, which was one of the original six Classic Malts that were sold together to pubs in a display plinth. A few years ago the company realized that they had miscounted their stock of Lagavulin and once the Classic Malts allocation had been dealt with there was not much left for everyone else. So Caol Ila stepped into the breach. Much of the output from the distillery going into blends is unpeated and occasionally appears as such in the form of special bottlings.

Caol Ila 12-year-old 43% ABV

One of the reasons Caol Ila is such a good blending malt is its oiliness, and this is oily – but in the nicest possible way. At this age it is lively, with sooty peat, some citrus fruits and a little burnt bacon-rind all adding to a rich tapestry of flavours.

Caol Ila 18-year-old

43% ABV

There is a view that peat is most expressive when young, and once it's been aged for more than 15 years it loses some effect. If the imperious Lagavulin 16-year-old provides a counter argument then the release of the 18-year-old last year kicks it into touch. This mix of age, sophistication and oily smoke show that a peated whisky never needs to be too old to rock and roll.

Caol Ila 25-year-old 59.4% ABV

An Islay classic – with the oils, seaspray, smokiness, barbecued trout with lemon, burnt bacon and oak all in evidence and all playing a role in making this one of the very best malts you can buy.

Caol Ila Moch 43% ABV

This no-age-statement whisky brings an altogether soft side to Caol Ila's peaty offerings. The nose is wispy, with baked apple and sherbet, There are sweet citrus fruits on the palate and gentle waves of woodsmoke. The finish is sweet and pleasant. In recent years Diageo has released some wonderful unpeated malts from this distillery and this one is another fine example of its flexibility.

CARDHU
www.malts.com

Cardhu's main claim to fame in recent years has stemmed from an unholy row caused when its owners Diageo added malt from other distilleries to it and branded it as Cardhu Pure Malt. That story has been regurgitated *ad nauseam* elsewhere so let's not bother with it here.

Cardhu is in Speyside and it makes the best 12-year-old malt in the region. The distillery is the symbolic home of Johnnie Walker and it has an amazing history. Originally founded by whisky smuggler John Cummings and his wife Helen at Cardow farm in 1811, it was first run by Helen, and then her daughter-in-law Elizabeth, who became famed for her whisky making and marketing ability and who expanded the distillery into a major operation. This remains one of the few times that women have run whisky distilleries, made all the more amazing given that it happened during the Victorian era, when women tended to play a far more submissive role in society.

Elizabeth's son, John Fleetwood Cumming, took over from her and was the first person in Speyside to own a car. He was driving it back to the distillery when he encountered Willie, the distillery's handyman, coming the other way on his bike. Willie, who had imbibed a few drams of Cardhu and had never seen a car before didn't quite know how to avoid it, so steered first left, then right, before riding off the road altogether and ending up in a ditch.

Cumming stopped his car and rather than check to see that Willie was alright or to apologize for driving him off the road, unfairly berated him for being drunk instead: 'yer a disgrace to yersel', yer a disgrace to yer family and yer a disgrace to my distillery,' he said, to which Willie replied: 'It's a wonderful thing this whisky. It puts some of us in big flashy cars, and it puts others of us in the ditch.'

The number plate of that first car can still be seen in Speyside on a blue Mercedes. A few years ago the owner turned down an offer from London-based porn magazine and sex-show promoter Paul Raymond for the number plate. He had realized that if the number was attached to a car with the rivets in the right place the number SO110 would look very much like Soho.

Cardhu 12-year-old 40% ABV

Hard to find outside Spain, but this an absolute must for fans of Speyside malts. This is the whisky equivalent of the chocolate factory of Johnny Depp's Willy Wonka in the 2005 film *Charlie and the Chocolate Factory*: an oral mass of happy bright colours and an overdose of the sweetest, fruitiest most delectable flavours you could ever imagine.

Cardhu 15-year-old 40% ABV

Cardhu 12-year-old with the volume turned up. Fuller and with an added third dimension over the 12-year-old, this expression has some nuttiness among the malt. Vanilla and oak both make an appearance here in another very palatable and fruity malt.

Cardhu Amber Rock 40% ABV

Don't believe all the fake news about no-age-statements – they're not all bad. In fact this one regularly top scores in my blind-tasting events. The spirit is matured in ex-bourbon casks so there is more vanilla than in the 12-year-old.

CLYNELISH
www.malts.com

The coastal road from Inverness to Wick has been described as Scotland's forgotten coastline, but it is home to a string of excellent distilleries, including Glen Ord, Glenmorangie, Balblair and Dalmore. Clynelish is here, too; a distillery that is sometimes not given the credit due to it partly because it's a relatively new distillery built in the 1960s and overshadowed by the ghost of Brora, which occupied the same site for a few years but was finally put down and replaced by Clynelish. Shame really, because it produces very good whisky. No doubt its day will come.

Clynelish 14-year-old 46% ABV

With green fruit and some melon on the nose, zippy lemon sherbet and fruit on the palate, this expression is given an extra dimension by its strength, together with traces of pepper and peat to round it all off.

Clynelish Distiller's Edition 46% ABV

This has been put into big sherry casks and it shows, with the Clynelish at the heart of the mix struggling to keep its head above the influence of the cask and just about succeeding. Arguably, Clynelish does not need this treatment, but it is worth trying because I suspect some people will fall in love with the unusual mix.

CRAGGANMORE
www.malts.com

Depending on how you define the region, well over half and up to two-thirds of Scotland's distilleries are in Speyside. We associate distilleries there with fruity, sweet, honeyed whiskies but it was not always that way. Before the Industrial Revolution, distilleries would have used peated fires to dry the barley. But Scotland's whisky has a long and close association with trains and as the railways spread into Scotland they brought with them cheaper commercial fuels such as coal. On the mainland peat was made redundant and its use only continued on the islands because trains do not generally travel through the sea. Cragganmore was one of the first distilleries to build a railway siding into the heart of the distillery, ensuring an efficient method of bringing in supplies from the mainland and shipping out malt. The distillery's whisky was chosen by Diageo to represent Speyside in its Classic Malts collection.

Cragganmore 12-year-old 40% ABV

If you are of the view that Speyside whiskies tend to be predictably fruity, easy drinking and unchallenging, then this should change your mind. It is a surprisingly complex malt, with heather and spring meadow on the nose, while on the palate you will find deep fruits, oak and wisps of smoke.

THE DALMORE
www.malts.com

You know those signs that say 'you don't have to be mad to work here but it helps'? Well they were invented for places such as Dalmore. Located in the northeast of Scotland on the Cromarty Firth, it's as wacky and kooky as a whisky distillery gets. While many distilleries are logically constructed and contain a balance of wash and spirits stills, Dalmore is anything but. Its stills come in a range of shapes and sizes and distilling is a hit-and-miss affair, with different runs coming off at different strengths. Making malt here is the whisky equivalent of flying a kite in a gale. It's a demanding process

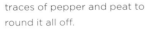

made more complicated by the unpredictable water supply. Water travels down to the distillery from a little reservoir, but on its way the water must travel over a wall. When the water levels fall below the level of the wall, the water stops flowing completely, so global warming, therefore, is not the distillery's friend.

Making spirit here is a tough ask, so you can excuse a certain degree of ordered chaos. The resulting spirit, though, is robust, fruity and the starting point for some of the finest-tasting single-malt whisky in the Highlands.

The Dalmore 12-year-old 40% ABV

A burnt caramel, rich orange and mandarin taste and some oaky notes make this seem older than its 12 years, but it is a big, full malt with lots of flavour, most notably a sprinkling of cocoa dust and some charming spicy notes.

The Dalmore 15-year-old

40% ABV

The nose is reminiscent of a church on Easter Sunday morning, with polished oak, fresh flowers and a hint of sherry. On the palate there are bucket-loads of fruit, with tangerines and satsumas in the mix. Vanilla, cinnamon and some woody tannins all contribute to a big, bold and spicy whisky. Delicious.

The Dalmore 18-year-old 43% ABV

Released late in 2009, this is a step up for Whyte & Mackay because it's bottled at 43% ABV instead of the company's favoured 40%. It has a bold and meaty nose with a trace of sulphur and then intense orange and red berry fruits. The palate is a big and busty mix of fruit, chewy malt, oak and spice – all rather wonderful. This is a heavyweight of a whisky.

The Dalmore 40-year-old 40% ABV

Historically, whisky stills in the Highlands are small. While barley was in abundance in the Lowlands and big commercial malt stills were built to produce the volumes of malt needed to service the growing blended whisky market, in the Highlands barley is harder to grow so there was less of it to turn into whisky. Smaller stills also suited the illicit distillers because they could be transported or hidden from the gaugers more easily. But the more the spirit comes into contact with copper, the more fats, oils and flavour compounds are removed, creating lighter, more floral malts. Short, squat stills allow more to pass though into the final spirit, making for an oilier, meatier and fuller malt. Robust malt is better suited to standing up to the influence of the cask, and that's why you can get the likes of Dalmore and Macallan maturing 40, 50 and even 60 years and they still taste good. This has a shy nose at first, and you don't want to be adding water to a whisky this old, so work with it. Eventually there are some orangeade and lemonade notes. The taste is elegant, delicate and citrusy. Added to this there are some dark chocolate, nutmeg and plummy notes for good measure.

The Dalmore King Alexander III 40% ABV

Legend has it that one of the Mackenzie clan saved King Alexander from death during a hunting trip and as a way of thanks he granted the Mackenzies the right to use the royal stag's head in its livery. When the Mackenzies became involved with The Dalmore, the stag's head emblem was taken up and now appears proudly on all bottles. In commemoration of this, whisky-maker Richard Paterson has married casks of The Dalmore of different ages and of different types. As a result the whisky has all sorts going on, with plums, red liquorice, vanilla and red-berry fruits on the nose and a big hit of stewed fruits, oak, cherry and spice on the palate. Oh, and if you're wondering what the different casks were, the malt was matured in wine, madeira, sherry, marsala, Kentucky bourbon and port casks.

The Dalmore Cigar Malt 44% ABV

Now and again the world of whisky is shaken by a row, and here is a case in point. Owners Whyte & Mackay discontinued it because it was seen as an anachronism. The malt's many fans disagreed and clamoured for its return – and here it is. This version contains slightly older malts to the previous one, but has many of the same characteristics: lots of burnt orange zest, rich sherry notes and char. Earthy and robust.

Dalwhinnie 15-year-old 43% ABV

Dalwhinnie does not come in a range of ages, but that is because its owners discovered long ago that its perfect age is 15. This is one of the truly great malts, traditionally part of the Classic Malts range. It is a rich, full and mouthcoating malt defined by two very different traits: intense honeyed sweetness wrapped around the fruit and malt centre, and a peaty earthy carpet to rest it all on. That combination – sweet and earthy – is what great Highland whiskies are about.

The Dalmore Dominium 43% ABV

This special edition of Dalmore is finished in Matusalem sherry casks (González Byass) and the trademark orange and toffee notes of Dalmore are tempered by a fragrant and spicy note on the nose, and by citrus and exotic spices on the palate.

Dalwhinnie Distiller's Edition 43% ABV

Tasting this after the 15-year-old is like watching The Rolling Stones do 'Undercover of the Night' for an encore after they have ended their set with 'Jumpin' Jack Flash', 'Satisfaction' and 'Sympathy for The Devil'. It is better than many other malts, but you have just pretty much experienced perfection so this cannot help but be a tad disappointing. That said, the oloroso influence works well, and there is still plenty to enjoy, particularly for fans of the core whisky.

DALWHINNIE
www.malts.com

Arguably the funniest sign in the United Kingdom is the one that greets you at the tiny village of Dalwhinnie just off the A9 on the road up to Aviemore. 'Dalwhinnie – twinned with Las Vegas', is what it says. In winter, when the snow is a metre (three-feet) deep and the icy gusts from the Cairngorms reach into your soul, the village is a remote and barren place and really far removed from the glitz and glamour of Las Vegas. Thankfully God invented whisky for such occasions, and the malt at Dalwhinnie is the ideal tonic for such extreme conditions. The distillery can no longer claim to be the highest in Scotland now that Braeval has reopened, but sipping a 15-year-old at altitude is a marvellous experience.

Dalwhinnie's sign is not the funniest I've ever seen. That honour goes to a house door near Cork in Ireland. It says: 'This is the back door. The front door is round the back.'

DEANSTON
www.burnstewartdistillers.com

It is cool to be green these days, so Deanston has an advantage over many of its competitors, one that its owner has hit upon and taken full advantage of. The distillery is like no other, beside a fast-flowing river it is a tall, foreboding eighteenth-century cotton mill of the dark satanic variety. It was founded by the great industrialist Richard Arkwright and it channels water from the river to drive a wheel and power its own electricity plant, so successfully that it provides light and heat for both the distillery and the local community. The old Deanston sold very well in the United States a while back, but was not stunning. The replacement is an altogether richer, fruitier affair. It is like Speyside, with spicy, nutty notes and eco-friendly packaging.

Deanston 12-year-old 46.3% ABV

The replacement 12-year-old Deanston is a vast improvement on the original standard Deanston: a softer and more rounded, fruity palate and a longer finish.

DUFFTOWN
www.malts.com

Clever people, the malt marketing folk at Diageo. Having backed down in the row over Cardhu a few years ago, they came up with another way of spreading their limited stocks further afield by encouraging people to drink malts they might not have otherwise chosen. A few years back the Singleton of Auchroisk built up a considerable following before it was eventually withdrawn. Now the Singleton is back – but what you are drinking depends on where you drink it. In Asia the malt in the bottle is a sherried version of Glen Ord. In America it's Glendullan, while in Europe it is Dufftown you will encounter.

Singleton of Dufftown 40% ABV

This is a bit like the quiet bloke who comes down to the pub to watch soccer with the lads. All perfectly pleasant and harmless, but you would not really miss him if he was not there. This is a workman-like Speysider with nothing worthy of criticism but nothing to get excited about. It is included here, though, because it is an easy-drinking entry-level malt – a tame pony to teach novices how to sit in the saddle.

FETTERCAIRN

Fettercairn is a rustic Highland distillery that has not had the best press in the past. This is a little unfair. One celebrated whisky writer was so critical of the malt from here that he has not been invited back. Which in turn means he has never updated or reassessed his criticism. Perhaps he should. Some of the whisky in casks at the distillery suggests that Fettercairn has a lot to offer as a single malt. A few years ago a new range of four malts was released

in new packaging. The malt has adopted a unicorn emblem as a reference to the Ramsays – distillery owners who were noted for their philanthropist tendencies. Fettercairn was sold on to the Gladstone family, and Liberal Prime Minister William's familiarity with whisky led to legislative reforms that abolished the malt tax, allowing the sale of whisky in bottles to the public, and tax laws, so distillers were no longer taxed on the 'angel's share' (the 2% of spirit that evaporates during maturation). There is plenty to thank this distillery for, so the Fettercairn fight-back starts here.

Fettercairn 24-year-old 44.6% ABV

An awkward malt, which initially hides behind a slightly rubbery, sulphury nose but in time gives way to a taste of tangerine and grapefruit, some cocoa and some prickly spices. It is like prising conversation out of a sulky schoolboy and finding he is remarkably bright and interesting – just lacking in confidence. A strange but ultimately worthwhile experience.

Fettercairn 30-year-old
43.3% ABV

The best of these three old releases is a delight: surprisingly young-tasting, with zest of red apple and soft pear, some melon and orange fruit and eventually a subtle wave of spice. The age only starts to make itself known very late on. In the finish there is blackcurrant sherbet. Fettercairn – poor? Oh no.

Fettercairn 40-year-old
40% ABV

Classic old Highland whisky without a blemish. Early on it is surprisingly soft and gentle, with grapefruit and lemon and some savoury notes, but it builds with oak and spice adding to the body and gives way to raspberry and glacé cherry. The finish is long but gentle, with spice and oak.

GLENCADAM

www.angusdundee.co.uk

The traditional view of a distillery setting up close to a primary water source is turned on its head by Glencadam. This Highland distillery, close to Brechin on Scotland's coast, pipes water 48 km (30 miles) to meet its distilling needs but the malt made here does have a distinctive creaminess, using an unpeated malt.

Glencadam 10-year-old 46% ABV

Sweet strawberries with ice cream on the nose, pleasant and easy malt and spice on the palate, with some raspberries, strawberries and redcurrants. The spiciness remains through the finish.

Glencadam 15-year-old 46% ABV

Arguably the definitive Glencadam bottling, here the extra age gives the malt a fuller and richer mouthfeel. The berry notes are still prevalent on the nose, but on the palate the oak makes its presence felt and with time tannins and spices battle against the berry fruits, leaving a long oaky and spicy finish.

Glencadam 25-year-old 46% ABV

A rare and unusual bottling of Glencadam because there are some distinctive sherry influences. Indeed, this is a classic big Christmas pudding of a whisky, with sherry-soaked raisins and mulled wine on the nose, leather, raisins, plummy fruits and spices on the palate, with tasty strawberries and ice cream in the fruity finish.

THE GLENDRONACH

www.glendronachdistillery.com

Talk to people with long memories in and around Huntly, and they'll talk of GlenDronach as a big, proud, dark, sherried whisky, a million miles away from the somewhat anaemic 12-year-old that kept the brand's name alive. For many years the distillery's owners Allied Domecq did not seem to know what to do with it, and for years it seemed to drift, unloved and uncared for. When Allied was broken up, Teacher's and Ardmore went to Beam while GlenDronach, a key component in the blend, went to Pernod Ricard. It felt like a divorce, and the distillery's wretchedness was summed up on the quaint maltings floor, where cardboard figures had been placed to show visitors what a working maltings was like. Then in 2008 the team behind BenRiach got its hands on the distillery and wasted no time in restoring the distillery to its former glory. The following years a new range of standard bottlings and a number of special releases – yes, big, dark, sherried ones – were released. They have helped put GlenDronach well and truly back on the distillery map.

The GlenDronach 8-year-old The Hielan 46% ABV

As you come to expect from this management team, this takes GlenDronach away from its sherry comfort zone. The grapey and nutty notes are still there, but creamy vanilla is also there thanks to the use of some bourbon casks. It's all very warming and excellent value for money.

The GlenDronach 12-year-old 40% ABV

Some mint toffee on the nose, with sherry, berries and citrus fruit. The taste is reminiscent of blackcurrant and cranberry, there is some pepper and an earthiness that ensures the overall effect is not too sweet. A savoury finish with some peat.

The GlenDronach 15-year-old

(2009 RELEASE) 46% ABV

The new version of the 15-year-old is deep brown, leaving the drinker in no doubt what is coming next. There are distinctive wisps of sulphur on the nose but this doesn't detract from a grandiose and complex nose that includes sherry, floral notes and chicory coffee. The taste is also intense and challenging, with sweet fruitcake at first, then a wave of chilli and paprika, and finally some woodiness, astringency and plummy smoke. The finish is about three Ps: plums, peat and pepper. Wonderful.

The GlenDronach 18-year-old

(2009 RELEASE) 46% ABV

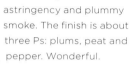

Not for the faint-hearted this. You want big old-fashioned sherry-cask malt? You've got it. There are earthy and rootsy aromas with some distinctive sulphur on the nose, but don't be too put off – the taste is all about plum, stewed fruits and raisins. There is some astringency from the wood late on, some peat and menthol and some spices on the finish.

The GlenDronach Peated

(2009 RELEASE) 46% ABV

A massive departure for GlenDronach and not just because of the peat. This malt is matured in bourbon casks and is then transfered to oloroso to give it more recognizable sherry notes. It's like adding a peaty brass section to the core rocking GlenDronach sound. And it works. GlenDronach is now part of the Brown-Forman empire. Before it was sold on it had built up a reputation for unpredictable and, at times, challenging releases. Let's hope that continues. The early signs have been good.

GLEN ELGIN

www.malts.com

Several towns lay claim to being the 'capital' of Speyside but Elgin's claim is as good as any. Elgin is, according to its website, Scotland's smallest city and its friendliest, and has a fascinating history based around its cathedral. But it also lies close to several distilleries and is home to outstanding independent bottling company Gordon & MacPhail. The company's large shop in the town is well worth a visit if you are in the area, especially if you are looking for something different, whisky-wise. Glen Elgin distillery lies in a small village on a road into the town and has been long associated with the White Horse blend. It has a substantial following as a single malt, too, and its reputation as a rich, fully flavoured and honeyed malt has been enhanced by some special bottlings in recent years, including a cask-strength bottling as part of Diageo's Manager's Choice series in 2009.

Glen Elgin 12-year-old 43% ABV

This is an example of classic Speyside at its best. You don't see it very often, but if you like clean, sweet, malty and plummy whiskies then you need to seek this one out. An unsung hero.

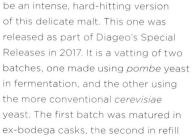

Glen Elgin 1998

61.6% ABV

A version of a 1998 Glen Elgin was released in 2009 at 11-years-old, and it proved to be an intense, hard-hitting version of this delicate malt. This one was released as part of Diageo's Special Releases in 2017. It is a vatting of two batches, one made using *pombe* yeast in fermentation, and the other using the more conventional *cerevisiae* yeast. The first batch was matured in ex-bodega casks, the second in refill European oak butts. The result is a very creamy and honeyed whisky with lots of delicious fruity notes.

GLENFARCLAS

www.glenfarclas.co.uk

Glenfarclas is to whisky what Bentley is to cars – excellently made, to the highest standards, in the traditional manner. You do not mess with classic style, so there are no gimmicky finishes from the distillery, no malt alchemy in its labs. Glenfarclas is one of the last family firms still making whisky in Scotland and it survives by simply being the best at what it does. And what it does is produce big, bold, fruity, sherry-influenced Speyside malts. Family member George Grant has taken on the ambassadorial role for the distillery and is increasingly its public face, though he has threatened to cut back on the travel. It's not all it's cracked up to be, he says, especially when you are detained at immigration in the Far East twice – once for carrying a plastic bag full of white powder, which turned out to be barley flour, and once for carrying a suspicious-looking lump of peat.

Glenfarclas 10-year-old 40% ABV

There is some orange and lemon on the nose here, followed by Christmas cake, rich malt, some orange notes and a warm and delightful finish.

Glenfarclas 12-year-old 43% ABV

A rich and full sherry influence here, with stewed plums and apricots, honey, cinnamon and nutmeg. This is a perfect winter warmer.

Glenfarclas 15-year-old

46% ABV

The extra strength and age adds another dimension to the malt here. Tangerine, marzipan and red berries complement the sherry trifle and Christmas cake mix. Some oak adds tannin and spice, to give the overall flavour balance and shape.

Glenfarclas 21-year-old 43% ABV

A slight departure from what has gone before, the intensity of previous bottling is replaced by a candy-ish flavour, less sherried and perhaps with more vanilla and yellow fruit notes.

Glenfarclas 25-year-old 43% ABV

Glenfarclas responds well to old age. I was given a small bottle of whisky from the year of my birth by John Grant at a Speyside festival: from 1961, at 44 years old, as well as an advance sample. Sublime, it one of the best whiskies I've ever had – toasty, spicy and fruity. I opened the bottle around my 50th birthday.

Glenfarclas 30-year-old 43% ABV

The nose is surprisingly soft and rounded with some marmalade and oak notes. The oak is noticeable in the taste, too, with crystal barley, pepper and earthiness.

Glenfarclas 40-year-old 43% ABV

A big wave of pink grapefruit, burnt toast with chunky lime marmalade on the nose, and rich orange marmalade, dark orange chocolate and Turkish Delight on the palate. A very lucid flavour for one so old.

Glenfarclas 105 60% ABV

A weighty, intense classic malt and the epitome of clean and crisp sherried whisky. Clearly you need some added water, and this releases raisin, date and plum flavours, sweet, spicy orange notes and some delicious crystallized maltiness at the end.

GLENFARCLAS FAMILY CASK

Glenfarclas might not be experimenting with weird casks and strange finishes, but that does not mean it is not capable of being a pioneer in the world of malt. The Family Cask range has no parallel in whisky – 43 single-cask bottlings covering 43 consecutive years from 1952–94. This is the equivalent to the long-awaited complete archive set of recordings that Neil Young has been promising and which has been appearing in dribs and drabs – a chance to plot the complete history of a distillery. Unsurprisingly, over such a lengthy period of time, there is huge variety on display. And among the casks are:

ABOVE John and George Grant show off all 43 expressions of the Glenfarclas Family Cask collection, covering 1952–94.

1993 Cask 11 58.9% ABV

Nose: metallic, sulphur.
Palate: sherry, sharp astringent oak, dark, intense finish.

1991 Cask 5623 57.9% ABV

Nose: Almost European liqueur-like fruit, sweet.
Palate: Rich, mandarin orange, creamy, oak.

1989 Cask 11721 60.0% ABV

Nose: Powerful, rich orange, fruitcake, sulphur.
Palate: Rich, sweet, rounded and very fruity.

1988 Cask 7033 56.3% ABV

Nose: Odd, herbal, oil paints.
Palate: Soft fruit, pear, liquorice.

1981 Cask 29 52.4% ABV

Nose: Chinese spices, tingling.
Palate: Plum fruit, menthol.

1979 Cask 146 52.8% ABV

Nose: Sweet, honey and sherbet.
Palate: Honey and lemon, smooth and rounded.

1978 Cask 587 50.3% ABV

Nose: Linseed oil, nuts, mandarin.
Palate: Rapier-sharp spice, bitter fruit, liqueur-like.

1976 Cask 3111 49.4% ABV

Nose: Ginger biscuit, date, cake mix, European-style fruit.
Palate: Sweet, full and fruity; dates and late pepper.

1975 Cask 5038 51.4% ABV

Nose: Blood orange, hot mince pie filling.
Palate: Orange fruits, liquorice, soft toffee.

1972 Cask 3546 51.1% ABV

Nose: Dusty and musty, smoky, resinous.
Palate: Mint, sharp spices, wood; hot.

1969 Cask 3188 55.6% ABV

Nose: Spent match sulphur, toasty, candy, shrimps.
Palate: Sweet, metallic; raisin, dark cherry, menthol.

1962 Cask 2647 52.0% ABV

Nose: Dry sherry; cocoa, dark-chocolate orange, limes.
Palate: Rum-&-raisin chocolate, mint, sherry, cocoa, oak.

1959 Release III Cask 3227 50.9% ABV

Nose: Mahogany polished office.
Palate: Dark chocolate, treacle toffee.

1957 Release III Cask 2 46.2% ABV

Nose: Stewed fruits, date, oak, dark treacle, nutty.
Palate: Intense marmalade, menthol.

1954 Cask 444 52.6% ABV

Nose: Chestnut, oak, root vegetables.
Palate: Cocoa, dark chocolate, bitter oak.

1952 ED2 Cask 2115 46.5% ABV

Nose: Herb garden, plums, raisins.
Palate: Sweet, salt and spice; tannins.

Key whiskies

Glenfarclas 10-year-old 40% ABV
Glenfarclas 12-year-old 43% ABV
Glenfarclas 15-year-old 46% ABV
Glenfarclas 21-year-old 43% ABV
Glenfarclas 25-year-old 43% ABV
Glenfarclas 105 60% ABV
Glenfarclas Heritage 40% ABV

ABOVE Glenfarclas is an independent family-owned distillery.
BELOW The distillery is known for its excellent sherry-cask-matured malts.

GLENFARCLAS

Ballindalloch, AB37 9BD
www.glenfarclas.co.uk

Very few of the distilleries of Scotland are owned privately, but two of the best known and loved Speyside distilleries remain in family hands: Glenfiddich is owned by William Grant & Son, and Glenfarclas is owned by the Grant family.

The Grants, most of them called George or John, have managed the distillery ever since 1870 when one of the Georges and his son, who is one of the Johns, took on the distillery, as well as the farm it was sited on. The current George represents the sixth generation of the family.

Glenfarclas can be found in the heart of the rural idyl of Speyside, in a remote region criss-crossed with historical smuggler' trails and in the shadow of the impressive Ben Rinnes, from which it sources its spring water. The name Glenfarclas means 'valley of the green grass' and that's exactly where it nestles. From the exterior to looks very much like a farm, and its size is deceptive. This is no craft distillery – it produces 3.5 million litres (nearly 1 million US gallons) of spirit, which makes it mid-table when it comes to the size scale of Scottish malt distilleries. As with all distilleries, demand is high, and in 2017 the family opened another ten dunnage warehouses, raising the total it has by a third.

In recent years across the world of whisky there has been a move to experimentation with unusual casks, and of finishing malt in a range of barrels that had previously held anything from rum to cognac and from beer to sweet wine.

Not at Glenfarclas. The Grant family has no intention of trying to fix something that's not broken. Glenfarclas is made in casks formerly used for the production of sherry. There's something reassuringly traditional about the packaging as well, and when the distillery releases an older and therefore rarer whisky, it has avoided expensive packaging and gimmickry, such as a crystal top or a free decanter, aiming instead to keep the price as low as possible so that regular drinkers can afford to taste it. The one sop it has made to modern trends, however, was the introduction of a no-age-statement whisky under the name Heritage.

Glenfarclas is a rugged whisky, surviving longer than average periods in the cask, so the distillery has been able to release very old expressions. Amazingly it released a 60-year-old in 2014 and has regularly released whiskies aged 50 years old.

If plotting the history of a distillery's malts is your thing, then the Family Cask Collection from Glenfarclas should be right up your street. This was a fascinating trek through history, with a release from every year from the 1960s to the turn of the millennium. The range was surprisingly varied, with taste and colour significantly different, quite possibly defecting the casks available to the company at different points in its history.

The whisky from Glenfarclass is released at a variety of ages but the whiskies tend to be rich, sweet, fruity and with earthy spice notes. The iconic 105 (a British proof measure equating to 60% ABV), is definitely a treat not to be missed.

ABOVE A tour at Glenfarclas: it makes great sherried whisky.

GLENFIDDICH
www.glenfiddich.com

Lovers of whisky have a great deal to thank William Grant & Sons and its number one malt Glenfiddich for. Familiarity breeds contempt and it is understandable that experienced malt lovers might feel the overwhelming urge to move swiftly on but please don't. Pause for a minute and pay tribute to the malt that kicked it all off.

Talk to family member Peter Gordon about how William Grant & Sons has consistently sensed the way the wind is blowing and continually got it right when making big make-or-break decisions and he'll modestly tell you it's been through luck rather than design. I don't buy that. It's a bit like the 'lucky' fisherman who keeps catching the best fish because by chance he's always in the right place at the right time. And from the 1960s, when the company set about putting single malt into the spotlight, right up to the launch of cool and trendy Monkey Shoulder, William Grant & Sons has been instrumental in the development of modern-day malt whisky.

It's hard to believe now, but before the 1970s there was no real single-malt market. Single malts were sold in Scotland and close to the distilleries where they were produced, but their influence was minimal. But, William Grant & Sons had a problem. To make its blended whiskies it relied on grain whisky from its rivals. So what would happen if the suppliers turned off the tap?

The company made two huge decisions in the early 1960s – it built its own grain distillery at Girvan, and it bottled Glenfiddich as a single-malt whisky. It had already come up with the distinctive three-sided bottle. Then, to help explain the world of whisky, the company also opened up the very first visitor centre.

Glenfiddich has been a heavy hitter ever since, and has stayed among Scotland's single-malt whisky producers, though today the likes of Glenlivet and Roseisle (see p.92) also produce masses of malt. Visit the distillery and you'll find a state-of-the-art site geared up for tourists, with guided tours in a range of languages and an excellent restaurant and shopping facility. But William Grant & Sons has maintained its investment in fine malt whisky, and not only is the flagship 12-year-old better than it has ever been, but there is a range of exciting expressions that show the distillery's diversity and the outstanding talents of the whisky makers here. Glenfiddich is a a classic example of the Speyside style, with lots of sweet fruits.

Glenfiddich 12-year-old 40% ABV

The way malt whisky changes over time is rarely discussed. Better cask management and a greater understanding of production and maturation on the one hand, better yielding but arguably blander and more homogenous barley strains on the other, mean the spirit in the bottle today will not be the same as it was 20 years ago. Booms and busts matter, too, eg. the times when a standard 12-year-old will contain more rare and aged whisky than at others, depending on malt supply and demand. No doubt this whisky has changed in recent years and is now better than it used to be. Well-made but unchallenging, entry-level malt – fresh and fruity with vanilla.

Glenfiddich 15-year-old Solera Reserve 40% ABV

Unfortunately, this whisky will always remind me of a prospective candidate for the British Conservative party who joined a group of whisky writers for a short leg of a sponsored walk from Glenfiddich to the Craigellachie Hotel in Speyside. As I walked with him he argued that we should not be raising money for Africa any more because everyone was so rich there now they all had sunstrips on their cars – thanking the British for their new wealth, and that he thought that whisky would be a more viable product if the Scots just added flavourings to industrial alcohol. This is a fine example of Speyside malt, with vanilla creaminess plus soft fruits, sweet barley and a touch of oak. It is beautifully crafted.

Glenfiddich 18-year-old 40% ABV

A full fruit bowl of over-ripe squelchy fruit, with plums, raisins, apricots and grapes all in the mix, and some toasty oaky notes make this a sophisticated and stylish drinking treat.

Glenfiddich 21-year-old 40% ABV

Many of my favourite whiskies are aged 17 or 18 years, but for some reason Glenfiddich does not seem to fully hit its stride until 21. This whisky would probably be my pick of the entire core range, though there are some beauties in the rarer and older vintage range. Boiled sweets, new office and lemon cleaner or polish on the nose, lemon and honey on the palate, plus sweet malt, oak and a touch of menthol. The finish is quite zingy, with lemon and grapefruit in evidence.

Glenfiddich 50-year-old 46.1% ABV

Should a whisky that retails at $15,000 a bottle and that has pretty much all gone anyway, be included in a book like this? That's a big debate and one to be held over a dram or two, though probably not with this particular whisky. Okay, I'm there – yes it should. Once this has gone, it will have gone forever, and there should be a record of it somewhere.

People from all over the world were invited to the launch – one bottle arrived accompanied by a piper, then guests were invited to swoon over it. We had songs and a dramatic and quite brilliant recital of *Ode To a Haggis* by Glenfiddich public relations manager Libby Lafferty. All this was in honour of one whisky. It could have been a disaster, an overdose of sentimentality resulting in a massive anticlimax. But it wasn't, simply because this whisky is stunning. At 50 years old, it is imbued with spritely sweet grapefruit, honey and citrus.

Amazingly, you can trace the thread of this malt all the way forward to the petulant teenager that is Monkey Shoulder. It is like watching the scene in Martin Scorsese's *Shine A Light* when Mick Jagger upstages Jack White, the master showing the pupil how it should be done. Is whisky ever worth $500 a shot? Of course not. Is this a blemish-free, perfectly matured piece of art in a glass and history in a bottle? Very much so. This was distilled before the age of single-malt whisky had fully dawned – and it is an honour to have tasted it.

Glenfiddich 125th Anniversary Edition 43% ABV

This was created to celebrate the 125th anniversary of the opening of the distillery. It contains both peated and unpeated malt, and they have been matured in European sherry and American bourbon oak. The result is a malt that swings from vanilla to smoke to oak, all over the top of a fruity and complex range of flavours.

Glenfiddich Age of Discovery Bourbon 19-year-old 40% ABV

Originally released for the travel retail sector, this is one in a series exploring different cask types. This bourbon shows tropical fruit and lots of sweetness. There are some attractive spices, too.

Glenfiddich Age of Discovery Madeira 19-year-old 40% ABV

You can't beat sweet when it's like this! This is all jellied fruits, sweet dessert ginger and cinnamon and chilli spices. Juicy currants and some dry oak give this a richness and full-bodied finish. Very nice indeed.

Glenfiddich Rare Collection 40-year-old 43.6% ABV

This whisky does not give up its treasures lightly, and you have to chase the nose a bit. But it's surprisingly soft and subtle, with some lovely yellow fruit flavours, as well as honey and vanilla. There are few signs of age, no negative oak or spice notes and a lingering and lovely finish. Quite outstanding.

ABOVE Glenfiddich can produce around ten million litres (2.6 million US gallons) of spirit a year.

BELOW One of the distillery's traditional warehouses.

GLENFIDDICH

Dufftown, Keith, AB55 4DH
www.glenfiddich.com

How important is it to be the world's biggest malt whisky distillery? Judging from the battle for that title between Glenfiddich and Glenlivet, the answer would seem to be 'very'.

A few years ago at the turn of the millennium, when Glenlivet made about six million litres (1.5 million US gallons) of whisky spirit a year, there were audible gasps and a heavy dose of cynicism when Pernod Ricard's management team announced at a press conference that it had plans for Glenlivet to grab top spot from Glenfiddich, its Speyside rival.

At the time it seemed highly unlikely but in 2014, with its production up to 10.5 million litres (2.8 million US gallons) a year, it achieved its goal.

Game over? No chance. William Grant & Sons was having none of it. The following year it was back at the top of the tree with a staggering annual production of 13.7 million litres (3.6 million US gallons), it is holding off all comers, for now at least.

In a world where craft and quaintness are taken as virtues, Glenfiddich's familiarity has bred a considerable amount of contempt, and that's not just sad, it's very unfair. As you might expect the distillery is large and commercially friendly, and it boasts excellent facilities. In the summer there are large tour groups learning about the plant and the region in an array of foreign languages. It is a hands on, bright, interactive centre for tourists.

But it's so much more. For a starter, Glenfiddich is one of only a handful of family-owned distilleries. What's more, Scotch whisky enthusiasts have a lot to thank it for. In 1963 it was the first whisky to be marketed as a Scottish single malt, and a few years later the introduction of its iconic triangular green bottle played a major part of bringing single malt to new markets and competing not just with blends, but other drinks styles, too, bringing Scotch whisky off the optic.

A family company it may be, but William Grant & Sons has not been slow in adopting new ideas or reacting to trends, pretty much ahead of everyone. The family has described itself as fortunate, but there are plenty who don't buy that. This is the company that gave us Hendricks, a gin with a reputation for being craft, before craft gin was a

thing. Monkey Shoulder is a blended malt that was wowing 20-something-year-old bar people before malt whisky became cool again. The family also bought Tuthilltown Distillery in New York just as American craft distilling was taking off, and invested in Irish whiskey brand Tullamore DEW and built a distillery for the brand in Ireland, well in advance of the explosion of Irish micro-distilling.

So it is with Glenfiddich malts. In addition to an extensive core range, there have been a large number of special releases over the years, including a number of vintage expressions up to 50 years old, experimental malts such as whisky finished in IPA beer casks, and a number of special finishes in casks, including former madeira and red wine casks. I also take the view that the regular 12-year-old expression is at the very top of its game at the moment.

ABOVE Glenfiddich: we have a lot to thank it for.

GLEN GARIOCH

www.glengarioch.com

Glen Garioch (pronounced 'geery') is a hidden gem, something of an unsung sibling in the Beam Suntory stable, though that might be changing. Having rebranded and repackaged Auchentoshan a few years back, the company has turned its attention to this highly underrated distillery. You'll find it north of Aberdeen, in the village of Oldmeldrum. It is a small but perfectly formed distillery with a smart, newish visitor centre (see also p.90). Glen Garioch is a Highland whisky but it has had something of an identity crisis – with a distinctive peaty note playing hide and seek.

Glen Garioch Founder's Reserve

48% ABV

Crikey! A new bottling focusing on the fact that this distillery was originally established in the late eighteenth century, but if Morrison Bowmore is keen to win over new drinkers to this malt, it sure is taking a difficult route. This is a true Highland laddie, dominated by big spicy, peaty and earthy notes. Easy it is not, but for me it sits in a special category of old-fashioned Highlanders, alongside Ardmore, Benromach and Glencadam. No bad thing at all in my book.

Glen Garioch Virgin Oak

48% ABV

It takes a big whisky to hold off the overpowering effects of virgin oak, and this one is. The cask is made of North American oak and as you'd expect there is a dusty toasted oakiness, and some vanilla. The pepper-spice stays under control and orange and milk chocolate notes get to make an appearance.

GLENGLASSAUGH

www.glenglassaugh.com

In the heady days of 2008, when malt was at its most buoyant and everybody was after a distillery, Glenglassaugh was snapped up by a private consortium. Its new owners inherited a distillery in a stunning location (it has access to a small private beach) but with virtually no stock at all and with a serious vandalism problem. But they didn't muck about. They invested heavily, recruited industry heavyweights and released three vintage bottlings. They also released 'works in progress' and young whiskies under the names Revival and Evolution.

Glenglassaugh 21-year-old 46% ABV

Boiled-lemon candy and vanilla on the nose, this has a core taste of orange, citrus fruits and crystallized barley, with supporting roles for mint, cinnamon, chilli and oak. The finish is disciplined and polite.

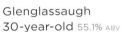

Glenglassaugh 30-year-old 55.1% ABV

The pick of the bunch, with all the ducks lined up in a neat and balanced row. There's lots of delicious orange marmalade, stewed fruits and plums on the nose, and it has a zesty sherbety taste, with pineapple and melon up front, tannin and spices later. The finish is long and fruity with just the right amount of oak to balance it all up.

Glenglassaugh 40-year-old

44.6% ABV

Dark berries, fruitcake and plum on the nose, a creamy toffee and vanilla heart on the palate, with berries, chilli and tannins in the mix. The finish is refined and long, with the plum and oak holding out longest.

GLENGOYNE

www.glengoyne.com

Glengoyne is Glasgow's other distillery, but it is located a few miles north of the city, straddling the Highland line – the distillery being in the Highlands, the warehouses across the road in the Lowlands. The distillery is owned by independent bottlers Ian MacLeod, whose Islay malt Smokehead (which has been very successful) is attracting younger drinkers in to the single malt world. This is ironic, because for a long time Glengoyne made an asset of the fact that it is peat-free. A few years back they even hired a luxury boat and sailed to the Islay festival with a banner that urged whisky fans to drink peat-free whisky – the real taste of malt. Glengoyne is a lovely distillery and it employs some of the most charming people in the industry. It offers a comprehensive range of tours and whisky experiences – from the basic tour to a blending course.

Glengoyne 10-year-old 40% ABV

Another entry-level malt with a clean and crisp malt bite, very refreshing. Wet straw and heather give way to a touch of oak and sweet crystallized ginger, as pure as the water that tumbles down the rocks at the back of the distillery.

Glengoyne 12-year-old 43% ABV

The Glengoyne 12-year-old was added to the range in 2009 and has become a firm favourite ever since. The distillery makes a virtue of the fact that it uses no peated barley in its production, fairly unusual for a Highland whisky (though the distillery is on the dividing line between Highlands and Lowlands). This has a clean and refreshing green-apple taste, lots of crisp barley and just a small amount of spice late on. This is a beautifully made malt whisky, with flavours all working at their cleanest and sharpest limits. Very more-ish.

Glengoyne 15-year-old 43% ABV

Lighter, sweeter and more citrus-driven than you might expect from Glengoyne. There's something very artisanal about this one, with malty and oily notes playing off rustic citrus notes. A welcome addition to the range.

Glengoyne 18-year-old

43% ABV

What a big decision to replace the much loved 17-year-old with a new 18-year-old expression. Traditionally the team here like big, smelly, browny-black, sherried casks from this distillery – we know that because a few years back each of the team was allowed to choose a cask for bottling and without exception they were all sherry monsters. This is not like that at all, although there are obvious sherry influences. Add in marzipan, stewed apples and orange marmalade and this isn't a bad addition at all.

Glengoyne 21-year-old

43% ABV

Restraint is order of the day – this is a delightfully juicy mix of juicy barley, rich raisins and black grapes on the nose, with dried fruits, grapefruit marmalade and a wave of oak and pepper to taste. The finish is long: honey, red fruit and oak.

Glengoyne Cask Strength Batch 4

58.7% ABV

This is an intense and pure version of Glengoyne and packs a powerful fruity punch. There is plenty to delight here, including cooking apple, marzipan and some vanilla. The malts eventually give way to pepper spices.

Key whiskies

Glen Garioch 1797 Founder's Reserve 48% ABV
Glen Garioch 12-year-old 48% ABV
Glen Garioch Renaissance 15-year-old 51.9% ABV
Glen Garioch Renaissance 16-year-old 51.4% ABV
Glen Garioch Virgin Oak 48% ABV

ABOVE With its traditional distilling process and friendly visit centre, Glen Garioch is hugely popular.

GLEN GARIOCH

Oldmeldrum, Inverurie, AB51 0ES
www.glengarioch.com

There is an argument that the Glen Garioch distillery is Scotland's best kept secret. It's a classic case of out of sight, out of mind, though it may well be the case that its status as a hidden gem is starting to change.

The distillery is owned by Morrison Bowmore Distillers, which in turn is part of the Beam Suntory empire. In terms of familiarity, for years it tended to come third in a three-horse race, placed soundly behind Bowmore and Auchentoshan. That's a real shame, because Glen Garioch is special. It is one of Scotland's oldest distilleries, having been established in 1797. And although it was expanded in the late 1800s, as its owner sought to take advantage of the growing demand for blended Scotch whiskies and needed to secure his malt stocks, the distillery only makes 1.37 million litres (361,916 US gallons) of spirit annually – around a tenth of the output of Glenfiddich.

The distillery can be found in the heart of the sedate Aberdeenshire market town of Oldmeldrum, which lies to the east of the A9, off to the right as you journey north from Aberdeen towards Speyside. It's about 27 km (17 miles) from Aberdeen and is the closest distillery to the city.

But, the region around the distillery is distinctly rural. The Valley of the Garioch has a surprisingly mild climate by Scotland's standards, there is a plentiful amount of sunshine and not too much rain, and so the region has long been renowned as the finest barley-growing area in the country. At one time there were six distilleries here. Now just Glen Garioch remains, and at a couple of points in its chequered past, its survival wasn't guaranteed.

Now, with a makeover, more focus from its owners and the support of a major international owner, it is quite possibly in the best health it has ever been. Although a new visitor centre was added to the distillery at the turn of the millennium, it is still a small and quaint distillery, and its owners have put a strong emphasis on the fact that it is a traditional distillery with close to no automation whatsoever.

Made up of the dark and distinctive brickwork so common in the Aberdeenshire region, it is doused in history but is a warm and comforting place to visit. Probably more through fate than

design, it's possible to follow a logical and ordered tour through the premises, the route tastefully decorated by information points and examples of Doric – the strong dialect still spoken by some people in the northeast of Scotland.

The distillery tour ends with a tasting and the opportunity for visitors to bottle and label their own single malt. The choice of different styles of Glen Garioch is a good indicator as to how varied and diverse the whisky is. One reason for this is because when the distillery was reopened in 1997 it changed to producing malt without the use of peat. Before that peat was used for drying and at least some bottlings veered away from the Highland style and towards the style of whisky being made at sister distillery Bowmore.

But there is also diversity at the distillery, created by the array of casks used in the whisky maturation. Glen Garioch joins a select handful of distilleries that have the ability to flip from light, clean, sweet bourbon-cask malts to distinctly earthy, gutsy and agricultural ones. First Suntory's and now Beam Suntory's commitment to the distillery has been borne out by its investment in a complete revamp of the whisky range and the release of several new vintage expressions. In 2013, 11 single-cask expressions were released.

WELL, FANCY THAT...

The Glen Garioch distillery is situated in an area where Doric is still spoken. Doric is an old dialect that can be very hard to understand. In the Disney film *Brave*, one of the characters spoke Doric, and the running joke was that nobody could understand him. There are dictionaries and online guides, but what makes it difficult is that different words may be used from town to town. 'Doric' is thought to come from the Greek word for 'rustic' or 'rural'.

GLEN GRANT
www.glengrant.com

One of five distilleries in the Speyside town of Rothes, Glen Grant is now owned by Campari and continues to enjoy immense popularity in Europe, and particularly Italy. It would surprise many in Scotland to learn that it is one of the top-five selling malts in the world. It is a lovely distillery to visit, particularly in late spring or early summer, because it has extensive gardens. By the side of a little bridge there is a safe built into the wall. Major Grant kept a bottle of whisky here and would take guests out for a dram among the flowers and trees. The house style may be described as light and soft. The Italians like it at five years old (probably because at such a young age it is the nearest that Scotch gets to grappa), but the 10-year-old is more suited to most malt-lovers' tastes.

Glen Grant 10-year-old 40% ABV

Dry and shy on the nose, followed by a crisp, herbal and light fruity taste on the palate, this one has a medium-long finish to enjoy.

GLENKINCHIE
www.malts.com

The nearest distillery to Edinburgh can be found at Pencaitland, and is a Lowland distillery making light, gingery whisky.

Glenkinchie 12-year-old 43% ABV

The nose is cereally and sweet here, with some damp straw and a hint of spice. The taste is distinctly spicy but rounded and smooth, with some ginger notes. This is one of the single malts that works as an apéritif whisky.

THE GLENLIVET
www.theglenlivet.com

A few years back Glenlivet's owners announced that it intended to challenge Glenfiddich for the number-one malt spot, but the claims were regarded by most of the cynical journalists present at the press conference as marketing bluster. But, in 2010, the distillery put the finishing touches to an expansion programme that now allows it to produce pretty much the same amount of spirit each year as Glenfidddich and Diageo's 'super distillery' at Roseisle (a state-of-the-art plant designed to produce malt for blending). The Glenlivet was already a big player, up there as one of the three great Glens, alongside Glenfiddich and Glenmorangie. It is a great distillery that produces fine malt – a shame, then, that its 12-year-old has been so badly devalued by years of discounting into the superstore trade. Only Glen Moray has fallen further from malt's high table.

The Glenlivet 12-year-old 40% ABV

Another classic Speysider, with aromas of fresh green apples and a touch of grapefruit; a soft, sweet fruity taste and a pleasant and clean finish.

The Glenlivet 15-year-old French Oak Reserve 40% ABV

Now we're motoring. This is an outstanding expression of Glenlivet, all zippy spice from some virgin French oak, and scatter-gun oak and malt, like a couple of playful kittens tumbling over each other. Feeling depressed and into rock music? Then get yourself an album by Australian cosmic rock giants Wolfmother (either will do, but the debut album is easier to get to grips with), pour a weighty (but obviously responsible) glass of this, turn off the lights and listen to the Sabbath-Zeppelin hybrid, while the spices zip about your mouth. Try not to smile until you've swallowed. There. Everything seems better now, doesn't it?

The Glenlivet 18-year-old 43% ABV

If the Nadurra (below) is a fun pillow-fight of a whisky, this is the sensible big brother asking you to keep the noise down. It's exactly what you'd expect the 12-year-old to grow up to be. Oak, honey and spice add sophistication not found in the younger malt. But the fresh apple fruit is still there.

The Glenlivet 21-year-old 43% ABV

The flavour here is much fuller than in younger bottlings, very rich and chewy. If the 18-year-old is a fit athlete of a whisky, this is it with a beer gut, less disciplined, but fun to spend time with – a soft and smooth malt with citrus fruits, a nuttiness and some oak. Yet another twist to the Glenlivet story.

The Glenlivet XXV 43% ABV

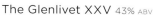

This is a rich and enveloping malt with big candy, toffee and vanilla notes alongside the trademark fruits. Oak and spice give away clues to the whisky's age – but overall it is sublime and enjoyable.

The Glenlivet Nadurra 16-year-old 48% ABV

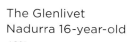

There is a cask-strength version of this, but this is the one to go for. You have to hunt for the Glenlivet characteristics because this malt is a law unto itself, a mix of ginger, paprika, white pepper and chilli, all sprinkled over ginger barley. You know how trendy chefs are into mixing pain and pleasure and creating egg-and-bacon ice cream and that sort of thing? Well this is whisky's answer to that – a sort of chilli-flavoured chocolate, with ginger wine in the mix.

GLENMORANGIE
www.glenmorangie.com

The lattice-work symbol on the Glenmorangie bottle is an image of an old Pict standing stone (to be found in a field close to the distillery). The images on it show female warriors on horseback, symbolizing power and high rank, and suggesting that the Picts were a matriarchal society. Sitting at the foot of the stone with a glass of fine Glenmorangie is, without doubt, a special and spiritual experience and is throughly recommended. A few years back, it was said that Glenmorangie was driving fast towards a brick wall, its warehouses full of inferior whisky going nowhere quickly. The turn around since then has been remarkable. Taking full advantage of the skills of whisky-genius Dr Bill Lumsden, Glenmorangie has become an industry leader in wood management. Spirit was put in better wood, and existing whisky was finished and transformed in a range of different casks. Glenmorangie is now synonymous with quality whisky. Under the new ownership of Louis Vuitton Moët Hennessy (LVMH), a new range of core malts and three finishes was introduced in ultra-modern bottles. More recently Lumsden and his team have started to experiment with new whiskies – going back to the future to explore old styles and reinvent them in new and exciting ways.

Glenmorangie 18-year-old 43% ABV

Sharper than the 10-year-old, with clean citrus fruits on the nose and an overall taste that is a mix of orange, oak and citrus fruits. The finish is clean and lengthy.

Glenmorangie 25-year-old 43% ABV

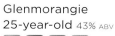

If you are going to splash out for a whisky of this age you have got to be sure that it steps up a division. Without doubt this does – up there with Macallan 25 and Highland Park 25 as a monumental malt worthy of every one of its 25 years. This is stately, dignified and complex with a honeycomb heart, enough oak and spice to give shape, orange and stewed fruits in the mix and a dusting of cocoa.

Key whiskies

The Glenlivet 12-year-old 40% ABV
The Glenlivet 15-year-old French Oak Reserve 40% ABV
The Glenlivet 16-year-old Nadurra 48% ABV
The Glenlivet 18-year-old 43% ABV
The Glenlivet 21-year-old 43% ABV
The Glenlivet XXV 43% ABV

ABOVE As its popularity and sales have grown, Glenlivet has been expanded, and now – effectively – has two distilleries under one roof.

THE GLENLIVET

Castleton Of Blairfindy, Glenlivet, Ballindalloch, AB37 9DB
www.maltwhiskydistilleries.com

On my first day at work as editor of *Whisky Magazine* I received a letter of complaint from an outraged reader. Apparently the magazine had published a picture of a pair of pot stills that we said were at Bunnahabhain but were actually from Bruichladdich.

I nearly resigned on the spot.

At the time it was beyond me how anyone could tell the difference between one pair of pot stills and another. And I felt there was something unhealthy about a grown man identifying two lumps of copper at one place over two lumps of copper down the road. This was, it was clear, obsessive – the whisky anorak's version of the Page Three photograph in the British tabloid *Sun* newspaper. But, of course, every distillery's stills are different, each still room unique. Like the whiskies they make, distilleries have much in common with each other, but we thrive on the differences between them. And while they all go through the same process in pretty much the same order, the differences between them can be vast.

One of the main differences is in atmosphere, created in part by size, in part by the layout and in part by the noise, or lack of it. So, while Bunnahabhain, say, or Pulteney, clatter and clang, others such as The Macallan or The Glenrothes seem to hum. The former are bustling and busy, the latter, calm and graceful. I've always put The Glenlivet in the 'quiet' category. But if the old still room is relatively silent, nothing quite prepares you for the new still room, which in 2010 effectively doubled the distillery's output and made it the biggest single-malt distillery in Scotland. It is like a library.

Where once malt spirit production required several people with a number of skills, today the modern distillery can be operated by one person, and if health and safety regulations allowed it, they could run it from home and not come to the distillery at all. Modern computers have taken on so much of the burden of production that at the Glentauchers distillery everything has been maintained in the traditional way, so staff can be trained in skills that might otherwise become redundant.

At The Glenlivet, the newer of the two still rooms is like something from a science-fiction film. One desk is placed at an angle on a raised platform, to oversee the new stills. A bank of computers tells the operator exactly what is going on in the room. Nevertheless, just in front of the desk are the traditional spirits banks that you would find in any distillery.

'When we were planning the new still room we involved staff in decisions as to where to put the desk and that sort of thing,' says Chivas distilleries manager Alan Winchester. 'It's not often you get the chance to include people in that way. They wanted the spirits banks where they could see the spirit flowing, even though the computer tells them that it is. It's a link to the old ways.'

They don't want to make much about their size, pointing out that all the company has done by reopening Braeval and Allt A Bhainne and extending The Glenlivet is replace the volumes it lost when it was forced to sell off Glen Grant and Ardmore during the purchase by Allied a few years back.

But, it makes what is one of Scotland's most impressive distilleries even more so. It also produces some of the world's finest whiskies and some that pretty much define Speyside. A ridiculous pricing policy in British supermarkets may have devalued The Glenlivet 12-year-old but expressions such as the 15-year-old French Oak Reserve, the Nadurra 16-year-old, the 18-year-old and the 21-year-old are all heavyweight champion malts.

But there are other reasons to visit here, too. A small but beautifully executed interactive visitor experience is a highlight of one of the most charming visitor centres in the industry, and The Glenlivet is trading on its historical role as the birthplace of the modern Scottish malt whisky industry by opening up a series of smugglers' trails so that you can relive more dangerous times for whisky while immersing yourself in the unspoilt natural beauty of the Glenlivet valley.

Add to all of this a calm and not-too-noisy tour and there's an argument that The Glenlivet is the epitome of rest and relaxation. Oh, and if you are interested, some pretty distinctive pairs of stills, too.

Glenmorangie Astar 57.1% ABV

   !

On the face of it, another experimental departure for Glenmorangie, an intense barley-fuelled, cask-strength malt. If Signet is all about urban sophistication then Astar (right) would seem to be all about rustic gruffness. Add some water, though, and the Glemorangie characteristics come flowing through, with a range of barley and honeycomb. The spices that make an appearance early, and then just keep popping up, are a big plus.

Glenmorangie Milsean 46% ABV

Pronounced 'Mill-shun', this means 'sweet things', and is just what this is. A Beach Boys of a malt, an oral equivalent to pretty harmonies. Spending 2.5 years in port barriques, the result is an all singing, all dancing cherry, mango, tropical fruit and sweet grape treat. Far too drinkable, too. God only knows what we'd do without it...

Glenmorangie Nectar d'Or 46% ABV

Putting malt in a cask that has been previously used for wine, rum, port or madeira for the last few months of its maturation is a skill. And Glenmorangie's finishes are exemplary. This one is finished in Sauternes (sweet white wine) casks. Wine casks don't always pair well, but this works far better than some of the big red wine casks. Sweetness, cinnamon and spice take what was a great whisky to an even more glorious place.

Glenmorangie Original 40% ABV

This is the original 10-year-old repackaged and it's as reliable as a Harley Davidson. There is a lot going on, with a honeyed nose, sweet-malty centre and candy-like core. Rounded, easy-drinking, characterful whisky with hints of orange and nuts.

Glenmorangie Quinta Ruban 46% ABV

Here the finishing cask is port and again the lovely orange and barley core is enhanced by sweet fruit and an extra richness, so that sweet and dry battle for attention, to pleasing effect. This is up there with the wonderful Balvenie 21-year-old as the best port finish available.

Glenmorangie Signet

46% ABV

   ?

This is not so much a roller-coaster ride as the whole funfair in one glass. What's happened here is that Bill Lumsden and his team have thrown away the Glenmorangie rule book and set out on an adventure, exploring every channel within the tight rules of whisky making. They have used toasted and chocolate malt, virgin oaks to add spiciness and casks of different types and sizes. And they have come up with the most exquisite and hedonistic malt imaginable.

It is rich and gloopy, and is whisky's equivalent of those handmade, boutique, dark chocolates you get that have been infused with fruit flavours and aromatics. Awesome whisky making and there's more to come. Dr Lumsden has just shared another 'work in progress' with some of us, and it's a different beast altogether. These are exciting times that we live in.

Glenmorangie Tusail 46% ABV

The man behind this whisky is, again, Dr Bill Lumsden and like the team at Bruichladdich he's intrigued by terroir and the role that barley from different regions makes to the taste of malt whisky. In this case he has tried to travel back in time. This is the result of Glenmorangie's experiments with old-grain strains and it recalls another era. The barley is Maris Otter, and it is traditionally floor malted. The result is an ovaltine-style whisky, creamy and soft, but with distinctive chocolate-barley notes. There are some distinctive oaky hints here, too.

GLEN MORAY

www.glenmoray.com

Glen Moray has been making its own steady way since it was somewhat unceremoniously dumped by LVMH and picked up by La Martiniquaise. It is located in the Speyside town of Elgin, tucked back at the end of a standard residential area. It's a dinky, pleasing distillery and it makes perfectly fine 12-year-old and some rather special older releases. But the distillery has been criminally undervalued, its 12-year-old sold at under half its market value through superstores. So let's look at this: you distil fine spirit, put it into quality oak casks and mature it to the same standards as other malts for a minimum of 12 years. Then you flog it off as a cheap superstore brand. What does that do for the morale of the talented team at the distillery? LVMH finally sold the distillery so it could focus on its more premium malts, and Glen Moray is under new ownership. It has been very quiet in recent times – and hopefully a reappraisal and repositioning process is underway.

Glen Moray 12-year-old 40% ABV

This defines a Speyside malt – plenty of sweetness, plenty of fruit, plenty of crystallized barley and a blemish-free and pleasing mouthfeel, taste and finish. There has been a series of distiller's editions from this distillery over the years that have been truly outstanding. They are extremely hard to find but if you do stumble across one, then it is definitely worth investigating. A limited-edition 1974 pot-finished malt is particularly recommended.

GLEN ORD

www.malts.com

Glen Ord is something of a hidden gem, occupying a site to the north of Inverness overlooking the Black Isle, and it has suffered from something of an identity crisis over the years, having been bottled under several different names. Most recently it has been reformulated to include a higher proportion of malt matured in sherry wood and bottled as the Asian representative of The Singleton range.

The Singleton of Glen Ord 12-year-old 40% ABV

Glen Ord is located close to Inverness in the northeast of Scotland and the whisky has become quite difficult to find as a single malt because Diageo has used it as its Singleton malt for the Far East market, and particularly Taiwan. If you do find this version, expect a robust, fruity and reasonably sherried malt with some plummy fruits. The Singleton version, should you come across it, is sweet and has even more sherry. There is little evidence of an earthy Highland backbone, but this is pleasant enough.

The Singleton of Glen Ord 15-year-old 43% ABV

Offering exceptional value for money, this is something of an all rounder, combining rich and fruity Speyside flavours with delicate spice and oak. The extra age gives body and depth.

The Singleton 18-year-old 40% ABV

This is a relatively new addition to the Glen Ord portfolio – and is a beauty. With a gorgeous range of exotic and tropical fruits and lashings of sherried berries, there are attractive oaky tannins and spices, too. Clean and fresh.

The Singleton 28-year-old

58.3% ABV

Hickory, surprisingly youthful barley and some estery notes on the nose, with a full and sweet taste combined with cocoa and coffee notes. Late on some tannin and spice but it is all well-balanced and ordered. A revelation.

Key whiskies

Glenmorangie 18-year-old 43% ABV
Glenmorangie Original 40% ABV
Glenmorangie Nectar d'Or 46% ABV
Glenmorangie Quinta Ruban 46% ABV
Glenmorangie Signet 46% ABV

ABOVE Glenmorangie is something of a rarity in Scotland, because the water it takes from the Tarlogie Springs is hard.

GLENMORANGIE

Tain, IV19 1PZ
www.glenmorangie.com

Glenmorangie is whisky royalty. It is The Rolling Stones of single malt – a commercially successful business on the one hand, but retaining rootsy credibility on the other.

It is one of the three great 'Glens' along with Glenlivet and Glenfiddich, though the distillery itself isn't as big as either of them. And nor is it in Speyside. You'll find it up on what has been called Scotland's forgotten coastline, on the road heading north from Inverness to Wick.

The region is wild and remote, and dripping in history. Throughout the region there are links to its Pictish past – a full-size handcrafted replica of a Pictish standing stone lies close to the distillery. An image of it appears on the Glenmorangie label.

The distillery itself is close to the shoreline and is in a relatively sedate location at one end of the bustling town of Tain, on the south shore of Dornach Firth, to which it is inextricably linked. Until 2017, you could watch the mass of birds feeding on the spent lees and pot ale the distillery pumped in to the sea through a large pipeline. That's no longer the case now though. These days an environmentally friendly anaerobic digestion plant converts the by-products into gas, which is used as fuel for the distillery's boiler. The distillery is also part of a scheme to reintroduce the European flat oyster to the Firth for the first time in 170 years.

Nearby is the distillery's famous water source, Tarlogie Springs. It contains pure water that may have spent up to 1000 years passing through limestone and sandstone rock to reach the surface. The water is therefore hard, unlike the waters that serve Speyside to the south. Visitors who choose the upmarket heritage tour at the distillery are taken there. It's remarkably small. The spirit that the distillery produces as a result of that water is clean and fruity.

Glenmorangie is the fourth best-selling single-malt whisky and has grown in popularity in recent years, particularly in countries such as the United States. The distillery makes about six million litres (1.6 million US gallons) of spirit a year, sizeable but not huge. But the distillery's reputation is based on the fact that it has carved out an enviable reputation for quality rather than quantity. Glenmorangie's owner is LVMH, a company renowned for luxury, and since it bought the distillery and its sister, Ardbeg (on Islay), it has given free rein to the highly gifted and imaginative whisky maker, Dr Bill Lumsden, to explore stylish and exciting whiskies.

Glenmorangie has always been ahead of the game when it came to launching whiskies with no-age-statement on them, though the age of expressions such as Original and Lasanta are not kept a secret. The company view is that age is not important and that the focus on a malt should be entirely about its quality. And Glenmorangie has an admirable track record in this department. Stunning whiskies such as Signet have ensured the distillery's reputation for craft and quality, and in recent years Dr Lumsden has explored all sorts of avenues, recreating historical styles of whisky by employing rarely used barley strains, leaving casks to cook in the sun and maturing and finishing malt in unusual combinations of casks. Since 2009, there has been an annual Private Edition release of an unusual expression of Glenmorangie, each with a Gaelic name. Experimental bottlings have looked at malts made with barley grain from specific Scottish farms.

Glenmorangie is open to the public and offers a series of different tours and tasting experiences, including the heritage tour, which also offers lunch in Glenmorangie House and the tasting of some of the distillery's rarer expressions.

WELL, FANCY THAT...

A great deal is made of the soft waters of the River Spey and its tributaries. and many distilleries claim that soft water is essential to distillation. Tell that to the brewers of Burton-on-Trent, who argue that beer fermentation requires the opposite (whisky is made from beer). Or to the folk at Glenmorangie, who use the distillery's own water source at Tarlogie Springs. The 'hard' water here provides qualities in stark contrast to most other distilleries.

THE GLENROTHES

www.theglenrothes.com

You would struggle to find two places that have less in common with each other than Texas in the United States on the one hand and St James in Mayfair, London on the other – but they do have a bizarre link. St James Street is home to Berry Bros & Rudd, a traditional wine merchants with a long and colourful history at the heart of affluent London. In recent years it has added fine spirits to its offering, and it has the long-term rights to the outstanding Speyside Glenrothes distillery. A few years ago, Berry Bros company director Christopher Berry Green was made a Freeman of the State of Texas by the then governor George HW Bush.

'Between 1842 and 1845 Texas was the Lone Star Republic and had embassies and legacies across the world,' says Glenrothes ambassador Ronnie Cox. 'In London it was on the first floor of our offices in St James. So in recognition of this, in 1996, Mr Berry Green, who was a tall, former Grenadier Guard and very British, was presented with a pair of garish cowboy boots and a ten-gallon Stetson, which I doubt he ever wore. In return, he gave George HW Bush an unpaid invoice from 1845 for three months rent.'

Glenrothes is a big distillery – they call the still room The Cathedral – but most of its output has traditionally gone into blends. Now, though, it is being recognized in its own right, partly because of the quality of the malts it is putting out, and partly because of its distinctive grenade-style bottles with handwritten labels. The people behind Glenrothes are not above having some fun with the brand, and enjoy matching each vintage with music of different styles, including jazz, blues, new-wave, Americana and rock. So in the spirit the company intended, here are some classic rock pairings.

The Glenrothes 30-year-old 43% ABV

This takes no prisoners, after a slow-burn start. At first there are damp leaves and faintly musty aromas and then some sherry and citrus fruits. But it explodes on the palate, with lemon sherbet, aniseed, sweet mint and some drying astringency. The finish is long and intense. Soundtrack: 'Mistreated' Deep Purple.

The Glenrothes Robur Reserve 40% ABV

The aromas here include apricot jam, some lemon zest and honey. The creamy taste has citrus and yellow fruits and some soft spices. Very pleasant, very Speyside and very ordered. Soundtrack: 'Make Me Smile (Come Up and See Me)' Steve Harley & Cockney Rebel.

The Glenrothes Select Reserve

43% ABV

This is a mix of various vintages and so is more consistent than some of the distillery's other malts. Something of a greatest-hits package. Sweet barley, vanilla, mince pies, sherbet and orange on the nose, dried fruits, spice, sugar and sherry on the palate, and a gentle pruney finish. Soundtrack: 'Purple Rain' Prince.

The Glenrothes 25-year-old

43% ABV

Here is a truly adorable nose of sweet-candied fruits, lemonade, orange and lemon rind and spearmint. The taste is pretty extraordinary, too – tropical fruits, some sugar-like spice and an oaky carpet. The finish is long and sweet. Soundtrack: 'California Dreamin' The Mamas and the Papas.

The Glenrothes 1994 43% ABV

This whisky is reminiscent of a freshly cleaned dining room, with aromas of lemon cleaner and polish. It is oily and rich in the mouth, with flavours of melon and lemon, and hints of toffee. A breezy, summertime whisky. Soundtrack: 'Made of Stone' The Stone Roses.

The Glenrothes 1992 43% ABV

This is another light and easy-drinking malt, with a flowery nose sprinkled with sherbet and fruit. On the palate it is rich and fruity, with pineapple, liquorice and melon. All in all a sparkly, summery, feel-good malt. Soundtrack: 'Dancing in the Dark' Bruce Springsteen.

The Glenrothes 1984 43% ABV

This is a more delicate example of Glenrothes, with delicate vanilla and wood sap. The taste is sweeter than you might expect, with sugary barley, vanilla ice cream and some caramel sauce. Ends with a pleasant dash of oak and spice. Soundtrack: 'Wrecking Ball' Emmylou Harris.

The Glenrothes 1991 43% ABV

This is an enticing malt, with some welcoming aromas, which include soft toffee, vanilla, blackcurrant and blueberries. The taste has caramel, some tannins, cherry and redcurrant and stewed fruits. The colour is chestnut. Soundtrack: 'Solsbury Hill' Peter Gabriel.

The Glenrothes 1981 43% ABV

The oddest of the Glenrothes vintages, this has some sulphur and cask vagrancies on the nose, reminiscent of stewed beanshoots. A woody taste, with some dried fruits the sweetness thins out to leave a peppery finish. Soundtrack: 'Welcome to the Machine' Pink Floyd.

The Glenrothes 1987 43% ABV

This one is probably the least complex and most predictable of all the vintages but this is not a criticism – it is floral and almost perfumey, with orange and grapefruit notes and a simple, medium-long but pleasantly sweet finish. Soundtrack: 'I Want You To Want Me' Cheap Trick.

The Glenrothes 1978 43% ABV

The nose is a bit off-kilter, with a strange mix of sherbet fruits and earthy chestnut flavours, but the complex taste makes up for it. Lots of fruits, liquorice, aniseed and vanilla. The finish goes on and on, and it is very pleasant. Soundtrack: 'More Than a Feeling' Boston.

The Glenrothes 1985 43% ABV

This is a different Glenrothes to what has gone before – an earthy, savoury nose with chestnuts, apple core and mushroom. The taste is much more attractive, with over-ripe peach and apricot, honeycomb, burnt toffee and a distinctive oakiness in the delicious mix. Sound track: 'In the Evening' Led Zeppelin.

The Glenrothes 1972 43% ABV

Another vintage that starts off with rootsy and earthy aromas reminiscent of stewed vegetables, but the malt is creamy and full in the mouth with fruit, vanilla and liquorice and some late spice and tannins. The finish is the best part – long and balanced with sweet fruits, spices and oak. Soundtrack: 'Nice n' Sleazy' The Stranglers.

GLEN SPEY
www.malts.com

One of several Speyside distilleries that exists primarily to provide malt for blending. It is not easy to find as a single malt, but Diageo did release a 12-year-old as part of its Flora and Fauna range.

Glen Spey 12-year-old 43% ABV

Full and sturdy, fruity malt, with a spicy finish and a solid malty base. Smooth, honeyed and tasty.

GLENTURRET
www.the famousgrouse.com

Glenturret is one of Scotland's oldest, most rustic distilleries, but it is also home to The Famous Grouse Experience, a completely interactive visit for all the family. The overall effect is akin to dressing a farmer in a space suit. The distillery itself is small and traditional. Much of the malt goes into The Famous Grouse, but there is a hard-to-find single malt, too.

Glenturret 10-year-old 40% ABV

Solid enough; somewhat two-dimensional Highland malt, with honey, crystallized barley and gentle oaky tones.

HAZELBURN
www.springbankdistillers.com

If Springbank is the scuzzy street punk of Campbeltown and Longrow is its salty sea dog, then Hazelburn is its dapper young gentleman, a triple-distilled unpeated and sweet malt on a day trip.

Hazelburn 8-year-old 46% ABV

Hazelburn is triple-distilled at Springbank in Campbeltown, so the overall taste is smooth and rounded. This is a Malteser-in-a-glass, with honey flowing through it.

HIGHLAND PARK
www.highlandpark.com

Everyone should visit Orkney at least once. The islands are littered with burial sites, ruins and stone circles, signposts to history are at every turn, and you can trace human struggle and suffering from the earliest settlers thousands of years ago to the protected war grave in Scapa Flow. The islands are also home to two distilleries. Highland Park is whisky's greatest all-rounder, its malts noted for the balance of peat, oak, fruit, honey and spice, making it easy to argue objectively as to why the 18 and 25-year-olds, in particular, can lay claim to being the world's greatest malts. The 21-year-old won best single-malt whisky in the World Whisky Awards. Recent unconventional expressions mean new releases are always exciting.

Highland Park 12-year-old

40% ABV

The standard 12-year-old Highland Park is like a colourful fashion show, featuring many designers. First you get honey and barley, then fruit, a touch of wood and spice and a sexy, sensual peaty smoke finale. Some performance.

Highland Park 15-year-old

40% ABV

Again, trademark honey to the fore and a support act of oak and smoke, but the extra years give the malt more of a caramelized toffee centre.

Highland Park 16-year-old 40% ABV

This is more restrained than the younger bottlings and the nose has developed some range and citrus notes. The honey is there on the palate but this time with toasty, cereally notes, an orange-candy centre and then some pleasant smokiness. The malt ends as it started, with a finish that is delicate and short.

Highland Park 18-year-old 43% ABV

Malt whisky's equivalent to rock band REM's 'Man on the Moon'. Loud bits, quiet bits, passion and perfect harmonies – a little bit of something for everyone and, as a whole, instantly familiar, while different to everything else in its field. Perfect.

Highland Park 21-year-old 40% ABV

Brought down from a higher strength, but still a masterpiece, with the oak playing a big role but malt and honey still the dominant tastes.

Highland Park 25-year-old 48% ABV

This has changed significantly from the big heavy fruit-and-oak driven 25-year-old from a few years back. With lemon flu powder and grapefruit on the nose, it's quite delicate overall. And a game of two halves on the palate: first up is honey and candy sweets followed by citrus notes. Then a triple whammy of spice, peat and oak take your tastebuds to a different level. The finish is an intriguing amalgam of all that has gone before.

Highland Park 30-year-old 48% ABV

It seems there are two very different styles of old Highland Park. This one, like the 25-year-old above, comes from the citrus stable, but is an altogether more assured bottling than its slightly younger sibling. The citrus fruits dominate the nose, but there is some peat and honey there, too. Honey and vanilla dominate the taste, but there is enough oak and peat to prevent it from being too sweet and wispy.

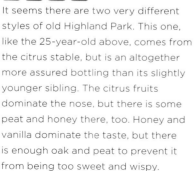

Highland Park 40-year-old 48% ABV

Another twist again. On the nose there is scented wax candle, pot pourri and sweet citrus fruits. The palate combines exotic and citrus fruits, honey and peat. The big five – peat, fruit, spice, oak and honey – face up to each other in the finish to see which can go longest without blinking. It's the peat that wins.

Highland Park Dark Origins 46.8% ABV

Dark Origins is a combination of 60% European oak and 20% American first-fill sherry casks, and 20% refill sherry casks. The result is another big, rich and sherried Highland Park. There is dark chocolate, cocktail cherry and a big beating peat heart. Sherry and peat work excellently together here.

Highland Park Einar 40% ABV

Punchy, given its strength, this Highland Park is matured mainly in American oak. There are tropical fruits on the nose, and bonfire smoke. On the palate, orange and lemon notes, buttery vanilla and more smoke prevail.

Highland Park Valkyrie 45.9% ABV

The first of a series of legendary viking bottlings, this is a smoky and spicy treat, with a rich, fuller taste than the standard 12-year-old. The spices pack quite a punch and the sherry casks used in production are evident. Highland Park fans will love this.

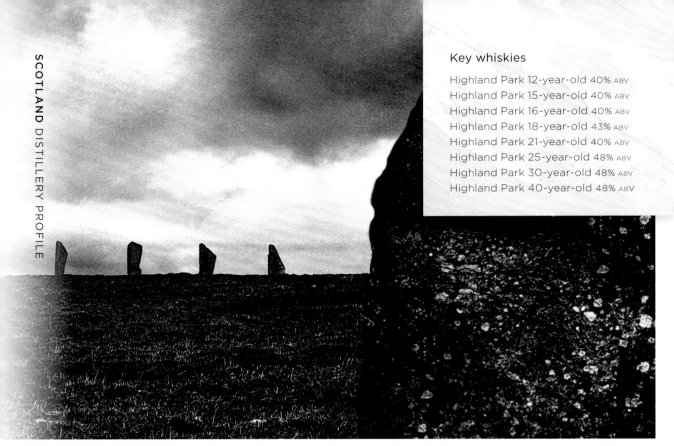

Highland Park 12-year-old 40% ABV
Highland Park 15-year-old 40% ABV
Highland Park 16-year-old 40% ABV
Highland Park 18-year-old 43% ABV
Highland Park 21-year-old 40% ABV
Highland Park 25-year-old 48% ABV
Highland Park 30-year-old 48% ABV
Highland Park 40-year-old 48% ABV

ABOVE The Orkney Isles are rich in history and spirituality. The Ring of Brodgar, is made with stone not native to the islands.
BELOW Quiet... whisky sleeping.

HIGHLAND PARK

Holm Road, Kirkwall, Orkney KW15 1SU
www.highlandpark.co.uk

Over the last five years or so Britain has lost a number of top-class beer breweries, each of them shut because they were considered 'economically unviable.'

This excuse has become depressingly familiar, and reflects a sizeable shift away from culture and community and to the relentless and selfish pursuit of money. Plus, as we increasingly try and trade and/or compete with nations that pay their workers a pittance and can mass-produce components for next to nothing, uncaring capitalism has grown stronger. Next time someone tells you the local factory or business closure is inevitable, say two words to them: Highland Park. Truth is, when companies are committed to something beyond the cash figure at the bottom of the page, miracles can happen. Whisky is full of them. And when it comes to economics, how can it make sense to produce whisky on the tiny islands of Islay, Jura and Skye?

And most of all, what sort of business model allows for a regular convoy of vehicles to travel the full length of Scotland on narrow roads to its furthest point, then sail through rough northern waters to a group of islands best-suited to sheep-rearing, and all for the sake of an alcoholic drink?

It is because distillery owners – and this includes giants such as Diageo and Pernod Ricard – are committed to maintaining a malt-whisky industry, noted for its diversity and regional variations.

Highland Park is a case in point – a malt distillery that makes no sense whatsoever until you taste the whisky that comes from it. As Scotland's most northerly distillery, it is sited at the heart of a group of islands where history is marked out by archaeological sites, stone circles and ruined villages that predate Egypt's pyramids. The islands are characterized by wind and water and there are few trees there due to the unforgiving climate. The surrounding seas are littered with wrecks, including much of the German fleet scuppered towards the end of World War I, and that of the Royal Oak, which was sunk by a U-boat with the cost of more than 800 lives. You can still see the masts of fishing vessels sunk to block channels and stop U-boats entering Scapa Flow, and some of the islands are linked by roadways placed over massive concrete slabs that were piled up in the narrow waterways by Winston Churchill to thwart the submarines when the fishing boats failed.

The distillery itself is a cosy, dark-brick distillery with twin working pagodas – a haven of warmth and welcoming aromas set in the harshest of environments. Owner Edrington has been investing heavily in it over the last couple of years so new pagoda roofs, a modern and stylish distillery shop and a smart tasting room sit next to old traditional stone walls and homely but antiquated offices.

The beating heart of the distillery lies high up in its maltings, however. Here, in a forgotten and dusty room full of crumbling old distillery equipment is a rectangular window. Through it is a room illuminated in eerie orange. Wispy smoke wafts across it, and on the floor golden nuggets of barley feed on the peat smoke that is rising up to them. This is the honeycomb heart of the distillery and its whisky – and it is utter magic.

Honey is at the heart of Highland Park whisky, but so is the peat, which is cut from a moor close to the distillery. You can see it being cut in spring and drying in the fields over summer, an umbilical cord between the malt and the land on which it is produced. And if the sun shines and the sea turns Caribbean-turquoise blue, then grab a hip flask full of 18-year-old, head to the port and watch the procession of ships bringing barley and carrying away waste products and whisky spirit.

It is enough to have the accountants sweating in their sleep. And it is testament to how whisky makers are committed to investing in their industry.

WELL, FANCY THAT...

The Pictish village at Skara Brae consists of eight dwelling areas dating back to 3200BC. Huge stones used to create ancient stone circles are not from the islands, but no one knows how they were transported there.

JURA

www.isleofjura.com

Highland Park on Orkney might claim to be the most 'uneconomic' whisky distillery, but Jura can give it a run for its money. In recent years it has not been fashionable to say it, though maybe the times are changing: there are more important things than the blind pursuit of money. Such things include happy communities, the dignity of honest labour and an expectation that the state has a duty of care to its people. Many, many businesses would not survive without being subsidized, but what is and is not helped out financially is the essence of politics.

The distillery on Jura makes no sense economically because it is on an island off an island. Great big lorries must negotiate little back roads and a feisty car ferry to ship in grain and ship out spirit, as well as effluent, because the distillery's wastage cannot just be dumped offshore. But it's thanks to distilleries such as Jura that the world of whisky is such a diverse and stimulating one. Jura has a lot of deer, even more adders and the most bolshy cows in Britain. If you go there, they will remind you that you are the visitor by refusing to get out of your way.

It's a brave company that decides to scrap its entire core range and replace it with a whole new set of whiskies, particularly if your old whiskies had performed well, but that's what Whyte & Mackay did with the Isle of Jura in April 2018. The four-strong core range is now a five-piece outfit, with additional members in some travel-retail markets. So, are the new whiskies any good?

Jura 10-year-old 40% ABV

I was no fan of the original 10-year-old and in my opinion this is a vast improvement. The changes are evident from the nose: a mix of sherried berries, treacle and pear drops. On the palate the malt is light and easy, but there is a subtle mix of orange fruits, cocoa and light smoke. It's fresh and clean, with berry fruits on the finish.

Jura 12-year-old 40% ABV

Some years ago while sailing down the Sound of Jura, the captain let me take the helm. I'll never forget the excitement of that moment. Then a fellow traveller gave me his iPod and played me Alabama 3's 'U Don't Dans to Tekno Anymore'. A blast of their album 'Exile on Coldharbour Lane' and a sizeable (but obviously responsible) dram of Islay malt remain my 6pm Saturday evening treat. This whisky is a revelation, with an autumnal nose of dates, dark berries, plum and Waldorf salad. The taste has a savoury aspect to it, with some earthiness, tannins and spice and further depth provided by menthol and treacle toffee.

Jura 18-year-old 44% ABV

After 18 years in American white oak, this malt is finished in red wine casks and it shows. This is a delight: a full-bodied, wine-rich whisky with sherry trifle, toffee and dark chocolate.

Jura Journey 40% ABV

A brand new no-age-statement whisky, and it works – grape and very gentle smoke aromas, a vanilla palate, then lemon, lime and clementine, all on an earthy backbone.

Jura Seven Wood 42% ABV

Seven woods? Seven? Yes, indeed, but six of them are different types of French oak. The small step up in alcoholic strength is significant here, giving this expression of Jura. Peach, cooking apple, pantry spices and wispy smoke on the nose; a delectable, subtle taste of clean orange fruitiness, redcurrant and gentle smoke.

KILCHOMAN

www.kilchomandistillery.com

The launch of whisky from Islay's first new distillery for more than 100 years was some occasion. Representatives from all of Islay's other distilleries were there, friends travelled across the world, whisky writers and enthusiasts rubbed shoulders and the whisky arrived on a tide of emotion. For the team behind the project its arrival was greeted with relief – successfully overseeing the birth of a new whisky takes blood, sweat, nerve and very deep pockets. Kilchoman, though, got on its feet quickly and has gone from strength to strength. The distillery lies to the west of the island and is a pretty, dinky operation, complete with a small shop.

Kilchoman Machir Bay 46% ABV

Wow, how quickly they grow up! Machir Bay is Kilchoman's signature malt, matured for six years in first-fill ex-bourbon casks, it's married and then finished in oloroso sherry butts. The result is a punchy, peaty malt that is right at home on Islay. But, the finishing process gives some red- and tropical-fruit notes. Industrial smoke is ever present. A treat.

KNOCKANDO

www.malts.com

Knockando is something of an enigma. Not a particularly large distillery, it is the core malt in J&B, but it has a surprisingly big fan base of its own. Fans are drawn to its complexities – nuttiness and floral notes, honey and an engaging earthiness, which all contribute to a fascinating malt.

Knockando 12-year-old 43% ABV

Like being out in the long grass on a summer's day, with light grassy and heathery notes, some sweet fruit and a dry and brittle malt.

KNOCKDHU

www.ancnoc.com

Knockdhu is now owned by Inver House, but when the company bought it from Diageo it agreed to change the name of its malts to AnCnoc to avoid confusion with Knockando. It is a Highland distillery but sits right on the boundary of Speyside: its postal address is in Speyside although the distillery is not.

AnCnoc 12-year-old 40% ABV

This is an interesting malt. Taste it in isolation when you have had nothing else to confuse your tastebuds and it is quite rugged, with clean-cut barley, some herbal notes and a rising crescendo of spices before a long and complex conclusion. Taste it after a meal and it can flounder. Overall, though, it's an impressive whisky.

AnCnoc 16-year-old 46% ABV

Pineapple candy, vanilla, crystallized barley on the nose, lots of citrus and yellow fruits in the centre, a long, spicy-sweet conclusion.

AnCnoc 1994 46% ABV

A real dessert of a whisky, with rich vanilla ice cream and butterscotch sauce, deep sweetness and summery malt.

AnCnoc 1993 46% ABV

More oak and spice than the 1994, but otherwise from the same stable. Clean, sweet barley with candyfloss and ice cream after.

AnCnoc 1975 50% ABV

The nose is subtle and sophisticated, with citrus fruits, noticeably lime, vanilla and honey. A pleasant mix of balanced flavours on the palate, with berries, honey and gentle oak and spice.

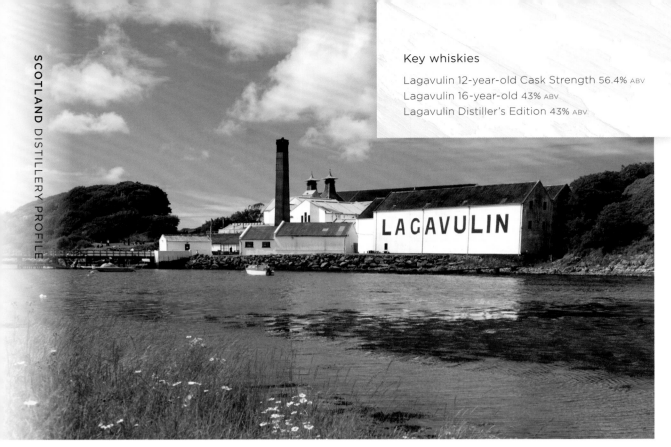

Key whiskies

Lagavulin 12-year-old Cask Strength 56.4% ABV
Lagavulin 16-year-old 43% ABV
Lagavulin Distiller's Edition 43% ABV

ABOVE Lagavulin is one of three peated distilleries located next to one another on the southern shores of Islay.
BELOW The stills produce the distinctive spirit that characterizes the final whisky after 16 years of maturation.

LAGAVULIN

Distillery Cottages, Lagavulin, Isle of Islay, PA42 7DZ
www.discovering-distilleries.com

It is a late summer's evening on the western whisky island of Islay, and darkness has shrouded the distillery in darkness.

In the pretty courtyard there is laughter, the babble of chat and the sound of tinkling glasses. The whisky is flowing liberally and guests help themselves to an impressive buffet. This is Lagavulin hosting a céilidh to mark the end of the Classic Malts Cruise – an annual three-leg, three-week pleasure sail attracting up to 1000 boats and bringing the world together for a celebration of whisky and sailing, linking up the distilleries of Oban on the mainland, Talisker on Skye and Lagavulin on Islay.

Speak to anyone who has taken part in the cruise and they will talk of new friendships, the thrill of sailing on Scotland's wild western waters and the fun and laughter of it. But, even by the Classic Malt Cruise's standards, the final céilidh at one of Scotland's most magisterial distilleries would be intoxicating, even without the whisky.

We had arrived by boat into Lagavulin bay earlier in the afternoon, our boat bobbing wickedly as an increasingly ashen-faced skipper battled to steer us through two posts marking the only section of waterway deep enough to let us in to the natural harbour. The sense of history is all-encompassing.

When the Lords of the Isles ruled the western waterways they made their home here, and the ruins of their castle lie close to the distillery. The prominent white walls and bold black lettering of the distillery itself are seen to be carved deep in to the land, and there is evidence of several distilleries in the region stretching back to the time of the Jacobite uprisings. Savour the craggy shoreline and you cannot help but feel little has changed geographically in the ensuing 275 years.

Lagavulin is the centrepiece of Islay's holy trinity of peated whiskies, all lying within a couple of miles of one another. It sits between Ardbeg on one side and Laphroaig on the other. If Islay is to whisky what heavy metal is to rock music, then Lagavulin is its Led Zeppelin, a loud battering ram of a whisky but with nuance, subtlety and sophistication if you look for it. This mix of 'volume to 11' peatiness and rich vein of fruity sweetness stems from the long maturation period and the use of selected sherry casks. Unusually for any malt but especially for a peated whisky, where old age isn't necessarily a friend, the standard Lagavulin is aged for 16 years, though a number of surprisingly diverse 12-year-olds have teasingly been drip-fed in limited batches on several occasions in recent years. Blink and you will miss them though.

For all its majesty and charisma, Lagavulin is actually a dinky, intimate distillery, where the emphasis is on quality rather than quantity. Owners Diageo has Caol Ila at the other end of the island geared up for large-scale production. Here the emphasis is on quality. The year 2010 may well be regarded as a pivotal year for the malt, too. During the 1990s, the distillery started producing a malt with a phenolic content of 50ppm, but reverted back to the original formula of 35ppm a while later. The heavier 50ppm was bottled throughout the first decade of the millennium, but 2010 saw the first 35ppm whisky complete its 16-year maturation journey and arrive in the bottle.

There is one word of warning about the tour at Lagavulin. While the warehouses are a highlight, do not be taken in by talk of the whisky maturing here. Only a tiny amount is stored in those warehouses, mainly for show, and Diageo takes virtually all its new-make spirit away in tankers to be matured on the mainland – not very romantic, but practical. And as anyone familiar with Lagavulin can testify, there's no discernible negative effect on the final whisky. Sipping a glass of it on the deck of a sailing boat in front of the distillery as the sun sets is right up there as one of my favourite whisky experiences.

WELL, FANCY THAT...
The rocky shoreline is a challenge to even small boats, so in times gone by casks had to be floated out to a puffer ship, which would carry the stock over to the mainland.

LAGAVULIN
www.malts.com

Lagavulin is one of Islay's holy trinity of big peated whiskies and it lies in the southeast of the island, hugging the shoreline. It doesn't go for lots of different expressions but that is because once you have got to where the 16-year-old is, the only place to go is down, and there is not much room on the tasting ledge for anything else.

Lagavulin 12-year-old
Cask Strength 56.4% ABV

Intense, sharp and peaty, with the odd citrus note on the nose, a full and mouthcoating peat and a hit of oil on the palate. The finish crackles and flares with peat and fruit.

Lagavulin 16-year-old
43% ABV

Up there with the very best whiskies in the world and a place in my personal top ten, Lagavulin 16-year-old has a nose that flies like a butterfly and stings like a bee, with some sweetness on the nose and palate but a sledgehammer punch, with big peat and some brine. Salty seaweed lingers, giving way to sensational, oily, grilled bacon and an exquisite smoky conclusion. As with Miles Davies, you either get it or you don't.

Lagavulin The Distiller's Edition 43% ABV

To continue with the music analogy, would you add an orchestra to a definitive Miles Davis track? Messing with this malt is like playing pontoon and twisting on 20. Lagavulin lovers fall into two camps: the traditionalists who argue you do not dance with the devil no matter how good the moonlight, and those who argue that this is indeed the extra ace. Sherry casks give this a rich intensity and some extra sweetness, but remarkably none of the peat is lost.

LAPHROAIG
www.malts.com

Quite possibly the least subtle of The Big Three, it is still hard not to love Laphroaig if you like peated whisky. There has been a debate among lovers of this malt about whether it has been 'dumbed down' in recent years. But there is plenty to be encouraged about. The Quarter Cask bottling is an intense heavy hitter and does not break the bank. The most emotional moment in updating this book for a second edition was dropping Laphroaig 27-year-old. Possibly my favourite ever whisky, it has not been spotted in years, and when it is it's priced around $6000.

Laphroaig 10-year-old 43% ABV

A classic iodine-charged medicinal and peaty nose, with a big, grungy taste and through the brooding clouds of peat, some sweet and succulent barley. The finish is long and peaty.

Laphroaig 10-year-old Cask
Strength 57.3% ABV

Laphroaig 10-year-old is the flagship expression for this distillery, but some fans of the malt reckon it has lost its way in recent years, and they haven't been enamoured by some of the no-age-statement whiskies either. But, I think the distillery is still in credit due to the Quarter Cask and this beauty.

Restrained peat, salt and tar on the nose, but a firecracker of a taste, particularly with a little water. This is a sort of scorched-earth policy of the mouth, with hot chilli peppers flattening the few tastebuds still standing after the peat has jumped up and down on them a few times. It is the oral equivalent of soccer fans running riot. When the peat and pepper depart, you can still hear them chanting, out of sight.

Laphroaig 18-year-old 48% ABV

Sometimes the best whisky moments come when you least expect them. Somebody recently gave me a CD by Soulsavers, a band who I knew nothing about at all, beyond the fact that the line-up features Josh Homme of The Screaming Trees and various dreamy solo albums. I tasted this while watching out of my window as the snow fell when the fifth track 'Some Misunderstanding' came on. It's eight minutes long, mixes beautiful interwoven vocals, rolling sludgy basslines and sharp, twisted, gritty guitar. Just like this whisky, the music mixes pure sweet grist and grain, liquorice and hickory and growling pepper and peat. Quite possibly the best whisky-and-music match I have ever experienced. And this is quite possibly one of the best-ever whiskies.

Laphroaig 25-year-old 50.9% ABV

Be warned: the age of this whisky means that the peat has not only been tamed, but it cowers back for a good part of the drinking experience. That is not necessarily a bad thing because there are plenty of pleasant and sweet directions in which the core malt takes you. The nose is almost grapey, and on the palate there are some oak and dark-chocolate notes. When the peat does arrive, it crashes over the palate like a spring tide crashing past the harbour walls and swamping the beach with frightening speed.

Laphroaig 30-year-old 43% ABV

Hard to find, but the age has imparted a complexity rarely seen in Laphroaig. It has a full, rich taste and the peat still sits at the head of the table, but is surrounded by oak, fruit and spice.

Laphroaig Quarter Cask 48% ABV

After about six years maturation, the whisky is put in to smaller casks, increasing the amount of contact between wood and spirit. This speeds up maturation but more importantly it intensifies the flavours in the whisky. So that by eight years and maybe a bit more, you have all the flavours of a 10-year-old but with the volume turned up, and, better still, you retain some of the youthful barley at the core.

LINKWOOD
www.malts.com

Linkwood's output is mainly used for blended whiskies and, in particular, Johnnie Walker. But, occasional single-malt bottlings do emerge, and these are surprisingly refined and floral on the palate.

Linkwood 12-year-old 43% ABV

If you have got a good imagination, then you could describe the St Andrews area of the English city of Norwich as the Soho of the east (London's Soho, that is). Okay, a very good imagination. It has a shop selling Chinese food and drink, a Sinsin's Love Shop and an Ali Bongo's – so that's sort of like Soho isn't it? But it also has a great pub, the Rumsey Wells, run by brother-and-sister team Dan and Katie. It is a traditional boozer, with great ales and food, and it puts on great live music, attracting a cool student crowd.

It is also where the Norwich Whisky Club used to meet. I tasted this whisky for the first time at a club meeting, while world-class saxophonist Snake Davis played soprano sax for us. Snake has appeared on recordings by Take That, M People and Heather Small, and has toured with the likes of Annie Lennox and George Michael. To taste a new whisky while listening to such sublime music guarantees a relationship with that whisky for life.

This is a summery Speyside malt with green-pear and apple notes and some clean and fresh barley – until that is, a sharp wave of pepper arrives late on. Utterly irresistible.

Key whiskies

Laphroaig 10-year-old 40% ABV
Laphroaig 10-year-old Cask Strength 55.7% ABV
Laphroaig Cairdeas 2017 57.2% ABV
Laphroaig Lore 48% ABV
Laphroaig Quarter Cask 48% ABV
Laphroaig Select 40% ABV
Laphroaig Triple Wood 48% ABV

ABOVE Laphroaig is one of three distilleries hugging the southern coast of Islay – and all three of them (Ardbeg and Lagavulin are the other two) make big, peaty malt whiskies.

LAPHROAIG

Port Ellen, Isle of Islay, PA42 7DU
www.laphroaig.com

You can fly to the west coast island of Islay – it takes about 20 minutes from Glasgow – but the best way to arrive, particularly if it's your first visit, is by ferry.

The drive from Glasgow, up past Loch Lomond, across to Inverary and then down the peninsula to the port at Tarbert, is tedious and lengthy. But it's worth enduring just for the first glimpse of the coast of Scotland's whisky island, and you can never tire of seeing the island's holy trinity of whisky distilleries one after the other: Arbeg, Lagavulin and Laphroaig, each nestling close to the shoreline, their walls white and inviting, the distillery name boldly displayed in large black lettering.

These are the island's heavy-hitting peat whiskies, though these days all the other distilleries offer at least some heavily smoked whisky. Arguably the most famous of the three, and certainly the biggest, is Laphroaig. Favoured by royalty – it is Prince Charles' favourite malt – Laphroaig has calmly made and matured its malts while the economic tides have swirled around it, and today it shares a roof with some of the world's best American and Japanese whiskies as part of the Beam Suntory empire. Not that you'd notice from a visit. It may be that you'll look at the world map in the visitor centre or view the thousands of little flags in the grounds and wonder quite how so many people from far-flung outreaches of the world have made the pilgrimage to the distillery. But, just as it has always been, there are no other signs of corporate globalization.

In fact the folk at Laphroaig are keen to stress that this is a traditional distillery making whisky the traditional way. It even has its own maltings, though only about 20% of the malt needed for making the 3.3 million litres (871,768 US gallons) of Laphroaig spirit each year is malted on site.

The distillery was one of a number of legal distilleries established as the laws governing whisky production were relaxed. It was opened in 1815 by a pair of farmers, Donald and Alexander Johnston. They named it Laphroaig, after its location, 'broad hollow by the bay'. It stayed in family hands for the next 139 years, when the secretive Ian Hunter, the last in the family line, passed it on to the one person he trusted to guard the distillery's secrets and maintain its high production values. That person was Bessie Williamson, a graduate who had taken a summer office job at the distillery, and ended up staying 40 years. Hunter bequeathed the whole distillery to her on his death, but after a few years at the helm she realized that the distillery would need investment to continue to grow. So she sold it, staying on until she retired in 1972.

Little at the distillery has changed since that first sale in 1967, though the distillery did expand, and between 1967 and 1972 three new stills were installed, bringing the total to seven. Those seven stills – three wash stills and four spirits stills – have provided malt whisky ever since, and in recent years have been working at maximum capacity. Plans for expansion have been discussed since 2016.

But, if the distillery has stayed pretty much the same, the malt hasn't, and neither has its packaging. There has been a series of new releases ever since a 40-year-old expression was introduced in 2001. Not all of them have been a total success, and some of the no-age-statement malts have come in for criticism – but, that said, Laphroaig Quarter Cask is highly regarded. And there have been some excellent experiments with sherry-cask whiskies. Laphroaig is also a whisky that can taste wonderful at very young ages (Quarter Cask and 10-year-old Cask Strength) and at well beyond 25-years-old, eg. the hard to find but absolutely magnificent 27-year-old.

ABOVE Laphroaig's stills: little has changed over the years.

LONGMORN

Iconic single-malt whiskies enjoy the same sort of loyalty as sports teams or rock bands do. Mess with the whisky at your peril, as the owners of Longmorn found out. Longmorn enjoys cult status, or at least its 15-year-old expression does, made all the more intense and perhaps charismatic by the fact that the distillery is usually closed to the public. So, opening the distillery and launching a new expression at one Speyside festival made for a major event. What should have been a celebration turned sour as die-hard fans of the 15-year-old roundly rejected the new premium-priced 16-year-old. They had a point. I was first introduced to Longmorn by the French whisky writer Martine Nouet, who uttered the immortal 'Let me introduce me to your new mistress...'. Since then, all has gone quiet on the Longmorn front and the mistress has become a dowdy madam. Pity.

Longmorn 15-year-old 45% ABV

Hard to get now, but definitely the expression to go for from this distillery. It's one of those malts where the age is not reflected in the whisky. The oak is held back by the juicy, grassy, green fruity centre. Balanced and refreshing Speyside-style.

Longmorn 16-year-old 48% ABV

Considered by some as a blatant attempt to take advantage of the growing market for premium malts, the 16-year-old is bigger and fruitier than the 15-year-old, but is in some respects flabbier and less focused. No negatives, the whisky is good – but not like the original.

Longmorn 17-year-old Cask Strength 49.4% ABV

Apple, pear, maple and vanilla on the nose here, with yellow and apple fruits on the palate, plus custard, toffee and some oak. Spices arrive later.

LONGROW

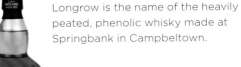
www.springbankdistillers.com

Longrow is the name of the heavily peated, phenolic whisky made at Springbank in Campbeltown.

Longrow 10-year-old 46% ABV

An oddball this, where smoky peatiness and a sweet-barley core work side by side, but never totally in harmony. Intriguing though, and worth investigating because it is distinct from the peated island malts.

Longrow 10-year-old 100 Proof 57% ABV

This one is much more like it. An earthy, rootsy flavour underpins a rich, intense and very oily mouthcoating mixture of sweetness and malt. Water lets the smoke out.

Longrow 14-year-old 46% ABV

Smoke and peat on the nose, plus fudge, with coal tar, peat and bonfire to taste, and distinctive seaside notes. A deli of a whisky for savoury-malt lovers. Oak and spice showing later.

Longrow CV 46% ABV

Arguably the best of the Longrow range, with a proper charcoal-peat delivery and a delightful oily and rustic note – tastes as if it is handcrafted by artisans. Funny that...

Longrow Gaja Barolo 55.8% ABV

I think as a rule whisky and red wine prove that, while you can mix the grain and the grape, you have to keep them at arm's length much of the time because they will fight like cat and dog. But, this is an example of a puppy and a kitten rolling in playful abandon. Lots of smoke-and-wine flavour, and a totally original taste. The whisky here is only seven years old, so it is untamed. It works very well.

THE MACALLAN
www.themacallan.com

Few distilleries enjoy the iconic status that Macallan does. And yet, in recent years, its owners have changed the look of its core expressions and completely overhauled some of its range. On the one hand, there is the gilt-edged Speyside distillery, which has few equals when it comes to special and rare, collectable bottles – the distillery that has been capable of commanding more loyalty than almost any other and that has consistently sat at the very head of the premier cru Scottish distilleries. And on the other, it is the one that first moved away from its sherried past, with the launch of a whole new portfolio of lighter, more bourbon-cask-influenced whiskies, and then ditched some of its younger age-statement whiskies altogether, replacing them with four colour-coded whiskies.

The argument put forward by the distillery's owners for the move was that European drinkers wanted lighter spirits and had moved naturally to its Fine Oak range of malts. But, that does not hold any water when you look at trends in dark spirits generally and the success of the likes of Glenfarclas and GlenDronach distilleries, in particular. That said, there is nothing wrong at all with the Fine Oak range and the diversity helped bring a new generation of drinkers to the Macallan table. The second move, to no-age-statement whiskies also led to some head scratching. Hadn't the industry spent years convincing the public that the colour of a whisky was a guide neither to age nor quality?

For all that, though, some of the world's best whiskies still come out of this distillery, so it's still very much in credit. You just wish it would throw off the marketing claptrap.

The Macallan 10-year-old
40% ABV

The original 10-year-old punches well above its weight, dripping in style and sophistication without commanding a premium price. Take a bottle of this whisky, a bottle of Aberlour and a bottle of BenRiach 12-year-old and you have a pretty good cross-section of the different Speyside styles. This is sherried with orange, red berry and plum fruits.

The Macallan 12-year-old 40% ABV

Rich Christmas cake, fruit crumble and spice, with some orange in the mix and a taste shaped by toffee and candy notes.

The Macallan 18-year-old
43% ABV

This is another contender for the title of the world's best single malt, whatever that means. There are plenty of Macallan lovers who will tell you that this is not the heavyweight it once was, more of a David Beckham than a Wayne Rooney. I could not tell you, as I do not get this expression at all and do not have a long enough history with it. Undoubtedly, though, this is premier league stuff all the same – lots of sherry, oak and spice.

The Macallan 25-year-old 43% ABV

A venerable old-boy whisky, with rich sherry, plenty of oak and a clean orange core.

The Macallan 30-year-old 43% ABV

No malt commands the sort of respect that Macallan does, but there were mumblings when the lighter version of the malt was introduced, and when age-statement whiskies were replaced by whiskies named by their colour. This, though, is the real deal. Christmas in a glass, not just because of the big sherry and fruitcake notes, but also because of the spicy aromas of clove, the cinnamon-laced punch and Liquorice Allsorts at its centre. If the Macallan is the Rolls Royce of whiskies, then this is its Silver Cloud – an ageing, classy model.

The Macallan Fine Oak
10-year-old 40% ABV

The Fine Oak range marked a radical departure for The Macallan, and offered a lighter version of what had always been a full-sherried malt. A higher percentage of bourbon-cask whisky in the mix works remarkably well, showing off the malt craftsmanship. Clean barley, cedarwood and orange on the nose; citrus and spice to taste.

The Macallan Fine Oak
12-year-old 40% ABV

This has aromas of butterscotch, vanilla, orange fruits and other citrus fruits. The taste is of grapefruit and orange before a big wave of spices arrives. A great example of how sherry and bourbon casks can perfectly complement each other.

The Macallan Fine Oak
15-year-old 43% ABV

A soft nose with squidgy yellow fruit, a big mouthcoating taste of ginger barley, tinned peaches and some oak and spice late on. Altogether, this is a rich and satisfying malt, and proof positive that the Fine Oak concept can be every bit as rewarding as the other traditional Macallans.

The Macallan Fine Oak
18-year-old 43% ABV

The nose is soft and mushy and not very impressive, but the taste is much better, with a sweet-and-sour, rich fruit and chewy barley giving way to intense pepper and oaky tannins. It all pulls around, however, for a most pleasant finish.

The Macallan Fine Oak
21-year-old 43% ABV

An ideal whisky for warm summer days, this one, it has lots of playful barley and zippy citrus fruits on both the nose and the palate. It is certainly refreshing, and the oak very much takes a back seat.

The Macallan Fine Oak
25-year-old 43% ABV

An assertive nose combines stewed fruits, dark chocolate and cocoa, plus summer berries. The taste is a Ferris wheel of flavours – with all sorts of sweet exotic fruits, ordered and pleasant spices, hickory and liquorice – and just enough oak to give the whole shebang some weight.

The Macallan Fine Oak
30-year-old 43% ABV

And here's another big, sleek and stylish whisky. Still elegant, but also a little rough around the edges, giving it a healthy dash of character. The sherry and red-berry notes are all present and correct, but there are some notes of yellow and citrus fruit, too, and on the palate it's all about chunky-orange marmalade and oak. Heady stuff that is rich and golden in colour.

The Macallan
1824 Series Amber
40% ABV

One step up from Macallan Gold, this is more full-bodied and the malts in it are more mature and balanced. The nose is very pleasant, with Danish pastry and rich sultanas. On the palate there is still raisin but also green apple and cinnamon. Quite chewy and very drinkable.

The Macallan 1824 Series Gold 40% ABV

The entry-level malt, this is underwhelming and contains whiskies of a number of different ages, though I'd bet my life that most are from the younger end of the scale. There are some fruity confectionery notes, gentle spices and a touch of vanilla.

The Macallan 1824 Series Ruby 43% ABV

The oldest whisky in the series is something of a venerable old lady. Classic church pew, dark berries, orange marmalade and prunes. Sherried malt the old-fashioned way.

The Macallan 1824 Series Sienna 43% ABV

By far the best in the series. Bigger, richer and fuller, with juicy raisin and delicious citrus bouncing off a toffee and honey base. Full, rounded and never cloying, this is great.

MILTONDUFF
www.maltwhiskydistilleries.com

Miltonduff is one of the two key distilleries for production of Ballantine's, the other being Glenburgie (rebuilt a few years ago). The two distilleries can now be run by one operator, who can see every part of the production process from his desk; technology has now reached a point where, were it allowed, a distillery need not be manned at all. Such automated plants remove the need for traditional distilling skills, and some distilleries have reacted by reverting completely to traditional whisky-making methods.

Miltonduff 15-year-old 46% ABV

A perfectly palatable and enjoyable Speyside whisky with a twist. Sweet and fruity for the most part, it takes an odd salty, nutty turn half way through. Like finding a knot in a rope.

MORTLACH
www.malts.com

One of Scotland's most enigmatic distilleries and one that produces a whisky that is always worth getting excited about. The distillery is not open to the public, and little of its considerable output is bottled as single malt. But this is a core whisky in Johnnie Walker, and is a whisky anorak's dream due to the triple-distillation process for a sizeable fraction of the distillation. The distillery has worm tubs – the traditional condensation method which is thought to ensure a meatier, more robust spirit.

The whisky often appears in specialist bottlings as intensely sherried and is unpredictable: oily, meaty or sulphury. Once noted for its classic 16-year-old, different expressions were introduced in 2014.

Mortlach 16-year-old 43% ABV

On one level this is a street urchin, but get past the unkempt nature of the malt and it is surprisingly sophisticated. There is sherry, spice, oil, menthol and an endearing, welcome touch of sulphur on both the nose and the palate, with fruit, cocoa and chilli late on. Not for softies.

Mortlach 18-year-old 43.4% ABV

In recent years Diageo has taken pleasure in showing off Mortlach's lesser known personalities. But, this is what Mortlach is famous for: big and active sherry-cask notes. Cherry, coffee, dark chocolate and berry fruits all battle it out over an oily base. Oaky spices round it all off. Great.

Mortlach 25-year-old 43.4% ABV

In the film *End of The End*, Black Sabbath perform a touching version of the ballad 'Changes'. This is Mortlach's equivalent: when all the bombast and power is put on hold, and a delicate side is revealed. There's tropical and Starburst fruits and the oak and spice are held in check.

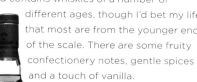
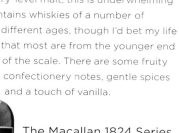

Mortlach Rare Old 43.4% ABV

The entry-level whisky in a super-premium range of Mortlach releases. The nose is sweet, with fudge, raisin and some spice. The whisky is rich and oily in the mouth, with liquorice, currants and kitchen spices. Glacé cherries are evident, too.

OBAN
www.malts.com

Oban is a port on Scotland's west coast and is the gateway to the Western Isles. The distillery is small and compact, hidden behind the towen's main street. Nearly all of Oban's output is bottled at 14 years.

Oban 14-year-old 43% ABV

Another quirky and unique malt, big on fruit and sherry – on both nose and palate – but with at least a smattering of west coast and Highland earthiness. Sweet conquers peat here, but enough smoke and peat stop the sweetness elsewhere becoming too dominant in the mix.

Oban The Distiller's Edition 43% ABV

The debate about whether you should mess with a special whisky too much is assuredly kicked in to touch by this distiller's edition, which uses sherry casks and adds a spiciness and clean, green fruitiness to the sweetness of the standard 14-year-old. It succeeds in pulling off that trick of still being distinctly Oban, but is very much a quality whisky in its own right, with its own personality and character.

OLD PULTENEY
www.oldpulteney.com

Pulteney is Scotland's most northerly distillery and, if you travel by road, you go so far through the Highlands you come out the other side and the landscape goes flat again.

Old Pulteney 12-year-old 43% ABV

This was once described as the ultimate whisky for which you should throw away the cork – and this is spot-on. I know several people who have set out on an (obviously responsible) afternoon or evening session with a group of friends and a bottle of this, and belatedly discovered that they had all but drained the bottle. It is the saltiness in this easy-going, citrusy malt that does it, coupled with a spectacularly short finish. As someone pointed out to me, it is a bit like Pringles crisps – the whisky seduces you with its sweet-and-sour combination. You want to resist, but it's futile.

Old Pulteney 17-year-old 46% ABV

Many years ago, the herring were so plentiful around Wick that the sea turned silver, hence the distillery's, and this whisky's, gold and silver theme. The herring created a buoyant and thriving industry, and at one time Wick had the biggest port in Europe. So great was the trade that the area (Pulteney) was built to house the hundreds of immigrant workers who moved here. Thomas Telford built roads and bridges to service the trade. And the Scottish fishwives followed the herring as they travelled all the way down the east coast and into England. Today you can visit the Time & Tide museum in Great Yarmouth and learn of the link between Wick and East Anglia, and occasionally you can meet someone of Scottish descent whose grandmother followed the fish and fell in love with the region, one of its inhabitants, or both. There is nothing left in Wick now, of course, except this distillery. But this whisky is a fitting salute to another lost part of great British industrial history. It's a much more intense version of the 12-year-old, with some oiliness, chocolate, soft toffee and rich fruit.

Old Pulteney 21-year-old 46% ABV

The tide was well and truly in with the 17-year-old and while this is a wonderful whisky, it is like going back to the 1960s and asking Hank Marvin to follow Hendrix. Lots of honey, just enough wood, plus some orange and candied fruit, salt and treacle toffee. Very good indeed.

Old Pulteney 30-year-old
45.8% ABV

Hard to know what to make of this – it is a very different Pulteney, adding more to the distillery's admirable diversity. It's very delicate and soft, with lemon and grapefruit that belie its age. It is all a little fragile, but more spritely than it has any right to be. The spice is still there but it plays quite a back role.

ROYAL BRACKLA
www.dewars.com

Royal Brackla was bought by John Dewar & Sons 12 years ago, but no stock was included in the deal, so only very young malt exists. But the promise is certainly there, so this is one to watch.

Royal Brackla 10-year-old 40% ABV

Youthful, fresh, sappy malt, with some heather and floral notes, a touch of spice and a sweet core. It is included here because it is one of the best examples of young and untainted barley.

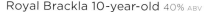

ROYAL LOCHNAGAR
www.malts.com

This distillery lies close to the Balmoral Estate, Scottish home to the Queen. It is Diageo's smallest distillery, but is one of the prettiest and it's packed with character.

Royal Lochnagar 12-year-old 40% ABV

Royal Lochnagar is one of only three distilleries allowed to include the word 'royal' in its title, thanks to the patronage of Queen Victoria. The distillery is small and traditional, with worm tubs and old wooden washbacks – and it makes a traditional Highland whisky. The 12-year-old provides easy drinking, a rich-honeycomb heart, sherry fruits and a warm finish.

Royal Lochnagar Selected Reserve 43% ABV

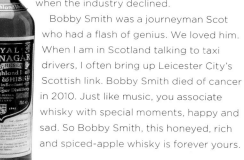

I happened to be tasting this when my brother called me to say Bobby Smith had died. That name will mean little to most people, but Smith played soccer for Leicester City in the 1980s (and for Edinburgh side Hibernian for many years, too) and was part of the great Jock Wallace City sides of yesteryear. Years before I fell in love with whisky, Leicester had a special relationship with Scotland. Wallace, who had been a legend at Rangers, gave Leicester one of its greatest spells in the game. He brought in fiercesome fighting Scots such as Gary McAllister, Ally Mauchlen, Iain Henderson and personal favourite Alan Young. He mixed them up with a bunch of enthusiastic puppies including one Gary Lineker, future England international player.

I lived in Market Harborough and our crowd knew one of the players, Andy Peake, so we always felt we had a direct line to the heart of the club, and we went home and away, often travelling with the exiled Glaswegians from Corby. Their parents had been moved en masse from Scotland to the English Midlands to work in the steel factories, but faced mass unemployment and poverty when the industry declined.

Bobby Smith was a journeyman Scot who had a flash of genius. We loved him. When I am in Scotland talking to taxi drivers, I often bring up Leicester City's Scottish link. Bobby Smith died of cancer in 2010. Just like music, you associate whisky with special moments, happy and sad. So Bobby Smith, this honeyed, rich and spiced-apple whisky is forever yours.

SCAPA

www.scapamalt.com

Witnessing the resurrection of a whisky distillery is rare, and an experience not to be missed. And so it was that I found myself on the Orkney Isles, clambering over bricks and debris in driving wind and rain. The roof for the main part of the distillery was off, and birds had taken over the still room to messy effect. But two features stood out: the large window, which overlooked the brooding Scapa Flow and the black buoy marking where the sunken Royal Oak had come to rest, and the big Lomond still in the centre of the still room. The Lomond still was a feature of some distilleries in the 1960s. It fell in to disuse, because its plates often clogged up and were difficult to clean. Today the distillery is refurbished and the still room is fully functional. The Lomond still is in place, but functions as a conventional still these days.

Scapa Glansa 40% ABV

Over the years Scapa has been on the periphery, enjoying cult status as a 14-year-old, then struggling as a 16-year-old. And now we have this, an easy-drinking malt with a peaty tang and no-age-statement. It's been partially matured in casks that had contained peated whisky, so the smoke's there, but there's lots of vanilla and fruit, too.

Scapa Skiren 40% ABV

Scapa is one of Scotland's most northerly distilleries, located in the Orkney Isles, which have strong Norse links. The name here comes from the Old Norse word for 'glittering bright skies'. A dapper, smart-suited malt, all smoothness, sophistication and cool. Apple pie on the nose, salted caramel on the palate, with apple and spice. Hints of tropical fruits, too. Very easy drinking.

SPEYBURN

www.inverhouse.com

Speyburn is owned by Inver House and has been used as an entry-level malt. It is not seen very often, but an occasional older bottling suggests that this distillery is an undiscovered gem. Time – and the plans of the parent company – will tell.

Speyburn 25-year-old 46% ABV

This has an unusual aroma, with a slight off note nestled under lemon, grapefruit and orange, and hints of oak. The taste is soft, honeyed and rounded, with some oak and spice. The finish is refreshing and really quite fruity.

SPRINGBANK

www.springbankdistillers.com

Once there were scores of distilleries in Campbeltown, which is the peninsula running down the west coast of Scotland. Whisky was exported across to the United States from there, but over time the quality of the malt deteriorated, people stopped wanting it, and one by one the distilleries disappeared. Today there are three distilleries in the region. This is the biggest and most successful.

It is actually three distilleries in one, because the triple-distilled Hazelburn and the intensely peated Longrow are also produced here. Springbank itself enjoys iconic status, with serious whisky drinkers attracted by both its unique taste and the rustic and boutique nature of the distillery.

Springbank 100 Proof 57% ABV

Like the 10-year-old with the volume turned up. This is an oral orchestra, and although each section is working in harmony overall, it is fun to focus on each component part individually, particularly the peat and spicy notes, which give the whisky its character. There are some vanilla and soft toffee notes in the mix, too.

Springbank 10-year-old 46% ABV

This is as complex as a whisky this young gets, with honey, barley, candied lemon, earthy peat and salt and pepper all contributing to a malt that has an appealing bitter-sweetness to it.

Springbank 15-year-old

46% ABV

Outstanding, rich and full-flavoured, with a soft, sweet, crystallized peach nose and oily, fruity palate that again pulls the impressive trick of being sweet and savoury all at once. To taste, red and tropical fruits can be found, and a rustic grunginess provides weight to the whole drinking experience.

Springbank 16-year-old Rum Wood

54.2% ABV

Arguably the best bottling of Springbank there is, with all the exotic fruits, vanilla and coconut cranked up to the highest level and almost in conflict with big peat and pepper notes, like duelling fencers scampering across our palate. A big, mouthcoating and assertive whisky, and not one for wimps.

Springbank 18-year-old 46% ABV

The nose here is surprisingly soft and delicate, with grape, some green fruit and a touch of smoke. But, the taste is massive, with an early hit of black pepper, some unripe banana in the centre and cocoa and smoke towards the end. Peat is most noticeable on the finish. Not much impact from oak for the age, but overall it's less sweet than other bottlings.

Springbank Vintage 1997 54.9% ABV

Toffee, vanilla, peat and green banana on the nose. The taste is very intense and needs unlocking with water, but when you do so there is oak, smoke, vanilla ice cream with soft toffee sauce and tropical fruits.

STRATHISLA
www.maltwhiskydistilleries.com

Flooding in November 2009 forced its owners to give the visitor centre a complete makeover. But this is a very pretty distillery anyway, and one of Scotland's most photographed. It is also home to Chivas Regal.

Strathisla 12-year-old 43% ABV

Another definitive Speysider, with a delicate ginger barley and grapey nose and a rich, sweet, yellow-fruit taste, with some red berries and barley at its core and a wisp of smoke towards the finish.

TALISKER
www.malts.com

You should not trust the Internet. It has no editor, and it can circulate information at an awesome speed, even when that information is wrong. When I first became editor of *Whisky Magazine*, a new James Bond film portrayed the hero as a Talisker drinker. Judi Dench as M also sipped single malt, so I thought it would be a good cover story. Talisker, was – I was told – James Bond's preferred tipple in the Ian Fleming books.

And so we did a cover story, after some difficult negotiations with the management of Pierce Brosnan, as the actor did not want to be associated with a strong spirit.

A few years later I was telling a group of people how drinking single-malt whisky had started in the 1970s when someone asked me how it was that James Bond would have sipped single malt when the Ian Fleming books were written in the 1960s, before Talisker would have been generally available. Good question, so I consulted the Internet.

There are thousands of references to Bond and whisky. Trouble is, they all stem from my original feature. There is no reference to Talisker in the Fleming books. It is not true. By the time of the next James Bond film, our super spy was drinking Finlandia Vodka. It is called product placement.

Talisker 10-year-old 45.8% ABV

An electric storm of a malt, crackling with pepper and spice, and flickering with cocoa and sweet barley. It has an almost metallic quality, and it bounces around the palate like savoury sherbet, as uncompromising, unforgettable and unique as the island of Skye – from where it comes.

Talisker 18-year-old 45.8% ABV

We've opened a bottle of this for Father Christmas (Santa Claus) for the past three years because, in our house, we know how seriously Santa takes his whisky. No more needs to be said about it. This is one of the world's very best whiskies, richer, fuller and with more depth than the fiery 10-year-old, but with the pepper and peat still very much to the fore and an intensity to die for.

Talisker 25-year-old

54.2% ABV

The nose is reminiscent of cracked pepper and salt on lemon-drizzled trout, and on the palate the pepper is still there, but sits snugly alongside citrus, ginger barley, vanilla and some oak. The tearaway 10-year-old has settled down into an old man who still has some attitude.

Talisker 30-year-old 49.5% ABV

The peat and pepper have settled down in this whisky and have taken more of a back seat, making it one of the most intriguing and unusual Taliskers you will ever taste. Oak is unsurprisingly in the mix, and there are some light, even floral notes, alongside the spice.

Talisker 57 North

57% ABV

This is a cask-strength bottling, which is sailing somewhere between Skye and Islay (exactly where I first tasted it), so the trademark pepper and peat are still there, but they are joined by sea breeze and brine, smoke and seafood. This is a rough and rugged malt as big and hardy as a Scottish trawlerman.

Talisker Dark Storm 45.8% ABV

Proof, should it be needed, that non-age-statement whiskies are automatically a dumbing down. This malt has been matured in heavily charred casks, and wave after wave of spice and smoke crash over a sweet citrus base.

Talisker The Distiller's Edition 45.8% ABV

The extra maturation in sherry casks makes for an intriguing and ultimately rewarding malt, with fruit filling out the flavour over the 10-year-old, but without sacrificing the peat and chilli burst so important to Talisker. Like the 18-year-old, this expression is richer and fuller than the standard bottling.

Talisker Storm 45.8% ABV

Not as assertive as the 10-year-old, but not as two-dimensional and metallic either. It's softer and creamy, with salt and pepper, lemon and chilli spice.

TAMDHU
www.tamdhu.com

Most of this sizeable distillery's malt used to go into blends, including The Famous Grouse. The distillery was closed for a while and then sold to independent retailer and Glengoyne distillery owner Ian MacLeod. It's now being bottled as a single malt. The whisky gets really exciting in older expressions. If you like your whisky fruity and sherbety, then this may well be for you.

Tamdhu 40% ABV

No-age-statement, but this is clearly young, with fresh barley, sweet honey and a thrilling lemon-and-lime sherbet core. Outstanding.

Tamdhu 25-year-old
43% ABV

Oily, sweet, plummy and with enough oak and spice to hold the honey and sweet fruit in check. Very underrated and worth seeking out.

TAMNAVULIN
www.whyteandmackay.com

Tamnavulin is now owned by Whyte & Mackay, and was reopened in 2007, but since then it has struggled after being badly damaged by snow in the winter of 2009–2010. Stock is limited and most of the pre-2007 output tends to be reserved for adding to blends.

Tamnavulin 12-year-old 40% ABV

Another malt that is more often than not destined for blends and therefore hard to find in its own right. Owner Whyte & Mackay does little to support it. The taste is of digestive biscuits, light spices and a menthol note – making this the ideal early summer's evening whisky.

TOBERMORY
www.tobermorydistillery.com

The only distillery on Mull, and one of the few places where you can see sea eagles and golden eagles. The distillery has had a chequered past, and has changed style and image more times than David Bowie. Traditionally it was light on peat, though the peaty Ledaig exists. The most recent change to style came when the strength of the whisky was raised to 46.3% to avoid the need for chill filtration. The double effect of higher alcohol and retention of flavour compounds have made the standard bottling a weightier, harder-hitting animal.

Tobermory 10-year-old 40% ABV

You expect the big peaty whiskies to divide opinion, but not something as simple and straightforward as this. And yet there are people who choose this slightly salty, very subtly fruity and faintly smoky whisky above all others. Equally, there are just as many who cannot stand it. As with Jura, the reason may lie in the dairy-ish nose, although the taste is thoroughly fresh and fruity.

Tobermory 15-year-old 46.3% ABV

This is rich in sherry and Christmas cake flavours, with spice and orange dominating the nose and taste. Some oak prevents the malt from being too one-dimensional, but if you do not like sherry you really will not like this.

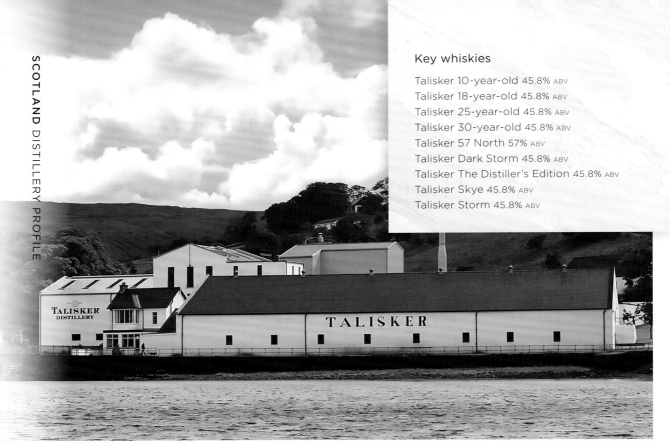

Key whiskies

Talisker 10-year-old 45.8% ABV

Talisker 18-year-old 45.8% ABV

Talisker 25-year-old 45.8% ABV

Talisker 30-year-old 45.8% ABV

Talisker 57 North 57% ABV

Talisker Dark Storm 45.8% ABV

Talisker The Distiller's Edition 45.8% ABV

Talisker Skye 45.8% ABV

Talisker Storm 45.8% ABV

ABOVE Talisker – one of the world's most famous and distinctive malts – is well-suited to its rugged environment.

BELOW Its whisky's signature peppery, smoky taste is much in demand.

TALISKER

Carbost, Isle of Skye, IV47 8SR
www.malts.com

It might have a bridge joining it to the mainland now, but visiting the island of Skye is still like entering another world. As with so much of Scotland, it's a place with attitude.

In fact the northwest of Scotland is all a bit other-worldly. In the eighteenth and nineteenth centuries, lairds drove many of the poor residents off this land to make way for sheep – driving Scots across the world as far afield as New Zealand and the United States. It's a rough-and-ready region, which threatens in bad weather and sparkles in sunshine, as the coastal waters turn blue. When the sun's out you could imagine you were on a rugged Greek island if it wasn't for the temperature.

Stuff happens here, especially at night. Goats' eyes suddenly appear in your headlights; a white owl swoops in front of you; the Northern Lights provide a dancing light show. If it feels darker here than many other places, then that's because it is. There is little light pollution in Wester Ross.

Even by the region's dizzying standards, Skye still excels. Its jagged shoreline, unpredictable, challenging and rapidly changing weather, its rocky crops and the black, flinty Cuilin mountain range – the island's backbone – all make for an atmosphere that can send shivers down your back. And not just because of the icy rainwater dribbling down it. No wonder Bonnie Prince Charlie chose to sail over the seas to it when he went on the run. What a place to hide in.

If you were to create a malt whisky to reflect such a harsh, uncompromising and inhospitable place, it would be Talisker. It is a big, rugged, gritty malt that reflects the Isle of Skye perfectly, but is at the same time a welcome warmer of a whisky. No matter what the elements throw at you, a good glass of Talisker will see you through.

The distillery is owned by Diageo and, as you'd expect, everything at the distillery is in immaculate condition. If you visit a lot of distilleries you'll recognize some of the drinks giant's signature furnishing from other sites – sometimes Diageo keeps its distilleries so well they tend to come across like museums.

But, this is a petty quibble, and with Talisker's production at full stretch as its owners vainly attempt to keep up with demand, everyone's putting in the extra yards.

The distillery was founded in 1830 by Hugh and Kenneth MacAskill, the sons of a doctor who had settled on the island five years earlier. Distilling on such a remote and difficult island, even with a bridge to the mainland, has not been easy. Barley has to be brought across from Glen Ord, for instance.

Unsurprisingly, for most of Talisker's history it has operated alone on the island, though there were plans for a Gaelic-speaking distillery in the early part of the millennium, and a sizeable distillery started producing whisky spirit at Torabhaig in early 2017.

As with so many other whisky companies, Diageo has extended the range of Talisker bottlings in recent years, releasing limited-edition, aged releases, single-cask and distillery-only bottlings, plus some special releases. Talisker is moderately peated and is noted for its distinctive peppery notes, so not all of the experimental releases worked. Port Ruighe, for instance, is finished in ruby port casks and doesn't work at all. On the other hand, the weighty 57 North, marking the distillery latitude and bottled at the unusual strength of 57% ABV, is a fabulous peaty and briny malt that nods to the island of Islay, and two no-age-statement releases, Storm and Dark Storm, are both worthy additions to the main range.

WELL, FANCY THAT...

Talisker's history stems from one of the most unsavoury periods of Scottish history. Founders Hugh and Kenneth MacAskill were classic Clearance landlords, and from 1825 they set about forcibly shifting the resident population from their farms, either to new settlements at Carbost and Portnalong or off the island entirely. As well as replacing subsistence farmers with more profitable sheep, they opened their Talisker distillery in Carbost in 1830 using the people they had cleared out of their farms as its workforce.

RACHEL BARRIE

Benriach Distillery Co.

Rachel Barrie likes a good challenge. In a glittering and illustrious career of more than 25 years she has worked with some of the very best whisky makers, and for some of the world's most impressive drinks companies.

But she's at her happiest when working with a small distillery and helping to take it from underdog to top dog. It's one of the delights of the world of whisky that small distilleries can exist and thrive while part of a larger company. So, working for a big boss doesn't have to be an obstacle at all. Barrie's turned it into an art form. It seems that no matter where she works, she is drawn to the underdog, relishing the challenge of getting people to take notice. Which is just as well, because although she works for Brown-Forman, the Kentucky-based owners of Jack Daniel's, her remit covers the three Scottish distilleries that form The BenRiach Distillery Company under Brown-Forman's control: BenRiach, GlenDronach and Glenglassaugh.

Barrie studied chemistry at university before getting her first job in whisky at the Scotch Whisky Research Institute. She was ahead of her time, because today the science route is the norm for would-be distillers. But, any suggestion that she is a product of boffin theory and not hands-on practice go straight out of the window when you look at the people she has worked with, and the passionate and allegorical way she talks about whisky, constantly comparing it to living creatures.

She was given her first job by the late-great Dr Jim Swan, and she says she learned so much from him, describing him as a genius.

'I have such fond memories of him,' she says. 'I was just in awe of him. With Jim, I learned about how things work, but also learned to work with nature – to think it and feel it. He had it all. Entrepreneurial spirit, great imagination and scientific knowhow.'

She moved to Glenmorangie (now owned by LVMH), where her education continued while working next to Dr Bill Lumsden. He has been putting the arguments about no-age-statement to bed years before it even became a term, by creating wonderful malts finished in a myriad of different casks. While others were clumsily hiding poor-quality

whisky by turning them pink in port casks, Lumsden kept raising the bar. But it was here that Barrie was to achieve her first major success, raising the quality of the company's blend Baillie Nicol Jarvie to such an extent that critics began to notice. That takes some doing with a blended whisky. Talk to her about that period, though, and its the rebirth of Islay distillery Ardbeg that really excites her. She was in the perfect position to see a distillery go from zero to hero, and it's that thrill that has fired her ever since.

Barrie's next move was to Morrison Bowmore, part of Suntory. It's no shrinking violet of a company, but Barrie's influence over the company's malts was in evidence very quickly. The much-neglected Auchentoshan was given a complete makeover and we started to see unusual and limited-edition bottlings. She put the wonderful Glen Garioch on the whisky map. And when Bowmore lost its way, she moved in. Under her guardianship, wonderful expressions under The Devil's Cask and Tempest series were released – big, heavy-hitting whiskies delivered at cask strength. Even the 15-year-old Darkest seemed to go up a notch, bringing sherry and peat together in what is malt whisky's hardest party trick. When the chance came to work with another great whisky maker, Billy Walker, ready to replace him when he retired, and to oversee whisky production at three whipper-snapper distilleries, it was too good for Barrie to resist. So, in 2017, she joined The BenRiach Distillery Company and started sampling the many casks held by BenRiach, GlenDronach and Glenglassaugh. She reckons she has nosed 150,000 casks, and her career has bridged the period from when women in the industry were rare to the point where women in whisky jobs is the norm and not even worth discussing.

'The aim is to take a distillery and make it the pinnacle, revered around the world,' she says. 'Master blenders and master distillers, we are all guardians of quality, continuing the legacy and tradition and protecting whisky for the future.'

TOMATIN

www.tomatin.com

You rarely hear much about Tomatin, but in its heyday it could make more than 12 million litres (3.2 million US gallons) of spirit a year, making it Scotland's largest distillery. Even today it's one of Scotland's larger producers, but much of the spirit goes back to Japan. The distillery is in the north of Speyside and is not the prettiest, but it does welcome visitors.

Tomatin 12-year-old 40% ABV

The aroma of this whisky is light and delicate, the flavour surprisingly rich and robust, with a nutty malt. There are also some noticeable sherry tones and a pleasant, fruity, malt finish.

Tomatin 14-year-old 46% ABV

Flip, and verily, flop. Tomatin is one of Scotland's more intriguing distilleries, prepared to release an oddball like this in to its core range. This contains some whisky matured in tawny-port casks. This starts life as a juicy, fresh-salad sandwich and then goes all dessert, with vanilla, pepper and berry fruits marching proudly in to the finish.

Tomatin 18-year-old 43% ABV

This is the malt that elevates Tomatin to the premiership, a weighty whisky at the top of its game and deservedly an award winner. Juicy currants, sweet spice and vanilla on the nose. The malt is rich, oily and mouthcoating, with lots of sherry fruit, red berries and oak. The finish is fruity and woody.

Tomatin 25-year-old 43% ABV

Fluffy apple, vanilla and lemon on the nose; the taste is of vanilla-ice-cream sundae, with chocolate and hazelnuts, a wave of late pepper and an ordered and balanced finish. This was a revelation – a very good whisky indeed.

Tomatin 30-year-old 49.3% ABV

Released in very limited quantities, this is hard to find. Baked apple, cinnamon and cloves on the nose, and a complex and intriguing mix of spice, oak, orange, citrus, plus nuts and sherry, with a long, characterful finish.

Tomatin Cask Strength 57.5% ABV

Tomatin has been moving up through the gears in the last five years or so, and this is proof that the distillery is in fine fettle. It is made from a mix of bourbon- and sherry-cask malts, with full-on vanilla, spice, orange and berry fruits in an assertive, gleeful malt. Top stuff.

Tomatin Legacy 43% ABV

An experimental whisky, this one, with the malt matured in virgin oak casks as well as ex-bourbon ones. If you could taste colour, this would taste of yellow. It's all light and sweet, with some spring-meadow notes giving way to sweet citrus, pineapple and melon. The finish is all sugar and spice.

TOMINTOUL

www.tomintouldistillery.co.uk

Way back before Highland and Speyside whisky went legitimate, the reputation of malt from the region became known as far away as London. There was a thirst for the rich, sweet malts in the bars and taverns of Glasgow and Edinburgh, and smugglers would bring whisky on horseback through the Glenlivet valley. The story goes that on one visit the king of England asked for a glass of Glenlivet, shocking his Scottish hosts and elevating the reputation of the distillery. Other distillers, keen to cash in on its perceived reputation, added the word 'Glenlivet'. Tomintoul still includes the descriptor 'Speyside Glenlivet' on its label, and has every right to do so, because the two distilleries are sited very close to each other and some distance from other Speyside producers.

Tomintoul 10-year-old 40% ABV

A light, easy-drinking malt and so gentle it could be from the Lowlands. Perfectly drinkable but a little underwhelming and with some decidedly sweet toffee notes. This may be for people who don't like malt whisky, or whose experience is in blends.

Tomintoul 16-year-old 40% ABV

This one is much, much better, with lemon, orange and green fruits on both nose and palate, and a pleasant level of spiciness – probably from the wood. It does not hang around long at the end, though, but is pleasant and rounded.

Tomintoul 27-year-old

40% ABV

A stocky and rich malt, with orange marmalade on the nose and a pleasing taste that includes fudge, vanilla and light fruits. Given the age, there is not a great deal of oak coming through, but it is noticeable at the finish.

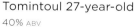

Tomintoul Peaty Tang 40% ABV

More than just a tang of peat, but not a full-blooded, Islay-style whisky either. This is a two-trick malt, with an earthy, rustic character from the peat and green fruits from the Speyside malt. It all tastes a little like a smoky Irish whiskey (they do exist).

TORMORE

www.tormoredistillery.com

This is a really weird distillery. It is only just over 50 years old and when it was built, its owners were happy to pay for not only a state-of-the-art distillery, but an ornate and showy one, too – one that almost begged for visitors to come and marvel at it. It has ornate clocks with moving parts and four different Scottish songs to mark each quarter hour. And yet it is not open to the public and never has been.

Tormore 12-year-old 40% ABV

Another light, unassertive and gentle toffee-ish single malt, this has some straw and yellow fruit notes. Nothing wrong with it particularly, but you would not miss it if it disappeared. A whisky for those who are not crazy about big-tasting drams.

TULLIBARDINE

www.tullibardine.com

Tullibardine was reopened by a consortium in 2003 and since then there has been a flood of different bottlings and the release of other products, such as whisky beers. In 2011, the distillery was sold to French drinks company Pica.

Tullibardine 1993 40% ABV

A restrained nose, complete with floral, almost perfumy notes. On the palate there are delicate spicy notes, some honey and oak. The finish is polite and ordered.

Blended whisky

Single malt is the Scotch whisky style that gets most of the attention, but the country also produces three other styles that are happy getting on with what they are doing without shouting loudly about it at every opportunity.

By far and away the biggest category of these is blended whisky, the one that put Scotland on the map worldwide, and that still accounts for the vast majority of whisky sales. One of whisky's greatest ironies is that while most whisky lovers pay homage to single malt and are dismissive of blends – which they consider inferior – in fact most single malts only exist because of the blended sector. Our ability to enjoy a single malt in its own right is made possible by the economic realities of selling a great deal of blended whisky to fund the single-malt process.

It is quite understandable that single malts should grab the headlines. For they read individuality, variety, unpredictability, stimulation. For blends read reliability, consistency and palatability. Single-malt whiskies are Angelina Jolie or Johnny Depp, blends, more often than not, are Jennifer Aniston or Hugh Laurie.

To ignore the category, though, is to overlook whisky making at its very best. Blends are like the circus – there is a lot of tired, clichéd and uninspiring rubbish out there, but just occasionally you stumble on the Cirque du Soleil, a perfect blend of balance, strength, creativity and grace. If you buy a bottle of 'Clan Sporrantosser' for less than the price of a can of strong lager from a dodgy convenience store, then expect it to be little more than caramelized vodka, matured for three years and a minute in a cask that has been filled more times than a window cleaner's bucket. Splash out for a special blend,

though, and you get more twists and turns than a season of *Game Of Thrones*, and more layers than a boxful of onions.

Blends do not have to mean blands and, indeed, at their best they are every bit the match of the very best single malts. Once you have found a favourite, the one that has you 'ooo-ing and aah-ing' every time you come back to it, then those values of consistency and reliability do not look quite so frumpy, do they?

To make blended whisky you need grain whisky, which is made in a different style of still to single-malt whisky, known as the continuous, column or Coffey still. The resulting spirit has a less-defined taste than new-make malt spirit, but when mixed with malt it smooths and rounds its rough edges. On its own it can be pretty uninspiring, but it has been described as being like a blank canvas, so if you can add enough colour through a top-quality oak cask it is possible to create something that is fresh, new and vital. The best examples of these are found in the independent sector and are often more than 30 years old.

The final style of Scotch whisky is a mixture of malts from different distilleries. In more sensible times, these were called 'vatted malts' but the term came to be considered to be too 'industrial'-sounding. For reasons best known to itself, the Scotch Whisky Association (SWA) ignored suggestions of alternative names, such as mixed malts, married malts, mingled malts or just malts whisky, spuriously claiming with a somewhat amazing chutzpah that its research indicated support for a new term – blended malt whisky. This is a different category to blended whisky because blended malts contain no grain whisky.

Got that? Don't worry, you are not alone. No one has.

100 Pipers 40% ABV

The traditional Scottish song '100 Pipers' was written about Bonnie Prince Charlie and the Jacobite Uprising of 1745 and tells of how the clans marched on England, swimming across the Esk.

'His bonnet and feathers he's waving high,
His prancing steed naist seems to fly
The nor' win' plays wi' his curly hair
While the pipers play wi' an unco flare'

I can't help wondering whether if they had stopped looking at what his hair was doing and concentrated on fighting with swords, rather than playing with pipes, the Uprising might not have been such a total disaster. The song this blend is named after has survived the centuries, though, and with a symbolic 45 years (the Uprising was called the '45) behind it, the blend is in pretty good shape, too. It's light and toffee-ish and is used by owners Chivas as a good entry blend for new markets.

The Antiquary 12-year-old 40% ABV

At 12-years-old, this contains a mix of premium spirits and aged grain, and it really is something of a stonker. It's from Tomatin distillery, a large Japanese-producer, and is big, full and peaty – easily among the best in class for the price. The Antiquary, with its reference to the writing of Sir Walter Scott, used to be a superior premium blend, but is now, stylishly packaged and immensely pleasant to drink, one of the best whisky deals you can find.

The Antiquary 21-year-old 43% ABV

Good golly! An intense, big mouthfeel – the sort of full taste you expect from a Japanese blend, but without the earthiness. There is peat, though, along with lots of sherry and berry. Excellent indeed.

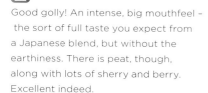

The Antiquary 30-year-old 46% ABV

This comes in a deep-blue velvet box that is a bit like the interior of an old Victorian theatre: designed to be voluptuous and lavish but bordering on tacky and dated. Not unlike the blend actually. This is a whisky that is akin to hitting the cross bar with a 30-yard (27m) scorcher in soccer – nearly brilliant, but in the end dropping frustratingly short.

Bailie Nicol Jarvie 40% ABV

This is made by Glenmorangie and it's another big-bang-for-your-buck blend. The vital ingredients for good-quality blended whisky are: good-quality malt, a large proportion of it and a skilled blender. You get all of that here. Look hard enough and you will find a Scottish road tour in the glass, with Speyside, Highland and Island malt in the mix. This is mainstream malt that stands up on its own, with the citrus notes, in particular, a total delight.

Ballantine's 12-year-old 40% ABV

Years ago there was a British beer advert that ended with the slogan 'the pint that thinks it's a quart'. This is the whisky world's equivalent, a blend so well made and established that it is produced in a range of expressions in the same way as single malts. This is a honeyed, creamy and stylish entry-level blend, with some oak.

Ballantine's 17-year-old

43% ABV

There is an argument (supported by this writer) that 17 and 18 years are the ideal age for Scotch whisky. By this age the cask has given up most of its secrets, the oak has added enough to the whisky's body, but is not beating up the smaller and weaker flavours, and everything has reached a perfect pitch. Like a band at its peak, playing in perfect harmony.

Ballantine's 21-year-old 43% ABV

This is almost as good as the 17, with plenty of melody and harmony, but perhaps a little more individuality. This has some truly scrummy candy, bourbon layers and lots of shifting shadows – smoke, oak, spice, hickory, red berries.

Ballantine's 30-year-old 43% ABV

This is to whisky what Paul McCartney is to the modern rock scene. It sits on a pedestal, one of the few really great stars, to be treated with the greatest of respect and a degree of reverence. There are times when a vertical whisky tasting (a tasting of different expressions from one brand) is akin to climbing up a castle on top of a hill. Each time you reach a new level you gasp at the view in front of you and immerse yourself in the beauty. Then you head on up again and it gets even better. This is the view from the highest parapet.

Bell's Original 40% ABV

One of the very great names in blends, and therefore included here on the strength of provenance and history. With huge popularity in the United Kingdom this is a smooth operator, with light oak, cereal and spice notes. As always with Diageo whiskies, very well made.

Ben Nevis Blended At Birth 40-year-old 40% ABV

This is a unique whisky that deservedly picked up a Masters Award in *The Spirit's Business* Whisky Masters Awards 2009. It is different because the grain and malt spirits are mixed as new-make then matured for 40 years, as opposed to the normal blending of the finished whiskies. Sophisticated, fruity, cocoa and oak, this blend demands a chance to be tasted alone. Outstanding.

Black Bottle 40% ABV

Quite possibly the best-value Scotch whisky on the market. In 2013, owners Burn Stewart moved to a less peaty and more fruity version of this whisky and, although repackaged, it still doesn't get the adulation it deserves. This is a cracker.

Black Bull 12-year-old 50% ABV

Speyside is much in evidence in this wonderful blend from Duncan Taylor, with green apples, toffee, vanilla, pear and eventually some sherbety fruit notes that you often get with Tamdhu (which I know is in the 40-year-old, but I am not sure is here). This is a zingy, zippy summer delight of a blend and well worth seeking out if you can.

Black Bull 40-year-old 47.6% ABV

'It's a blend Jim, but not as we know it.' Containing a sort of malt whisky 'greatest hits' including Highland Park, Glenlivet, Bunnahabhain, Springbank and Glenfarclas, plus some zesty Tamdhu, this is 90% malt and tastes it. A monster of a whisky, with strong apple and pear up front and then a wave of other fruits and spice. The oak is there, but is not in the least bit dominant. Exceptional.

Black & White 40% ABV

Glenrothes brand ambassador Ronnie Cox used to work on Black & White and was once asked to attend a promotional event in the United States. 'They flew me over on Concorde and I went straight to the event,' he recalls. 'And the bloke organizing it goes "we have someone specially flown over from the UK to talk to you now. Ron Cox!" So I get up to talk and have just started when someone stands up and says "are you gay?" "No I'm not," I say, "I'm as heterosexual as you are." "That's my point," says the man. "I'm gay and this brand is a dead horse, but I can sell it to my gay customers." ... I attempt to carry on. But another man stands up – a big black man. "This brand is totally dead but I can sell it and you know how?" he says. "I say to the white bartender give me one of you and one of me. I'm black and you are white, so give me a Black & White. That works." I knew at that point I hadn't got a chance with that crowd.' This is a sturdy, old-fashioned blend with a hearty malt core and some well-crafted peat and smoke around it.

Blue Hangar 30-year-old 45.6% ABV

A blend put together by Berry Bros & Rudd, which has been consistently excellent over the last few years and has caused a degree of confusion because it is also bottled as a vatted, sorry, blended malt. This unfurls like a good-quality single malt, with oak, oil and a fruity centre. Quite sharp and spiky, too – a blend for people who do not like blends.

Buchanan's 12-year-old 40% ABV

Buchanan's is a premium blend owned by Diageo that does well in South and North America. This 12-year-old is something of a whisky sandwich: its nose and finish is rich and full, its centre citrusy, with some grape and sherry notes. Pleasant, though.

Catto's 12-year-old

40% ABV

The citrus is still there and this is refreshing and enjoyable enough, but there is not a great deal of depth and little evidence of the 12 years in wood.

Catto's 25-year-old

40% ABV

Delicious rich and sherried whisky, with burnt fruitcake, dark caramel, oak and spice. Full and assertive yet gentle and mellow on the finish. Excellently made – a venerable old whisky.

Catto's Rare Old Scottish 40% ABV

Catto's is not a household name in the way that some of the old family blends are, but it still has a pedigree stretching back some 140 years. This standard version is fresh and juicy, with distinctive cidery apple and citrus notes in mellow grain.

Chivas Regal 12-year-old 40% ABV

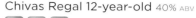

Another of the truly great blends, Chivas is owned by Pernod Ricard and has pretty much worldwide distribution. With Speyside whiskies such as Strathisla and The Glenlivet at its heart, this is unsurprisingly very clean and fruity and nicely honeyed. The finish is too restrained for this palate overall though.

Chivas Regal 18-year-old

40% ABV

The distinctive Speyside green fruits are in place here, and there is a honeyed, creamy mouthcoating feel about the whisky, too, with some heather and floral notes. It is nicely balanced, mellow and polite.

Chivas Regal 25-year-old 40% ABV

Undoubtedly the best in the range, but then you would expect that. Strangely enough it is the most lively and zingy, too, despite its age – with green, red and orange fruits, an elegant layer of spices and clean, chewy barley at the finish.

Clan Campbell 40% ABV

Launched just over a quarter of a century ago, this is a new boy on the block. Owned by Chivas it contains Aberlour and other Speyside whiskies, and has been successful in some countries where young, light and fruity whiskies are popular. A refreshing whisky, begging to be served with ice, and therefore suited to warmer climes.

The Claymore 40% ABV

A Whyte & Mackay second-division brand, sold in the standard market, but if you take that into consideration it is not bad at all. It is traditional and Highland in style, which means that it is full and fruity, possibly because of the inclusion of Dalmore in the mix. A solid 'centre back' or 'prop forward' of a blend.

Compass Box Aylsa Marriage 40% ABV

John Glaser set up Compass Box with a vision to take whisky into new and exciting areas and he has succeeded in abundance. Many of his creations, call them boutique whiskies if you want, are blended malts but this is a blend, albeit not a normal one. It is truly sweet, reminiscent of vanilla slice with squidgy cream, or perhaps traditional Bakewell tart.

Crawford's 40% ABV

You do not see Crawford's too often in the major markets so presumably it is doing licence-holders Whyte & Mackay a job in developing some overseas territories. This has an intriguing lemon-and-pepper combination going on.

Cutty Sark 40% ABV

There are few more famous or iconic brands than Cutty Sark. In 2010, control of it was handed over to Edrington and the long-term lease of The Glenrothes was given to Berry Bros & Rudd instead. Berry Bros originally introduced the blend for its wine-drinking customers who were put off by prevalent peatiess ruining their palates. So, Cutty Sark was designed to be fresh and clean: it was the world's first light whisky. This version meets the bill perfectly, with clean fruit, honey and vanilla.

Cutty Sark 12-year-old 43% ABV

It's a shame that the Cutty Sark visitor experience isn't open to the public. It's wonderfully dated and great entertainment. It includes the Berry Bros London shop, where Mr Berry will talk to you; or enter a speakeasy and listen to an American World War II soldier tell you 'You can get a Cutty Sark down the street, buddy, but you'll have to wait in line'. The range of brand advertisments give a strong sense of how big it once was. This version is full and fruity, with honey on the finish.

Cutty Sark 15-year-old 40% ABV

During Prohibition, the gangs running the illegal drinking dens – and having to make do with poor-quality bourbon mixes – welcomed the opportunity to bring in Scotch. One supplier, William S McCoy, based in Bermuda, supplied Cutty Sark to many parts of the United States. His product was known for quality and his name is credited with the expression 'the Real McCoy'. This expression is smooth and rounded, with some honey and toasted oak, but is perhaps just a little too polite.

Cutty Sark 18-year-old 43% ABV

Oak and sherry notes drift around the edges, wood and honey mix at the middle and there is a blend of sweet molasses, spice and a sharper lemon note to end. Pure from start to finish.

Cutty Sark 25-year-old 45.7% ABV

Another classic and a perfectly balanced blend. Honeycomb malt and chocolate-like-Maltesers flavours form the core of the whisky but there are significant spices, too. A real treat.

Dewar's 12-year-old 40% ABV

The impact that the Dewar's family has made on whisky has been considerable, and none more so than Tommy Dewar. He was only the third person in the country to own a motor car, was a pioneering champion of whisky and travelled across the world promoting his brands. He had a less attractive side to his personality, too, as a Conservative MP who campaigned vigorously on behalf of an immigration law aimed particularly at London's East End Jewish community. But, he actively supported sport initiatives and was responsible for the building of the Aberfeldy distillery, where today you can visit the excellent and informative Dewar's World of Whisky. The standard version of Dewar's is pleasant and sweet, with Aberfeldy-trademark honey singing through a robust and fruity body. Stylish.

Dewar's 18-year-old 43% ABV

This is a fine and fairly assertive blend, with sweetness from the grain to the fore, and just enough citrus fruit, oak, hints of smoke, hickory and spice to create a noisy big-band sort of a whisky.

Dewar's Signature 43% ABV

Based around an aged 27-year-old Aberfeldy malt, this is one of my very favourite whiskies, and absolute proof to any doubters that blends can feature among the very best Scotch whiskies. Perhaps it is the malty feel of the whisky upfront, but it is more than that. It unfurls in the mouth like someone turning over cards, a jack of citrus fruit here, a king of spice there, the queen of oak and an ace of sweet, honeyed, chewy grain. Good heavens – a royal flush of flavour.

Dimple 12-year-old 40% ABV

Now owned by Diageo, this brand was known as Haig Dimple and it has a long and glorious history as a premium blend. Dimple is a triumph of marketing and few brands inspire as much sentimentality as this one. The distinctive bottle and the advertising slogan 'don't be vague, ask for Haig', along with some definitive brand adverts from the 1950s to the 1970s, has created an army of people who all but equate Dimple with quality blends. This whisky expertly mixes dried fruits, spice, toffee and a little bit of oak.

Dimple 15-year-old 43% ABV

The 12-year-old's big brother is just what you might expect: full and fruity, with some cocoa notes and hints of smoke. Worthy of the name – and the brand's premium status.

The Famous Grouse 40% ABV

Owned by Edrington, owners of Highland Park and The Macallan, The Famous Grouse is Scotland's number-one blend and has been triumphantly competing with the leading blending houses over the last 125 years. It is a surprisingly full and robust blend and also a surprisingly sophisticated one, with the emphasis on the balance between rich, meaty malt and delightful soft and sweet grain.

The Famous Grouse
The Black Grouse 40% ABV

A fascinating aside for The Famous Grouse, with smoke and peat joining a base of toffee, fruit and caramel. Overall it's grungy and chewy. The name refers to a threatened rare species of grouse found on the west coast islands and Edrington are working with the Royal Society for the Protection of Birds to help conserve the bird via whisky sales.

The Famous Grouse Gold Reserve 12-year-old 40% ABV

I'm not sure what the future holds for this expression of The Famous Grouse as it is quite hard to find and its owners were not particularly enthusiastic about supplying samples of it. A shame really, because the mix of orange and lemon fruits with some hefty oak, sweet toffee and wisps of smoke makes for a winning combination.

The Famous Grouse Scottish Oak Finish 44.5% ABV

Whiskies matured in Scottish oak are exceedingly rare. But, I cannot think of any of them that were not outstanding, and this is no exception. The oak seems to add a spiciness to honeycomb. Imagine a chilli-flavoured honeycomb bar. The grain softens the impact in this blend, but it is pretty awe-inspiring stuff. This is a limited edition and very hard to find. If you do find it, make sure to try it.

Grand Macnish 40% ABV

With its distinctive, quaint bottle and the fact that there are 40 whiskies in the blend, this is a good choice to spoil the blend drinker in your life with. It is something a little different to the standard tipple, and specialist whisky shops stock it. Macduff International make it, and it has a sweet fruity taste.

Haig Gold 40% ABV

Like Mickey Rourke in *The Wrestler*, this blend has seen better days. Indeed, it was a champion once, the leading whisky for a generation. Now it is a bit-part player, part of the vast Diageo stable, and only thriving in some of the remoter southern European markets. A perfectly palatable but light blend, it has soft fruit, spice, wispy smoke.

Hankey Bannister 40% ABV

Amazingly Mr Hankey's and Mr Bannister's wine-merchant business has its roots stretching back more than 250 years. The name is now owned by Inver House, and is the umbrella for a range of blends that, at the higher end, are of extremely high quality and continue to win awards and critical acclaim. This entry level blend is another good break from the norm: pleasant, rounded fruit and mellow finish.

Hankey Bannister 12-year-old 40% ABV

Fruit, vanilla, honey, a touch of spice and oak and a balanced and attractive finish.

Hankey Bannister 21-year-old 40% ABV

Fresh green fruit and a vigorous flavour combination disguise the age here, until a malt-oak and spice complexity arrive. The finish is seemingly graceful, with flavours working hard beneath.

Hankey Bannister 25-year-old 40% ABV

Tastes like the big brother of the 21-year-old, with the same array of flavours but with the intensity and quality turned up a notch. The oak and delightful vanilla notes make this a stand-out, however.

Hankey Bannister 40-year-old 43.3% ABV

This was voted the world's best blend a couple of years ago, and promptly disappeared, though another version has been put out since. It has enough weight and body to appeal to single-malt lovers, with rich oak, malt and spice. It's a complex beast, too, with deep citrus and a long, rounded finish.

Islay Mist 12-year-old 40% ABV

Another Macduff International blend, mixing rich, peaty malts from Islay with some Speyside and Highland ones, and rounds them all up in a smooth grain net. It is a stylish piece of work, though, and pulls off the clever trick of delivering on rich flavour – both medicinal and linctus notes are present – offering up 'a spoonful of sugar to help the medicine go down'.

Isle of Skye 21-year-old 40% ABV

The best of a range of Isle of Skye blends from Ian Macleod: whisky's Artful Dodger, a mischievous street urchin, with charming good nature at its heart. Sugar and spice, it annouces its presence, though how much Talisker is here is unclear. Keeps you interested.

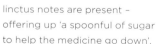

J&B Jet 40% ABV

Wonderfully packaged in sleek black with red touches, this looks the part. To taste, there is a distinctive Speyside influence, some assertive notes and a mellow and rounded finish.

J&B Rare 40% ABV

J&B (Justerini and Brooks) is part of the Diageo empire. It has always been a bit cutting-edge, this version was launched as a light whisky for a new type of drinker in the 1930s, and Diageo has used the brand for a series of innovative launches. There was a clear version, for instance, aimed at appealing to younger vodka drinkers, while Nox was a triumph of style over substance, packaged to stand out on nightclub shelves. And then there was Ultima, which was just that – a mix of more than 125 whiskies. This one is hugely popular in world markets and has sweet tinned fruits, vanilla and honey, plus appealing smokiness, all held in check by the grain.

John Barr 40% ABV

If this had originally been made by anyone else other than the company that became Diageo there would be a case for 'passing off' – everything about it screams Johnnie Walker Red. It was introduced to replace that very brand when Diageo's predecessors DCL got into a dispute with the European Union and withdrew Red Label. Now with Whyte & Mackay, it most likely includes Fettercairn and Jura. A curiosity found only in selected markets.

Johnnie Walker Black Label 40% ABV

As editor of *Whisky Magazine* a few years back I asked ten blenders to name their favourite blend by a rival company. I recall eight said Black Label, and one of the two blenders who did not was the blender for Black Label. This really is iconic, a masterclass in blending, with a touch of everything, including a delightful wave of spice from Talisker and peat from Caol Ila. I am not a blending expert, but I am told Caol Ila is loved by blenders because it is oily and full-flavoured, so makes a successful foundation for a blend. There is Speyside fruit here, and it is clear that only top-grade 12-year-old-plus whiskies are present. A heavy hitter for sure.

Johnnie Walker Blue Label 40% ABV

The journalist and presenter Piers Morgan annoys a lot of people but I love him. He is opinionated, brave and an outstanding journalist, prepared to stand up for his principles and with the uncanny knack of being able to get people to open up, and not only tolerate awkward and difficult questions, but answer them.

A few years ago he was approached by Johnnie Walker Blue's marketing people, which was, as he said in one of his books, a bit of a no-brainer. Why would you not take money (and no doubt whisky) to say nice things about a blend he drinks anyway? As part of his ambassadorial duties he interviewed the world-famous Italian referee Pierluigi Collina in front of an invited audience, the idea being that if you take different components and bring them together, you create something new – geddit? Morgan asked Collina what it was like to send off a world-renowned soccer superstar. The Italian gave a lengthy answer about the regret at ending the performance of an artist and depriving the crowd of a craftsman...

'Oh come on,' interrupted Morgan after a minute or so, 'when you've got that red card in your hand, and you're waving it in his face... it must be better than sex isn't it?'

Priceless Piers. Beforehand the guests were invited to numb their mouths with chilled water, then to sip Johnnie Walker – as the whisky warmed the mouth, its flavours took over. The most expensive of all this range has no-age-statement because the age on the label must refer to the youngest whisky in the mix. Here there is a proportion of very young whisky – to pep up some very old grand malts. An oral kaleidoscope, peat gives way to pear and melon, sherbet dip, liquorice, oak. Not cheap, but sublime.

Johnnie Walker Gold Label 40% ABV

Diwali is the Hindu celebration of good over evil and marks the return of Lord Rama to his kingdom after defeating the demon king. It is known as the Festival of Lights because it is celebrated with the lighting of small lamps, and it is traditional to exchange gifts with loved ones. One of the ultimate gifts a son can give his father at this time is a bottle of Johnnie Walker, and sales to the Indian market at Diwali are huge, so much so that when a batch of homemade whisky passed off as Johnnie Walker led to the death of several people, Diageo put out advertisements written in a number of Indian languages across the British trade press, reassuring Asian customers that the official bottlings were not tainted.

The Gold Label contains whiskies that are at least 18 years old. No expense has been spared. I can't help thinking that when people moan about the fact that one company owns so many distilleries they should consider whether this blend would exist if the situation was different, and whether the world is a better place for its presence. It most certainly is, and worthy of a top place on whisky's highest table – all whisky, not just blends.

Initially, this is surprisingly youthful, rich and zesty, then the full fruit, berry and smoke all kick in and kick off. Diageo's marketing people suggest you keep the bottle in the fridge and serve it chilled. Then hold it in the mouth, and let it warm so the flavours reveal themselves one by one. You could do that. Or just enjoy it. World class.

Johnnie Walker Red Label 40% ABV

Funny what sticks in your mind. I remember clearly my father's indignation at no longer being able to buy this version of Johnnie Walker, and how he was being presented with a choice of paying more for the Black Label, which he did not like (too peaty) or changing brands. It says masses about the power of a top brand that my father seemed genuinely offended that his loyalty could be repaid in this way. I think of him standing in the kitchen complaining to anyone who would listen (me) every time I hear of an American football franchise upping sticks to move cities. He blamed 'the grey gnomes of Europe' and I've been cynical ever since about Britons blaming Europe for everything.

Nowadays this one does pop up in British airports and specialist shops. Srangely the peaty taste my father objected to in Black Label but presumably wasn't there in the late 1960s is key to the current Red Label.

The Last Drop 52% ABV

Johnnie Walker is a snip next to this. This will set you back some £3000 or $4000, and there is not much of it (hence the name). But, if anyone ever tells you that at the high-end, premium whisky cannot match the world's best cognacs, tell them about this. It is another curiosity.

There are 12 grains and something like 70 malts in the mix here, and they all date from 1960 or earlier. But they were blended in 1972, when they were a minimum of 12 years old, and then returned to the cask for a further 36 years, when the whisky was rediscovered by accident and bottled at 48 years old. Its price comes from its rarity but it is the most honeyed, rounded, smooth and wonderful blend I have ever tasted.

Amazingly, every oak note is positive and good, with no sharpness or unpleasant tannin at any point.

If you buy a full bottle they give you a miniature so you can try it and decide whether you are going to keep the big bottle as an investment or drink it. That's not a choice, that's torture.

Lauder's 40% ABV

This does not claim to be anything it is not. In fact, it is a straight-ahead, well-made session blend – good for mixing. It's made in the heart of Glasgow and it is a far better prospect than the cheap blends you find in superstores and convenience shops.

Old Parr 12-year-old 40% ABV

Named after Thomas Parr, who is said to be have lived to 152 years old, this is normally sold in overseas markets. A juicy, fruity and exceptionally well-balanced blend, showing raisin, toffee and an earthy underbelly with a whiff of smoke.

Old Parr Superior 43% ABV

I tasted this while listening to Johnny Cash's final recording, 'American Vol VI: Ain't No Grave'. By the time he made the CD he was so ill he could only record on certain days. Clearly close to death and struggling to find the strength to sing, you can tell. I defy anyone not to have a lump in the throat or a tear in the eye by the time he sings Kris Kristofferson's 'For the Good Times':

 'Don't look so sad, I know it's over. But life goes on and this old world will keep on turning. Let's just be glad we had some time to spend together. There's no need to watch the bridges that we're burning'.

 This whisky is a fitting tribute to the great man – big and old-fashioned, rich and fruity. There is sherry all the way through. It is a little rough round the edges but a class act right until the end. Yep, this is good enough for Johnny.

Pig's Nose 40% ABV

Pig's Nose was part of the same management buy-out from Whyte & Mackay as Sheep Dip (see p.150), and while on the face of it both brands might appear to be novelty acts, they both reflect high-quality whisky-making by W&M's master blender Richard Paterson. Find a stockist for either or both and you will also find a loyal fan base. This is smooth, tasty, gentle and well constructed.

Royal Salute 21-year-old 40% ABV

Royal Salute is owned by Pernod Ricard and is all about top-quality premium whisky. Lavishly packaged in royal blue and gold, this blend includes some of the company's finest Speyside malts, but don't assume it will be a softly, softly, honey-and-fruit medley. Whether consciously done or not, this occupies a different place to older bottlings of sister blend Chivas Regal, and there is some real bite, and creamy chocolaty tones that give it an identity all of its own.

Royal Salute Hundred Cask Selection 40% ABV

Another big, big blend that would hold its own in any malt company, not least because it knocks the spots off most malts simply because of its complexity. The chocolate theme remains here, but there are all sorts of twists and turns, from fresh and zesty malt notes and from splashes of spice, oak and smoke. This is a roller coaster ride of a blend and delightful on every level.

Scottish Leader 12-year-old 40% ABV

This is owned by Burn Stewart and, like Lauder's, it does not claim to be anything it is not. Indeed it is whisky's answer to AC/DC former singer Brian Johnson – a salt-of-the-earth, no frills, honest-to-goodness blend that delivers exactly what you would expect.

Something Special
40% ABV

Another Pernod Ricard blend, aimed at the premium blended market, especially in South America – and it's impressively packaged. It also has Longmorn as its core malt, and as expected there is rich fruit, though soft fudge and vanilla ice cream are not far from the surface. With spice adding to the mix.

Stewarts Cream of the Barley
40% ABV

Among a certain generation of Scotch drinkers, in Scotland, this remains king. It once enjoyed wide distribution as a 'rack whisky' and is surprisingly malty. It is young but captivates with a touch of chilli and smoke. A little niche all of its own.

Teacher's Highland Cream 40% ABV

An old bruiser, this is a heavyweight blend from another era and one that divides opinion. The high malt content and gritty, grainy heart are welcomed by lovers of robust whiskies, but many naturally drawn to blends find it too rough and aggressive. I would argue it is one of the few blends that can be enjoyed neat, not for the subtleties or nuances of an aged Johnnie Walker or Dewar's Signature, but because of its malty, craggy honesty. Like sitting on a rugged coastline when the wind is up – not for everyone, perhaps, but for some eminently more preferable to sunbathing on a sunny day.

Teacher's Origin 42.8% ABV

Teacher's was a silent giant for a long time, and even when Allied broke up and it ended up as part of the Beam empire, little was heard of it. But that started to change in 2010 with the launch of two new Teacher's products and a general increase in its media profile. The move is long overdue and I for one am delighted. Of the two new releases this is the one that is cause for the greatest excitement. Teacher's Origin is genuinely different and a blast of fresh air for blended whisky. It is based on four principles – a high malt content of about 65%, as opposed to many blends that are 40% or less; a bold and characterful core malt, in this case the savoury, peaty and challenging Ardmore; quality barrels including the same quarter casks that produced stunning Laphroaig and Ardmore; and a range of aged whiskies, in this case from 5–13 years. It is not an easy ride – the Ardmore means there are oily, peaty, fishy and savoury notes to contend with – but give it a chance to grow on you and chances are you will be locked in for good. Tasting is like fishing – for every big catch you have to land a few minnows. This is like finding a monstrous brown trout after a day catching sprats.

Té Bheag Connoisseurs' Blend
40% ABV

And talking of unusual fish, this is a west-coast sea bass, fat and fleshy, dripping in brine, reeking of sea, oily and slinky and utterly irresistible. There is some peat, spice and soft fudge. Oh, and if you are wondering, you pronounce it 'Chay Veg'.

VAT 69 40% ABV

My dad's favourite joke in the 1970s was 'what's the Pope's phone number?' and this is what he used to drink once Johnnie Walker Red Label ceased to be an option. Is it still going? A million cases say yes, though only in a few selected markets. A medium-bodied and drinkable blend with a nice one-two between sweet grain and chewy malt.

White Horse 40% ABV

My late father's second-favourite joke involved this whisky and ended with the punchline: 'What? Derek?' No one has done more work with matching whisky with food than Diageo. And a few years ago the company used to stage large dinners with a different malt for each course. One meal, based around curry, was held at Terence Conran's Bluebird Café in London, and is memorable for me because it was the night when Diageo's Nicholas Morgan introduced me to what is now my favourite pairing: Lagavulin and Roquefort. The evening was also memorable because at the dinner was Charles MacLean, whisky writer, after-dinner speaker and genial *mein host* beyond compare. This evening, though, he had a bee in his bonnet. He had issues over the way I was editing *Whisky Magazine* as a consumer magazine rather than trade one. That is because that's what it is, I told him.

'Oh no it's not,' he replied, and thus began a five-hour debate that started at the restaurant, continued in the taxi and ended in the hotel bar over several drinks. Gradually everyone went to bed until it was just us, but still Charlie wanted to continue. Then suddenly he sat bolt upright and said 'there's a mouse!'

I turned round but there was nothing there. Five minutes later it happened again. Same thing. And again. And by this time I was having serious doubts about Charlie's state of mind. But on the fourth time I turned round and there was a mouse, staring intently at us and eating a crisp.

'Look Charlie,' I said. 'Even the hotel mouse has got fed up waiting for us to leave so let's go to bed and tomorrow send me an email and I'll address your points.'

'Tomorrow?' says Charlie. 'Good golly, man! I won't remember any of this in the morning!'

No email arrived and the matter was never referred to again. White Horse is another Diageo blend and it's a big and busty whisky, with plenty of fruit, honey, smoke and spice.

Whyte & Mackay 30-year-old

40% ABV

A big, rich, venerable blend packed with oaky, spicy flavours, good old-fashioned Highland malt and a substantial sherry hit. In many ways a traditional style, but an impressive blend in an impressive bottle.

Whyte & Mackay 40-year-old 45% ABV

World-class whisky making by any standards and a perfect balance of all the great ingredients whisky has to offer, not least the rich Christmas cake notes from sherry cask, full fruit from big Highland and Speyside whiskies and the most exquisite oaky notes. Another classic example of how blends can, in their truest form, knock virtually all other whiskies into touch.

Whyte & Mackay Special 40% ABV

Charlie MacLean is a lot of things, but if you asked most people who know him to make a list, 'AC/DC fan' would not be on any of them. So I was a bit surprised when Whyte & Mackay's international public relations manager Rob Bruce told me he had got tickets to see the band and that Charlie would be coming along. Charlie looks like a World War I bi-plane pilot, complete with moustache, is a gentleman in the best sense of the word and is in his element in fine-dining rooms surrounded by articulate, wealthy bon viveurs. But, Charlie is also a chameleon, and from the off it was clear he was going to have the time of his life. The image of AC/DC's Angus Young writhing on his back on a platform underneath an 18m (60-feet) high busty Rosie while Charlie guffawed heartily at the madness of it all, will be with me forever – and comes back to me every time I hear the words 'Whyte & Mackay'.

This is an easy-to-like blend, unchallenging and very palatable, with lots of over-ripe fruit and a rich, sweet and pleasantly lengthy conclusion.

Whyte & Mackay The Thirteen

40% ABV

Here, orange and citrus fruits suggest The Dalmore, while red berries suggest some sherry influence and there are yellow fruits and spice, with a rounded, full-grain backbone.

RONNIE COX
Berry Bros & Rudd

As oddities go, the plaque on the wall of Berry Bros & Rudd takes some beating. It commemorates the three year period in the 1840s when the building was home to the Texas Legation – a sort of Embassy for the State as it sought its independence.

Berry Bros & Rudd is in St James Street, Mayfair, across the road from St James Palace – it is a quintessentially English bit of London, round the corner from The Ritz and surrounded by high-class restaurants and cigar retailers. Berry Bros is soaked in history. It still has the scales that were used to weigh the leading lights of society and there are wine collections in the cellars stretching back decades and generations. If you are really fortunate you can dine in Napoleon's Cellar, where there is an escape tunnel that was built as a quick getaway for Emperor Napoleon III, who took refuge there while in exile in the 1840s. He lived in fear of assassins and used it as a base to plot his return to France. And there, in the alleyway, is the plaque that confirms that Berry Bros & Rudd rented a building to the Texan Government all those years ago.

The site is also where you'll find Ronnie Cox. And if you're really lucky you might get to attend one of his wonderful dinners. If I were to pick a table for the perfect dinner party, Ronnie would be among the guests – probably sat between firebrand activist and newspaper columnist Owen Jones and the wonderful American crime writer James Lee Burke. Cox is a genial host, an excellent raconteur – and as batty as a fruitcake.

Give him half a chance and he will tell you great stories about how blended whisky Cutty Sark was designed as a peat-free alternative whisky for Berry Bros' wine customers who wanted to taste fine Scotch but did not want to taint their palates. He will tell of how Sam Bronfman, larger-than-life American head of Seagrams, rudely burst in on a company lunch to demand to buy the business and was politely and firmly rebuked, and how the management approached Highland Distillers to ask if they could develop one of its whiskies that hadn't been bottled as a single malt before, thus starting the fruitful Glenrothes-Berry Bros partnership.

Then there's the story of how Mr Berry travelled on the same ship as Prohibition-advocate Pussyfoot Johnson, how they had an altercation and how Johnson wrote a letter of rebuke on ship's paper urging Mr Berry to train his son for the cloth rather than the wine trade, which he assured him, was 'a vanishing business'.

Cox is one of the whisky industry's true gentlemen and although you would not necessarily sense it from his educated accent and attire – he is more of a tartan trews sort of guy, rather than a kilt-wearing one – he has Scotland and whisky running through his veins, distilled and matured over generations.

It is fitting that he is the face of The Glenrothes because he has an association with the town of Rothes stretching back to when he was a little boy. Indeed, the house that the distillery owns brings back memories from his childhood.

'It was the old manse and I had been there as a boy,' he says. 'When I was six I got a small rocket on a spring as a gift from a cornflake packet; with it I managed to hit the Presbyterian minister on the head right in the middle of a sermon – a frightening moment.'

That The Glenrothes will be tied to Berry Bros and Ronnie Cox for many years to come is great news. With such a marriage of outstanding talent, the malt can't fail to go from strength to strength. But the company is looking forward, too. It has teamed up with Texan craft distillery, Ironroot Republic, to bottle a Berry Bros Texan Legation whiskey. Mayfair has never seen anything like it.

WELL, FANCY THAT...
Ronnie Cox has a long association with the whisky industry, stretching back seven generations. He has worked in hot spots such as Panama and Colombia. He has twice had a gun held to his head and he tells great stories of corrupt officials and dodgy distributors.

William Grant 12-year-old 40% ABV

William Grant owns Glenfiddich and The Balvenie. So, even in its relatively young guises its blends fly. This is a tango between malt and grain, with the malts showing citrus and green-fruit zestiness and a creamier fuller fruit, and sweet and clear grain. Sweet, rounded, full and fruity.

William Grant 15-year-old 43% ABV

Basically the 12-year-old with the volume turned up. The extra age adds texture and a fuller oak influence, but basically everything else is perfectly balanced and in its proper place.

William Grant 25-year-old

43% ABV

Outstanding. A distinct sherry nose, a healthy level of spice and plenty of oak, but wrapped up in the sweetest, softest grain imaginable, so the result is a gossamer-like blend that coats the mouth with honeyed fruit, then leaves behind a woody and wonderful aftertaste. It is like a musical concerto in three movements.

William Grant Ale Cask 40% ABV

If you have ever tasted Innis & Gunn beer, then this is where it originated from. William Grant made beer to season the casks for this blend and then threw the beer away. That was until someone in management spotted staff siphoning off the beer and drinking it. It was tasted, found to be excellent and the rest, as they say, is history. By such happy accidents are some great inventions born. This is great. The beer takes away a level of sweetness and adds a malty, earthy and slightly savoury level to the blend, leaving all its core characteristics intact. It is the whisky equivalent of a Rugby Union team playing a Rugby League team at league. Odd but fun...

Blended malt

For many the world of whisky is intimidating. The large number of distilleries, many expressions emanating from them, age statements, special finishes, complex label wording... is the drinking equivalent of map-reading in Tokyo. So, when a group of friends came up with the idea of presenting whisky in modern and simple packaging, and focusing purely on taste, it offered Scotch whisky a route into the future that would bring on board a new generation of whisky drinkers.

The vehicle the friends chose to hitch their idea to was the vatted malts category, where whiskies contain a mixture of malts from different distilleries. Marketed under names such as the Smoky Peaty One, the Rich, Spicy One or the Smooth Fruity One, these new-look whiskies were introduced to a fresh audience. Although there was nothing new about the category, the new whiskies looked like they had the potential to revolutionize our approach to whisky drinking.

Then the SWA got involved, imposed a new term for a mixture of malt whiskies from different distilleries on the trade, and in the process caused so much confusion that the progress of the category ground to a complete halt. The term – now enshrined in law – for these mixed malt whiskies is blended malt whiskies. This is different from blended whiskies, as blended malt whiskies use only malted whisky, whereas blended whiskies have a large quantity of grain other than malted barley. The new terminology is misleading because most of the population know little or nothing about whisky beyond the fact they think single-malt whisky is better than blended. Leaving aside that this is in itself wrong, if they do opt to buy a 'special' whisky they tend to bracket the blended malt whisky category with blends.

This is a big shame, as some of the most exciting experimentation is going on in this category. Compass Box, Douglas Laing and Wemyss, in particular, have taken malt whiskies into exciting new areas eg. Compass' Canto Cask Series. It is a category of whisky worth watching – often offering great value and some seriously fine whisky.

Angel's Nectar 40% ABV

For years the blended malt category has looked awkward and ungainly when compared to other whisky styles. In the United States, many commentators have stopped making a distinction between bonds and blended malts. But, this may be changing. New blended malt Copper Dog (see p.147) has invigorated the category, and William Grant seems to have breathed fresh life into its Monkey Shoulder brands. This whisky won't harm the category either. Angel's Nectar is a blended malt produced by an independent company headed by former Glenmorangie man Robert Ransom, and – inspired by the spirit that evaporates during maturation – is an imaginative attempt to create what the Angel's Share might taste like. It brings together clean, sweet and fresh Speyside fruit-bowl malts, with heather, spice and Highland earthiness. A good session whisky.

Barrogill 40% ABV

I'm no royalist, but it is hard to immerse yourself for eight years in whisky and not grow a sneaking respect for the Prince of Wales. He loves whisky. He has visited a good number of Scotland's distilleries and has casks maturing in most of them. And if he seems stuffy and formal when meeting the suits, that is not the case when he is out among the workers. Talk to a warehouseman or distillery worker who has met him and they will tell you of his genuine interest, his knowledge of whisky and his enthusiasm to hear and learn more. He does not like fuss. Distilleries expecting a visit are instructed to make sure that invited guests arrive well before he does and are given a drink. Guests are told to carry on chatting and not to stop what they are doing when he arrives. Barrogill is a mix of malts from the northern Highlands and is endorsed by the prince, who is Duke of Rothesay as well as Prince of Wales, and it is even liveried in the royal colours. It is a robust, full and weighty whisky, with some peat, lots of savoury tones and some tingling spice on the finish.

Big Peat 46% ABV

Do not be put off by the somewhat tacky label – it cost independent producers Douglas Laing a fair few sales over Christmas because the whisky comes without a box and looks a bit amateurish. But the whisky is amazing and it deservedly won the best blended malt category in the 2010 World Whisky Awards. It contains Ardbeg, Caol Ila, Bowmore and the extremely rare Port Ellen. Big, rich, peaty and very good indeed.

The Big Smoke 40% ABV

Released by independent bottler Duncan Taylor and another heavy hitter for Islay lovers, with smoke, peat, seaweed and barbecued fish.

Clan Denny Islay 46% ABV

This was a big hit when it was first launched, and it has been rediscovered by Douglas Laing, though this goes further than the original bottling. It is a fantastic, big, rich, sweet and peated mix containing malt from seven Islay distilleries (the original had just four). These include Ardbeg, Bowmore, Bruichladdich, Bunnahabhain and Caol Ila. If you have ever asked yourself why you would bother buying a blended malt of your favourite distilleries when you could just as well buy a single malt bottle of each, this is your answer.

I'm drawn back to Islay time and time again, and often sit with a dram and debate in my head about which is my favourite distillery. This is in many ways greater than the sum of its parts, like watching four jazz musicians playing together and bringing out something new and fresh in each other. Sure, if you are in the mood for Coltrane or Davis nothing else will do. Sometimes a medley is enough, though. This is a malt medley and then some.

Clan Denny Speyside 46% ABV

Like the Clan Denny Islay, but this time substitute peat for fruit. Again, big, clean, rich and tasty, this is every bit the match of the Islay bottling, though more mainstream. Less Coltrane and Davis and more Clapton, Beck, Page and maybe Jack White of the White Stripes (there is some younger stuff in here, I am sure of it).

Compass Box Flaming Heart 15th Anniversary Edition

48.9% ABV

There have been several versions of Flaming Heart since it was first released in 2006. This one came out in 2015 and Compass Box put out the exact amounts of each whisky in the mix – more than a quarter of it is a 30-year-old Caol Ila. The SWA didn't like that, so Compass Box launched a campaign to allow transparency in whisky. Quite close to being my perfect whisky, this is stunning stuff, using the finest mainland and island whiskies. What we have here is blackcurrant, melon and tropical fruits all wrapped up in a ball of smoke and peat and kissed away with liquorice, hickory, chilli and cinnamon, and an oiliness that coats the mouth – absolutely the 'business'. Compass Box makes this in limited batches and it sells quickly each time. Hopefully, though, the company will come back to it again and again.

Compass Box Oak Cross 43% ABV

This is another personal favourite, but for altogether different reasons. Here the heads of the bourbon cask have been replaced with new French oak (the cross reference in the title). The effect is a dusty, dry, fruity and highly spiced whisky. Late on there is some Battenberg cake and milk chocolate. Tastes like it should be expensive. It is not. Oh, and as with all Compass Box products, it is beautifully packaged, too.

Compass Box Optimism 44% ABV

A limited-edition whisky, so it is hard to know whether you can still find it, but this was released as an antidote to all the depression that a recession brings and could be described as 'happy juice'. It is all bright, zingy, refreshing and sherbety malts and has a rich and sweet taste, with some delicious peaty notes.

Compass Box The Peat Monster

46% ABV

Does what it says on the tin – lots of big and bold smoke and peat flavours, and among the char and oil there is some very pleasant fruit and spice, too.

Compass Box The Spice Tree 46% ABV

Every time I write something nice about the SWA I get a wave of negative replies from whisky enthusiasts who despise the organization. Does it have any idea what a large number of whisky enthusiasts think of it? We try to be nice about it, we really do, but the feeling is that it always goes after the little guy, wielding a sledgehammer to crush a nut. This is a case in point. The original version of this was matured in casks where some fresh oak staves were put inside the existing cask. You cannot do that, said the SWA, because you are adding oak. It would have been okay to replace existing staves with new oak, and Compass Box legally replaced the heads of casks with new oak for Oak Cross. But the company could not put extra staves in. Now John Glaser and his team have come up with a new and legal way to bring Spice Tree back.

This is another extraordinary whisky not least because we really do get a spice rack of flavours – from clove, ginger, nutmeg and cinnamon at one end of the spectrum, and chilli, paprika and black pepper at the other.

Copper Dog 40% ABV

A mix of eight Speyside malts put together by Diageo for The Craigellachie Hotel, this is designed as a maverick entry-level Scotch whisky. It is an easy-drinking fruit bowl of a whisky, with honey, orange, ginger and gentle spice. Great as a simple mixer – say with fresh apple juice, but it won't frighten the horse if it's consumed neat over ice.

The Famous Grouse
10-year-old 40% ABV

If you are an English Rugby Union fan, turn away now. Ever since I first went to Eden Park in Auckland in 1988, shared beers with Welsh and Kiwi fans in the gardens of total strangers close to the ground, and watched the best sporting team on the planet, then and since, annihilate Wales, scoring more than 50 points for the second week in a row, I have loved the All Blacks. My love of their way of playing the game has led to countless great shared rugby moments with fans across the world and to the consumption of far too many whiskies with knowledgeable and intelligent fans of the game. But there is one exception: the English.

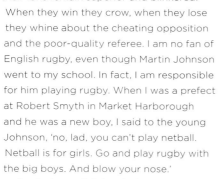

Maybe they are not the arrogant public school fans of old, but English rugby is dull and their fans remain superior and blinkered. When they win they crow, when they lose they whine about the cheating opposition and the poor-quality referee. I am no fan of English rugby, even though Martin Johnson went to my school. In fact, I am responsible for him playing rugby. When I was a prefect at Robert Smyth in Market Harborough and he was a new boy, I said to the young Johnson, 'no, lad, you can't play netball. Netball is for girls. Go and play rugby with the big boys. And blow your nose.'

This might be a lie. So, I was delighted when The Famous Grouse invited me up to a Calcutta Cup game in 2006, showed me round The Famous Grouse Experience and introduced me to this blended malt. Then off we went to the game – or rather off to the bar first, before the game. It did not kick off until early evening by which time the Scottish fans had consumed pretty much the entire beer and whisky allocation for Great Britain for that year. And frankly, the English did not have a chance. The Scots built up to the game by filling the pitch with bands and pipers, sent on a whole army of fire-waving Bravehearts, and banished the English team to a small corner of the pitch.

When they actually got around to the rugby the Scots won – a famous victory; remember, this was when the English team was actually very good. I recall sitting in the corridor of my hotel (so as not to disturb the family, who were in bed by the time I managed to find my way back from the celebrations) and toasted the day with a glass of this and a big juicy rare steak. Great memories.

This has blackcurrant and soft fruits in the mix and is nowhere near as good as it tasted that night. But that's whisky for you.

Johnnie Walker Green Label 15-year-old
43% ABV

Now you see it. Now you don't. Now you do again. Diageo relaunched this as its big hitter in the blended malt category shortly after the SWA introduced the new terminology. I seem to remember we were taken to a big

stately home or castle and played lawn croquet in the pouring rain; and I'm still not really sure why. Then Diageo discontinued it. And then they brought it back in more than one form, this being one of them. Whenever I taste this – and I really love it – I'm reminded of steep, muddy forest paths by gurgling brooks in the shadow of mountains on a wet spring day. As you'd expect from Johnnie Walker, this is a masterclass in whisky making, and just about as good as blended malts can get – give or take the odd Compass Box offering. On the palate, you'll find dark chocolate, cereal, coffee and wispy smoke. Truly outstanding.

Johnnie Walker Island Green
43% ABV

Not so much a walk in the forest now, and more of a paddle in the sea. Baked peaches and cream, prunes and berries all peering through a healthy layer of smoke. This is made using malts from Clynelish, Glenkinchie and Cardhu, but it gets its personality from an increased share of Islay malt Caol Ila. Beautifully put together.

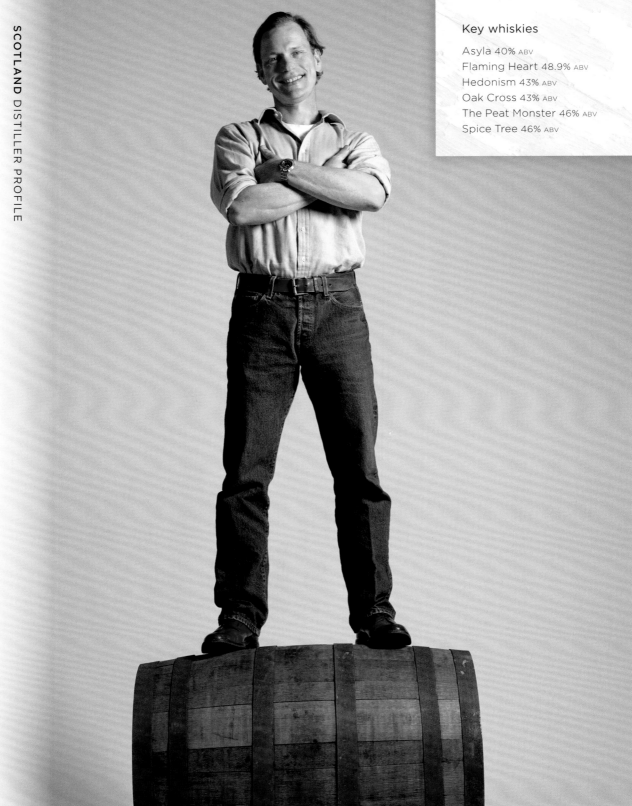

Key whiskies

Asyla 40% ABV
Flaming Heart 48.9% ABV
Hedonism 43% ABV
Oak Cross 43% ABV
The Peat Monster 46% ABV
Spice Tree 46% ABV

JOHN GLASER

Compass Box Delicious Whisky Ltd

On the face of it, it doesn't look much – an incongruous blue building with art-deco pretensions in a faceless industrial estate off the Chiswick High Road in west London, England.

But, go through the doors and you are in a whisky Aladdin's cave. This is the home of Compass Box, Britain's only true boutique whisky maker, and before company founder John Glaser has even defined the terms for our meeting, he's off, bubbling with enthusiasm and reaching for the sample glasses. First up, a Laphroaig from 1998, with vanilla and peat to die for, followed by a quite stunning vatting of Glen Elgins he has got his hands on over the years, its nose – liqueur-like tropical fruits – is like nothing else I have come across. Surely he must be tempted to bottle both these outstanding samples as they are?

'That would be so me-too,' he says. 'What would be the point of that? We attempt to do something a bit different rather than just do independent bottlings. Better to keep hold of these whiskies just for our friends.'

Compass Box was formed at the start of the millennium by Glaser, then in his mid-30s, to create new and exciting whiskies and present them in stylish, upmarket packaging. Compass Box remains small but it has been punching above its weight for years now, giving whisky enthusiasts such stunning whiskies as Flaming Heart, Oak Cross, Peat Monster, Spice Tree, Asyla and Hedonism.

Armed with a supply of fine-quality malt from some of Scotland's best distilleries he has pushed the whisky envelope outwards, experimented into new taste channels and tested the very boundaries of Scotch whisky. Not without controversy: occasionally he has fallen foul of the SWA, but inadvertently he has become a champion for the small producer and of the craftsman.

'Perhaps it's my background and I should get on with just making whisky,' he says with a shrug, 'but it's important that a line is drawn between artisan producers and brands and the big brands and mass producers speaking the parlance of artisan producers while making industrial products.'

Glaser's belief that as whisky drinkers learned more about whisky there would be more of a demand for small-scale whiskies from across the world has well and truly been borne out. There has been an influx of small companies who are chipping away at the dominance of the enormous international drinks companies.

'If you think of the hegemony of French wines over the rest of the world thirty years ago versus the world of wine today, you get the picture,' he says. 'We've seen more people who love whisky crossing from avid consumer to whisky producer. We've seen continued growth in small, entrepreneurial whisky-making companies. The consumer perception of what whisky can be, stylistically, is evolving, as new producers push at the envelope of the craft.'

The message is clear: Compass Box is doing fine but if you fancy joining it, come on in. In the meantime Glaser is living his dream, crafting fine whisky. We lunch at a local pub but before we leave he asks the barman to pour us a draft gin, that was being produced on a tiny still down the road, in the buildings where Michael Jackson used to run his beer and whisky business. Micro-distilling: you can see the temptation in his eyes.

'We have looked at distilling ourselves,' he says 'but we decided against it because we're so small. But it remains a dream and I'm not against distilling in London or somewhere else in England. We have started filling our own casks with new-make spirit so we have greater control over the process, so who knows?' Then a cheeky gleam enters his eye.

'If we took a cask of Clynelish and matured it in London, what could we call it? It wouldn't be Scotch if it was matured in England, but could we call it whisky? Or English whisky? Or Scottish malt spirit matured and bottled in England?' He laughs but I swear I hear something else, too. Not a bunch of SWA lawyers spluttering into their Scotch on the rocks perhaps?

Monkey Shoulder 40% ABV

The blended malt sector has the potential to bring a whole new generation of drinkers to whisky, and this brand provides the proof. Because a mixture of malts can come baggage-free and it does not need to have intimidating labels that many people don't understand, it is possible to present whisky in a totally different way. When the whisky in the bottle tastes like this, then the job is twice as easy.

The name sounds slightly off-beat and zany but it is actually as traditional a reference as you could possibly get, referring to an old distillery affliction – effectively repetitive strain injury in the shoulders caused by manually turning the malt, causing sufferers to hunch. The whisky in the bottle is a mix of un-aged Balvenie, Glenfiddich and Kininvie, and producer William Grant has deliberately focused on the soft, sweet pear-and-apple flavours in its malts, making for a light, refreshing and easy-drinking whisky that tastes great when chilled. It is great neat, but, of course, youths being youths, they will insist on mixing it, so the company has created an impressive and inventive list of Monkey cocktails.

So successful has the Monkey Shoulder campaign been that in some areas bars apply to become Monkey bars – preferred stockists for this malt. So, in effect, bars are asking to be allowed to sell Monkey Shoulder and to pay William Grant to do so. That is very clever and, if it is not the future, I don't know what is.

Rock Oyster 46.8% ABV

Rock Oyster is Douglas Laing's blended malt based on whiskies from the Islands, specifically Jura, Islay, Arran and Orkney. Laing's intention was to capture the essence of the Scottish coast, with its distinctive saline and seaweed flavours and breezy freshness, and he has succeeded. This is drinking by the seaside, with seaweed, salt and pepper and some fruity notes. Very enjoyable.

Scallywag 46% ABV

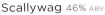

Scallywag is Big Peat's pet dog, but he's chalk to his owner's cheese. Where Big Peat is all about Islay, this is a Speyside blended malt, with a high proportion of sherry casks and a number of American oak ones, too. The sherry influence is heavier on the nose, and on the palate the fruit is joined by some spice.

Sheep Dip 40% ABV

Another wacky name, and another one that has a stronger link to whisky's heritage than at first it might appear. It has been the patriotic duty of Scottish whisky makers over the last 1000 years to avoid paying tax to the English, and they have demonstrated considerable skill at doing so. One way was to mark casks of whisky as sheep dip, for ridding sheep of vermin and infestations before shearing. If there was duty due on sheep dip it was far less than it was on whisky. Simple really. And again this is young and fresh, with a range of Speyside and Highland malts brought together without blemish and with the meekest touch of spice. Now marketed independently.

The Six Isles 43% ABV

As the name implies, this blend takes malt from six of the whisky-making islands of Scotland, which (when it was launched) was all of them, though now there is a new distillery on Lewis. You associate the islands with peaty whisky but this is not always the case – Tobermory on Mull, Arran on Arran and Scapa on Orkney all make predominantly peat-free whisky, and Islay has its share of unpeated malt, too. That said, though, this focuses on the peatier end of the spectrum. The nose doesn't give too much away, but, boy, does this kick on the palate. There are some citrus notes, a rich, oily undercurrent and pepper spices late on.

Timorous Beastie 46.8% ABV

The fourth of Douglas Laing's regional blended malts, and it's anything but a timorous beastie. This is made up of Highland whiskies, including The Dalmore, Glengoyne and Glen Garioch. This is a rough-and-ready, earthy treat, with candied apple and orange fruits. Some heather in the mix, too.

Wemyss Malts
The Hive 12-year-old 40% ABV

The clue's in the name. The Wemyss range of blended malts named with a descriptor has grown up since the last edition of this book, and now they're 12 years old. The Hive replaced The Smooth Gentleman, and this version is a delight, something of a Speyside greatest-hits package. Honey, yes, but a fruit bowl, cinnamon and nutmeg.

Wemyss Malts Peat Chimney
12-year-old 40% ABV

This whisky lives up to the billing, but offers more than just Islay peat. There are traces of woodsmoke in the mix, some barbecued meat and citrus notes, toasted oak and black pepper. There is also a very attractive sweet note, too, but with fruit in the mix, too. Mango chutney perhaps?

Wemyss Malts The Spice King
12-year-old 40% ABV

I always felt that previous versions of The Spice King were to spicy whisky what korma is to Indian curry. This is much more of a Madras offering, with strong peppery notes from the off.

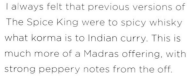

Grain whisky

There is a view that single-grain whisky is lining up for its place in the sun. If you find an old-grain whisky that has been matured in a good-quality cask, it can be quite sublime, bringing the finest elements of Scottish grain with the rich vanilla and candy notes of an American oak cask, a Scotch-bourbon hybrid to die for.

Aged grains of 30 years are less expensive than their single-malt whisky counterparts. Look out for independent bottlers such as Duncan Taylor and Gordon & MacPhail.

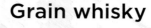

Compass Box Hedonism 43% ABV

Most grain whisky goes into blends and what little ends up being bottled on its own is mainly produced by independent bottlers, and much of it is very old. This is a vatting of grains, from the grain distilleries Cameron Bridge, Carsebridge and Cambus. There is nothing younger than 14 years old and some of the grain is more than 25 years old. By this time the grain has taken on some of the flavours of the bourbon casks they have been matured in. This is a delightfully sweet, vanilla and coconut dessert whisky with some gentle oil and oak. A pleasant change.

The Famous Grouse
The Snow Grouse 40% ABV

Unsurprisingly from The Famous Grouse family, though you would be hard pressed to make any real connection. This is another one of Edrington's experimental releases, and is a whisky designed to be kept in the fridge and served chilled. It's a refreshing enough drink, has a sweet, two-dimensional taste, and has very little to do with whisky as we know it. Make of that what you will.

USA
&
CAN
ADA

f all the great whisky regions of the world, the United States is potentially the most exciting.

Not only is United States whiskey in rude-good health at the moment, but it is undergoing a whiskey revolution, too. All sorts of weird and wonderful whiskeys are being released across the country currently; many of them challenging our perceptions of American whiskey, and offering a range of 'whiskeys' that are new, exciting and even controversial. The United States has form in this area. A few years back, a new wave of micro-breweries did for its beer industry what punk-rock music did for bloated corporate rock – shook it by the throat, scornfully cast it aside and replaced it with something altogether more vibrant and exciting. Now the same is happening to whiskey, albeit on a smaller scale. In the United States, whiskey has tended to mean bourbon and a few add-ons, and bourbon has tended to mean Kentucky. These days, though, new micro-distilleries have been established across the country, unfettered by tradition and convention and not afraid to take whiskey in whatever direction they see fit. The best of them are picking up awards domestically and several are winning over whiskey fans across the world.

So, a classic case, then, of out with the old, in with the new? Actually, no. They're built of sterner stuff than that down in Kentucky. You know the song that goes 'I get knocked down, but I get up again...'? That's Kentucky. It is a state littered with the crumbling remains of fallen distilleries, its history books packed with great whiskey-making names that have been battered and broken, but which have a habit of popping up again within the portfolios of the surviving distillers. Economic tornados and social hurricanes have battered Kentucky's whiskey industry, but this is a state built on limestone rock, and it will take much more than a few hundred upstarts in Portland, San Francisco, Colorado or New York to rock it off its axis.

Indeed, Kentucky has risen to the challenge. Across the state there are casks made of maplewood, ash and hickory filled with maturing spirit; there are barrels containing single malt, pure wheat and rye whiskey and spirit made with oats and even white (sweet) corn. And then there's the more traditional bourbon: rich, flavoursome, magnificent – and in as good a shape as it has ever been. And, it's getting its own wave of new craft distillers – it's hard to match this wonderful state for its cohesive sense of purpose, its intensity, quality of whiskey and empathy with, and understanding of, grain spirit. Just as single-malt

PREVIOUS Buffalo Trace: one of America's most historic distilleries.

ABOVE Copper Fox barrels: new distilleries are giving the old boys a run for their money.

ABOVE One of the iconic stills at Jack Daniel's.

whisky will be dominated by Scotland for generations to come, so, too, will Kentucky dominate American whiskey – and play a key role as it moves forwards to a new level on the world stage.

When you think of Kentucky, you tend to picture green fields, glistening chestnut geldings, fields of corn and picket fences – and in part, this is true. The distilleries of Woodford Reserve, Maker's Mark, Four Roses and Wild Turkey are situated in deepest rural Kentucky, and Tom Moore, Kentucky Bourbon Distillers and Heaven Hill are a stone's throw from the historic town of Bardstown. But, there is another Kentucky, too. Louisville lies to the very north of the state, the historic and symbolic Ohio River that separates north and south flowing on its border. It is a growling, vibrant city, a mix of old, down-and-dirty industry and modern skyscraper-based business, faceless retail malls and independent student-dominated suburbs. Whiskey first reached out to the world from here. Brown Forman and Heaven Hill have their headquarters downtown here.

When the first edition of this book came out, Louisville was a hipster city, but it was one that pretty much ignored its whiskey roots. That has now completely changed. The fledgling Urban Bourbon Trail with a handful of members, now has 40 bars and restaurants and is turning applicants away. No self-respecting bar in the city doesn't offer bourbon flights, and the streets are lined with advertising posters promoting whiskey events. Whiskey Row, its buildings preserved from another era, has sprung back to life, with the likes of Evan Williams and Michter's opening visitor attractions, and a new wave of distillers bringing whiskey production back in to the heart of the city. In 2007 the tourist authorities in the city largely ignored bourbon. Today, it sits alongside horse racing as the state's number one priority. When The Oscar Getz Museum opened in late 2018 (a bourbon museum and tourist centre for the Urban Bourbon Trail, with exhibition space designed by the team that built Dublin's Guinness Experience), bourbon's rebirth was complete.

It could be argued that Louisville isn't just the whiskey capital of America, it's the whiskey capital of the world. It is in this context you realize that bourbon is looking forward and not back. Its distilleries might still be monuments to hospitality, history, polite manners and gentle country ways, but here in Louisville the businessmen are finding new ways to sell their whiskeys, and marketing an increasingly diverse portfolio.

Bourbon

The United States' native spirit must contain at least 51% corn, although it would usually have considerably more, and it must be matured in new white-oak barrels, which may be toasted and/or charred. Straight bourbon must be matured for at least two years, and the drink is bound by strict rules on distilling strengths and the strength it can go in to the barrel. Nothing can be added at all beyond grain, yeast and water, meaning that the rules for bourbon are stricter than those governing Scotch single-malt whisky.

ABOVE Buffalo Trace's warehouse contain some of the most exciting and experimental whiskeys in the United States.

Ancient Age 10-year-old 40% ABV
www.buffalotrace.com

'Ancient Age' is the old name given to what is now Buffalo Trace. The site, on the banks of the Kentucky River and close to the state capital, is where the traditional world of Native Americans and the new settlers met head-to-head. Buffalo Trace is so named because it lay on the old buffalo trails. The region offered the settlers much, but their arrival and eventual settlement was not without bloody incident. Frankfort is named after Stephen Frank, who was killed by a Native American party while camping with other settlers.

This bourbon is a delicate balancing act of soft corn, spicy rye and chunky fruit, particularly citrus, all held together by some delightful oils.

Baker's Aged 7-year-old 53.5% ABV
www.jimbeam.com

One of four whiskeys in Jim Beam's small-batch collection, named after Baker Beam, Jim Beam's great-nephew and a master distiller in his own right. Made using a 60-year-old yeast strain and matured for seven years, an age at which some would argue the bourbon has taken all it can from the wood in terms of fruit, vanilla and sweetness. The recipe is the same as the standard Jim Beam, but it comes off the still at 125 proof. This strength gives a big, upfront flavour with anisette, liquorice and a crisp, fruity heart while the maturation gives it a chunky fullness.

Balcones Blue Corn Bourbon 64.5% ABV
www.balconesdistilling.com

The earliest bottlings of this were fresh, raw, different... and under-cooked. But, a few years on, this young bourbon, made with Texan blue corn, has settled down, and all the pluses are still there, but with a rich, thick, consistent sweet corn core. Caramel, baked apples and lots of spice make this something of a treat.

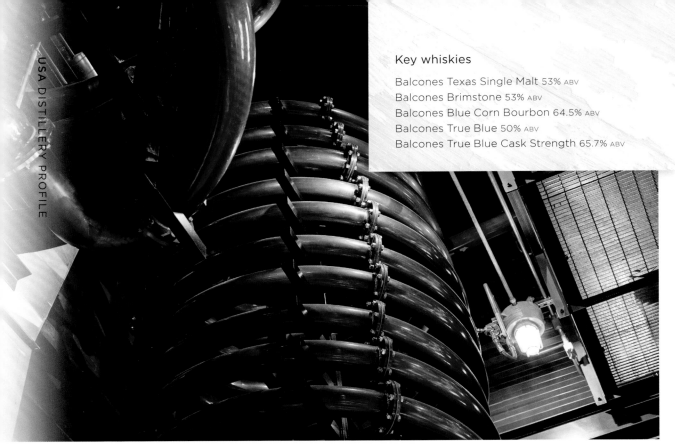

ABOVE Balcones has led the way in American single-malt production, but makes great corn whiskey, too.

BELOW Testing new samples at Balcones.

BALCONES

225 S 11th Street, Waco, Texas 76701
www.balconesdistilling.com

Whiskey from Texas? Really? Yes, sir, and the big, brash cowboy state has a special, but somewhat incongruous, relationship with one of Britain's oldest wine and spirits companies, Berry Bros & Rudd of Mayfair, London.

When Texas declared itself a republic in the 1840s it set up three legations.

In London, the legation was at 4 St James Street, the diplomatic address of Dr Ashbel Smith, appointed ambassador to London by Sam Houston. The property was owned by Berry Bros & Rudd next door and was rented out by it.

Texas hasn't forgotten how Berry Bros helped it, and when George HW Bush was governor of the state, he visited the retailer and presented one of the Rudd family with a huge Stetson cowboy hat. In return Mr Berry presented the future president with a bill for the outstanding rent of $160. That's not the end of the story either. Some time afterwards 26 Texans dressed in buckskin arrived at the shop and repaid the debt, with Texan dollar bills.

Today, Texas is making some of the best craft whiskey in the whole of the United States, much of it is made with native baby blue corn, or with barley dried over a mesquite twig fire.

Balcones is at the very forefront of the boom in American distilling. It was founded in 2008, some way ahead of the craft-distilling revolution in the United States, and it did its growing up in public, falling into traps and stumbling in to pot holes as it went, not least the acrimonious fall out between distillery founder Chip Tate and his investors, a series of unpleasant law suits and the eventual ousting of Tate from his own distillery.

Chip Tate is now back with a new distillery project, but he learned the hard way that growing your business and meeting the demands of making whisky, keeping the books, organizing sales, focusing on marketing and public relations and representing a brand as an ambassador are not always compatible, and their execution is fraught with danger.

Meanwhile Balcones has just kept growing, and its reputation has been built on the back of its highly successful whiskey brands, which have been picking up awards ever since they were first launched. They fall in to two distinctive categories: corn whiskeys and Texas single-malt whiskey. Balcones makes a bourbon, as well as a flavoursome and unusual blue corn whiskey. But, the most distinctive and notable corn whiskey is called Brimstone, made using an innovative process by which the whiskey rather than the grain is smoked using Texas scrub oak.

Its single malts are often bottled at cask strength, and they have managed to kickstart an American single-malt category, where malt whiskey is matured in a variety of conditions depending on where in America they are – in virgin-charred white-oak casks, as bourbon is. There have been a number of special and one-off bottlings, and the continued success of the distillery means that it has had to move to a new and larger distillery site.

With several other distilleries operating in this state, Texas is steadily carving out a reputation for quality whiskey.

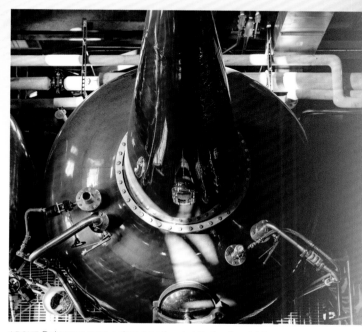

ABOVE Balcones uses column and pot stills for its whiskeys.

Basil Hayden's 8-year-old 40% ABV
www.jimbeam.com

When Basil Hayden travelled to Kentucky from Maryland the state had been in existence for just four years and George Washington was still president. The marketing material reckons this bourbon is made to a recipe perfected back then, which is, of course, fantasy. What is true though, is that the recipe is that of Old Grandad, which was originally distilled in the 1880s by Richard Heydon – note the different spelling – who named it after his grandad, Basil. It is Basil's picture that appeared on the old Old Grandad label.

What you will find in the bottle is a healthy amount of tasty rye, as much as a third of the mashbill. The spirit is taken off the still at 120 proof, much lower than Old Grandad, and is casked with no water. There is a distinctive pepperiness about this, but the lower strength means more fruity flavours, particularly citrus, and the eight years maturation ensures some delicious woody notes.

Benchmark Old No. 8 40% ABV
www.buffalotrace.com

A curiosity, this. The bourbon has appeared as just Benchmark, and as Benchmark Old No. 8. Some but not all bottlings have the word 'McAfee's' before the name.

That's the case here. It is said that the McAfee Brothers travelled to Kentucky as early as 1773, identified a site near Frankfort and then left surveyor's benchmarks for subsequent settlers to find.

This bourbon was part of the Seagram stable before its demise and has ended up at Buffalo Trace near Frankfort, not far from where the McAfees laid down their markers. This version of the bourbon is an easy-drinking and inoffensive tipple, with strong, sweet vanilla and some soft toffee notes.

Blanton's Single Barrel No 209
46.5% ABV
www.buffalotrace.com

Arguably the first single-barrel bottling and therefore the very first drops of what has become a torrent towards premium bourbon. Bottlings of this sort are to official whiskeys what bootleg CDs are to the music industry. Every barrel is different and, certainly in the case of Blanton's, differences between them are significant, which is where the fun lies.

This particular series of bottlings was started by former distiller Elmer T Lee, who worked with Colonel Albert Blanton, and who spent more than 50 years making fine handcrafted bourbon. Elmer continued to choose the finest casks for this bottling in to his 90s. Sadly he passed away in 2013, aged 93. Most bottlings are taken from casks stored high up in warehouse H, but they vary in age and so the bottle carries no-age-statement. This one has a soft nose with exotic fruits upfront. Next follows a big wave of spicy rye, a dark treacle undertow and ends with a honey-and-liquorice combo to die for. Excellent.

Booker's 6-year-old 63.5% ABV
www.beamglobal.com

Number three in Beam's small-batch quartet and arguably the best – but what a great argument to have. Booker Noe died a few years back and is sorely missed. His son Fred still works with Beam and a few years ago he was forced, against his better nature, to speak to a group of festival visitors while the PR people replaced some samples. He spoke about his father, about the special qualities that made him so loved and about his legendary generosity. Finally he told how they went to him one night as he lay sick and offered him a whiskey, but he declined. 'That's when we knew he was leaving us,' said Fred. 'Because he no longer cared for a bourbon.' This is a fitting tribute to him. It is a big, characterful bourbon just like Booker, rich in vanilla, fruit, spice and with a honeycomb-candy heart that is battered, but withstands the influence of the oak. Everything a sledgehammer bourbon should be.

Buffalo Trace 45% ABV
www.buffalotrace.com

Ever had an experience that you will always associate with a particular whiskey? For me it's this bourbon – and Jon Bon Jovi.

It was in Sydney, Australia, during the Keep The Faith Tour. I was working for *The New Zealand Herald* and had seen the first of three Sydney shows the night before the interview. He was a journalist's dream. He spoke of many things, including how he'd trade his rock-star status for a few nights playing guitar for one of his and my heroes Southside Johnny, as a member of the Asbury Jukes, in front of 200 people. That night he referred directly to our conversation on stage and mentioned me by name, and at the after-show party I toasted him with Buffalo Trace. Two weeks later he rang me to say he'd gone on the road with Southside Johnny and the Asbury Jukes. What a star.

This bourbon is, like Bon Jovi, pretty damn good. It rocks when it wants to, but a sweet fruitiness makes it pretty mainstream, too. Easy on the palate, but that doesn't mean that there isn't greatness here.

Bulleit 40% ABV
www.bulleitbourbon.com

A few years ago, Tom Bulleit (great-great-grandson of original Bulleit distiller Augustus Bulleit) held a party for journalists in the suburbs of Bardstown. One small group of journalists arrived to find that Tom wasn't there yet, so they planned to come back two hours later. When they walked into the house where the party was, they found no one there. After some moments, they heard laughter and talking in the neighbouring garden. They had entered the wrong house.

'That could have gone either way,' one of the Bulleit entourage said later. 'In Kentucky if the householders had found you they would have pulled a gun – or offered you dinner.'

Bulleit is made at the Four Roses distillery: the fruitiness suggests so. The recipe is said to be based on Augustus's original one. Populist bourbon with lots of honey and vanilla.

Eagle Rare Single Barrel 10-year-old 45% ABV
www.buffalotrace.com

Eagle Rare is another single-barrel bottling and, while there are big differences between each bottling, you can be pretty confident that what you are going to taste will be outstanding. Originally launched by Seagram and now part of Buffalo Trace, Eagle Rare was arguably the first super-premium bourbon. A new version is released every autumn, but demand tends to outstrip supply; you have to move fast to get hold of it because it is hard to find. When you do, you will encounter a citrus and orange nose with an almost liqueur-like quality. Exotic fruits, floor polish and sweet grain make it an easy-drinking bourbon with just enough oak to lend shape and structure.

Eagle Rare 17-year-old 45% ABV
www.buffalotrace.com

Every Autumn Buffalo Trace releases five rare and special bourbons as part of its Antique Collection. They are small-batch whiskeys and vary from year to year, but whiskey lovers know to expect something special from them. Unsurprisingly, demand for them is exceptional. Eagle Rare 17-year-old is right up there with the very best. Named after the great American symbol, the Bald Eagle, Eagle Rare is meant to share similar values – the pursuit of life, liberty and happiness. When it soars, the 17-year-old is up there with the very best bourbons. But there is considerable variance. You should expect to find trademark woodiness and substantial rye spice, but after that, all bets are off. It's well possible that a particular expression will have a big, silky, spicy body and a long, leathery finish. But other releases have been floral and grassy, offering an altogether more gentle and soft experience. There's no better or worse here – the whiskey is always sublime – but expect to be surprised.

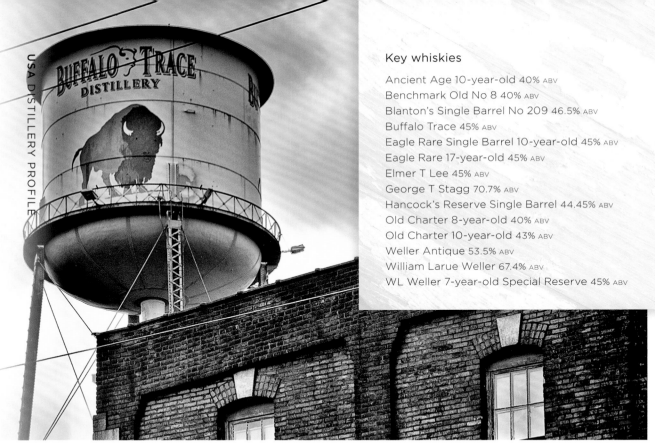

Key whiskies

Ancient Age 10-year-old 40% ABV
Benchmark Old No 8 40% ABV
Blanton's Single Barrel No 209 46.5% ABV
Buffalo Trace 45% ABV
Eagle Rare Single Barrel 10-year-old 45% ABV
Eagle Rare 17-year-old 45% ABV
Elmer T Lee 45% ABV
George T Stagg 70.7% ABV
Hancock's Reserve Single Barrel 44.45% ABV
Old Charter 8-year-old 40% ABV
Old Charter 10-year-old 43% ABV
Weller Antique 53.5% ABV
William Larue Weller 67.4% ABV
WL Weller 7-year-old Special Reserve 45% ABV

ABOVE Buffalo Trace's iconic tower: some of Kentucky's greatest distillers have produced bourbon here.
BELOW The distillery offers a thorough and lengthy Hard Hat Tour.

BUFFALO TRACE

113 Great Buffalo Trace, Frankfort, Kentucky 40601
www.buffalotrace.com

Distilleries are to whisky writers what children are to teachers – you know you should not have favourites but sometimes you just can't help it.

And even by Kentucky's exceptional standards the visitor experience at Buffalo Trace is special. No matter which of the three tour options you take, you are in for a world-class whiskey treat. If you have the time, though, and are in good health, make sure that you take the Hard Hat Tour. It does exactly what it says on the tin, and is a delightful trek up and down ladders and rickety staircases, into the heart of the distillery and through its warehouses.

Buffalo Trace occupies an immense site on the edge of Frankfort, the state's capital, and is another of those places with links to some of the great names of bourbon. Formerly called Ancient Age, the roll of honour at this distillery includes George T Stagg, William Larue Weller, Colonel Albert Blanton and Thomas H Handy. Tennessee whiskey maker George Dickel was based here for a while, the Van Winkle range of old bourbons are maturing on site. They make Buffalo Trace here, of course, but also Sazerac Rye, Eagle Rare and Hancock's.

If you think that once you have seen one distillery you have seen them all, then Buffalo Trace and its amazing guides will make you think again. Strange artwork, stunning views and a quirky micro-still, now used to create all sorts of single-barrel experimental whiskeys – all add to the colour. Extra attractions on the tour include a visit to the barrel room and a meeting room that looks like a classroom in a nineteenth-century schoolhouse.

'You might think that what a distillery fears most is fire, but it's not,' says Freddie Johnson who, like his fellow guides at the distillery, is a gushing font of bourbon knowledge. 'The biggest fear is a bad cooper. You get the barrels wrong or end up with leaks, and it can wipe out your whole profit.'

At the back of the meeting room is a bookcase that turns out to be a secret door leading into warehouse C. It's whiskey's answer to Harry Potter's Room of Requirement and, once through it, you will find all manner of mini-casks and strange creations as the distillery team test new whiskeys for future release.

But, the best part of the tour is the visitor centre, which tells the story of the distillery and includes some stunning photos stretching back 150 years. On one wall there is a list of every distillery ever opened and/or closed in Kentucky, including scores that never reopened after Prohibition. Close by there is a full-size picture of a worker inspecting barrels for leaks with a torch. This is Jimmy Johnson, Freddie's father.

'They brought him in to roll out the six-millionth barrel since Prohibition,' says Freddie. 'And he got to touch the millionth barrel all those years ago, and the second-, third-, fourth- and fifth-millionth after that.'

Freddie's grandfather also worked at the distillery, working alongside Colonel Blanton – and there several other families where generation after generation helped to pour out the spirit and roll out the barrels here. No other distillery quite captures such a sense of history. When you look at the black-and-white pictures on the visitor centre wall, at the workers from 140 years ago, and you read the list of great distilleries, many of which are now reduced to rubble, you feel like you're passing through history on a conveyor belt that was here before you stepped on to it and will continue to roll on by when you step off. It gives the workforce a sense of duty – to take pride in producing fine bourbon.

WELL, FANCY THAT...

Buffalo Trace is so named because the distillery is sited at a point where once great buffalo herds, following a traditional migration route, slowed down to cross the Kentucky River, at a natural ford, making them perfect targets for Native American Indian tribes.

ABOVE The distillery is one of the largest in Kentucky.

Elijah Craig 12-year-old 47% ABV
www.heaven-hill.com

The nose is surprisingly wispy and subtle, with traces of cherry and mint, and some pine and forest flower notes. Given its age, this is nowhere near as bold as it might be, but the oakiness holds in check the sweet vanilla heart; the overall taste is rounded, smooth and more-ish. With its traces of glacé cherry and spearmint, this is very much a band effort, with no soloists.

Elijah Craig 18-year-old 45% ABV
www.heaven-hill.com

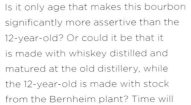

Is it only age that makes this bourbon significantly more assertive than the 12-year-old? Or could it be that it is made with whiskey distilled and matured at the old distillery, while the 12-year-old is made with stock from the Bernheim plant? Time will tell. This puts up a strong argument against those who say bourbon doesn't work older than 10 years. You should be a fan of oak in your whiskey to appreciate it, but it's is no wooden battering ram; plenty of spicy rye, peach, tangerine, liquorice and a squelchy, oily base to carry it off. Stunning.

Elmer T Lee 45% ABV
www.buffalotrace.com

Elmer T Lee is a bourbon legend. After serving in the armed forces after Pearl Harbor he returned to university in Kentucky, before starting work in 1949 at what was the George T Stagg distillery. He worked with two recipes that have remained largely unchanged, plus a rye recipe. We tend to think of Single Barrel and Small Batch bottlings as relatively recent developments, but Elmer T Lee can be credited with starting the trend 25 years ago. This one has lemon, orange and sour-apple notes, then a wave of spice, before a smooth finish marked by a perfumy quality and some soft fudge. Dangerously quaffable.

Evan Williams 43% ABV
www.heaven-hill.com

Heaven Hill's Heritage Center on the outskirts of Bardstown was built a few years ago and is a good introduction to bourbon in general, and the Heaven Hill story in particular. A large barrel-shaped tasting room is the ideal place to sample the distillery's bourbons, and a well-stocked shop ensures that you can take one of the iconic brands away with you. Here you will find the stories of Evan Williams and Elijah Craig. But make sure you maintain a healthy dose of cynicism when you read them. Williams was born in Wales, settled in Virginia and moved into the unchartered territories within the state during the 1780s, some years before they were renamed Kentucky. Whether he was the state's first distiller is questionable, but he was certainly among its pioneers, providing the United States with a rich and evolving distilling heritage that stretches back 220 years.

This standard black-label bottling is a big seller and as good an entry-level bourbon as you'll find. It's bourbon for people who have discovered Jack Daniels or Jim Beam and want to move on – easy-going, sweet and toffee-ish, with some pear and apple flavours – unchallenging and pleasant enough – the bourbon equivalent of mainstream country singer Garth Brooks perhaps?

Evan Williams 12-year-old 50.5% ABV
www.heaven-hill.com

Twelve years old is a weighty age for a bourbon, and the strength of this bottling gives it extra gravitas and power. This is made up of casks specially selected by the late Parker Beam and his son Craig from Heaven Hill's iron-clad warehouses at the Bardstown site and is not widely available. It is a bold and assertive bourbon and drier than many of its competitors. There is a juicy berry fruit aspect to it, as well as just enough tannins to keep everything in check, moderate vanilla notes and a delightful wave of spices courtesy of the rye.

Evan Williams 23-year-old 46.75% ABV
www.heaven-hill.com

The Watson Twins from Louisville record torch-song country and blues songs. The perfect way to enjoy their music is to pour a glass of something like this, dim the lights and let the music and bourbon dazzle your senses. This is therapy of the highest order; after 30 minutes, no problem seems too great. This whiskey is hard to find, but great to savour. You'll encounter kiwi fruit, guava, then hickory and finally sweet chilli and cayenne pepper. As delightful, complex and varied as the twins themselves, this is a heaven-made match.

FEW Bourbon 46.5% ABV
www.fewspirits.com

The name FEW is ironic – from the initials of Frances Elizabeth Willard, a key figure in the Temperance Movement, who ensured that this distillery's home town had Prohibition for a century. This is a craft bourbon and isn't flawless, but the vanilla, toffee and herbal notes are delightful, with a long, lingering, spicy finish.

Four Roses 40% ABV
www.fourroses.us

The sentimental story of how this bourbon got its name involves a marriage proposal from the distillery founder to a southern belle being accepted by the symbolic wearing of four roses on a ballgown. More interesting is the fact that it stands out from more assertive bourbons like a ballerina stands out in a rugby scrum. It's very fruity, with orange in the mix, some fruit peel, cinnamon and creamy vanilla. You have to look for it, but there is enough rye there to provide a solid backbone. Bourbon's equivalent to Annie of 'Get your Gun' fame: quite feminine but pretty feisty, too. Often accompanied by a rendition of 'My Old Kentucky Home' at the annual Four Roses Let's Talk Bourbon Breakfast.

Four Roses Mariage 58% ABV
www.fourroses.us

Based on the French wine concept of blending two wines to create something new and better, this Mariage from 2009 is arguably the fruitiest bourbon ever made. Llike chewing on alcohol-soaked orange jelly babies, with a liqueur-like intensity; a charry, toasty aspect and plenty of oak tones calm the sweetness. Best of all, a gloopy oiliness allows flavours to linger.

Four Roses Single Barrel
50% ABV (VARIES)
www.fourroses.us

For many years you couldn't buy Four Roses in the United States beyond the regions where the workforce lived. Its roll out in recent years has therefore been dramatic. But people still need convincing that this is a very different whiskey to the blend that dominated liquor-store shelves when the Bronfman family and Seagram took over. It was common to see distillery staff handing out samples at liquor stores across the state on Saturday mornings. A bland blend this most certainly isn't. This is Four Roses at its sharpest and cleanest, with all the grains playing an active part, the fruits giving it the chewiest of centres, and just enough oiliness to hold it all together.

Four Roses Small Batch 45% ABV
www.fourroses.us

There's nothing wrong with the standard yellow label, but when you move to the Single Barrel and Small Batch versions you start to realize how very good this bourbon is. Four Roses uses two recipes and five different yeasts to create ten different whiskeys. Of these ten, three are selected for the Small Batch. The citrusy notes from the standard version remain, but this is like mixing alcohol with fruit jellies. Bringing a new generation to the world of bourbon.

Garrison Brothers
Straight Bourbon 47% ABV
www.garrisonbros.com

We expect big bold whiskeys from Texas, and the bottle here suggests more of the same. Not at all. If Balcones is a Saturday-night bar-room brawl of a whiskey, this is Sunday morning church – subdued, with flowers and incense.

George T Stagg
70.7% ABV
www.buffalotrace.com

Part of the Buffalo Trace Antique Collection, and, frankly, the star quarter-back. Each autumn there is a mad rush for the new bottling. Little makes its way into Europe and what does is considerably more expensive. But it's worth it, one of the world's truly great whiskeys, a true thoroughbred with no obvious weaknesses whatsoever. It's rich in honey, oak, cinnamon, cloves, orange peel, marzipan, cocoa, sandalwood, tobacco pouch and candy stick; for me, it's all about cherry in dark chocolate, hickory, red liquorice and pepper dust. Sip and savour without water. An all-but-perfect bourbon

Heaven Hill 40% ABV
www.heaven-hill.com

Some bourbons including this one are matured first and then filtered through maplewood charcoal just before bottling. They can be called bourbons because the filtering is after distillation and maturation so the whiskey-making process is unaffected. This is different to Tennessee whiskeys, where the charcoal filtering is is carried out on the newly distilled spirit BEFORE it is matured. This bourbon is mellow, inoffensive and under-whelming. Best served as an early evening apéritif on a summer's night

Henry McKenna Single Barrel
10-year-old 50% ABV
www.heaven-hill.com

Single barrel, so nothing's guaranteed when you buy a bottle, but if it's anything like this, then you're in for a treat. It has an applejack nose, and is liqueur-like, with pruney-*rumtopf* notes. Intense. The taste on the palate is full, concentrated and intense, too, with baked apple and concentrated syrup. The ideal music to accompany it? Try Kentucky's Broadfield Marchers, comprizing brothers Mark and Dustin Zdobylak. They play jangly, post-Byrdian pyschedelic rock reminiscent of REM at their best. Their mix of exuberant youthfulness and respect for tradition is a perfect foil for this wonderful whiskey.

High West American Prairie
Reserve 46% ABV
www.highwest.com

There is a big debate in the United States about whiskey companies that buy in whiskey spirit and bottle it as their own. If it's transparent, that's no different to independent bottlers elsewhere. When the whiskey's this good who's complaining? This is a mix of 6- and 10-year-old bourbon. It's a rollicking ride from start to finish, with wood, spice and fruit battling each other the whole way.

Hudson Baby Bourbon 46% ABV
www.tuthilltown.com

If you've seen the film *Baby Driver* you'll have an idea of what's going on here. This whiskey is all cocky, strutting, no cares in the world bourbon: a little rough round the edges but very likeable. It's sweet, with marzipan on the palate and a touch of pepper spice. It has improved significantly since the first edition of this book.

Hudson Four Grain Bourbon 46% ABV
www.tuthilltown.com

For more than 200 years, the gristmill at Tuthilltown used water power to grind grain in to flour. But, in the late 1990s a small group of whiskey aficionados acquired the property and converted one of the mill granaries in to a micro-distillery, and set about learning the craft of distilling. It took them a couple of years to negotiate the legal hurdles put in their way, but by 2004 they were making spirit. So successful has the company been that it was bought by Scottish distilling giant William Grant. Tuthilltown's main achievement has been in getting some of New York's trendier drinkers to take a fresh look at rye and bourbon. Four Grain Bourbon is balanced, feisty and exciting.

IW Harper 43% ABV
www.fourroses.us

Some whiskeys are for sipping, some for slugging – but only responsibly of course. Some are for daytime, others for evening or late at night. Some are reflective, some raucous; some passive and subdued, others edgy and active. If you can find this, it's smooth and elegant, and my listening suggestion is 'Face a Frowning World', a tribute to Estil Cortez Ball, an Appalachian country singer from Virginia who sang secular and gospel country songs. Now that's a classy night in.

Jefferson's 8-year-old 45.1% ABV (VARIES)
www.mclainandkyne.com

McClain & Kyne (part of Castle Brands in New York), imply they make bourbon in Bardstown. They don't. But, they are buying good-quality bourbon, and this small batch uses just 8-12 barrels for each bottling. Perfectly palatable, with hickory, rye spice and pleasant sweetness. Tastes mature without being over-oaky, with a delightful fruity finish.

Jim Beam 40% ABV
www.jimbeam.com

Like Jack Daniel's, Glenfiddich, Famous Grouse, Teacher's and Jamesons, the standard Jim Beam suffers from contempt because of its familiarity. This is grossly unfair. World-class whiskies become world class for a reason. Next time you walk in to a bar and you realize your whisky choice is limited to the above, make a point of going for one of them anyway. It will be then that you remember just how good each is, and how you'd forgotten about it. With Beam you'll get brown sugar, a significant alcohol bite and a sweet corn centre that is not so obvious in many other bourbons.

Jim Beam Black 8-year-old 43% ABV
www.jimbeam.com

Proof if ever it were wanted that big does not necessarily mean bland. This is aged for twice as long as the standard white-label version, and it's premier-league stuff, capable of holding its own in a blind tasting against any mainstream bourbon under ten years old. Christmas cake, ginger drizzle and liquorice come into play here; juicy berry fruits and raisins dip in and out of the mix; and there is just enough wood and rye to make this a complete experience. Incredibly complex and well balanced, this is Exhibit A for those who think eight years is the perfect age for bourbon.

Jim Beam Devil's Cut 45% ABV
www.jimbeam.com

The Devil's Cut refers to the whiskey that soaks in to the cask and that remains in the cask after it has been dumped. Historically it could be washed out with water and was known as grog. Nothing quite that crude is done to extract it here, but the woody, earthy spirit is mixed with Beam 6-year-old to create a robust and intense oaky bourbon.

Key whiskies

Bernheim Original 45% ABV
Elijah Craig Small Batch 47% ABV
Evan Williams 1783 43% ABV
Evan Williams Bottled In Bond 50% ABV
Georgia Moon Corn Whiskey 50% ABV
Henry McKenna Single Barrel 50% ABV
Larceny 92 Proof 46% ABV
Mellow Corn 50% ABV
Old Fitzgerald Prime 43% ABV
Parker's Heritage Collection 61% ABV
Pikesville Supreme 40% ABV
Rittenhouse Rye 40% ABV

ABOVE The visitor centre at Heaven Hill is located in the Bardstown heartland of Kentucky bourbon production...
BELOW ...while Heaven Hill's actual production takes place in Louisville.

HEAVEN HILL

PO Box 729, Bardstown, Kentucky 40004
www.heavenhill.com

Visit California, Louisville when it is raining, and you can't help thinking that whoever named it had a strange sense of humour.

It's a grim, run-down inner-city suburb that has nothing in common with the Sunshine State on the US West Coast. But, it is home to Brown-Forman's big distillery and the Bernheim plant where Heaven Hill now produces its spirit – not without incident. The plant flooded a few years ago and gun incidents aren't uncommon here.

'One time they had been over at Brown-Forman and the security guys had chased them off,' says Heaven Hill's head of corporate affairs Larry Kass. 'They came down here and fired two bullets into the fermenters. They were caught by the police but the fermenters had to be emptied to be repaired because they were leaking. The slugs were never found. Now that's what you call bullet bourbon!' and he bark-laughs in distinctly Kass-like fashion. Life at Heaven Hill is not usually as lively.

Nevertheless it is hard to imagine a whiskey distillery more removed from the standard country image on show throughout Kentucky. Heaven Hill moved here at the end of the last millennium after its distillery was destroyed by fire. They bought the site from United Distillers (merging with spirits giants UDV to form Diageo), and inherited a distillery that is both huge and high-tech. There is something incongruous about finding a check-shirted Craig Beam seated in an office surrounded by computer screens and automated production equipment.

Craig's role within the company is to ensure that the passage from grain delivery in Louisville to whiskey maturation out at Bardstown and then back for bottling is a smooth one and all the traditional values of brands such as Evan Williams, Elijah Craig, Rittenhouse and Henry McKenna are maintained. He oversees the second-biggest quantity of ageing bourbon in the world. He does it by bringing the old production skills and methods into the modern environment. It is a classic case of old meeting new and hopefully taking the best from both. For instance, across from Beam's office is the refrigerated room where the yeasts are kept; there is always an air of mystery about yeast, because

it is at the heart of whiskey-making magic, and it contains a whiskey recipe's deepest secrets. That applies just as equally in a high-tech monster plant as much as it does in a farm-hut micro-distillery. At Bernheim, two buckets on the floor contain the raw yeasts, but, in the refrigerator itself, there are scores of packets of dried yeast. Made in Belgium.

'I'm not too sure how Craig feels about dried yeast but it works for the plant,' says Kass. 'The original yeast is sent all the way from Belgium because this place is considered the best. Only Craig knows the exact yeast strain though. It was handed down by Parker Beam's father Earl from the old days, when they would have to weigh it down and drop it to the bottom of the lake to keep it cool in summer. Earl would make up the yeast in a bucket and then cover it with a cloth and put a monkey wrench on top to hold it down. And that monkey wrench always faced the same way. You didn't mess with the monkey wrench.'

The way distilling skills and habits are handed down through the generations are much in evidence here. Craig shares his grandfather's obsession with cleanliness, too, even in the new plant. That is how it all started for him, he says.

'There was this old building that needed cleaning down so I got to do that with some friends,' he says. 'Pigeons had been roosting in there for years so we had to wade through the muck to clean it out. We'd come out looking as black as coal miners.'

Craig represents the eighth generation of family distillers and his great-grandfather was the brother of James, better known as Jim. He is immensely aware of the dual responsibility of carrying such a famous bourbon name and being responsible for some of its most famous brands.

'But that's why we take such great care doing what we do,' he says. Kass agrees: 'Heaven Hill has strong family connections through the Beams and through the Shapira family that owns it. It is important for everyone to keep the old traditions alive, not just with bourbon but with rye, wheat and even corn whiskey, no matter where it's made.

Key whiskies

Baker's Aged 7-year-old 53.5% ABV
Booker's 6-year-old 63.5% ABV
Knob Creek 9-year-old 50% ABV
Jim Beam 40% ABV
Jim Beam Black 8-year-old 43% ABV
Jim Beam Devil's Cut 45% ABV
Jim Beam Rye 40% ABV

ABOVE Visitors to Kentucky can visit the Jim Beam American Outpost close to the distillery. It includes a tasting room housed in a traditional clapboard building.

JIM BEAM

526 Happy Hollow Road, Clermont, Kentucky 40110
www.jimbeam.com

If you are in a fighting mood and you fancy kicking up a storm while downing a few bourbons at the Talbott Tavern, Bardstown, raise the issue of small-batch bourbon.

On paper it would seem to be a simple concept. Small batch, in theory, is exactly what it says it is – bourbon made from a small number of casks, with the emphasis on only using whiskey of the highest quality. Problem is, there is no legal definition of the term. And one man's small shack is another man's castle. At the big distilleries, such as Jim Beam, they probably make in a minute what Maker's Mark manages to make in a day, so how small, exactly, is small? Are distilleries such as Maker's Mark by definition small batch? And if a distillery makes ten million litres (2,641,720 US gallons) of spirit a year and directs 10% of it – one million litres (264,172 US gallons) – into its 'small batch' range, can that really count? Indeed, so vague is the whole concept that one respected whisky writer has even declared 'there is no such thing as a small batch'.

He's wrong, because there is. Or more exactly, there are. Smaller volumes of specially selected bourbons that are superior to their standard versions do exist. It is just that they exist under a number of different definitions. The confusion arises because many assume that the term small batch refers to the size of the production run, but this is not the case. If it were, Maker's and Woodford Reserve (if stock taken only from the new distillery were bottled), would qualify as small-batch distilleries.

At Four Roses, they have their own definition. The distillery produces ten whiskeys from two recipes and five different yeasts and marries them together to produce its standard bourbon. For its small-batch runs, Four Roses selects just four of the ten. That may well still be a massive amount of whiskey.

The term 'small batch' was introduced back in 1988 by Jim Beam as a way of describing a special whiskey that Booker Noe had created to set it apart from standard Jim Beam. This was at a time when there was no great market for premium bourbons, as there is now, and when single-barrel selections were few and far between. Beam has two huge distilleries producing millions of litres (thousands of US gallons) of spirit every year, and although the company website is not above some smoke and mirrors when it talks of returning to small-scale, handcrafted bourbon with its small-batch range, the company's whiskey professor is more forthright on the subject.

'Beam has big distilleries and production is twenty-four-seven and so in this sense production could never be small batch. But that doesn't mean the distillery can't make a small-batch bourbon.' The issue here is barrel selection. 'If you pre-plan what you are going to mature as single batch before you start maturation and put a part of your spirit production in a set number of casks in specific areas of your warehouse, then that constitutes small batch.'

It makes sense, particularly in Kentucky where temperature extremes mean that there are areas that will produce honey barrels – ones producing spirit of particularly high quality.

'It's not just a marketing trick. In 2008 we ran out of Knob Creek and there were shortages of it. If you look at the figures from the Kentucky Distillers' Association for that year, you'll see we had twenty-three-thousand barrels of nine-year-old bourbon, but we didn't pull any of it out and call it Knob Creek, because those casks weren't part of the planning for the small-batch run.'

Perhaps we shouldn't get hung up on definitions, anyway. The big boys produce bourbon to the same exacting standards as even the smallest makers. Are Booker's and Knob Creek fine bourbons? Yes, they sure are. And as someone put it while sipping moonshine at a barbecue a while back: 'Don't matter if it's one barrel or one thousand. Fine bourbon's fine bourbon, and rotgut is rotgut. No marketing man can ever change that.'

> ### WELL, FANCY THAT...
> **A version** of Jim Beam has been sold in one form or another since 1795. Today it is the world's most popular bourbon and the company can make 40 million litres (10.5 million US gallons) of spirit a year.

John J Bowman Virginia Straight Bourbon 50% ABV
www.asmithbowman.com

Classy stuff. This is a balanced, flavoursome bourbon that branches out in to all sorts of fun areas with a little water. This is vibrant, fresh and full of character. A whiskey at the very top its game.

Johnny Drum 43% ABV
www.kentuckybourbonwhiskey.com

A bit of a curiosity comes from the Kentucky Bourbon Distillers, which bottles for a range of other brands. Johnny Drum varies in strength, is normally bottled at four years old and is rare. But it is a jolly bourbon, made, we are told, from small batches of top-quality barrels, and it is rich, fruity, spicy and zesty.

Johnny Drum Private Stock
50.5% ABV
www.kentuckybourbonwhiskey.com

This has an intense and fruity flavour with hints of strong candy stick, leather, tobacco pouch and over-ripe fruit, together with a pleasant woodiness.

Kentucky Gentleman Straight Bourbon 40% ABV
www.heaven-hill.com

The nose here is soft and fruity, like tinned pears, with soft fudge in the mix. The makers claim that rye is higher in the mix than is sometimes the case; certainly the overall volume of the other blended grains is turned down. This whiskey is fine, but it won't kick or punch, preferring to make peace in the mouth, not war. Greener, fresher than classic bourbons, with shades of eucalyptus, it's still very drinkable, ideal for sultry summer evenings.

Kentucky Tavern 40% ABV
www.bartonbrands.com

The Talbott in Bardstown was my nomination in *Whisky Magazine* as one of the world's great whisky bars. They say that Jesse James held court here.

The whiskey, which is actually named after a totally different tavern, is quite endearing. Sweet apple and pear on the nose, not unlike Kentucky Gentleman, some very gentle spice on the green-fruit palate – bizarrely it is not dissimilar to some of the stuff they are bottling at Bladnoch in Lowland Scotland, or at Cooley in Ireland.

Knob Creek 9-year-old 50% ABV
www.knobcreek.com

There are two Knob Creeks in Kentucky. One is next to a gun range, the other is the creek running through the farm where Abraham Lincoln grew up. His father made whiskey, too.

The bottle is designed to look like a bootleggers' version, with newsprint on the label to ape the old newspaper that the distillery used for wrapping. The oldest and best of the Jim Beam small-batch range, Knob Creek is full of flavour, with endearing cocoa and dark-chocolate notes, honey sweetness and rye and oak, too.

Maker's Mark 45% ABV
www.makersmark.com

This is one of the most distinctive and softest of all bourbons, and so it should be, as it's designer-made and aimed to appeal to people who don't like bourbon. It is the creation of William Samuels, who bears the name of one of the great bourbon families, but had retired from whiskey making in the 1940s. When he decided to come back into the business he wanted to do something new and different, so consulted Pappy Van Winkle and settled on a high wheat recipe. The story goes that it was his wife who persuaded him to drop the family name from the bottle, to go for a distinctive wax seal and to model the product on the jewellery industry, with a stamp representing the maker. William's son Bill is still the brand's figurehead but these days the distillery is headed up by Bill's son Rob, and is part of the Beam empire.

Maker's Mark is made in relatively small batches. Nevertheless, bottlings tend to be pretty consistent, probably because this is the only Kentucky distillery that rotates its casks during maturation. This is an angel's delight of a whiskey, with soft bread and custardy notes. Bill Samuels claims that every member of the bottle-dipping team has his or her own wax 'signature' and he can tell who dipped each bottle just by looking at it.

Michter's US *1 Small Batch

45.3% ABV
www.buffalotrace.com

This is a celebratory whiskey and one perfect for toasting the bourbon revival in Louisville, Kentucky and the opening of a Michter's visitor centre on Whiskey Row in 2018. Michter's can trace its history to the early pioneering days of the United States, when rye would have been the whiskey of choice. Rye was what Michter's was known for, but this bourbon is a gem, with rich plummy notes and some feisty spice courtesy of the rye. Cracking stuff.

Noah's Mill 57.15% ABV
www.kentuckybourbonwhiskey.com

The Willett distillery has a long and chequered history in Bardstown and news that it was being restored was greeted with enthusiasm. But its owners agreed that they would not get into debt reconstructing it, so over the last few years they have been building a new still-house brick by brick. Now it seems the project is complete and the new Willett distillery is accepting visitors again.

Over the years the company has bottled bourbon for a number of companies and has had its own bottlings, too. This one is an award-winner and arguably the best from the Bardstown stable. Another small-batch whiskey bottled by hand and containing some rare and special

bourbon, Noah's Mill is a robust and full-tasting bourbon that is aged for about 15 years and has strong woody notes. A dash of water opens up an Aladdin's cave of flavours, however – banoffee pie, vanilla ice cream, with hot fudge sauce and crumbly fruitcake.

Old Crow 40% ABV
www.beamglobal.com

One of the greatest names in bourbon, 2010 saw Old Crow given a new lease of life when its owners Jim Beam relaunched it as a 4-year-old, gave it new packaging and pitched it up against Evan Williams.

James Crow was a physician who became a leading figure in the development of bourbon, developing many of the techniques employed by bourbon makers today to ensure consistency and quality. He was a skilled and charitable doctor, spent more than two decades at the Labrot & Graham distillery and is remembered as one of the pioneers of modern bourbon. However, he never owned his own distillery, and the Old Crow distillery sited in Glenns Creek was not constructed until several years after his death.

This version of Old Crow has some strong liquorice notes, retains its freshness and is clearly aimed at the mainstream, but it works as a session bourbon and is one to look out for.

Old Fitzgerald Prime 43% ABV
www.heaven-hill.com

Most bourbons that feature a name in their title tend to take it from a particular distillery owner or distiller. But not in this case, according to Sally Van Winkle. This is named after a security guard who used to help himself to bourbon from select casks to give to friends. He had excellent taste and his reputation for identifying good casks became well known. So, when a good-quality bourbon went down to the blending room, it would be known as a Fitzgerald. Eventually it was applied to a brand. There is fudginess here, plus sweet pepper and cinnamon.

Key whiskies
Maker's Mark 45% ABV
Maker's Mark 46 47% ABV

ABOVE Maker's Mark distillery, set amid deep countryside in Loretto, is a National Historic Landmark and one of Kentucky's longest established sites for bourbon production.

MAKER'S MARK

6200 Dutchmans Ln 3, Loretto, Louisville, Kentucky 40205-3285
www.makersmark.com

As you travel from Louisville in Kentucky to Loretto you pass a number of houses that have statues of the Virgin Mary standing in upturned bath tubs.

The story goes that a bath salesman visited these parts a few years back but couldn't get the local folk interested in investing in new washing facilities. But he found out that this region of Kentucky is devoutly Catholic, so assuming the locals were more into spiritual than personal cleansing he hit on the shrine idea, sold his entire stock of baths and retired a wealthy man.

Loretto is home to both Maker's Mark distillery as well as some of the world's most expensive thoroughbred horse-breeding facilities. That's no coincidence either: the whiskey and the horses are here for the same reason. Kentucky is rich in limestone that enriches the grass with vitamins, making it ideal for developing healthy and strong bones in the horses. And it hardens the water and makes it ideal for distilling top-quality bourbon.

One of Kentucky's smallest and prettiest distilleries, Maker's Mark is very much at home among the wealth and beauty of the region. It was launched in the 1950s, but distilling has been carried on at the site next to Hardin's Creek for more than 200 years, making it the United States' oldest working distillery. It was established on farmland deep in rural Kentucky, and when you arrive there you are struck by how sedate and tranquil the neighbourhood is.

The distillery is a sedate and calming place, too, even when it is in full production. That's partly because everything is done on such a small scale. While the debate rages as to what constitutes 'small-batch bourbon', it remains a fact that at Maker's they produce as much bourbon in a month as sister distillery Jim Beam does in a day.

The whiskey-making process is gentler than at other distilleries, too. The corn is crushed, not by hammer as elsewhere, but by roller, because Maker's owners believe that the heat generated by hammering scolds the grain and makes it bitter. The grains are also cooked for longer, and brought to their cooking temperature over a longer period of time and a higher proportion of wheat and lower proportion of rye is used than for other bourbons, giving the whiskey a softer, sweeter and less spicy flavour.

For much of its history Maker's Mark only made one expression, aged for about six years. But in recent years it started rolling out Maker's Mark 46, the number referring to the number given to the level of charring rather than the alcoholic strength. The whiskey is matured as normal before being 'dumped' to empty the casks, which are then dismantled and rebuilt using new French oak staves to replace a few of the American ones before the whiskey is returned to the barrel. The result is a sublime, spicy, oaky whiskey. Once it is matured to the distillery manager's satisfaction and bottled, each bottle is dipped into the red 'wax' to give it its trademark cap, labelled and boxed by hand.

ABOVE Bottles are hand dipped with a wax-like plastic seal.

Old Forester 43% ABV
www.brown-forman.com

Old Forester's roots lie in the very earliest days of distilling. This was the whiskey – then spelled Forrester – that George Brown made at the distillery he founded in Louisville, and today is at the heart of the Brown-Forman empire. The whiskey's claim is that it was the first bourbon to be bottled. Before this time whiskey had been sold in barrels to wholesalers and retailers.

This tipple is a bit of an A–Z of bourbon flavours and covers everything from fruit-and-nut chocolate bar and vanilla ice cream to nutmeg, cinnamon, sandalwood and chilli spices. Class in a glass.

Old Forester Signature 50% ABV
www.brown-forman.com

Old Forester with the volume turned up, this is an intense and robust version of the standard bottling made up from a number of specially selected casks.

Old Pogue 45.5% ABV
www.oldpogue.com

Old Pogue is produced by another non-distilling company, despite the fact that the website displays a lovely old photograph of a Kentucky distillery and its home page claims that the bourbon is bottled in Bardstown by the Old Pogue distillery. Pogue is an old bourbon name and the people behind this bottling are descendants of the original distilling Pogues. A mainstream bourbon launched a few years ago, this manages to find a niche all of its own – and that is because it's thinner and less sweet than many other bourbons, having an almost apéritif-like dryness and unusual barley-meadow quality.

Old Rip Van Winkle
10-year-old 45% ABV
www.oldripvanwinkle.com

Sounds like a character from a nursery rhyme and indeed 'Rip Van Winkle' is the name of a short story by Washington Irving. It tells of Rip Van Winkle who escapes his nagging wife by wandering off into the Catskill mountains and encounters some strangely dressed men who are playing nine pins and drinking liquor, which Rip shares with them. Doesn't sound so odd if you have downed a couple of glasses of this bourbon (maybe this bourbon is meant to be the liquor in the story). It is aged to perfection and uses the distinctive Van Winkle wheated recipe, so it's soft, mellow and rounded with a rich, creamy toffee flavour and perhaps some chocolaty notes. There is a stronger 53.5% ABV version of this, too.

Old Taylor 40% ABV
www.jimbeam.com

I reckon that, if you asked 100 film buffs to name their favourite stars, Jeff Bridges would not figure very highly. Over his career, though, he's produced some absolute storming performances – *Arlington Road*, *Thunderbolt & Lightfoot*, *The Fabulous Baker Boys*, *The Last Picture Show* and *The Contender* are all great films. The Dude, his character in *The Big Lebowski*, has reached cult status.

In his most recent Oscar-winning offering, *Crazy Heart*, he is exceptional as a washed-up, back-bar country singer who slugs whiskey while watching his former band partner hit the big time with country-and-western slush. The soundtrack is by T-Bone Burnett, Stephen Bruton and Ryan Bingham, the film is a study in Americana, and if you are a fan of the new country genre, this hits all the right buttons.

I like to think that Bridges' drink of choice in the film is based on Old Taylor, because it's every bit as wizened, honest, genuine, traditional and soft at its centre as Bridges' character. A loveable-old-rogue of a bourbon, perhaps out of kilter with the smarter marketing whiskey world we now live in, but one to look out for and to savour at least once. It reminds me of Battenburg cake – all jam and marzipan. Good old bourbon as it should be.

Rebel Yell Small Batch 45.3% ABV
www.rebelyellbourbon.com

Once sold only below the Mason-Dixon line, Rebel Yell had a brief flirtation with international stardom in the early 1990s, when it made its way to Europe accompanied by a free rock tape. Yep, before CDs were the main musical vehicle. The brand wrapped itself in the Confederate flag and all but disappeared. Now it's virtually a new bourbon. Now owned by Luxco, it has been reinvented as a premium whiskey, and it's smartened up its image. In 2018 a distillery was opened in the historic town of Bardstown, Kentucky. This expression is great and not what you might expect. It's made to a William Larue recipe, and is wheated, soft and honeyed.

Ridgemont Reserve 1792 Small Batch 46.85% ABV
www.bartonbrands.com

The launch of this bourbon a few years ago signalled that times were a-changing at what was the Barton distillery. It is a premium bourbon, aged for at least eight years, and when launched its modern packaging was a clear statement of intent. The date refers to the year when Kentucky broke from Virginia and became a separate state, though a sizeable number of settlers had already arrived in the region and whiskey was already being made.

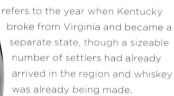

The bourbon itself is something else again. It's full-bodied and highly tasty, with just enough rye and oak to give it weight, but it's the creamy centre with vanilla pod and stewed apples that really delights. Some chicory coffee and hickory are in the mix, too. If it were a sports star, it would be the tennis great Roger Federer – immensely powerful and hard-hitting, but charming, soft and likeable, too.

Stagg Junior 67.2% ABV
www.buffalotracedistillery.com

George T Stagg is one of the world's finest whiskeys, and the annual release of the rare stock is one of the most important days in the whiskey calendar. Your chances of getting any of it are not great. Worry not. Stagg Junior is anything but an inferior sibling and is more readily available.

Take the strength for a starter. And this has been aged for eight or nine years, a long time for a bourbon. Taste-wise it's a bourbon master class, with the added delights of menthol and cherry.

Ten High 40% ABV
www.bartonbrands.com

In Kentucky many of the warehouses used to mature whiskey are tall, ugly buildings that dominate the skyline. They contain seven floors or more, and are wooden constructions. Given the huge weight of the scores of full barrels they contain, they are feats of engineering.

Each floor will differ from the next, with the hottest and most active ones at the top of the building, and the cooler ones lower down. Here, at Tom Moore, the warehouses have three ricks (or stacks) per floor, and they do not use the bottom three floors for bourbon at all. So the first rick used for whiskey is ten high (the first rick of the fourth floor) – hence the name of this bourbon. But, of course, they're well aware of the incidental gambling pun, too.

'I'd like to bottle a bourbon using barrels from the crow's nest at the very top of the warehouse' says Greg Davis. 'We could call it Black Jack because it would come from the twenty-first rick.'

No doubt it would be nearly black in colour, too.

This bourbon is a delight – very easy to drink, fruity and sweet. Great with ice and a perfect example of what some folk refer to as a sippin' whiskey.

Van Winkle Special Reserve
12-year-old 45.2% ABV
www.oldripvanwinkle.com

Prohibition, introduced in 1920, was part of a moral crusade that ended up nearly destroying a Kentucky bourbon industry employing good, honest and steadfast men, while creating a skilled and exploitative class of bootleggers, moonshiners and gangsters. Bizarrely, a number of distilleries were allowed to stay open to make bourbon for medicinal reasons, and at the same time the number of people being prescribed bourbon by their doctors grew massively. Whiskey may well have been the cause of the St Valentine's Massacre, when five members and two associates were shot dead by members of Al Capone's gang and hired help. To replace his bourbon empire Pappy Van Winkle went into business selling farm parts for a while – not very successfully.

This is the most accessible of the Van Winkle stable, a perfect after-dinner whiskey with a distinctive orange marmalade and sweet taste. There is also summer pudding and cream with some paprika and cinnamon spice in the mix.

Very Old Barton 6-year-old 50% ABV
www.bartonbrands.com

A few years back, whiskey writer Charles Cowdery and I were invited to a barbecue held by Bettye Jo Beam. She is well known in whiskey circles, and has been a keen competitor in the barrel-pushing competition at the annual bourbon festival. She married a Beam and her maiden name is Boone, so she's linked to two of Kentucky's most famous families. On hearing that we were coming, she asked Chuck if she could tell all her friends.

'No, Bettye, because that would be half the state of Kentucky,' replied Chuck. 'Okay then, what about family?' she enquired.

'That, Bettye, would be the other half,' said Chuck.

That barbecue was some event, but before we went I asked Chuck –

who knows masses about bourbon and whose opinion I respect greatly – what bottle I should take with me. He suggested this one, because it enjoys the respect of almost everyone.

'Very Old' in this case is just six years, and strangely the whiskey is bottled at three separate strengths. If you can get it, though, this is the one to go for. It is complex and challenging but never sharp or over-aggressive, and has a distinctive berry-fruit centre in a pepper and candy wrap. Another solid backliner of a bourbon, this is as solid and reliable as a Swiss watch.

Weller Antique 53.5% ABV
www.buffalotracedistillery.com

This bourbon is all about contrasts, with the soft honeyed and wheaten notes associated with Weller whiskeys meeting their match from an elephant-sized chunk of oily corn and oak flavour. There is no obvious winner between the two sides but the effect in the mouth is captivating and as it slips down the throat it is tempting to pour another drop so you can go through the boxing match experience again. Whenever I have a glass of this I also toast the late-great Keith Weller, who is something of a legend among Leicester City soccer fans and who was my hero and role model. He is remembered most for playing an English cup game wearing white tights – an act that echoes this bourbon with its confusing mix of macho brawn and effeminate gracefulness. He was something of a pioneer in American soccer, too, playing and/or coaching in a number of places, including Fort Lauderdale, New England, Tulsa, Houston, Dallas and San Diego. He died of cancer in 2004 at just 58 years old.

WL Weller 7-year-old
Special Reserve 45% ABV
www.buffalotracedistillery.com

William Larue Weller was one of the great early pioneers of bourbon. He was particularly noted for two things – using wheat in the grist rather than rye, creating a softer and more rounded bourbon and

for long ageing his whiskey. Weller and later the Stitzel-Weller distillery became synonymous with aged and top-quality bourbon, and all of the current bottlings from Buffalo Trace live up to the name. This is the youngest expression of Weller and it has a soft, fruity nose, a rounded and soft-honeycomb centre together with gentle ebbing-and-flowing waves of mild chilli. It is as soft and delicate as bourbon gets, but none the worse for that.

William Larue Weller 67.4% ABV
www.buffalotracedistillery.com

Every autumn, Buffalo Trace releases a group of special whiskeys under its Antique Collection series. They are snapped up, and all are exceptional. This year's offering from William Larue Weller is significantly stronger than normal, and, unlike the George T Stagg release, requires water to truly reach its heart. Even with a considerable dash of water it is x-rated stuff: the soft wheaten notes are swatted aside by huge high-cocoa-content dark chocolate, hickory, molasses and espresso coffee. Work with it and you will find some mint notes and plummy fruit. But you cannot escape the fact that it is to bourbon what the Indianapolis Colts are to American football – tough, uncompromising, ruthless and thoroughly brilliant in equal measure.

Wild Turkey 40.5% ABV
www.wildturkeybourbon.com

The story tells Wild Turkey was named after the bourbon that was brought to the annual wild turkey shoot. Turkey hunting, and attracting the male turkeys by impersonating female ones, is one of the most dangerous sports in the world. Not because wild turkeys are very vicious, but due to 'friendly fire'. Turkey hunters keep shooting each other because they're just as fooled as the turkeys are. Steady the nerves with this. It was introduced at a lower strength to appeal to the twenty-first century drinker, and is uncluttered, unchallenging and sweet. Nice with ice.

Wild Turkey 101 50.5% ABV
www.wildturkeybourbon.com

The ultimate rock-and-roll bourbon, and to fully enjoy this you need to crank up Lynyrd Skynyrd's 'Tuesday's Gone' or Blackfoot's 'Good Morning', sit back in your favourite chair, close your eyes and wallow in nostalgia. This is also the official passport to good times and friendship south of the Ohio River, certainly. If anyone in a check shirt asks you if you'd like a bourbon, just say '101'. Nothing else. Can't fail. The bourbon is a big-and-balanced mix of spice, candy, over-ripe yellow and orange fruits, dark chocolate, vanilla and cigar box, all held together by some chewy and oily undernotes.

Wild Turkey American Spirit
15-year-old 50% ABV
www.wildturkeybourbon.com

This is way out in the wilderness age-wise, but it is not what you might expect. Wood is there, certainly, but it is not over-domineering and is not the taste that you will take away. That comes from the Christmas cake and almost floral, fruity heart, the dagger-like rye hit and the gentler vanilla heart. A departure for Wild Turkey, this is certainly not to everybody's taste, but it is an interesting diversion nevertheless.

Wild Turkey Kentucky Spirit
50.5% ABV
www.wildturkeybourbon.com

There may well be a few bourbons from Kentucky that are not what they claim to be, but when Wild Turkey claims that Jimmy Russell personally selects the casks that go into this single-barrel offering, you can bet your last dollar he did. His nose for great bourbon is undiminished, repeatedly he dips into his distillery to produce a gem. This has trademark citrus notes, rye, sweet vanilla and spice.

Wild Turkey 40% ABV
Wild Turkey 101 50.5% ABV
Wild Turkey American Spirit 15-year-old 50% ABV
Wild Turkey Kentucky Spirit 50.5% ABV
Wild Turkey Rare Breed 51.4% ABV
Wild Turkey Russell's Reserve 45% ABV
Wild Turkey Russell's Reserve Rye 45% ABV
Wild Turkey Rye 50.5% ABV

ABOVE Grain is fermented in large vessels.

BELOW The legendary master-distiller Jimmy Russell samples one of Wild Turkey's casks.

WILD TURKEY

1525 Tyrone Road, Lawrenceburg, Kentucky 40342
www.wildturkeybourbon.com

Nobody rushes in Kentucky and when it comes time to retire, there seems to be no hurry to hang up the boots and head out on to the porch for a well-earned cigar and a bourbon or two.

If you want proof that bourbon makers live for their work and love what they do, just look at recent history: Elmer T Lee, Lincoln Henderson, Booker Noe, Parker Beam all worked until the end; Julian Van Winkle hasn't slowed down and Jim Rutledge retired from Four Roses, but is still involved in whiskey. Then there's Jimmy Russell at Wild Turkey, making bourbon for more than 60 years. When his beloved distillery was sold by Pernod Ricard a few years ago, you would have thought that would be the perfect time to call it a day. Not a bit of it.

'The owners had plans and wanted me to go to New York, Chicago and San Francisco in the following weeks,' he says. 'This is what I like to do, meet people who enjoy my bourbon, see the pleasure it brings them, travel to places to talk.'

'Mind you, you know you're getting old when you start working with your grandchildren, and I sometimes wonder when we fill the casks whether I'll still be around to see the whiskey being bottled.'

Russell is on site almost daily when he's not travelling, which is a less often these days, and splits his time between greeting visitors and playing an active role in producing spirit, which he now does with his son Eddie. There are few people anywhere in the world who understand their spirit the way Jimmy Russell does. He can tell how long the mash has been fermenting by the size of the bubbles, and he knows instantly if a batch of bourbon has strayed from the correct recipe or is the wrong strength. He also has a very precise idea of what great bourbon is. He doesn't care for spirit that has been aged for more than ten years, for instance, and his preferred bottling strength is 101 proof, not the more common 100 proof (the industry standard for a good while). The bourbon's name and its strength are interrelated, he says.

'The distillery was once owned by the McCarthy family and Thomas McCarthy was a keen wild turkey hunter,' he recalls. 'They used to go on shoots and everybody would contribute something to the food and drink for the trip. The story goes, McCarthy took a barrel of his bourbon one time and it happened to be at a hundred-and-one proof strength and everybody enjoyed it very much. The next time they asked him to bring more bourbon, so he found some the same strength and he referred to it as the wild turkey bourbon. Finally he christened it that way.'

Wild Turkey 101 remains one of the great old bourbons, but the distillery hasn't sat back and let progress leave it behind. Certainly, 101 is still going strong, but over the years the distillery has released a single-barrel bourbon, a rye, a liqueur and a number of special bottlings, including Tradition and Rare Breed. At the heart of everything, though, is big-flavoured Wild Turkey whiskey, because, says Russell, sooner or later everyone comes back to it.

'A few years ago they started experimenting with lighter whiskey and I never thought it would work,' he says. 'If I had not been wrong then, I would not be sitting here today. It's good that new things come along and keep people interested but what goes around comes around, and folk always come back to proper well-made bourbon.'

Wild Turkey has managed to maintain its integrity while keeping up with world drinks trends. Where that will take the bourbon next is anyone's guess, but whatever it is, you suspect Jimmy Russell will be involved right at the very centre. 'For sure,' he says. 'I'm in good health and I've got the energy. As long as that's the case I'll be here.'

WELL, FANCY THAT...

A distillery fire at Wild Turkey at the start of the millenium sent burning spirit into the Kentucky River; this was blamed for an environmental disaster soon after. Over 200,000 fish were killed by a blanket of algae that was thought to have fed on the alcohol and drained the river of oxygen. Wild Turkey faced a bill for nearly half a million dollars.

ALLISON PARC

Brenne

Allison Parc is an American who owns her own French whisky brand.
How did that happen?

What is your background?

I came into this industry on my own. However, in the early 2000s I had a burning desire to experience single malt made outside of Scotland that was using 100% local ingredients – to see if we could experience terroir in the whisky, much as you do with wines.

Prior to venturing into whisky entrepreneurship, I was a professional ballerina! The leap from ballet to booze did not seem so wild to me as it did to others. For me, I see a clear balance between science and artistry in both worlds.

How did you discover Brenne?

Originally, I thought I wanted to start an import company to bring single-malt whiskies – focused on using terroir and made in non-traditional countries – into the United States.

A few key collectors around the world knew about me and one of them pointed me in the direction of my now-distiller who lives in the Cognac region of France. When he and I met, I realized he was making a version of what eventually became Brenne, however, he had no desire to bottle and sell it. He was incredibly passionate about using only his heirloom barley grown organically next to his vineyards and his proprietary strain of yeast, which he also uses for his cognac fermentation. Once I learned that he was distilling this in the typical cognac stills verses traditional pot stills, I knew I had found what I had been looking for. The hardest part was ironing out how we would work together. Eventually I wired him my entire life's savings and took ownership of the whisky. We started working closely together on the barrel maturation of Brenne and then in 2010, I quit my job to launch my whisky company, which I did on October 1, 2012. It was a really wild time!

Please tell me a little bit about it.

While I essentially had the whole world as my canvas, France was particularly appealing to me. Terroir is a French word, and a way of being that is very much ingrained in the culture. France has such rich distillation history with calvados, armagnac and cognac that it seemed logical for the first terroir-focused single-malt whisky from a non-traditional whisky-making country to come from one of these places.

Brenne starts in the beautiful fields of the Charente region. We use two types of heirloom varietal barley grown organically next to the Ugni Blanc grapes. One of the things that makes Brenne really special is we only use French Limousin oak, both virgin casks and ex-cognac barrels, which attribute Brenne's incredible fruit-forward, crème-brûlée like notes.

What are the plans for the brand going forward?

I want to continue making great French single-malt whisky and bringing it to as many people as we can. There is an incredible amount of work over many years that goes into creating just one bottle of Brenne, so when I have an opportunity to share a bottle of my whisky with people, I always show up with gratitude, openness and excitement, so we can look each other in the eye and say cheers to those special moments in life.

> HEAR THIS...
> 'I want to continue making great French single-malt whisky and bringing it to as many people as we can.'

Wild Turkey Rare Breed

56.4% ABV (VARIES)

www.wildturkeybourbon.com

To catch a male wild turkey you need to impersonate a female; turkey calling has become a sport in its own right. There are competitions – many of them televized – where you can win big bucks. There are various categories and sounds include clucking, yelping, cutting, putting and cackling. This whiskey is a complete fruit bowl of flavours mixed with butterscotch, vanilla ice cream with soft toffee sauce, liquorice root and menthol.

Wild Turkey Russell's Reserve Bourbon 45% ABV

www.wildturkeybourbon.com

Jimmy Russell is one of the world's true great whiskey personalities and he is a bit like his bourbons: pleasant, soft and gentle on one level, but hardy, determined and with a great sense of purpose. He does not believe that bourbon gets better after ten years of maturation. But his preferred bottling strength is 101 proof (51.5% ABV). Odd, then, this is 45%. But, it's a corker, an oral roller coaster, the flavours build, then a crash of vanilla, citrus fruit, waves of sweet spices and polished wood. Very lovable.

Woodford Reserve Distiller's Select 43.2% ABV

www.brown-forman.com

The Kentucky Derby is the highlight of the social calendar. Local folk reach for their favourite bourbon – straight or in a Mint Julep, a drink associated with the event. High on the list is Woodford Reserve, and with higher-than-average rye content, a triple distillation process and about eight or nine years in the barrel, this is a full and rich fruity bourbon with delightful spiciness and enough oaky astringency to prevent cloying.

Tennessee whiskey

It is one of American whiskey's greatest ironies that the brand most people would cite as its most famous bourbon is not a bourbon at all. Jack Daniel's is a goliath of a brand and the whiskey world's most accomplished grifter, able with ease to bottle and sell millions of litres (gallons) of spirit while fooling its audience into believing that a few good ol' boys in Lynchburg, Tennessee are making and bottling whiskey exactly as Mr Jack used to. In fact, this is a huge operation, with close to 200 million litres (53 million US gallons) maturing on the vast site at any one time, and three bottling plants in operation. Not that you would know it from visiting – as millions do – because no other distillery enjoys an iconic status quite like this one. You know it's vast, of course, but this is Disneyland for whiskey drinkers and a million miles away from the Hard Hat Tours at Barton or Buffalo Trace.

Jack Daniel's is made in almost exactly the same way as a bourbon, but it doesn't qualify as one. Not because it's from Tennessee, but because at the end of the distillation process its producers break bourbon's strict rules by pouring the new spirit through a wall of maplewood charcoal. This process is a form of filtration, known as the Lincoln County Process, thus defining the whiskey as a Tennessee one and not a bourbon.

Some people say Jack tastes like bourbon and the technicalities do not matter. They do, though – especially to the people in Tennessee and Kentucky. Jack is not the only distillery in the state. George Dickel is a relatively large operation in its own right and produces whiskey using the Lincoln County Process but with a small difference – it chills the spirit before passing it through the charcoal, a process that allows even more mellowing. There have been a number of new craft distilleries, too.

ABOVE A view across the stunning landscape of Tennessee.

George Dickel No 8 40% ABV
www.dickel.com

This lighter version of Dickel is probably aimed at the mixing market, but it is pleasant enough on its own with ice. It is a smooth, easy-drinking whiskey with a balanced but laid-back mix of fruit, vanilla, rye and burnt oak. A lazy summer afternoon of a whiskey.

George Dickel Superior No 12
45% ABV
www.dickel.com

The Dickel distillery is only a short drive from Jack Daniel's and is now owned by Diageo, though the drinks giant seems to have a problem with American whiskey and has struggled to establish a foothold for this in the international arena. This is a perfectly decent whiskey, with floral and vanilla notes, soft sweet corn and toffee and chocolate in the mix. It also has a big mouthfeel and a surprisingly long finish.

Jack Daniel's Gentleman Jack 40% ABV
www.jackdaniels.com

The problem with spending years telling the world that Mr Jack got his whiskey right first time and you do not mess with a winning formula is that you leave yourself no room for manoeuvre when it comes to brand extension. So this version of the famous whiskey divides the room like no other. While Single Barrel is just regular Jack unplugged and acoustic, Gentleman Jack is a different expression because an extra level of mellowing has been introduced. This is the alcohol equivalent of Diet Pepsi.

Jack Daniel's Old No 7 40% ABV
www.jackdaniels.com

Whiskey enthusiasts get sniffy about this but really they shouldn't. It is quite remarkable that a strong-tasting dark spirit of any sort, let alone whiskey, should have established itself as the world's biggest spirit. Bland it most certainly isn't. It is true that most people mix it, but next time you get the opportunity to do so, sip it neat or mixed with a little ice. The vanilla, oak and liquorice triple-whammy is impressive whichever way you cut it. This, then, is the Harley-Davidson of the drinks world – a big, growling, rugged and iconic symbol of blue-collar working man's America.

Jack Daniel's Single Barrel Select ABV VARIES
www.jackdaniels.com

If Jack Daniel's is a Rolling Stones tour – a huge, glitzy worldwide greatest-hits package that delivers just what its audience expects – then Single Barrel is a Keith Richards solo gig – recognizably from the Stones but altogether rootsier, rougher, more intense and less predictable. It offers you the chance to get up close and personal. Each barrel not only differs from the next, but also differs significantly, and every barrel is chosen from the best parts of the best warehouses and every batch reinforces the view that Jack is a very-well-made whiskey indeed.

Jack Daniel's Single Barrel Rye
45% ABV
www.jackdaniels.com

Rye makes up 70% of the mashbill in what is a radical departure for Jack Daniel's. Deliciously fruity with spiky spice from the grain. Packed with flavour.

Key whiskies

Woodford Reserve 1838 Style White Corn 45.2% ABV
Woodford Reserve Brandy Cask Finish 45.2% ABV
Woodford Reserve Cherry Wood Smoked 45.2% ABV
Woodford Reserve Distiller's Select 43.2% ABV
Woodford Reserve Double Oak 45.2% ABV
Woodford Reserve Rye 45.2% ABV

ABOVE Woodford Reserve nestles in one of the prettiest and most secluded parts of Kentucky.
BELOW Unusually for bourbon, pot stills are used to make Woodford Reserve.

WOODFORD RESERVE

7855 McCraken Pike, Versailles, Kentucky 40383
www.woodfordreserve.com

At the pretty Woodford Reserve distillery, situated in Kentucky's famed bluegrass country, they are ringing in the changes and looking firmly to the future.

History seeps from every pore here. James Crow carried out some of the pioneering scientific work into bourbon on this site. He may not have invented the sour-mash process, but he mastered it and laid down the blueprint for consistency that is still maintained today. This was home to Elijah and Oscar Pepper, too. Major history. Master-distiller Chris Morris comments that may well be the case, but Woodford Reserve is a premium bourbon that looks to the future rather than the past.

'Sure this distillery is associated with Oscar and Elijah Pepper and with James Crow. But whatever they were making then was not what we know as bourbon now. We make Woodford Reserve here so we've taken down some of the displays about the past and replaced them with information on Woodford Reserve; we're focusing more on what we're doing now. That's what's important.'

Maybe, but it's not just Crow and the Peppers who haunt the distillery. George T Stagg is said to have distilled here, plus Colonel Edmund Taylor, who would later create Old Taylor at a distillery he built just down the road. The remains of distilleries are scattered around this part of Kentucky, known as Versailles. Some of them, such as Old Crow and Old Taylor, have taken on legendary status among bourbon enthusiasts. It is like a ghostly bourbon hall of fame here. Combine this with the sublime charm and beauty of the place and there are few distilleries on the planet as magical and mystical, few so entwined in such a rich tapestry of history.

Woodford Reserve is situated close to Glenns Creek. In summer red cardinals, the state bird, frolic on the picket fences. In winter chilly mists create eerie shrouds across the hills. This really is the heart of rural Kentucky and nothing can quite match the marriage of culture, history and beauty of the new Woodford Reserve distillery. But such a heady combination can be a swamp and you cannot blame anyone for trying to break free from the ghosts of history.

What Morris and his team are keen to stress is that this is a new distillery making a sophisticated and stylish premium bourbon ideal for the twenty-first century. It might be built from the ruins of Labrot & Graham, but owners Brown-Forman spent a small fortune on renovating this site. They do not even use the old name any more.

Woodford Reserve is Kentucky's smallest distillery, and its least typical. Instead of the standard, industrial-like column-still method of production, for instance, it has pot stills from Scotland. It distils three times, too. There is only one standard expression of the whiskey, but even then the distillery cannot make enough bourbon to meet the demand, so the new distillery's output is mixed with a significant – some would say high – proportion of 9-year-old whiskey made to the original Old Forester recipe at Brown-Forman's Louisville distillery.

But the real draw for bourbon fans is the Master Collection series. Each year for the past five years a limited-edition bourbon has been made purely with pot-still whiskey from the Woodford distillery, each one testing out a new angle. The first used four grains, for instance, one was finished in a wine cask, and another dispensed with the sour-mash process. Not all of them have worked, but they are always interesting.

'The last one was a big, weighty, oaky bourbon after a couple of lighter ones,' says Morris. 'So in 2010 we went with a sweeter bourbon finished in maple wood. We have pure rye whiskeys and single malts maturing, whiskeys made with white corn and oats, and whiskeys maturing in hickory and ash. Some will not work and we will not do them again, some will be outstanding.'

At their best, the special releases are enhancing an already greatly respected bourbon reputation. Morris and his team are tinkering on the margins, testing and experimenting as they look for new channels in the future. They are looking forward rather than back. But you know what? James Crow would surely have approved of what is happening right now.

Rye whiskey

Rye has a long and proud history in American whiskey but until relatively recently its popularity had declined and it had been marginalized. Over the past few years it has been enjoying a new wave of popularity, rediscovered by whiskey enthusiasts and bartenders who see it as an ideal base for several different cocktails.

In actual fact, there are three very different types of rye: Canadian whisky, which for a long time was actually referred to just as 'rye', is often made up of several ryes produced in Canadian distilleries, but these are blander and less spicy than American rye. American rye whiskey is made in the same way and to the same regulations as bourbon but must contain at least 51% rye in the gristbill. And finally, there are also a few examples of 100% rye whiskey. In this case the rye is malted so it is effectively a single-malt rye.

Corsair Ryemaggeddon 46% ABV
www.corsairdistillery.com

Corsair is at the vanguard of the craft-distilling revolution, but it has grown to a sizeable business, and now operates from three sites: two in Tennessee and one in Kentucky. The distillery makes a wide range of whiskey styles including oat and quinoa whiskey. This is an 80% rye whiskey, but with chocolate malt, and red whiskey. The result is a soft, easy-drinking whiskey, with dark chocolate, Christmas punch spices and some berries.

Devils Bit 47.7% ABV
www.mcmenamins.com

McMenamin's is a small pub and hotel company that runs its establishments in a quaint and old-fashioned manner, including its own micro-distillery that produces a range of spirits. It is exactly this sort of whiskey that shows the future is very bright indeed for the new wave of American distillers.

What makes rye such a stunning drink when it gets it right is the way it packs spikes and spices at its heart, but delivers on a crest of oil and oak, as is the case here. It is bold, assertive stuff. No drink can match it on its day.

Hudson Manhattan Rye 46% ABV
www.tuthilltown.com

New York was once famous for its rye, which was the whiskey used in the original Manhattan cocktail. So it is fitting that now small-batch distilling is taking place in the city once more, the whiskey makers should turn their hand to a proper, edgy rye.

This has an odd nose – aromatic wax candle, floral and floor-polish notes – all quite pretty. On the palate it is initially rootsy, with linseed oil coming before some orange jelly notes. This is all a bit unexpected until the spices arrive to pull it back on track.

Jim Beam Rye 40% ABV
www.jimbeam.com

This isn't Beam's best bottling but it has its place because beyond the tough, robust and grainy nature of the core drink there are aromatic and floral notes, and as a result it's a good starting point for anyone wanting to get to grips with rye. Reasonably priced, I understand Beam is upping output after some initial supply problems.

Kentucky Peerless Rye 53.7% ABV
www.kentuckypeerless.com

Kentucky Peerless is the cocky new kid on the block, strutting in to the centre of Whiskey Row in Louisville and not only fearlessly making whiskey under the noses of the old guard, but shamelessly dispensing with the sour-mash method of distilling bourbon used by all its peers, and putting spirit in to the barrel at a much lower strength. But this is a beauty: crisp, clean, fruity and spicy, very drinkable; totally blemish-free.

Old Potrero 18th Century Style Whiskey
62.05% ABV
www.anchorbrewing.com

According to Anchor, single-malt rye made back in the eighteenth century used heated-oak-wood chips to heat the staves to bend them. The heat would have toasted but not charred the inside of the barrel. That's what is done with the barrels here.

This is another amazing and totally incomparable whiskey. A sort of Campbeltown nose with liquorice. The taste is bold and mouthcoating, with oily hickory, cloves and lots of peppery spice. I reckon this would not only numb toothache, but may go some way to curing it, too. The medicinal notes are balanced by anisette, treacle toffee and apricot.

Old Potrero Hotaling's Single Malt Whiskey 50% ABV
www.anchorbrewing.com

The great San Francisco earthquake of 1906 destroyed 28,000 buildings and claimed countless lives. Some religious leaders blamed the entire event on the city's wicked ways. Oddly, though a number of churches were destroyed, Hotaling's distillery survived, despite the fact that there were thousands of litres (gallons) of inflammable liquid on site.

Old Potrero is the whiskey wing of Anchor Brewing, the cutting-edge San Francisco brewery headed by brewing genius Fritz Maytag, and their intention is to recreate whiskey as it used to be. To do this they malt rye and use it as the only ingredient – a 100% single-malt rye. And this is, quite simply, incredible. The nose is spiky and pithy, with a touch of water kick-starting waves of aromatics. Taste-wise it has a peat-like intensity of earthy spices mixed with chocolate honeycomb followed by floral notes and then finishing off with some orange and lemon chews.

Old Potrero Single Malt Straight Rye Whiskey 45% ABV
www.anchorbrewing.com

Over time whiskey makers learned that if they left the oak chips to continue to burn the inside of the barrels, the charring would allow even more flavour into the whiskey. This, then, is Anchor's attempt to recreate that style.

It has an oily putty-ish nose, with some meaty almost kebab-like notes. On the palate it is like mixing Talisker with Jamaican fruitcake – a delightful mix of berry fruits in soft cake, plus sweet pepper. It is delicate, too, with aromatic and floral notes. A total delight.

ABOVE Corsair experiments with different grains and woods.
BELOW Unusual stills contribute to unusual spirit flavours.

CORSAIR

601 Merritt Avenue, Nashville, Tennessee 37203
www.corsairdistillery.com

Since 2010 the world has gone craft distilling mad. And with a huge craft-brewing industry already locked in, no country has embraced craft distilling as America has.

It has been something of a tsunami: knocking down state laws one state at a time, and opening up a world of new challenges, exciting new spirits products and innovative methods of production. No one knows how long it will last, or how many distillers will survive in business, but at the time of writing the number of American craft distillers was somewhere between 1500–2000 and counting.

In the United States, the whole scene is on fast forward. Unlike Europe, where spirit has to age in oak for a minimum of three years (often a lot longer), America has few restrictions. Bourbon can be called bourbon the minute the spirit touches the side of the barrel, though straight bourbon takes two years.

In Europe, whisky has three distinct stages: one, the opening of the distillery and the first run of spirit; two, the day after three years when the distillery can call its spirit whisky; and three, the day the distillery bottles its first expressions.

In the United States all sorts of weird and wonderful spirits are being marketed as whiskey, many very young, and some not very good. Distillers are running roughshod over the standard definitions of whiskey, calling whiskey matured in port casks 'bourbon' and making 'single-malt whiskey' from hopped beer, when in both cases they clearly are not. So it's not all good news. That said, though, what the likes of Corsair are doing makes for an incredible, dynamic and lively whiskey scene.

The distillery describes what it makes as 'Tennessee whiskey', but the duo who formed the business started distilling in Kentucky because their home forbade it. When Tennessee changed its distilling laws Corsair opened in Nashville and now has two sites there, and so, having kept the Kentucky site, has three in total. Therefore, although the company grew out of the craft industry, it has spread its wings rapidly and is reaching out internationally as well as domestically.

The other key aspect about the new wave of distillers is that they are learning as they go, and their whiskeys are growing up in public. Early runs may have been small and ordinary, but subsequent bottlings have made real progress. This is the case for Corsair. Its whiskeys are significantly better than they were in 2012 – and they weren't bad even then. Best of all for adventure-hungry whiskey drinkers, though, is the willingness of Corsair to experiment with unusual grains such as oats and quinoa. Throw in some ultra-cool Rat Pack/ gangster-style, black-and-white packaging and some quirky names (Oatrage or Ryemeggadon, anyone?) and you're looking at a smart, well-marketed and youth-friendly range of whiskeys.

The core range is listed here (see left) but the distillery also makes experimental and seasonal whiskeys – such as a version made with buckwheat – as well as making beers, absinthe, rum and gin. Corsair offers tours, tastings and classes at all three of its distilleries.

ABOVE Careful work: Corsair bottles at various strengths.

Pikesville Supreme 40% ABV
www.heaven-hill.com

While we tend to think of Kentucky as the centre of American whiskey production it was not always that way. Tennessee clearly has a strong whiskey tradition, but so did Virginia, Pennsylvania, Indiana, Idaho and Maryland. Pikesville is named after the last rye to be made in Maryland and is meant to be based on that recipe. Even so, it has been made in Kentucky for 30 years and is part of the Heaven Hill empire. This is clean and zesty, with apple and pear sours, some rich candy chew and spice.

Rittenhouse Rye 40% ABV
www.heaven-hill.com

Rittenhouse's time seems to have come. Once one of the few brands keeping the rye style alive when everyone seemed to have turned their backs on it, Rittenhouse has not only survived but also started picking up the very highest international awards. What makes it particularly special for me is the fact that the three most available expressions of it are so different from each other. This is probably the poorest of the three, but doesn't mean it is not a great whiskey. The 40% ABV means it works as a good entry-level rye, although it is quite piky.

Rittenhouse 100 Proof Bottled-in-Bond 50% ABV
www.heaven-hill.com

Arguably the best of the three bottlings on offer here, because fruit has a bigger say in the mix and when battering against the rye it makes for oral fireworks. This is complex because a fruit bowl of flavours make their case one by one. Impressive stuff.

Rittenhouse 23-year-old 50% ABV
www.heaven-hill.com

Rittenhouse is made by Heaven Hill in Louisville, Kentucky, but the name is a reference to a square and park in Philadelphia, a city once associated with quality rye. It was one of five original squares planned by city founder William Penn in the late seventeenth century, and today it is at the heart of the city's most expensive and exclusive neighbourhood. It attracts visitors because it offers some of the best fine-dining experiences in the city, as well as luxury retail shopping.

This is a monster: a dusty, damp, oaky and musty room with a treasure chest packed with colour and flair. You have to work your way through the woody and spicy intensity to unlock the delights within, but boy is it worth it. Ancient by American whisky standards but undoubtedly a wonderful world-class whiskey.

Sazerac Rye 45% ABV
www.buffalotrace.com

Sazerac Rye's big brother is the weighty 18-year-old, which is part of Buffalo Trace's Antique Collection and a super-star. A bit like having Muhammad Ali for a big brother. But this is no wimpy kid or Sazerac Lite – the mouthfeel is big and assertive, and there is lots of spice and oak. Not particularly complex and far less challenging than many others in this category, that is no bad thing. Very well balanced, too.

Sazerac 18-year-old Rye 45% ABV
www.buffalo-trace.com

This is a linebacker in a skirt. One of the truly great American whiskeys, this would seem to be almost overwhelmingly muscular and brawny in terms of oak, spice and deep dark fruit. But, it is also surprisingly feminine around the edges – almost floral and honeyed at the heart. The peppery notes are a delight, and weave in and out of the oak and fruit unpredictably, meaning every sip is an adventure in taste.

Templeton Rye 40% ABV
www.templetonrye.com

The makers of this are based in Chicago, but claim that this rye is made to the same recipe as one that a town in Iowa produced during Prohibition. Its owners claim that the rye the town produced was so good that it commanded premium prices on the black market and became the drink of choice of Al Capone himself. It was sold in speakeasies in Chicago, Des Moines and as far afield as San Francisco.

It's a good marketing pitch. This version has only been available since 2004 and is a bit of a curio – well-made and enjoyable, it is sweeter and less spicy than most ryes and has a distracting smoothness. Definitely worth seeking out because it stands apart from other ryes.

Thomas H Handy Sazerac Rye 2017 63.6% ABV
www.buffalo-trace.com

The Sazerac was invented by Antoine Peychaud, who made it at his pharmacy in New Orleans' French Quarter. Originally it was made with brandy, absinthe and a secret mix of bitters. It became popular and was copied across coffee shops in the city. But its whiskey link came courtesy of Thomas H Handy, who bought the Sazerac Coffeehouse and added rye whiskey instead of brandy. He would have been proud of this. It is big, bold and has more up and downs than a baby in a bouncer. There are boiled-candy fruits and jagged ryes battling against each other, oak and alcohol punching in and out then traces of nutmeg, tarragon, chilli and mint.

The Buffalo Trace Antique Collection has become so rare that all five expressions released every year are on location. In recent years Master of Malt has sold its stock of this through a dram lottery, a bottle lottery and auction, raising funds for its chosen charity, Malaria No More UK. Please note: on the back of the lottery bottles is added the message 'I, [your lucky winning name], hereby swear not to sell this bottle – but to drink it with my chums. May my tastebuds and olfactory bulb shrivel and die if I should break my word.'

WhistlePig 12-year-old Old World Cask Finish 43% ABV
whistlepigwhiskey.com

Whistlepig has built up a great reputation since it was formed in 2007. It has combined acute business acumen, a nose for a great whiskey and total transparency to bring Canadian rye to the market. The company was formed by Raj Peter Bhakta, to create an outstanding rye whiskey brand. He recruited the ubiquitous master distiller Dave Pickerell, and began sourcing top-quality, 100% rye whiskey from Canada. The whiskey is finished in Vermont, blended and bottled at the WhistlePig farm. The 'Old World Cask' is made of spirit from three casks – whiskey matured mainly in madeira wood, but with a proportion from Sauternes and a touch of port casks. The rye is brought in by Whistlepig, but the company is responsible for the make up: it's a fruity, winey delight, with an easy finish. It is now distilling so expect great things in the future.

Wild Turkey Russell's Reserve Rye 45% ABV
www.wildturkeybourbon.com

Six years old but surprisingly set at a slightly lower strength than the favoured 101, this is nevertheless another giant. There is some unexpected honey, nuttiness and mint in the mix, some distinctive woodiness and lots and lots of spice.

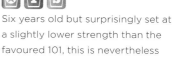

Wild Turkey 101 Rye 50.5% ABV
www.wildturkeybourbon.com

This the most bourbon-like rye on the market but is no worse for it. The trademark rye pepper is all present and correct but a wave of vanilla, liquorice and aniseed and some orange fruits make this rye easy and palatable. Bottled at Jimmy Russell's preferred 101 proof, there is enough weight and richness to make this worth seeking out.

Corn whiskey

Corn whiskey breaks all the rules when it comes to American whiskey production. It must include more than 80% corn, does not require ageing and if it is matured, the barrels must be either virgin oak or used – they cannot be new and charred or toasted as in bourbon production. This is the style of whiskey most normally associated with moonshine – and the marketeers do not shy away from this fact when they are considering such things as packaging and bottle labelling.

   Moonshine was produced on homemade stills and barely matured in casks – and the whole idea of drinking it young is part of the experience. That is at least partly due to the fact that corn makes for good sweet whiskey, like an alcoholic corn on the cob. If a drink genre ever reflected its culture it is this one – it is no-frills hillbilly whiskey and damn proud of its history and heritage.

ABOVE Corn is robust and gives us the bourbon base.

Balcones Baby Blue 46% ABV
www.balconesdistilling.com

Balcones is a heavyweight craft distillery in Texas and for some years now it has been hitting the ball out of the park with every release. The original Baby Blue was the distillery's first ever release and it was like a stroppy teenager: lots of attitude but a bit gangly, awkward and some way short of the finished article. Now, though, it's a firecracker, whiskey's answer to metal-band Stone Sour: big, butch and very left field. There's nothing like it, and if you like it, you'll love it. I love it.

Balcones Brimstone 53% ABV
www.balconesdistilling.com

And while we're in the realm of heavy metal, this is whiskey's answer to Marilyn Manson – a weird freak of a corn spirit that will offend as many as it impresses. Don't expect an easy ride. To get an idea of what to expect, grind a load of charcoal into a glass of American whiskey, scrape the burnt meat off the barbecue grill and mix that in, too, and drink. Sounds dreadful right? It's not. Not if you like Marilyn Manson.

Dixie Dew 50% ABV
www.heaven-hill.com

NASCAR racing is one of the biggest commercial draws in the United States, and it has its roots firmly entwined in the days of whiskey running. Cars would be converted to maximize storage space for moonshine, and the engines would be customized to ensure that if the law did try to catch up with the whiskey makers they could out-motor them and race to cross a state line where legal jurisdiction changed. Cue the long-running American television series *The Dukes of Hazzard*. Dixie Dew has a rough-gut youthfulness about it, some sweet liqueur notes and entertaining corn notes – corn on the cob in vodka, perhaps. An acquired taste and a basic one.

Georgia Moon 50% ABV
www.heaven-hill.com

The amateurish label, the jug-style packaging and the proud boast that maturation only took days should pre-warn you that this is going to be a cross-country motorbike ride, as rough around the edges as drinking whiskey gets. This is almost winey and vegetal, everything about it is short and sweet, and it's about as subtle as bare-knuckle boxing. Nonetheless, it feels and tastes pretty authentic.

Ironroot Hubris 58.9% ABV
www.ironrootrepublic.com

With its high strength, bewitching mesquite smoky notes and rich chocolate flavours, this isn't your typical corn whiskey. Spend some time with it and you'll learn to love it.

Hudson New York Corn 46% ABV
www.tuthilltown.com

New York Corn is smooth and sweet, and while lacking some of the bite and aggression of most Kentucky bourbon, is a pretty-good entry-level whiskey. The smart packaging has ensured a smooth passage for the whiskeys into some of New York's cooler bars, in turn bringing new drinkers to the bourbon category.

JW Corn 50% ABV
www.heaven-hill.com

Searching for rare corn whiskeys should be declared a sport. This one seems to have fallen off the map, but does turn up very occasionally. Older bottlings exist that contain 8-year-old whiskey, originally distilled in Indiana. More recently it's been bottled as a 4-year-old: sweet and much fruitier than Georgia Moon and with less oily corn notes. Almost certainly it is produced by Heaven Hill. JW refers to James Walsh & Co.

Mellow Corn 50% ABV
www.heaven-hill.com

If Georgia Moon comes across as a good impression of moonshine, this is at the other end of the spectrum. It is a soft, sweet and full corn whiskey, rounded and smooth, a gentle landing and green apples and treacle toffee on the palate. This is easy-drinking whiskey and tastes significantly softer than most bourbon.

Wheat whiskey

Wheat whiskey is made in the same way as bourbon, but the wheat content must account for at least 51% of the grist. Wheat is not a particularly common ingredient in bourbon, but it was what Bill Samuels Snr used to give Maker's Mark its softer, more female-friendly personality. Wheat whiskeys are also rare, but Heaven Hill has had significant success with Bernheim and some of the new generation of micro-distillers are turning to the style, most notably Dry Fly. The style is softer and sweeter than bourbon, more in keeping with a pure-grain whiskey.

ABOVE Wheat makes for a softer whiskey spirit.

Bernheim Original 45% ABV
www.heaven-hill.com

For many years, Heaven Hill stood apart in Kentucky as the lone producer of both wheat and corn whiskeys. But, now, as America wakes up to the potential of different whiskey styles, a new wave of both styles is upon us. Wheat whiskey is notoriously difficult to make. The grain is more delicate. But with careful handling, as this bottling shows, the results can be remarkably impressive. This is the American drinking equivalent of wrapping yourself in a soft-down duvet, a melt-in-the-mouth, orange-and-lemon sorbet, with a vanilla overcoat and honey and spice finale.

American single malt

American single malt isn't a contradiction in terms, but once upon a time it wasn't far off. Traditionally, American whiskey has been made with corn, wheat and rye, with a small amount of malted barley used as an enzyme.

There were one or two exceptions before the craft boom, but not many. Now, though, American single malt is building a new whiskey category as distillers distil barley as they do in Scotland, and then mature it as they would a bourbon – in new white oak. They're also getting very geeky about the type of barley they use!

Balcones Texas Single Malt 53% ABV
www.balconesdistilling.com

This is where American craft distilling comes of age. Balcones isn't the first American distillery to make single-malt whiskey, but it is the first to marry the malty grain notes with the candy, vanilla and oakiness associated with bourbon. This is big in every way, with baked apple, ripe pear and toasted oak. It's a single malt, Jim, but not as we know it...

Corsair Triple Smoke 40% ABV
www.corsairdistillery.com

Whiskey's answer to the Cadillac Three, a Tennessee trio bringing their individual magic to one place and maturing in to a truly great outfit. This whiskey has peated malt in the mix and nods to Scotland. But, it also has barley dried over beech and cherry wood, and is matured in new and charred American oak barrels. The result? A sweet, peat treat, with tobacco pouch, leather, vanilla, cherry.

McCarthy's Oregon Single Malt
47.5% ABV
www.clearcreekdistillery.com

If ever a distillery sounded like it was in Kentucky, it is this one. And if ever an American whiskey tasted less like bourbon, here it is.

This is a single malt that is a smoky monster, with engine oil, barbecued fish and a charriness on the nose. Taste-wise it is very sweet and rich in peat, but delightfully balanced by the grain. This is the drinking equivalent of American soccer – it appears to be very like the European game, but has been tweaked to give it a personality of its own.

Stranahan's Colorado Whiskey 47% ABV
www.stranhans.com

An unlikely alliance between a Colorado spirits connoisseur and a part-timer fireman who helped save his barn from burning down, Stranahan's is a single malt dressed in a Kentucky Colonel's finery. There's candy stick, vanilla, honeycomb, leather polish, spice and oak, but the whole mix has a barley malt heart. A bit like drinking very old grain whisky matured in bourbon casks – arguably providing the best of both worlds.

Wasmund's Rappahannock Single Malt 48% ABV
www.copperfox.biz

The Copper Fox distillery sits beneath the Blue Ridge Mountains of Virginia and distiller Rick Wasmund is on a mission. He learned his trade by spending some time working at Bowmore, but came back to America with a burning desire to use all he had learned and to take it to a new place. So, some of the malt here is dried over apple and cherry wood and it shows in the end product. Wasmund's is made barrel by barrel so there will be some variety in taste. Expect to pick up some oak and smoke, some unusual yellow fruit notes.

Westland American Oak 46% ABV
www.westlanddistillery.com

Westland has shot to the top of the chart of new wave American craft distillers faster than an Ed Sheeran single goes up the charts. The distillery seemed to come from nowhere – though its actual home is Seattle – and has already been swallowed by Remy Cointreau. This whiskey shows why. It is a classic example of the new style of American singe malt, adding bourbon characteristics such as vanilla and candy to a beautifully made malted barley spirit. Refreshingly different.

Westland Peated 46% ABV
www.westlanddistillery.com

This is the bridge between Scotch single-malt whisky and American single malts. Westland do peat extremely well. It has a number of special releases, and holds a Peat Reek Week each year. What we have is smoked vanilla ice cream, mixed with a fruit bowl that has been left too close to a smoky fire. Westland has discovered a unique flavour that is at once very smoky, nutty, minty and fruity.

Westland Sherry Wood 46% ABV
www.westlanddistillery.com

Amazingly, Westland has the biggest number of sherry casks in America, which gives you a sense of the scale of this distillery. This is matured in oloroso and Pedro Ximénez casks and is sweet, with red and black berries as well as some orange fruits. More 'me-too' than the other two single malts in the core range, but very well made even so.

Wood's High Mountain Tenderfoot Whiskey 45% ABV
woodsdistillery.com

There are a lot of clever things happening in American craft distilling, and while of it has still to make the grade, the innovation and experimentation can be incredible. It's normally assumed that a single-malt whisk(e)y is made with malted barley but it doesn't have to be. And grain can be malted, and as long as all the grains are malted, more than one grain type may be used. This is a single-malt whiskey because everything in it is malted and is from one distillery – the mashbill is made up of malted barley, malted rye and malted wheat. The resulting whiskey is all sugar and spice, with milk chocolate, honey, orange jelly and chilli. It ends a little like a cough sweet. Unusual and interesting.

Other American whiskey

Contrary to popular belief, bourbon doesn't have to be made in Kentucky, and nor is it the only style of whiskey made in America. For many years now a small number of distilleries have operated in other parts of the country making malt whiskey. Now a new generation of micro-distillers are experimenting with wood types, grains, special finishes, ground-breaking blends and hybrid products that mix production techniques from both single-malt whiskey and bourbon production. It is all reminiscent of what happened in America with beer a few years back, albeit slower and smaller. It would be impossible to cover them all here – some are producing on the tiniest of scales or intermittently, but this is a dynamic and exciting category all the same.

Charbay Hop Flavored Whiskey
64% ABV
www.charbay.com

Not strictly a whiskey at all because hops are used in the mashbill, giving a distinctive hoppy and floral aspect to the taste. But this warrants inclusion because it is one of several examples that shows where American micro-distillers might head – effectively creating new whiskey-infused drinks categories and potentially setting the world of whisky on fire. This is made in St Helena, California, and is big, bold and impressive.

Early Times 40% ABV
www.brown-forman.com

Another whiskey that is bending the distilling rules, Early Times is produced at Brown-Forman's Louisville distillery and disqualifies itself from being called bourbon because some of the spirit is matured in used barrels. The result is perfectly acceptable – a light, sweet vanilla ice cream with maplewood syrup and crushed nuts.

Angel's Envy Bourbon Finished in Port Casks 43.3% ABV
www.angelsenvy.com

Finished in port casks? Not bourbon then, no matter what this distillery might claim on its website. No matter though, because this is fine whiskey and a welcome addition to the American whiskey portfolio. Dark cherry and spices dominate the palate, but with a sweetness and traces of blackcurrant squash.

Edgefield Hogshead 46% ABV
www.mcmenamins.com

McMenamins is a hotel company in Oregon and prides itself on originality and authenticity. It has been brewing its own beer for 25 years now, making it an easy forerunner of the recent micro-brewery insurgency, and it now has an impressive 24 breweries producing 200 new recipes a year. It makes its own wine, roasts its own coffee and, as of 12 years ago, started distilling. This big soppy monster of a whiskey is proof that someone knows what they are doing. It is a toffee-rich and full-fruited single malt with a unique character and an unsubtle, uncompromising mouthfeel. Some honeycomb and wood enter the mix, too.

Catdaddy 40% ABV
www.catdaddymoonshine.com

Piedmont Distillers is based in Madison, North Carolina, and this is a triple-distilled flavoured moonshine. It is made by New Yorker Joseph Michalek who came to North Carolina and spotted an opportunity to reproduce the taste of some of the great illegal moonshine that was available at public events in the state. He won't say what spices and fruits are added to the mix, but technically this is somewhere between whiskey and flavoured vodka.

High West Campfire 46% ABV
www.highwest.com

High West has made its name not by distilling but by importing whiskey and mixing it into wonderful new shapes. Such producers are often criticized in the United States, but they are are just doing what Scottish independent bottlers do. This mixes bourbon, rye and peated Scottish single malt. This, then, is sweet breakfast marmalade, maple syrup cookies, raisins and spices, all smoked over, well yes, a campfire. Lovely.

New Holland Beer Barrel Bourbon
40% ABV
www.highwest.com

So not a bourbon then. This is made to a traditional bourbon mashbill and matured in virgin oak; so far so traditional. But, this is finished in barrels that contained stout, which is full-flavoured and full-bodied. There's a twist, too. The stout was made by New Holland and was matured in its bourbon barrels. The result is a very sweet whiskey, with milk chocolate, Crunchie bar, vanilla and sugar-coated corn flakes.

Rogue Dead Guy 40% ABV
www.rogue.com

Oregon-based Rogue is part of the new wave of great American beer makers and it makes some of the most exciting and tasty beers in the world, selling them in irreverent, almost punk-like, packaging.

Dead Guy was released by the company some years back to mark the Mexican Day of the Dead, and its rich flavours are the result of four different malts. This whiskey is distilled from that beer and is every bit as quirky. There is a delicious spiciness plus youthful fruitiness.

St George 43% ABV
www.stgeorgespirits.com

Made in Almeda, California, this is a single malt that so impressed a couple of members of my whisky club they made a detour while on holiday in the United States just to visit the distillery. St George is made in very small quantities and each batch differs from the next but it is distilled from a smoky brown ale, due to the barley being heavily roasted. Some malt is dried over alder and beech. The spirit is matured for three to five years mainly in bourbon casks, but also in French oak and port casks. It has been a while since I tasted it, but the batch I did was sweet, very fruity and quite complex with some cocoa, milk chocolate, toasted oak and a touch of mint on the finish.

Triple Eight Notch 44.4% ABV
www.ciscobrewers.com

Triple Eight distillery is part of Sisco Brewers on Nantucket Island, Massachusetts. The company makes a range of spirits and was at the vanguard of the micro-distilling revolution when it was formed in 1997.

The company's single-malt whiskey was created with the support of former Morrison Bowmore distilling consultant George McClements. The whiskey is finished in ex-Merlot casks – potentially risky – but the result is impressive, with soft tinned fruits and vanilla in the mix. It's been given the name 'Notch' because it's not Scotch. Geddit?

Whistlepig The Boss Hogg IV 59.6% ABV
www.whistlepigwhiskey.com

Subtitled The Black Prince 14-year-old, this takes its name from the English Black Prince, Edward of Woodstock, who enjoyed raising France and looting. Casks of armagnac were regularly brought back, and this 14-year-old rye whiskey is aged in armagnac casks. The length of maturation has softened the rye spice, but the casks lend date, apricot and sweet orange fruit to the overall flavour.

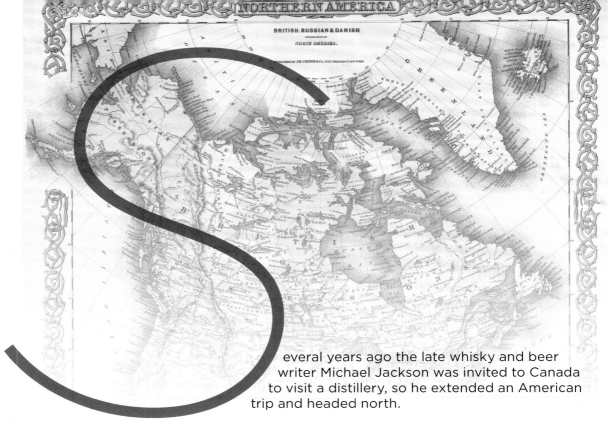

Several years ago the late whisky and beer writer Michael Jackson was invited to Canada to visit a distillery, so he extended an American trip and headed north.

But when he arrived at the Canadian border he was refused entry and quizzed about his reasons for entering the country.

'I'm a journalist and I want to write about a whisky distillery in Canada,' he announced.

Not good enough, he was told, to justify giving him an entry visa.

'Canada has journalists of its own,' he was told. 'Why would we let a foreign journalist come and do a job that a Canadian could do?'

Perhaps because an unbiased international whisky writer stating that Canada had great whisky to discover would have more authority in overseas whisky circles than if one of your own sang its praises, Michael pointed out.

In the end the Canadian authorities relented, but the story goes some way to explaining Canada's disjointed relationship with the rest of the world of whisky. To be fair, it has less to do with Canadian whisky and more to do with the over-officious and outdated protective nature of the country's authorities. Even so, Canadian whisky does not attempt to sell itself in the same way as Irish whiskey or bourbon does.

Or at least not in Europe, anyway. With Scotland dominating the world of whisky today, and Ireland providing it with much of its historical context, there is an assumption that other whisky markets should kow-tow to the 'old' markets. Not Canada. It has a proud whisky tradition of its own and knows which side its bread is buttered on – and that side is known as the United States.

Canadian whisky still sells by the ocean-load in the United States, and much of it is owned by international companies with large interests there. Beyond some key brands such as Canadian Club and Crown Royal, there is simply not that much of an incentive for Canadian brands to seek out markets elsewhere.

The American connection has helped define Canada's whisky. Although Canada is associated with rye, until quite recently whiskies from the country were nothing like the fierce, spicy and flavoursome American ryes that are exciting whisky enthusiasts across the world. Canada's whiskies have been lighter in style, easy-drinking, easy-mixing whiskies made through a complex process of combining many different whiskies, which are produced using an array of grains. Most Canadian whisky is blended, although there are a few grains and a notable exception at Glen Breton in Nova Scotia, where, unsurprisingly, the local folk look to Scotland's single-malt whisky for inspiration. The distillery achieved international fame (or notoriety depending on your point of view) when the SWA went to war with it and, in the eyes of many, made an ass of itself in the process (see right).

There are other reasons why Canada stands alone. Its liquor sales are controlled by the state, and its whisky-making industry, once characterized by hundreds of small distilleries, has in recent years been the story of drinks giants such as Diageo, Beam Suntory and Pernod Ricard. Some Canadian brands are owned by Kentucky bourbon producers, and some even include bourbon in their recipe, due to a somewhat bizarre law that permits a fraction of a Canadian blend to be made up with another fortified liquid or wine, which sometimes includes fruit juice or foreign whisky.

So it should come as no surprise that some parts of the Canadian whisky industry have an identity crisis and other bits appear complacent, satisfied and smug.

The final part of the picture, however, is made up by a growing number of innovators and trend setters within the country. Unfortunately, for many of us they are too small to make too much of a mark internationally, but they provide enough evidence that Canada as a whisky market is not finished quite yet. It just needs to get better at opening its doors to the world and telling us its story.

BELOW The Cabot Trail winds its way along the Gulf of St Lawrence at Cape Breton.

Canadian single malt

Glenora distllery is in Nova Scotia, and unsurprisingly, folks, they are proud of their links with Scotland. So when they decided to make malt whisky they imported Scottish barley Glen Breton and turned to Scotland for their stills. They have been producing whisky on and off for 20 years now, but it has been a bumpy journey. Lack of funds threatened to unseat them and they also attracted the ire of the SWA, which took umbrage at the words 'Glen' and 'Scotia' claiming the distillery was passing its whisky off as Scotch; its heavy-handed approach made few friends. Thankfully, the whisky is still flowing.

Glen Breton 10-year-old 43% ABV
www.glenoradistillery.com

The nose here is slightly doughy and oily, with a trace of orange and some honeyed sweetness. Taste-wise there is toffee and fruit and a gentle wave of prickly peat.

Comparisons with Scottish single malt are inevitable. This is slightly lower down the soccer league – more of a Hibs or Hearts than a Rangers or Celtic.

Canadian blended whisky

This dominant style of whisky is a combination of several different types of whisky, including a number of different rye recipes – often from the same distillery and mainly produced in column stills. Sometimes Kentucky bourbon is used in the mix.

Alberta Premium 40% ABV
www.beamsuntory.com

Complex, challenging whisky: orange, lemon, vanilla on the nose and a chewy toffee and rich fruit heart. Balanced, perfectly palatable, subtle and nuanced.

Alberta Springs 10-year-old 40% ABV
www.beamsuntory.com

If you have a sweet tooth then this is for you. A rye-dominated whisky, it's a perfect starting point to understand how different the Canadian version is to the American one. This is vanilla and caramel, with some pepper in the mix.

Canadian Club 6-year-old 40% ABV
www.canadianclub.com

This may well be the brand that caused the St Valentine's Day massacre, shipped in huge quantities by Al Capone from Canada to America during Prohibition. Undoubtedly it was established as a big player then and has maintained its position as one of the world's best-known whiskies. The whiskies are mixed after distillation and before maturation, and there are a number of expressions. This is oily and spirity with a fruity base; it does show its best and truest colours when mixed. Neat it's like chewing on olives.

Canadian Club Chairman's Select 40% ABV
www.canadianclub.com

Made with 100% rye, this is an Ed Sheeran whisky: a bit scuzzy, spicy and spiky, but ultimately aimed firmly at pleasing the masses. Everything is nicely balanced. Too nicely balanced.

Canadian Club Classic 40% ABV

Vanilla, yellow fruits and honey on the nose; raisin, berries, over-ripe banana and vanilla ice cream on the palate and icing sugar and cinnamon spice to top it all off. This is a real treat.

Canadian Mist 40% ABV
www.canadianmist.com

An oddball whisky from an oddball distillery that has achieved big sales in the United States. Made using corn and malted barley, it's then transported to Kentucky where it is mixed with a proportion of Kentucky rye. For what? A whisky that whispers, an innocuous, mild, sweet and fruity nothingness. Like any *X Factor* winner (with the exception of Leona Lewis); pleasant enough but easily forgotten.

Crown Royal 40% ABV
www.crownroyal.com

Now part of Diageo, this was created by Seagram's legendary drinks boss Sam Bronfman. It has a long and illustrious history – a thoroughbred blend, flowing with juicy grains, rich and delightful fruit and some stunning peppery notes. Unlike some of its national rivals it is not over-sweet either.

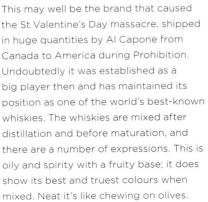

Crown Royal Special Reserve

40% ABV

www.crownroyal.com

It is hard to remain focused on the job in hand sometimes, and the mind wanders, especially when you are faced with some pretty ordinary whiskies that hand-on-heart you know will not make the cut. Before getting to this, for instance, I had three samples that will remain nameless, and while tasting them I found myself wondering what odds I'd get on Eddie Izzard becoming Britain's first transvestite prime minister. If you are reading this and wondering who on earth I am talking about, then that would suggest pretty good odds. If you are thinking he is just an oddball comedian and would never get elected as a politician, you're probably right. But, my reasonings are these: he is very intelligent, much-loved, has a social conscience and is debating standing as a Labour candidate in the future. He is an Internationalist and respectful of other cultures. I once took a French girl to see him on stage and such is the nature of his comedy that she spent the entire performance asking me to explain his jokes, so that being there was a waste of time for both of us. Weeks later she rang to say she went to see him again in Paris and he did the whole performance in French. And in 2010 he pulled off the almost-impossible feat of running 43 marathons in 51 days and raised more than £1 million for the UK's SportsAid – a quite awesome achievement made all the more so by the fact that he is chubby and he has bad feet from wearing high heels. This makes him a British national treasure. Yep, definite long-term prime minister potential I'd say. But perhaps I am just delirious after too much bad Canadian whisky.

Thank goodness we are back on track with this one, then – lots of fresh tropical fruits, traces of spice and rich, oily rye. Quite possibly my favourite Canadian whisky.

Forty Creek Barrel Select 40% ABV

www.fortycreekwhisky.com

The nose is young and spirity, not great, to be honest. Thankfully the taste picks up the pace, with an intriguing layered attack. On the surface it's as flat as a summer pond, underneath there are some grungier, meatier notes among the fruit.

Forty Creek Confederation Oak

40% ABV

www.fortycreekwhisky.com

A bold, winey, almost liqueur-like nose. It is rich, oily and you can taste a battle between the Canadian rye and the port and fruit influences. Almost chewy in its intensity, this one opens new doors for whisky from this part of the world.

Forty Creek Double Barrel Reserve 40% ABV

www.fortycreekwhisky.com

Soft, fruity and candied, with strawberry and sweet lime present early on, then a mix of fruits, some spice and some oil from the grain, as this complex whisky opens up. It is like going on the latest ride at the theme park, one that is like nothing that has gone before. But, whether you will like the experience or not is another matter. All credit to Forty Creek for daring to be different, though.

Seagram's 83 40% ABV

The number refers to 1883, the year the company was founded. This is a classic Canadian blend, with a sharp grainy core, some lemon notes and a rich and smooth taste that provides the perfect platform for mixers.

Wiser's Deluxe 40% ABV

www.jpwisers.com

One of the fruitiest whiskies to come out of Canada and one of the most pleasant: the oil-paint nose that characterizes a lot of Canadian whisky is a turn-off, but the soft grains, its honeycomb heart and attractive vanilla and oak alongside the rich fruits all work in this whisky's favour.

IRE
LAND

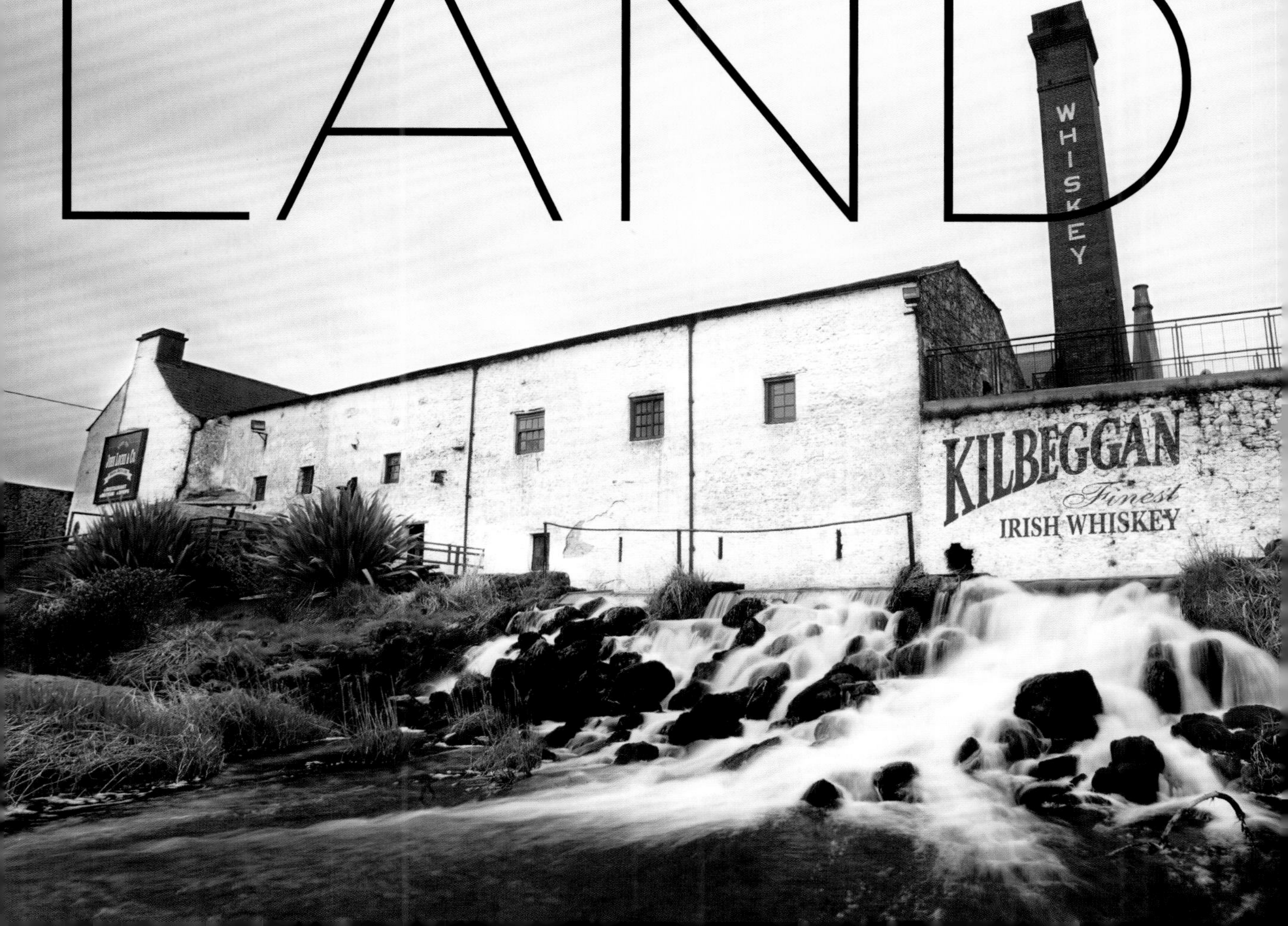

KILBEGGAN
Finest
IRISH WHISKEY

WHISKEY

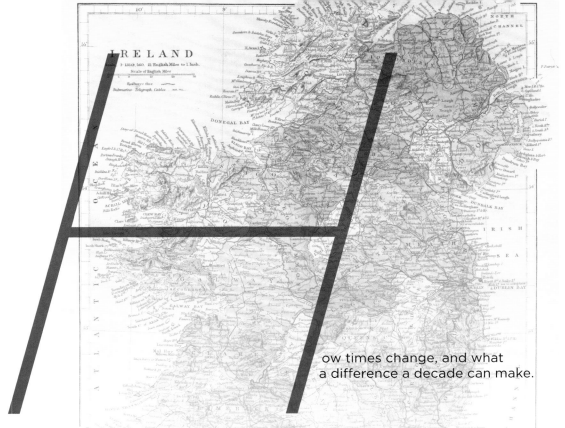

Aow times change, and what a difference a decade can make.

In the first decade of the new millennium the Irish whiskey industry was in the doldrums. Jameson was performing, but had all but maxed out; Bushmills was treading water. Maverick company, Cooley, was creating interest by messing with the standard Irish whiskey definition; there were a couple of independents, but little more. Globally the world of spirits has been turned on its head since then, and apart from the United States, no territory has undergone such a transformation.

There was a time not so long ago when you could visit whiskey distilleries in Ireland, but not ones actually producing any whiskey. At Midleton in Cork, it was possible to tour the huge disused distillery, and all but see and hear the ghosts of the workers who once produced spirit on the site, while in the background a new state-of-the-art distillery produced spirit behind closed doors. You could visit the old Jameson distillery in Dublin, an attractive enough museum, but without whiskey flowing through its veins; and at Tullamore and Kilbeggan you were transported to another more innocent time, when whiskey production was part of life on the Emerald Isle. And Ireland seemed incapable of pulling out of a production rut. It was

as if it had come to terms with being incapable of matching or surpassing the exciting Scottish single malts, and the increasingly confident whiskies of the rest of the world. But, today the world of Irish whiskey is transformed. John Teeling's independent Cooley has spawned an exciting and innovative exciting business run by his sons, Jack and Stephen. Teeling has now brought distilling back to Dublin, though it's not the only one doing so. Confidence is flowing through the country, and Dublin is home to a string of new whiskey distilleries. In fact, there are distilleries opening right across the country, both in the north and south of the island. Bernard Walsh has built a stunning plant in the heart of the Irish countryside, a new Tullamore distillery has been built by William Grant & Sons, and Beam Suntory has bought the Cooley distillery.

It will be some years until the new crop of whiskeys reach their ideal age, but a steady flow of new releases from the existing producers and the return of drinks giant Diageo to the Irish whiskey category has ensured Ireland is back in the whiskey spotlight. Moreover Dublin has reinvented itself as one of the world's greatest whiskey cities. Exciting times indeed for lovers of Irish whiskey.

PREVIOUS Let it flow: Kilbeggan is part of a distilling renaissance in Ireland.

ABOVE Cooley is now part of the Beam Suntory empire.

Irish single malt

Until the launch of Cooley a few years ago, Irish single-malt whiskey had become something of a novelty, a tradition kept alive at Bushmills, north of Belfast. But, Ireland once had scores of distilleries, many of them making whiskey using only malted barley. Cooley and now Teeling have resurrected some of the lost names and given Irish single-malt whiskey a new lease of life through award-winning single malts such as Connemara and Tyrconnell. A number of new craft distilleries have also started emulating some of the diversity found in Scotland.

ABOVE Irish single malt, just one of the new Irish styles.

Connemara 40% ABV
www.connemarawhiskey.com

Gentle smoke, twigs, dry leaves, then a heady mix of apple, fresh barley, green fruits, a touch of smoke. The peat and savoury notes get stronger and more noticeable towards the end.

Connemara 10-year-old Sherry Finish 46% ABV
www.connemarawhiskey.com

Early on it is like cooking a cob of corn on an open fire – you get rootsy embers and a musty flavour, but then, on the palate, peat and plum grapple with each other and sherried notes march through the middle. But, the peat wins out. Extraordinary.

Bushmills 10-year-old 40% ABV
www.bushmills.com

The first two decades of the twenty-first century have challeged this northern distillery. The company has changed owners twice, and seemed to be ignored. But, it has quietly gone about its business making exceptional whiskey, and its popularity has grown as a result. This is its flagship: summer fruits in a glass, orange, yellow, green fruit and honey on the nose, with sweet grape, red fruit and red apple on the palate before dark cocoa and pepper arrive to give shape. Definitive Irish whiskey.

Bushmills 16-year-old 40% ABV
www.bushmills.com

The extra few years in the cask give this expression an extra weightiness, with oak and spice adding an extra dimension to the malt. Beautifully crafted, and elegant on the palate.

The Irishman Single Malt 40% ABV
www.walshwhiskey.com

I was tasting this whiskey when the sad news came through of the death of Cranberries singer Dolores O'Riordan; The Irishman has some things in common with the band: sweet, pleasant and inoffensive on the surface, but with the hint of something more challenging underneath. This one's for Dolores, all tinned fruit and cream, with hints of spice and oak.

The Irishman Single Malt 12-year-old 43% ABV
www.walshwhiskey.com

Irish single malt is still rare, and a 12-year-old something of a curio. This starts off strolling through familiar apple, pear and peach territory, then body swerves off towards more savoury territory. Not quite spicy and oaky, it does offer something different. Lots of toffee and vanilla, too.

Teeling The Revival 46% ABV
www.teelingwhiskey.com

A 15-year-old malt released to mark the opening of Teeling's new distillery in Dublin, returning whiskey production to the city for the first time in 125 years. It's a beauty. Aged in rum casks – Teeling likes rum casks – the nose is fruity, with a zesty, sweet pineapple, citrus taste. Oak arrives late, to underline the fruitiness rather than suppress it.

Teeling Single Malt 46% ABV
www.teelingwhiskey.com

Single malt it may be, but it contains whiskeys matured in five different ex-wine casks. Grape and red berry on the nose, it's busy, complex and excellent on the palate. Yellow and green fruits, strawberry and raspberry and a healthy dollop of pepper and cinnamon spice. Fruity and stylish.

The Tyrconnell 10-year-old Madeira Cask 46% ABV
www.thetyrconnellwhiskey.com

Extraordinary, world-class whiskey by anybody's standards, with a wonderful mix of fresh exotic fruits, sweet lime and sherbety fruit on the nose; tinned fruits and jelly to taste; ice cream and pear dominate the finish – going on and on.

The Tyrconnell 10-year-old Port Cask 46% ABV
www.thetyrconnellwhiskey.com

Another one that reaches for the stars, but falls just a tad short of the Madeira Cask. This has some rum-and-raisin notes and richness from the port.

The Tyrconnell 10-year-old Sherry Cask 46% ABV
www.thetyrconnellwhiskey.com

Dusty, lemon-polished wood on the nose, then sherry fruits, red and blackberries and some wood. Pleasant and balanced, slightly directionless given the brand name's high quality standards.

The Tyrconnell 15-year-old Single Cask 1850/52
46% ABV

Sweet melon, yellow fruits, vanilla and clean grain on the nose, a dash of chewy spearmint, and then toffee apple. Later on you will encounter other green fruits with a bit of pepper on the finish.

The Tyrconnell 15-year-old Single Cask 957/92 46% ABV
www.thetyrconnellwhiskey.com

Lemon, bitter orange, melon on the nose; rich to taste with demerara sugar, sweet fruits, some wood, spice and nutty almonds. The finish is pleasant and medium-sweet.

The Wild Geese Single Malt 43% ABV
www.thewildgeesecollection.com

If you have ever been around a brewery or better still, a cider-maker's, you will know the unusual aroma that is a mix of yeast, malt and slightly stale ale. It is not unpleasant, just unusual, and you get it on this whiskey, at least initially. Then toffee takes over and there are some fresh apple notes. The taste is actually quite meek after the intro, but perfectly pleasant, with apple and pear and some spice.

ABOVE Bushmills is a popular tourist destination and is close to the Giant's Causeway.

BELOW And is kept in a pristine state at all times.

BUSHMILLS

2 Distillery Road, Bushmills, BT57 8XH
www.bushmills.com

They don't mask a big fuss at Bushmills. As other distilleries make a song and dance about what they're doing, the folk at Bushmills reflect the modesty of the community they work in, and just get on with making fine whiskey.

That hasn't always been easy, but despite the odds against it at times, the distillery has still thrived. You can't look at the history of a business in Northern Ireland without addressing religion and politics. The troubles did have an effect on it – Irish Distillers didn't take press parties to the distillery at times, for instance – and yet Bushmills joined the south-based Irish Distillers in 1972, when the war was at its most bloodiest. Years before the Good Friday agreement brought the conflict to an end and the border posts were removed, Bushmills was part of a united Ireland, at least in whiskey terms.

That said, at times it seems to have ploughed a lonely farrow. You wouldn't call it a forgotten distillery or whiskey brand, because only Jameson is better known in the Irish whiskey category in markets around the world. But it seems to be content to just go about its business – and given it has successfully been making whiskey for more than 400 years, that should come as no surprise. After all, why fix what's not broken?

When it was part of Irish Distillers it was owned by Pernod Ricard, who then sold it on to Diageo as part of a deal to allow the French company to buy some of Allied Domecq's distilleries when the company broke up. Diageo owned it for around ten years, investing in the distillery and expanding its production. Then, to the surprise of many and in a move still hard to explain, it gave the distillery to the company that makes José Cuervo for just over $400 million, plus full ownership of the Don Julio tequila brand.

Since then the distillery has proceeded as if nothing has happened, though it has benefitted from further expansion. It seems the distillery's latest owner, who also has hundreds of years of distilling experience, looks set to maintain a hands-off approach.

The distillery itself lies 97 km (60 miles) north of Belfast on the way to the stunning north of Northern Ireland coastline and right next to one of the great wonders of the world, the Giant's Causeway. It's a highly attractive distillery nestling in a quaint part of rural Ireland. It is very old world and oozing with charm, and as a result, its size is deceptive. The various expansions mean that Bushmills is now a heavyweight distillery. It has ten pot stills and is capable of making 4.5 million litres (1.2 million US gallons).

It's a highly impressive operation, and there is no cutting corners here. It's easy to forget that triple distillation means that fuel costs are 50% higher than most of the distillery's cousins over the sea to the east. It is not unheard of for the master distiller to start his working week spot-checking oil prices.

Bushmills is very well geared to accommodating visitors, and its tourist offering is as friendly and welcoming as you might expect. It offers guests a Bushmills Brand Experience, which encompasses guided tours around a working distillery, tutored whiskey tastings, a specialist whiskey shop and a gift shop with an extensive range of merchandise. There is also a restaurant serving lunches, and Bushmills inspired treats throughout the day. The Distillery Tour Centre is open seven days a week.

If the opportunity presents itself, an exploration of the warehouses is very worthwhile. Although most of the archive material of the distillery was lost in a fire, it's still possible to track casks going back many decades, and the distillery can also point to the fact that there is nothing new to finishing whiskey in casks that were previously used by strange and exotic drinks – it was buying wine casks from Europe in the nineteenth century.

The core range of Bushmills products has not changed and the bottle is still recognizable, even if the design has been tweaked. But, in late 2017 the first new expression for five years was launched. Red Bush is matured in first-fill, medium-char, ex-bourbon barrels.

Irish blended whiskey

Irish blended whiskey is the signature whiskey style from Ireland but it is a different drink entirely from the blends produced by Scotland. In Ireland a blend is a mix of pot still whiskey and grain whiskey, and unlike Scotland, the various whiskeys are blended before going into the cask for maturation. Irish blends were traditionally regional, so that in Dublin it was Guinness and Paddy, in Cork and the southwest, Murphys and Powers. The two main distilleries in the south, the mighty and massive Midleton, and the smaller but flexible Cooley, are complex in that they produce grain and malt whiskies and then blend them all under the same roof, using different combinations of pot still and column still whiskeys to make different brands.

ABOVE Irish blended whiskey may be matured for decades.

Bushmills Black Bush 40% ABV
www.bushmills.com

Black Bush is an old and iconic whiskey – a fine example of what the country is capable of when it comes to full-bodied, blended Irish whiskey. There is a mountain of fresh fruits in the taste, but juicy sultanas and a clutch of savoury and sweet spices ensure that this twists and turns in a delightful manner from start to finish.

Bushmills Original
40% ABV
www.bushmills.com

If Bushmills is a prize-fighter of a whiskey, this is the street equivalent, a bare-knuckle bruiser trained at Ryan's gym and as rough and ready as you would expect. You can almost see the tattoos. That said, the grain at the core is vintage Ireland, and it is good value for money. File with Powers and Paddy in the 'unreconstituted' section of the whiskey library...

The Irishman Founder's Reserve
40% ABV
www.walshwhiskey.com

About as Irish as a leprechaun performing River Dance. Contains 70% malt and 30% pot still whiskey, this has candy and fruit on the nose, and a taste of apple and pear with evaporated milk.

Jameson 40% ABV
www.jamesonwhiskey.com

Currently a world trailblazer, burning a path for Ireland into new and exciting territories, as the world once more realizes that Ireland can produce world-class whiskey. This may be a standard and ubiquitous whiskey but do not let familiarity breed contempt – it is a beauty. All the rounded fruit content is there and present, but there are some luscious red berry notes from the sherry, some oiliness from the pot still whiskey and some spices and oak. This is the work of distillers at the very peak of their craft – and a total delight.

Jameson Crested 40% ABV
www.jamesonwhiskey.com

This is rebranded Jameson Crested Ten, and is the standard Jameson's elder brother. It has relatively high sherry-cask-matured, pot still whiskey. The resulting whiskey is a lively, fresh and spicy, with vanilla and honey in abundance. Very pleasant.

Jameson 12-year-old
Special Reserve 40% ABV
www.jamesonwhiskey.com

The years in wood give this a richer and fuller sherry content than the standard bottling, there is more pepper and spice, and a noticeable and delightful toasted oak content.

Jameson 18-year-old
Gold Reserve 40% ABV
www.jamesonwhiskey.com

For many years Jameson employed a man named John Ryan as a brand ambassador. His approach to promoting Irish whiskey to journalists was simple – don't force it on them, or try to market it. Just give them a wonderful Irish experience that happens to include whiskey and they will naturally fall in love with it. Some years ago we were put up at a hotel near Cork, where it was required to wear suit and tie for dinner. John Ryan was so appalled by the entertainment that he decided to take us to a 'real' pub in Cork. Before he went in he told us that we should leave when he told us to. So, we walked through the door in suits and ties and the pub fell silent and a group of leather-jacketed youths just stared at us. It turns out that we had gone into a staunchly Republican pub. Ryan orders a bottle of Jameson, produces an acoustic guitar and heads off to a back room where he proceeds to regale us with IRA and Republican songs. He offers the bottle round the bar and within minutes the regulars have joined our table for a whiskey and some rousing versions of songs about freeing Ireland and beating the Brits. He insists on ordering another bottle and then challenges we English to sing a song. There is only one volunteer, with a weak version of 'Ilkley Moor Bah't 'at' to the general amusement among our hosts. After more IRA songs, Ryan announces we are leaving. The locals insist their new Brit friends stay, but Ryan is adamant. So, to loud applause, pats on backs and shakes of hand we leave. That is whiskey for you. Another wonderful example of aged Jameson, with the green fruit flavours mingling with oak, spice and some quite delicious sweet honeycomb. Some red berries, too, all held together by the rich oiliness provided by the pot still whiskey. Outstanding.

Jameson Rarest
Vintage Reserve 46% ABV
www.jamesonwhiskey.com

Irish Distillers brought journalists from around the world for a hoolie to launch this most special of Irish whiskeys. They put us up in a new hotel near Cork that was so big it took 20 minutes to walk to your room. This made the round trip 40 minutes:

and that is my excuse for taking the decision in the early hours to ensure I did not miss an early morning plane departure by sleeping in the bar. The party included an exclusive concert by the amazing Sinead O'Connor who not only performed a surprisingly hit-friendly set, but sat on my table. Watching her sing 'Nothing Compares 2U' in a small venue while drinking this whiskey is up there with my best memories. The whiskey is stupendous, made with the finest and very old whiskeys and with a price tag to match. But it is the fruitiest, tastiest, oiliest, spiciest and fullest Irish whiskey you will ever taste. Best of all, its strength has been boosted from 40% to 46% ABV, giving it muscle power to compete with the top whiskies of Scotland, Japan and America.

Jameson Select Reserve
Black Barrel 40% ABV
www.jamesonwhiskey.com

Taking all the worldwide quality and balance of the standard bottle, this adds a big dollop of pot still whiskey, providing plummy, rich fruits to the mix. They may have upped the effects of oak, too, for extra depth. Brand fans will love it, and pot still whiskey fans will appreciate a full and affordable blend.

Kilbeggan 40% ABV
www.kilbeggandistillery.com

A value-for-money whiskey that puts up quite a showing. Cereal notes and fresh barley, but plenty of green fruit and the odd hint of lemon on the finish.

Kilbeggan 15-year-old 40% ABV
www.kilbeggandistillery.com

The man behind Cooley, which makes this whiskey, is not a natural whiskey maker – he made his money in, among other things, mining. He is just a little crazy and opened Cooley in 1987 because he thought it would be fun. One of his crazier ideas was to get Kilbeggan up and running again,

but in 2007 he did just that. Kilbeggan sits on the main route from Dublin to the west coast, and when the economy was booming, Friday nights through the region were one long traffic jam, as affluent Dubliners headed off to their boats. So, imagine their outrage when they found the road blocked by a pot still. Cooley brought traffic to a standstill for hours as they tried to put new stills in place. But whiskey is being produced again at the site. If it matures as well as this has, it will be worth waiting for. This has cereal, honey and rich oak notes as well as the trademark fruit.

Lambay Small Batch Blend 40% ABV
www.lambaywhiskey.com

Lambay is the name of a small island just off the coast of Dublin and this whiskey is a collaboration between Alexander Baring, who comes from the island, and Cyril Camus, who is part of the Camus family, which makes world-renowned cognac. This whiskey is finished in Camus cognac casks and is rich, rounded, bursting with grape and sweet berry.

The Irish whiskey market is filling up and there are no doubt plenty of releases trying to jump on a bandwagon. This isn't one of them. With style aplenty, it's well worth exploring.

Locke's 8-year-old 40% ABV
www.kilbeggandistillingcompany.com

If you have a sweet tooth then this should be for you. It is a solid, chunky, honey monster of a whiskey, with a pleasant and balanced mix of malt and grain.

Paddy Old Irish 40% ABV
www.paddy.ie

This is included here because Paddy is in the memory banks, a throwback to a quieter, more naive Ireland, when every village had at least one pub: like someone's living room, where you were made to feel completely at home. Every one of those pubs had an old

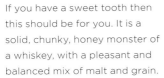

boy nursing a pint of stout and a whiskey chaser, studying the racing form. Give him the chance and he would tell you amazing stories from his past and offer sound advice. Paddy was that old boy. I am sure pubs like this still exist in Ireland but there have been huge changes over the last 30 years. As a brand this is going nowhere and it is an acquired taste – but it is a taste of history, an everyday blend with some pleasant pot still-induced moments, a straight-ahead maltiness mostly, and then a twist of pepper to finish.

Powers 12-year-old 40% ABV
www.powerswhiskey.com

A blend dominated by rich, mouthfilling, oily, grainy, pulsating, pot still whiskey – another traditional, classic Irish whiskey. But, this is relevant in the way that a big old Triumph Bonneville bike is relevant, powered on the twin engines of hard, solid grain and the pot still whiskey. Big, rich, fluffy, green fruit and a sharp and incisive wave of spice. Like Paddy, Powers is associated with a bygone era, of a rural Ireland where time passes slowly and men gather in village pubs to discuss the racing and sip whiskey and water. That's going now, but it may be that the tide has turned for the brand. Powers John's Lane was one of the pot still whiskeys that re-ignited an interest in the historic style, and perhaps expressions like this one will be rediscovered, too.

Powers Gold Label 40% ABV
www.powerswhiskey.com

There is an argument that with some whiskeys, particularly peat ones, years in the cask integrates the flavour but dulls the impact – a bit like when you add curry powder to meat. While young, all you get from the curry is chilli-burn and only over time does the spice become integrated and balanced. Thing is, if you like a big chilli hit, younger is best. This is what has happened here. It is much mellower, smoother and rounded than the original version, so that the oily pot still and pepper spice is more balanced and pleasant, but nowhere near the roller-coaster ride. Better than standard Powers? Debatable. I'm a raw chilli man myself.

Roe & Co 45% ABV
www.diageo.com

Roe & Co marks the return of Diageo to the Irish whiskey market, having sold Bushmills some years ago. This whiskey is a blend of single malt and grain whiskey and is as smooth and slick as a Craig David gig, sweet vanilla and tinned pears making for an easy, lush and satisfying whiskey experience.

Teeling Small Batch 46% ABV
www.teelingwhiskey.com

A blended whiskey with a high malt content and matured in ex-rum casks. The result is a slightly unusual but thoroughly enjoyable style with dark fruit and liquorice, plenty of spice and a creamy, rich mouthfeel. Smooth and sweet, too. The alcohol content is higher than most Irish blends and it gives the whiskey a welcome and warming kick.

Tullamore Dew 10-year-old 40% ABV
www.tullamoredew.com

A mainstream Jameson-like blend, with apple and pear fruits, nice grain and pot still notes and polite levels of oak and spice. It is perfectly drinkable and well put together.

The Wild Geese Fourth Centennial 43% ABV
www.thewildgeesecollection.com

To make the point about 400 years of hurt, this is a special bottling that is light, honeyed and rounded. It is slight and delicate, a tad fey, but if you look carefully, all the classic Irish whiskey traits are here – fruit, vanilla, oily grain and malt all make a showing.

The Wild Geese Rare Irish 43% ABV
www.thewildgeesecollection.com

The Wild Geese refers to the huge number of people who have left Ireland over the last four centuries to build Irish communities around the world. Whiskey is a relatively recent addition to the Irish offering and has been effectively designed to service what is perceived to be a demand for premium whiskey. It is made at Cooley for an independent company, and although the brand doesn't have much provenance, it is extremely well made. A great interplay between grain and malt, some fierce, shard-like, spicy notes and some hints of honey, lime and oak.

Writers' Tears Cask Strength 53% ABV
www.walshwhiskey.com

Bang! Everything an Irish whiskey should be, with the sweet green fruits and vanilla accompanied here by something altogether more tropical. Spices and some oaky tannins appear late on, and there are some orangey notes in the mix, too. Taste it while listening to Thin Lizzy's greatest hits and it'll have you dancing in the moonlight.

Writers' Tears Copper Pot 40% ABV
www.walshwhiskey.com

The word 'blend' is both much maligned and much misunderstood. It's just not true, when talking about Scotch, that blended whisky can't be very good. Most commonly known Irish whiskey is blended, but of pot still whiskey and grain whiskey. And then we get one such as this, where the mix is of malt whiskey and pot still whiskey. This is excellent, the pot still oils giving a depth to the sweet green fruits and vanilla ice cream. Far too easy to drink though.

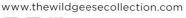 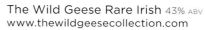  

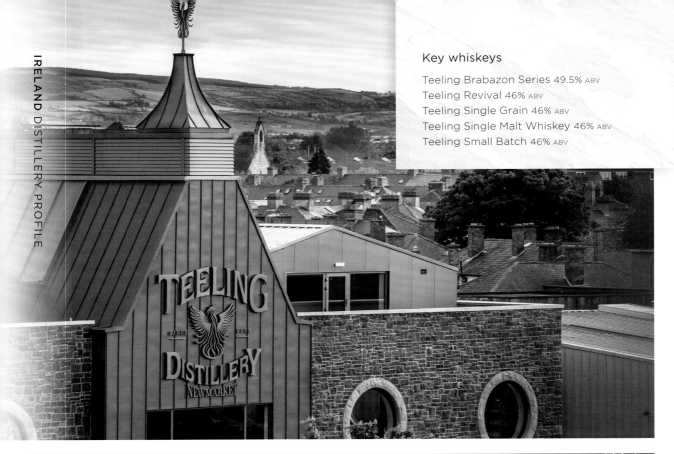

Key whiskeys

Teeling Brabazon Series 49.5% ABV
Teeling Revival 46% ABV
Teeling Single Grain 46% ABV
Teeling Single Malt Whiskey 46% ABV
Teeling Small Batch 46% ABV

ABOVE The exterior of the Teeling distillery.
BELOW Teeling calls itself The Spirit of Dublin.

TEELING

13–17 Newmarket, Dublin 8
www.teelingwhiskey.com

The current boom in Irish whiskey is part of a global move to craft distilling, but it also has a great deal to do with the Teeling family.

Ireland's once mighty whiskey industry had been reduced to just a handful of distilleries by the 1960s, and they grouped together to form what is now known as Irish Distillers. There were just two distilleries in production, Midleton near Cork producing pot still and grain whiskey in the south, Bushmills making single malt in the north. And in an understandable bid to differ itself from Scotland, Irish whiskey defined itself as unpeated, triple-distilled, mainly blended whiskey bottled at 40% ABV.

But, businessman John Teeling was to change all that. Looking for a new and exciting business, he turned to whiskey, opening Cooley distillery, a former industrial fuel plant on the Cooley Peninsula, and resurrecting some of the great Irish names of the past, Kilbeggan, Tyrconnell, Locke's and Connemara among them. Accompanied by his sons, Jack and Stephen, he ignored conventional Irish whiskey wisdom and launched peated whiskeys, whiskeys matured in unusual cask types and whiskeys at cask strength.

Wherever Irish Distillers opened a door, Cooley followed, offering international markets a diverse range of Irish options, so much so that eventually Irish Distillers responded by launching a range of new and exciting pot still whiskeys. Suddenly Ireland was interesting again. Perhaps inevitably, Cooley was sold to Beam Suntory as the global producers sought a route in to the Irish market. That wasn't the end of the story, though. Jack and Stephen left to form Teeling Whiskey, and with the whiskey nouse of head distiller Alex Chasko, they have been creating challenging and exciting whiskeys ever since, using stock bought from Cooley. A small amount is also being distilled at Kilbeggan, Ireland's oldest licensed distillery. The distillery is a tourist attraction, but a small still has been installed. Its approach to whiskey was to target Dublin, promoting itself as the spirit of Dublin, and supporting local events in the city. That claim became much stronger when the company built a distillery in the city and brought whiskey production back to it for the first time in 125 years.

You'll find it in the Liberties area of the city. In recent decades it had become a neglected part of the city, so Teeling's decision to move there was greeted with enthusiasm, and the area has started to enjoy a resurgence since, driven greatly by whiskey. It is now home to The Liberties and Pearse Lyons distilleries, Diageo has converted an old Guinness power house into Roe & Co distillery. And there is a whiskey trail, linking these distilleries and some smaller craft projects with the Whiskey Museum in Grafton Street, The Dingle Whiskey Bar nearby, and iconic bars such as McCanns. The distillery itself is a fully functional pot still distillery producing up to 500,000 litres (132,086 US gallons) of spirit each year. It's small and compact, but offers tours and has a small visitor centre and shop.

While Teeling waits for its stocks to mature it continues to provide first-class whiskeys. The distillery's flagship release is Teeling Small Batch, a flavourful blend, and the distillery also offers a single-grain whiskey matured in red wine casks. It also offers a range of more unusual whiskeys, including a regular series of malts, which are no-age-statement, but which the distillery says include malt distilled in 1991. Each one is a vatting of five different wine cask (sherry, port, madeira, white burgundy, Cabernet Sauvignon) finished Irish malt whiskeys. Teeling also caters for the premium end of the market with The Brabazon Bottling series, a limited-edition collection of unique Irish single malts capturing the full impact and flavour crafted through fortified-wine cask maturation.

With so many new distilleries at the earliest stages of production, the Dublin, and indeed Irish, whiskey story looks set to go from strength to strength. Whiskey is flowing through the city again, and new festivals and tourist offerings are giving fresh colour to what has always been an exciting and fun destination. Whatever happens though, and no matter how many distilleries come on board, Dublin will always hold Teeling in a special place in its heart.

Irish pot still whiskey

You would think it does exactly what it says on the tin – or more accurately, copper – but you would be wrong. Indeed it sounds like a bad joke: when is a pot still whiskey not a pot still whiskey? When it is made just in a pot still.

If ever there was a territory that needs to sort out its definitions, it is Ireland – and thanks to the formation of the Irish Whiskey Association (IWA) that's exactly what it has done. The problem comes from the fact that there are some who have claimed that if an Irish whiskey is distilled in a pot still it's a pot still whiskey. This is not only wrong, but hugely damaging to the Irish whiskey category. After all, that would mean that all Scottish single malt is pot still whisky.

Pot still whiskey is a style unique to Ireland, and contains a mix of malted barley and another grain, often unmalted barley, in the initial grist. This is then mashed, fermented and distilled in a pot still and makes for a rich, oily whiskey.

Method and Madness Pot Still 46% ABV
www.methodandmadnesswhiskey.com

The IWA is supporting new, exciting whiskey, like this one. It spends time in bourbon and sherry casks and is finished in French chestnut. A firework: Christmas cake from the sherry, tropical fruit from the bourbon cask, a musty creaminess from the chestnut and all-spice from all over. Amazing.

Redbreast 12-year-old 40% ABV
www.redbreastwhiskey.com

Redbreast is another classic, a marvellous example of rich, full, tasty pot still whiskey, with the grains and oils coating the mouth and refusing to let up. The spices dance, sherry bobs in and out, the oily pot still whiskey bursts out for a solo spot from time to time, liquorice and coffee have cameos and on it goes. This is the whiskey equivalent of Take That's 'Circus' tour – so much going on you have to try it all again. Awesome.

Barry Crockett Legacy 46% ABV
www.midletonveryrare.com

Named after the former Irish Distillers master distiller, this was first released in 2011 to kick-start a series of pot still releases from Irish Distillers. Unusually, it contains spirit matured in ex-bourbon casks and American new oak casks. The result is candy stick and vanilla in a crowd of spice, peach, apricot, honey and a subtle oiliness. Sophisticated, stylish.

Redbreast 12-year-old Cask Strength 58.6% ABV
www.redbreastwhiskey.com

One of the world's very greatest, the oral equivalent of being fired at with a confetti gun. Green fruit, rye spice, raisins, milk chocolate, sherry trifle and oaky oiliness all attack in glorious haphazard fashion. Utterly irresistible.

Green Spot 40% ABV
www.spotwhiskey.com

For years Green Spot kept the pot still category alive, along with Redbreast 12-year-old. Someone clearly understood the importance of this uniquely Irish drink. The name refers to the colour coding used to indicate the cask age. Easy-going and fresh; summer fruits, honey and a slightly scuzzy undertone. Classic stuff.

Redbreast 15-year-old 46% ABV
www.redbreastwhiskey.com

A limited edition, weighing in at 46% ABV and with a solid 15 years behind it. The nose has a grungy, tough, sulphury note to it at first, but this is merely a bit of macho posturing and a statement of intent. Give it a couple of minutes and it goes, like early morning mist, giving way to warming sunlight. The nose is fresh, clean, floral and fruity all at once, but the magic lies in the taste. Crisp red apples, under-ripe pears, some citrus notes and pepper form the centre of the taste and then something wipes everything to the side to leave a long fruity and spicy finale.

Redbreast 21-year-old
46% ABV

Intriguing, older addition to the Redbreast range, and while it's recognizably part of the family, it differs to the younger expressions. The spices in particular are more subdued, a touch of menthol/rancio give it extra depth, richness. The oiliness is spot on, and the fruit notes are tangy and satisfying.

Redbreast Lustau 46% ABV
www.redbreastwhiskey.com

The move from 40% to 46% ABV by Irish Distillers is welcome; the higher strength unleashes another layer of tastiness. This is a bit of a monster, but some of the subtler notes in the 12-year-old are submerged here. Redbreast normally consists of sherry casks with some bourbon casks, too. A collaboration between Midleton distillery and Bodegas Lustau; the

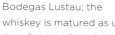

whiskey is matured as usual for 9–12 years, then finished for a further year in selected sherry butts. Berry fruits, dark chocolate and Battenberg cake dominate the taste.

Yellow Spot 46% ABV
www.spotwhiskey.com

If you've got a sweet tooth, then you may well love this. In addition to sherry and bourbon cask pot still whiskey, this contains whiskey matured in casks that formerly contained sweet malaga wine. Grain and grape are to the fore, too, and there are some delightful apple notes.

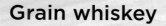

Grain whiskey

As is the case in Scotland, the term 'grain whiskey' in Ireland tends to refer to whiskey that is made with a grain other than malted barley, and in Ireland it is also taken to be a category distinct from pot still whiskey. There are plenty of people who believe that this style of whisky has great potential and is underrated. Irish and Scottish grain whisky are very similar and although Ireland doesn't produce much of it, Greenore has picked up awards around the world and is a leading player in the category.

Grain whiskey is most often produced in a continuous still as opposed to a copper pot still. Quality casks play a major role in the development of good grain whiskey and Greenore has achieved its success by double-distilling then maturing its grain whiskey in bourbon casks for at least eight years.

Greenore 15-year-old 43% ABV
www.kilbeggandistillingcompany.com

Elegant, rich, sweet, chewy, this is proof that grain on its own can still make a significant, impactful whiskey. This won the award for World's Best Grain in the 2010 World Whisky Awards, no wonder. It will never have great depths, but an interesting interplay between sugar and spice, a great sweet-grain core and woody notes stop it all becoming too cloying at the end.

Teeling Single Grain 46% ABV
www.teelingwhiskey.com

Irish grain whiskey is the elixir of the gods. This is the Van Morrison of whiskey: soulful, smooth, credible, complex and accomplished. This being Teeling, there's a twist: it is matured in Californian Cabernet Sauvignon casks, so under the smooth, sweet surface there is honey, strawberry jam, kiwi fruit. More please.

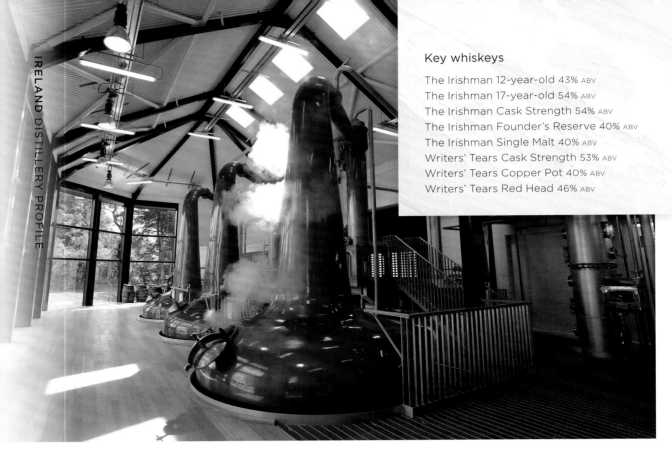

Key whiskeys

The Irishman 12-year-old 43% ABV
The Irishman 17-year-old 54% ABV
The Irishman Cask Strength 54% ABV
The Irishman Founder's Reserve 40% ABV
The Irishman Single Malt 40% ABV
Writers' Tears Cask Strength 53% ABV
Writers' Tears Copper Pot 40% ABV
Writers' Tears Red Head 46% ABV

ABOVE The lovely new still room at Walsh.
BELOW The Walsh distillery is designed to blend in with the local countryside.

WALSH

Royal Oak, Clorusk Lower, Carlow
www.walshwhiskey.com

These are heady days for Irish whiskey. Already the fastest growing premium spirit in the world, it is enjoying a resurgence that looks set to go from strength to strength.

A few short years ago there were just three operating Irish distilleries. In the coming years that number will hit 35, no doubt with more to follow. Those new distilleries are bringing tourists from across the world to the island of Ireland. Tourism in Ireland is in a good place, but whiskey tourism is doing even better, with substantial year on year rises. And with new Dublin and Irish whiskey festivals, and plans for official Irish whiskey trails, whiskey is back at the heart of the island's tourism offering, both north and south. Dublin is, of course, at the centre of the whiskey boom. Travel out of the city, though, and you can find pretty distilleries where whiskey spirit is sedately slumbering among the farm animals and the crops of rural Ireland. One such distillery is Royal Oak in County Carlow where, not to put too fine a point on it, Bernard and Rosemary Walsh are living out their dream.

Their story starts in 1999, when they set up a company to blend and bottle the perfect Irish coffee, after Rosemary had worked in a French ski chalet and served guests Irish coffee each evening. In 2005, the couple launched an Irish cream liqueur, and two years later, having signed a long-term supply agreement with Irish Distillers for the distilling and laying down of Irish whiskey stock to their specifications, they released The Irishman Single Malt, and The Irishman 70, a mix of 70% single malt and 30% pot still whiskey, an innovative and unusual combination that took Irish whiskey away from the standard Irish blended whiskey. Walsh whiskey was to move further into new territory with the creation of Writers' Tears, which is another pot still and single malt mix, and the launch of cask strength versions of both expressions. Both brands are highly respected and continue to win awards, most recently in 2018 winning gold medals and the title of Irish Distiller of The Year in The Wizards of Whisky World Whisky Awards.

Given that sort of history, a distillery was the logical next step, and it would have been odd if the Walshs weren't involved with the distilling revolution. Royal Oak Distillery was built after the Walshs agreed a €25million strategic partnership with Italian company Illva Saronno, which is owned and run by the Reina family and is renowned for its Disaronno liqueur. The idyllic site was purchased specifically, and work on a dedicated whiskey distillery, warehouses and a visitor centre started in 2014. The distillery combines tradition with modernity, its design deliberately empathetic to the rural environment it is part of, but with a distinctly twenty-first century feel about it. You can tell from everyone you meet there that they are revelling in their good fortune.

There's something else to note here, too. Whiskey is creating jobs in rural Ireland, and pumping money back in to the local economy. About 5000 people are employed directly or indirectly because of Irish whiskey, and that number is set to double by 2025. And there are spin offs for the countryside, too. Take Holloden House, the majestic eighteenth-century home on the Royal Oak estate for instance. It had fallen in to disrepair but the Walshs are in a long-term and highly expensive bid to renovate it.

Walsh is no micro-distillery. It has the capacity to produce 2.5 million litres (660,430 US gallons) of pure alcohol or eight million bottles of whiskey annually. The giant pot stills weigh between four and five tonnes (eight to ten pounds) each and scale up to 6.5 metres (21 feet) in height. The largest of the pot stills has a capacity of 15,000 litres (3963 US gallons). In all there is almost 30 tonnes (60,000 pounds) of copper and steel whiskey-distilling equipment installed at Royal Oak. The distillery is very rare for being manually controlled and producing all three styles of Irish whiskey in one still house, namely: pot still, malt and grain.

It'll be a while before we see mature spirit from the distillery, but, in the meantime, Bernard Walsh and his team continue to innovate and excite whiskey lovers, eg. Writers' Tears Red Head is aged whiskey matured in specially elected oloroso casks. As Irish whiskey evolves, Walsh is set to be in the vanguard. The next stage of a fabulous journey is underway.

NIKKA WHISKY

SINGLE MALT
MIYAGIKYO

宮城峡

宮城峡蒸溜所シングルモルト
仙台 宮城峡蒸溜所でつくられたモルト原酒

PRODUCED BY THE NIKKA WHISKY
DISTILLING CO.,LTD.,JAPAN

ウイスキー

THE
HAKUSHU
SINGLE MALT
WHISKY

AGED 12 YEARS

白
州

HAKUSHU DISTILLTILLERY

HIBIKI

SUNTORY WHISKY

JAPANESE HARMONY

A meticulous blend of select finest whiskies

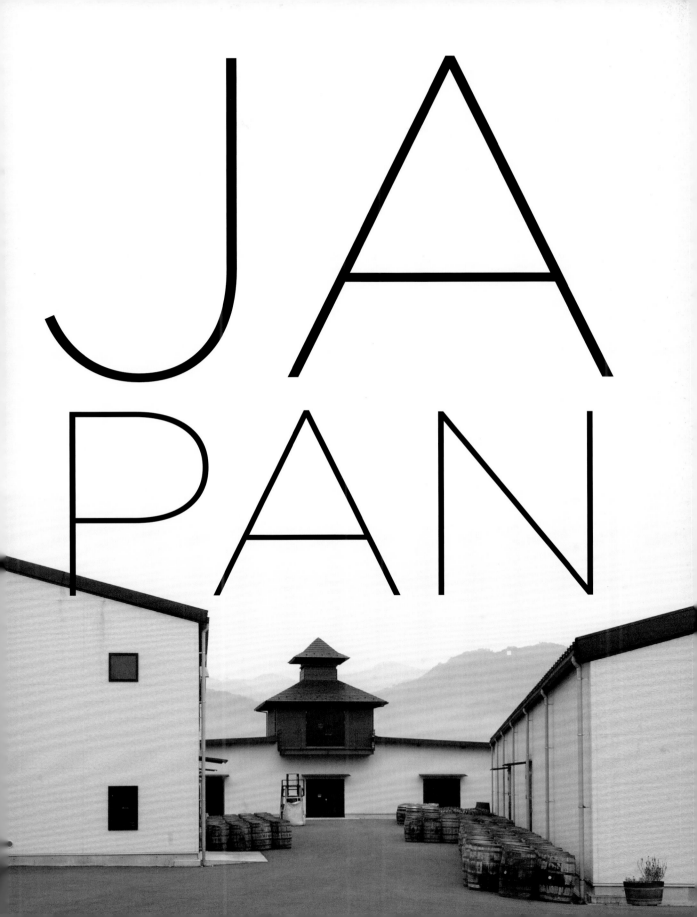

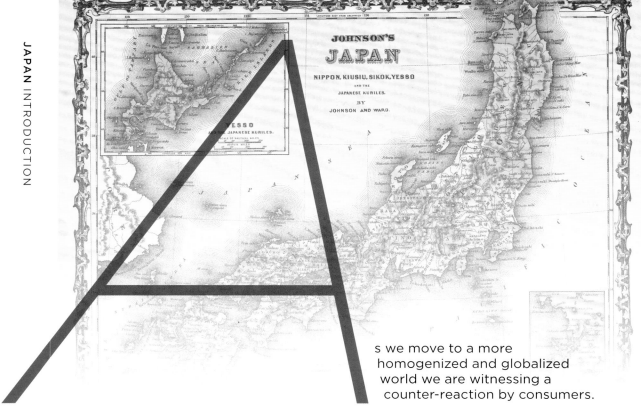

As we move to a more homogenized and globalized world we are witnessing a counter-reaction by consumers.

We have grown sick of travelling halfway round the world to a remote tribal village in darkest Peru only to find Carlsberg, Guinness and Bacardi on sale in the ramshackle bar.

Increasingly we are now seeking out products with a serious heritage and a traceabale provenance, drinks with a proper story to tell and a unique way of telling it. All this is very good news indeed for single-malt whisky, which has provenance and heritage by the bucket load.

But woe betide any drinks company that dresses its brands in the false clothing of heritage and provenance. When the public discover they are looking at a Top Man suit and not an Armani one, they will be uncompromising in their rejection of it. Craft 'distillers' that pretend they make spirit but buy it in from a huge commercial distillery, please take note. American owners of Canadian brands containing small amounts of American bourbon should pay heed.

Historically Japan's two biggest whisky-making companies, Nikka and Suntory (now part of Beam Suntory), have been criticized, too, for their approach to making some of their blended whiskies, which have sometimes included a significant proportion of Scotch whisky. In the future, as people take a greater interest in what they are drinking and where it comes from, they will take a dim view of hybrid brands with no meaningful story to tell.

Japan's problem in this area is created by the fact that the country has relatively few distilleries and a work culture that pretty much rejects the concept of cooperating with rival companies. The best blends contain a large number of different whiskies and in Scotland producers pool their resources to everyone's benefit.

They do not do that in Japan, so they only have two options: to create a number of different styles of whisky in each distillery, or to buy in whisky from other countries. Both options are in play.

Thankfully, no such problem exists with the country's single malts, and it seems that the word about how good the country's malts are is well and truly out. For some years now whisky writers have written glowingly about them, and they have scooped a clutch of major awards. But, growth has been relatively slow, partially because supply has been patchy. In the decade between 2008 and 2018 both Nikka and Beam Suntory have struggled to meet demand, and many world distillers have

PREVIOUS Most of Japan's distilleries are sited in pretty rural locations. This is Chichibu, just north of Tokyo.

been able to fill the gap for exotic whisky from unusual territories.

In recent years both companies have introduced no-age-statement whiskies to meet the demand, and both have moved away from their rarer and older whiskies, which have become incredibly expensive. In the case of Nikka, the aged bottles have stopped being produced altogether because the company faced running out of stock altogether.

Beam Suntory and Nikka have long dominated the market for Japanese whisky, but in recent years there has been smattering of other companies producing Japanese whisky. Mars Shinshu and Chichibu Number One Drinks Company is bringing new whisky to the attention of enthusiasts around the world.

Traditionally, Japanese whiskies have emulated the single malts of Scotland and are closer in style to them than the whiskeys of Ireland, the United States and Canada. But, in recent years they have increasingly developed their own style and character, and many have distinctive mushroomy-fungal notes. It sounds odd and may require a taste recalibration, but it adds distinctive and attractive characteristics to the whisky in the same way that the savoury and arguably discordant flavours contribute to the overall taste of olives or blue cheese. Most importantly for Japan, its whiskies are growing in popularity and people are buying in to their provenance, history and heritage. As drinkers continue to explore further afield, it all augurs well for Eastern whisky.

ABOVE Sampling maturing spirit at Yamazaki.

Japanese single malt

The Japanese have done with single malt what they have done with cars – taken the model, stripped it down, worked out how to make it and rebuilt it, not only matching much of the competition in the process, but surpassing it. Japan does not pretend it looked any further than Scotland for its whisky inspiration, its two biggest companies, Suntory and Nikka, were both effectively set up by an individual who learned his trade in the Scottish Highlands. Japan has been making malt whisky for a long time now but widespread critical acclaim and a clutch of awards suggests it has passed Canada and is now giving Ireland a run for its money as whisky's third most important market.

Chichibu IPA Cask Finish 57.5% ABV

Chichibu is bringing innovation and originality to Japanese whisky. This is one of many unusual malts from the craft distillery. Honey and citrus at its core, the beer barrel expresses in two ways: on the palate, the hops bitterness is discernible and the characteristic IPA grapefruit battles its way through late on.

Chichibu On The Way

55.5% ABV

Released in 2015, this is a mix of whiskies made by the fledgling distillery since it opened in 2008. It has fluffy apple and sweet pear on the palate, there are some delicate Japanese-style spices and a touch of oak. It's young, but those with high hopes for Chichibu will be delighted by this. It has a sweet, malty heart and it positively purrs.

ABOVE & OPPOSITE Reused casks are integral at Ichiro and include American, Japanese, French and Spanish oak examples.
BELOW New casks used in the distilling process are made from American oak and Japanese Mizunara oak.

CHICHIBU

49 Midorigaoka, Chichibu, Saitama

In a country where the whisky industry is so totally dominated by two companies, Chichibu is a rarity – an independent and free-spirited whisky maker, taking an individual approach to the industry.

The distillery was created by Ichiro Akutu, whose family has been making sake in Chichibu since 1625, and his grandfather, who represented the nineteenth generation of the family in the drinks business, built the Hanyu distillery in 1941. When his family's business ran into problems at the start of the new millennium, Ichiro saw it as his duty to pick up the baton and run with it.

'We sold the business, including the Hanyu distillery, at that time,' he says. 'But the new owner was only interested in quick business and had no desire to continue maturing whisky. I rescued the last four-hundred casks from the distillery before they were re-distilled. Whisky is in my blood.'

Having made the step into the whisky business, Ichiro set about doing things a little bit differently. He bought up remaining stocks of Hanyu and the closed Karuizawa and sold them off for considerable amounts of money. It was his idea to name the Hanyu stock after playing cards, with the higher value cards representing the oldest whisky stocks. A gimmick? Not at all, he says.

'When I visited bars in Japan I was struck by how difficult it is to remember the years and the numbers of single casks on the bottles,' he says. 'I wanted to find something distinctive that would look good on the back of the bar, but would also be easier to remember. That's when the card series came to me.'

Selling existing stocks of whisky is one thing, making it is another. But Ichiro has successfully gone down that route, too. He built a new distillery at Chichibu and the first fruits of his labours – young malt spirit, fledgling single malts and single-malt-and-grain whiskies – have been released to critical acclaim. Among the standard ex-sherry and ex-bourbon casks are some made with Japanese oak, and Japanese barley is also being used.

'Ultimately I want our whisky to be uniquely Japanese,' he says. 'Chichibu distillery is very small and I want the whisky to be handmade. I would like all my experience, and that of my ancestors, to be appreciated in each bottle from Chichibu. I have carefully studied every aspect of the whisky-making process at first hand. As well as working at Hanyu I have distilled spirit at Karuizawa and at BenRiach, and I want this to show.

'The intention is to release six casks from Chichibu annually, three for the domestic market and three for export,' he says. 'It's a small operation, but when I travel and see many people enjoying whisky it fills me with hope. I see young people enjoying whisky and I am pleased that Japanese whisky is being recognized. It makes me optimistic about the future.'

Chichibu The Peated

(BOTTLED IN 2013) AROUND 55% ABV

Young, single and free... well, not free exactly, quite expensive in fact. And that's if you can find it. If you can, don't miss out on what is a citrus-soaked, peaty, smoky delight. It growls like a dog protecting a bone, positively kicking off in your mouth. The fact it's only three years old means it has a zingy exuberance from start to finish. A confident, arrogant almost, statement of intent.

Fuji Gotemba 15-year-old 43% ABV

A strange nose that is part dry-shredded-wheat, part doughball. The taste is sweet and clean, with honey on vanilla ice cream and escalating mouthfeel before a wave of sweet spices and some oaky notes arrive later.

The Hakushu 10-year-old 40% ABV
www.suntory.com

Sometimes you taste a whisky and you taste a colour. A lot of Japanese whiskies are russet or autumnal brown. This one, though, is spring-like and green, with a wonderful crispness to it. Imagine pear crumble and custard followed by toffee apples. The palate has some earthiness underneath and is like an Irish Connemara whiskey.

The Hakushu 12-year-old 43% ABV
www.suntory.com

This has a very unusual and complex nose, with freshly cut leaves, clean and chewy barley, some citrusy notes and a touch of peat. The peat is noticeable on the palate but is not dominant. Among the fruits are some pleasant liquorice notes. All in all a little gem.

The Hakushu 18-year-old 43% ABV
www.suntory.com

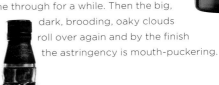

For many this whisky will be a step too far. Right from the first aromas – polished church pews, sawdust and some smoke – you can tell what is coming and it does. But, before that, it is like the sun making a brief appearance on a cloudy day, as bright apple and pear flavours and some enticing and tantalizing sherbety notes shine through for a while. Then the big, dark, brooding, oaky clouds roll over again and by the finish the astringency is mouth-puckering.

The Hakushu 25-year-old 43% ABV
www.suntory.com

This doesn't even try to compete with the oaky intensity of the 18-year-old. A big sherry trifle of a whisky, it seems as though a large dollop of fruity jam has pushed the wood back to the fringes. Oak is still there, and pepper and spice.

The Hakushu Distiller's Reserve 43% ABV
www.suntory.com

The no-age-statement by Beam Suntory to represent the distillery; while some no-age-statements represent a dumbing down of the distillery's character, this is a fine example of what Hakushu is all about. Both light and heavily peated malt is used: a smoky whisky, with clean and complex green fruit notes. Very good indeed.

Hanyu Single Cask 1991 57.3% ABV

By Japanese standards this has a surprisingly delicate and floral flavour, with sweet toffee and citrus notes on the nose and a big mouthfeel, with intense fruits and spices working their way through, and some menthol and liquorice notes. A fairly long, sweet, spicy finish.

Hanyu 1988 55.6% ABV

If you have ever heard Deep Purple performing 'Highway Star' on the band's live masterpiece 'Made In Japan' you will have a good idea of what to expect here. No messing, everything turned up to 11 and bang! we're off... This is the full-aged sherry shooting gallery, with wave after wave of power-chord marmalade up front, a wicked solo from dark cocoa and a pulsating spice and oak rhythm section.

Hokuto 12-year-old 40% ABV
www.suntory.com

The whisky equivalent of one of those disturbing television thrillers that you can't quite decide if you're enjoying or not, but can't bring yourself to turn off. Curious and unusual, with stewed fruits, oak and some dusty wood shavings on the nose, rose-petal water and sherbet on the palate, a stewed-prune heart, with pepper and oak late on. Long and spicy.

Ichiro Malt Eight of Hearts
56.8% ABV

Finished in an oloroso sherry butt, this looks like it should have a bark and a bite to go with its bold colouring. The nose is all dusty-old headmaster's office, but the taste is surprisingly fresh and jolly, with pepper, ginger, nutmeg and cinnamon all making an appearance and some juicy currants in the finale.

Karuizawa 17-year-old 59.5% ABV
www.karuizawawhisky.com

Stewed apples filled with mincemeat on the nose, with some nuttiness and dry sherry notes. But, it is a complex and evolving nose, and after a while it becomes zesty and sherbety. The whisky has a big, full flavour, but is nonetheless surprisingly gentle and rounded, with a nice balance, the right amount of oak and spice, plus lots of soft fruits, almost like a cordial. Long and warming.

Karuizawa 1986 Single Cask 60.7% ABV
www.karuizawawhisky.com

At first this whisky has damp, rootsy, fungal notes, with celery and truffles. With time, lemon and grapefruit appear; the refreshing citrus extends to the palate, which is a lot less grungy than the nose suggested. It has a big, rich mouthfeel with orange barley in the mix and a chewy, barley-note finish.

Karuizawa 1985 Single Cask
60% ABV
www.karuizawawhisky.com

A big, rich, autumn woodland of a nose, with musty mushroom, rich prune fruits and oak. But, nothing quite prepares you for the intense, fruity taste of this big whisky: plum, prune juice, intense red fruits and oak. With water, added sherry comes to the fore. A rich, sherried finish – Japan's answer to Scotland's A'bunadh for sure.

Miyagikyo 10-year-old 45% ABV
www.nikka.com

A poor start and dull nose, but this kicks into life on the palate with an intense dual between sweet fresh fruit and savoury spices. The fruit just about wins it.

Miyagikyo
12-year-old 45% ABV
www.nikka.com

Gooseberry, rhubarb and cocoa on the nose, then the softest and sweetest of starts when you taste it. Don't be fooled, though, because pretty quickly a razor-blade wave of sharp spiciness arrives and takes you through to a peppery conclusion.

ABOVE Harsh winter conditions are good for maturation at Nikka.

BELOW Natural beauty: Nikka's Miyagikyo distillery.

NIKKA

Kurokawacho 7–6, Yoichimachi, Yoichigun, Hokkaido
www.nikka.com

When Nikka announced in 2015 that it was discontinuing its range of aged whiskies it came as a shock.

Everyone knew that huge demand had put stocks under pressure. But Nikka announced that things had become so bad that it had to make a radical decision to avoid running out of whisky and going out of business altogether. It had been going so well, too. Less than five years earlier Nikka's Naofumi Kamiguchi had talked confidently about the future for his company's whiskies.

'Yes, we're going to be rocking all over the world,' he said. 'The sales of Nikka outside Japan are now starting. The first reaction is superb, we're confident it can spread further in the future.'

But, the optimistic outlook was misplaced for the craziest of reasons: the whiskies of Nikka and Suntory had been TOO successful. The growth in interest in Japanese whisky from 2005 had been phenomenal, the number of whiskies finding their way to all parts of the world was growing apace, and most importantly of all, the quality was mind-blowingly high. Tasting the extensive and diverse Japanese whiskies back then was a true delight – and no other country could boast such a consistent and uniformly high standard across the board.

Nikka is Japan's second largest whisky maker, but is dwarfed by Beam Suntory. It was founded in 1934 by Masataka Taketsuru, the same man who brought whisky-making skills to Suntory ten years before. Taketsuru learned his trade in Scotland and had a vision for Japanese whisky. He set up the country's first distillery in 1924, but ten years later found what he considered an even more perfect site for a distillery. To build Yoichi on Hokkaido he had to set up his own business, and so the company that was to become Nikka was formed. A second distillery, Miyagikyo, was built in 1969.

Although widely accepted and increasingly praised by the whisky-loving community, Japanese whisky is still a relatively small part of the overall whisky market. Its progress is on hold for now, but both the leading companies are seeking to address the shortage issues now.

'In three years the sales of Nikka exploded in France,' Naofumi Kamiguchi said. 'The whisky's reputation had grown across Europe and the sales were coming. Our friend Suntory is investing aggressively in its expansion, and in that sense Nikka is the follower. But we're proud of the quality of our whisky and in our opinion it is unique. We think, for instance, that our distinctive coal-fired distillation at Yoichi is helping us to make the best whisky in the world.'

Although modelled on the whiskies of Scotland, what excited whisky enthusiasts the most about Japan is the way that its malt were evolving and were heading off in their own direction. Japanese whiskies are designed to be consumed with food, and with that comes a distinctly Japanese way of drinking. *Mizuwari*-style means adding ice and water to dilute the whisky as a long drink – and this may become increasingly popular as understanding of Japanese whisky grows.

The distillers of Japan are a clever bunch, so they'll be working to pick up where they left off. Interest remains high, and there's unfinished business here. Japanese whisky, and the malts from Nikka will certainly be in the front line again some time soon.

'Our main issue will be making sure younger people drink whisky,' said Naofumi, before the stock issue took over. 'We have to recruit a new generation for the future, but we can do that. Certainly we are keeping up the high tradition of whisky making while never forgetting the need for innovation and improvement.'

That was then, and nothing's changed. Quality will out, no matter if it takes a while.

WELL, FANCY THAT...
Nikka founder Masataka Taketsuru and his wife are buried at the pretty Yoichi distillery, and after a daily television show about them in 2014 and 2015, tourist numbers have flourished.

Miyagikyo 15-year-old 45% ABV
www.nikka.com

Aromas of Christmas cake, dried fruit and sweet spices here, while the taste is mouthcoating, with plummy fruits, raisins and a pleasant malty core.

Miyagikyo Single Cask 1989 61% ABV
www.nikka.com

Just when you think you have got Nikka's Miyagikyo sussed, it throws up a curveball, as with this one. You expect sweet, easy-going fruity whiskies; what you get is a big, chubby, unbalanced but utterly intriguing and exciting whisky. A very pleasant surprise.

Miyagikyo Single Malt 45% ABV
www.nikka.com

Nikka's no-age-statement whisky will be the standard bearer for the distillery from now on. Elegant, floral and full-flavoured this has ginger stem and Malteser-like maltiness, traces of liquorice and spring meadow. Rich and complex.

Nikka Single Cask Malt 1991 58% ABV
www.nikka.com

The combination of a huge demand for quality Japanese whisky and the fact that Nikka has stopped producing all but a couple of core whiskies, encouraging enthusiasts to buy up everything they can, means finding a single-cask Nikka is all but impossible. But, a number of those enthusiasts run bars and proudly display stunning collections of the very rarest styles. You can find these bottlings if you look hard enough. A light, breezy whisky, this has candy, vanilla, banana and toffee on the nose; sweet fruit soda and blackcurrant Starburst to taste. A clean and sweet finish, with a touch of spice.

The Yamazaki 10-year-old 40% ABV
www.theyamazaki.jp

Surprisingly complex for what is effectively the distillery's standard flag-bearer. Sweet spice, fluffy apples on the nose; fresh, sweet lemon, melon, apple to taste. A clean, fresh, easy-drinking delight.

The Yamazaki 12-year-old 43% ABV
www.theyamazaki.jp

Starts with aromas of polished wood and pine then opens out with summer fruits on the nose. This marches into the mouth and occupies it. Luscious; as juicy as whisky gets: redcurrant, raspberry, blueberry, blackcurrant smoothie mixed with alcohol. The fruity finish is long and very warming.

The Yamazaki 18-year-old 43% ABV
www.theyamazaki.jp

I tasted this while staying at Center Parcs: it seemed totally appropriate, because the aroma is like damp leaves and an early morning forest stroll. Juicy raisin on the nose and lots of sherry and wood, dark chocolate, rum and raisin to taste. Astounding. Lurking under the surface are some meaty, grungy notes, probably from sulphur, but this only adds to the fun and festivities of this whisky. With a few thoroughbred whiskies in this Japanese section – and more than one from here – arguably this is the pick of the bunch.

The Yamazaki 25-year-old 43% ABV
www.theyamazaki.jp

    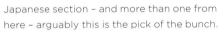 

Like a stately and imposing, dusty-old office. Full, rich sherry, raisins and berries, some dustiness and mustiness and a trace of mushroom. The taste is rich and mouthfilling, with plum chutney and orange rind. The finish is long and fruity, with a nice balance of oak and spice.

The Yamazaki Distiller's Reserve 43% ABV
www.theyamazaki.jp

Yamazaki is Beam Suntory's main distillery in Japan. This no-age-statement was introduced to represent it while aged stocks have all but disappeared. The sherry casks are obvious through lashings of red autumn fruits. A distinctly Japanese influence from delicate spice and a touch of oak. Beautifully made.

Yoichi 43% ABV
www.nikka.com

Nikka's no-age-statement malt is light and easy: sweet lemon and orange up front, apple and pear at the core and a mote, savoury, earthy finish. There's some peat in the mix, too. Solid.

Yoichi 10-year-old 43% ABV
www.nikka.com

We live in safe times. Nobody dare have an opinion on anything for fear of losing their job or being reprimanded. Which is why the 2010, live album 'White Stripes' is so important – it sounds like it might fall apart at any moment but never does, making for a thrilling ride. This is the whisky equivalent: the sherry, toffee, peat and vanilla should not work together at all, but they just about do.

Yoichi 12-year-old 45% ABV
www.nikka.com

Another intriguing mix of sherry and peat, though the sherry is by far the senior partner, with dried fruits and sultanas very much to the fore. There are also some vanilla and candy flavours here, too, and a rich sweetness, making for an outstanding, complex malt.

Japanese blended whisky

Japan has a long and proud tradition of making quality blended whisky, even though it has had to face considerable hurdles to do so. It makes blends in pretty much the same way as the Scottish whisky industry does – by taking a number of matured malts and mixing them with grain whisky before bottling. This is a bigger ask than it is in Scotland because there simply aren't the number of different malts to choose between. As a result, Japanese whisky producers have developed complex distilleries where several yeasts and recipes are used to create a range of different malts under one roof. Certainly the country is now producing world-class blends. Like other Japanese whiskies the country's blends are not shy when it comes to big, rich and full flavours.

ABOVE The Yamazaki whisky, made the Scottish way.

Akashi Red 40% ABV

There's an air of mystery about some of Japan's whiskies. Japanese producers keep their cards close to their chests and don't reveal more than they have to. We know that this is made at Eigashima or White Oak distillery, but after that, all bets are off. Still, it's a pleasant enough whisky, delicate, light and sweet, with grape and yellow fruits.

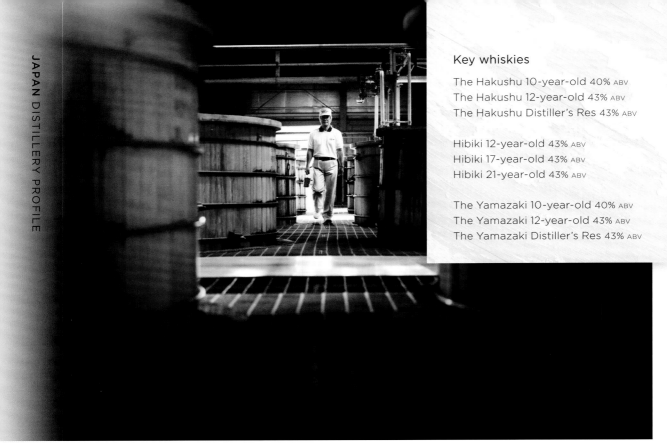

Key whiskies

The Hakushu 10-year-old 40% ABV
The Hakushu 12-year-old 43% ABV
The Hakushu Distiller's Res 43% ABV

Hibiki 12-year-old 43% ABV
Hibiki 17-year-old 43% ABV
Hibiki 21-year-old 43% ABV

The Yamazaki 10-year-old 40% ABV
The Yamazaki 12-year-old 43% ABV
The Yamazaki Distiller's Res 43% ABV

ABOVE The Suntory distillery, built in 1923, sits in the vale of Yamazaki and was the first malt whisky distillery in Japan.
BELOW Copper stills are used to create a superior Suntory. The distillery process is similar to that of Scotland.

SUNTORY

5-2-1 Yamazaki, Shimamoto-cho, Mishima-gun, Osaka
www.theyamazaki.jp
www.suntory.com

When Suntory's Dr Koichi Inatomi speaks about his company and the whiskies it makes, he does so with pride.

Dr Inatomi is something of a whisky legend. He's responsible for creating some of Suntory's finest whiskies, including the Hibiki range. Hibiki 21-year-old was awarded the title of world's best blended whisky in the prestigious 2010 World Whisky Awards and has won many awards since.

Now retired Dr Inatomi stayed on as a brand ambassador for Suntory's The Yamazaki and The Hakushu single malts and its Hibiki blends, becoming the perfect spokesman for a company that has not only put Japanese whisky on the map but has established it as a major and growing force in world whisky. He was added to *Whisky Magazine*'s Hall of Fame in 2016, the first way to sign off an amazing career. He's proud of the part Suntory made in the growth of Japanese whisky.

'These are very good days for Japanese whisky,' he says. 'It has made huge progress.'

But, there have been some big changes in recent years. Huge demand has sent the price of aged whiskies soaring, many expressions have all but disappeared, and Suntory itself is now part of Beam Suntory, currently a huge global player.

Japanese whisky might still be relatively new in many international markets, but it has a history stretching back to the 1920s and Suntory goes back even further than that.

'The company was formed by Shinjiro Torii as a wine-importing business,' explains Dr Inatomi. 'The name is taken from Torii and the symbol of the sun, which is very important to Japanese culture. Then in 1907 he launched a sweet wine called Akadama and it became very successful. The company still makes it. It provided the money to allow him to build Japan's first whisky distillery, Yamazaki.'

To help him make fine-quality whisky Shinjiro Torii turned to Masataka Taketsuru, who had spent some years in Scotland perfecting the techniques of distilling whisky. The rest, as they say, is history. Today, Beam Suntory has two distilleries, producing very different malt whiskies – Yamazaki between Kyoto and Osaka, from where both Yamazaki and the Hibiki blends emanate; and Hakushu, a giant and complex distillery that produces The Hakushu range.

Suntory's whiskies were hugely successful in Japan and remain very popular with, in particular, older Japanese drinkers. But one of the whisky world's greatest ironies is that while the rest of the world has caught on to the high quality of Japanese malt, younger Japanese drinkers have fallen in love with Scotch single malt.

'But this is often the way,' says Dr Inatomi. 'Younger drinkers in the bars of Glasgow don't often drink Scotch single malt. But one of the jobs we have to do is win over the next generation.'

In the meantime, Beam Suntory is putting time and effort in to bringing its whiskies to new territories, and it has done so with two no-age-statement whiskies. There were raised eyebrows when the decision was made to launch them, but they have ensured that Yamazaki and Hakushu can still be found on whisky shelves across the world.

'It does make me very proud,' says Inatomi. 'I have seen Suntory whiskies go from nowhere to the very top of the whisky world. These are exciting times indeed for our Japanese whiskies.'

ABOVE Suntory's iconic Yamazaki distillery.

Hibiki 12-year-old 43% ABV

www.suntory.com

On the nose, plum liqueur and exotic fruits; the taste is extremely gentle and sweet: zesty fruit and lots of vanilla. A very drinkable, refreshing summery blend. Spices give the experience some depth.

Hibiki 17-year-old 43% ABV

www.suntory.com

Unripe banana, red berries and vanilla on the nose; the green bananas extend to the palate. A big whisky, it coats the mouth, with other fruits arriving, some oak and spices having a say and a degree of stringency towards the end. Full and rounded – very nice indeed.

Hibiki 21-year-old 43% ABV

www.suntory.com

This was chosen as the world's best blended whisky in the 2010 World Whisky Awards. It's easy to see why: bold, precise, irresistible flavours. Orange marmalade and Christmas cake feature on the nose, while the palate includes glacé cherry, raisins and currants, all perfectly balanced and in tune.

Hibiki Harmony 43% ABV

www.suntory.com

Beam Suntory's no-age-statement Hibiki was always going to find it tough to fill the shoes of its older siblings. This has none of the polished depth and spicy oaky found in the world beating 17 and 21-year-olds. It's okay, though, as a smart combination of floral and fruity gives it a soft and sweet feel. Pepper and spice appear fleetingly.

Ichiro's Malt and Grain 46% ABV

It says on the bottle that this is a 'worldwide blended whisky.' Does that mean it has whisky from outside Japan in it? Some websites suggest aged whiskies from at least four other countries, which is intriguing. The blend itself is surprisingly light, but with some pepper and green fruit. Very light smoke adds some depth.

Nikka Rare Old Super

45% ABV

www.nikka.com

This is a brave whisky. Though no-age-statement, it claims to be old and rare and is veritably buzzing with aged oaky whisky. The nose is beguiling, but is little more than a curtain-raiser for the taste – it bursts with rich grain, big peat, sharp spice flavours. It says on the bottle that it's a smooth whisky – claptrap. This is a feisty, prickly wee beastie, with a few blunt edges. A truly delightful blend that is up there with the very best in its unusual category.

Suntory Kakubin White Label

40% ABV

www.suntory.com

Some whiskies seem perfectly suited for drinking in winter, others scream summer – and this one is in the latter camp. It's a light, drying, easy-drinking blend that tastes fine on its own or over ice, but really rocks when you mix it with soda. There are sweet citrus notes and milk chocolate.

Japanese blended malt

As with Scotland, this category refers to whiskies made up just of malt whisky with no added grain. There are a limited number of them in Japan – most of them from Nikka – although in 2008 the country passed a significant landmark, when a blended malt was released containing malts from rival companies. Traditionally, rival companies have tended not to cooperate with each other. The whisky in question picked up several awards but is no longer available. No matter. Without exception these mixed-malt whiskies are complex, challenging and worth trying.

ABOVE Nikka's Miyagikyo distillery.

Nikka Pure Malt 12-year-old 40% ABV
www.nikka.com

If you believe there is little point in mixing malts then try this, as it is definitely greater than the sum of its parts. The nose is all sweet fudge and soft toffee, but the taste contrasts with bitter-dark chocolate, chilli spice and an interesting peppery finish.

Nikka Pure Malt 17-year-old 43% ABV
www.nikka.com

By Japanese standards this is a surprisingly neutral whisky. You would never guess it was 17 years old, for a starter, with little coming from the cask. Instead it is sweet, smooth and pleasant. I was going to say it's a bit like listening to Coldplay, but it is not that bad, and the peatiness in the tail is a treat.

Nikka Pure Malt 21-year-old 43% ABV
www.nikka.com

The distinctive Japanese earthy-mushroom is here on the nose, while the taste is a masterclass in whisky making. Rich, juicy fruit over a delicious peaty base, enough oak to give proceedings shape and some bitterness for balance. The whole shooting match is soft and rounded. All in all, this is a cracker.

Nikka Pure Black 43% ABV
www.nikka.com

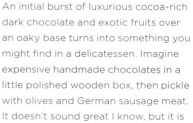

An intense, savoury nose with autumn forest, horse chestnut, damp leaves and dark treacle. The palate is complex and evolving: cherry throat lozenges, earthy peatiness, soft orange fruits, tinned peach and mango and spice. After such a flavour wave the finish is relatively slight: touch of fruit and spice.

Nikka Pure Red 43% ABV
www.nikka.com

An initial burst of luxurious cocoa-rich dark chocolate and exotic fruits over an oaky base turns into something you might find in a delicatessen. Imagine expensive handmade chocolates in a little polished wooden box, then pickle with olives and German sausage meat. It doesn't sound great I know, but it is a tangy taste sensation.

Nikka Pure White 43% ABV
www.nikka.com

Not quite sure about this colour coding, but I do know a good peaty whisky when I taste one. This is a belter: lots of rich oil, grilled trout, intense peat all wrapped in a sugar-and-spice blanket; a saltiness any Islay distiller would be proud of. If peat and smoke rock your boat, this is not to be missed.

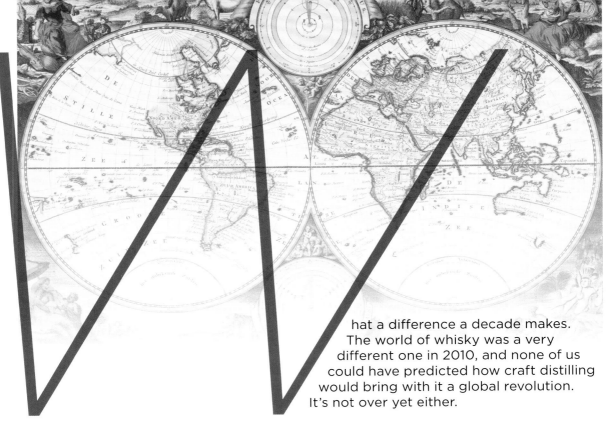

What a difference a decade makes. The world of whisky was a very different one in 2010, and none of us could have predicted how craft distilling would bring with it a global revolution. It's not over yet either.

Oh, there was a world-whisky scene in 2010. But, it was either very localized, or was made up of just a handful of distilleries that were exporting their whiskies to other countries. There were so few that they were thrown together in to a group that we called 'Rest of the World' (some dinosaurs still do), where, for the sake of the convenience of awards organizers, Australians were judged against Swedes and Belgians were paired up with Indians. We've come a long way. The small island of Tasmania has 30 distilleries alone, the Alpine region, still yet to realize its full potential, though it will, has as many distilleries as Scotland does. Many have yet to bottle their first whisky, others are only just setting out on the marketing and retailing part of their journey. There are a lot of dreadful whiskies out there now, and some distilleries have stagnated in recent years. There have been instances of growing pains, professional fall outs, take overs and closures. The world of micro-distilling has, at times, been a soap opera. But, if you're the curious type, it's been a blast, a tasty journey in to the future. And it continues. There has been so much to admire. World distillers are taking whisky in to new and exciting places, are bringing innovation and new thinking to whisky and some are

reminding the old world what attention to detail and investment in quality really looks like. Keeping up with all that has been going on is just about impossible, but, in the following pages, we've cast the spotlight on the distilleries that are already making world-class whisky or look destined to. It seems the perfect way to sign off the book, with eyes set firmly on the future.

PREVIOUS The Alpine region now produces fine single malt.

ABOVE Award-winning Säntis single malt owner Ken Locher.

ARGENTINA

La Alazana Sherry Cask 46% ABV
www.laalazanawhisky.com

Single malt

A pretty distillery on a farm; intent on making a Scotch-style malt. This marks a solid start. It's not very sophisticated and is still relatively young, but there are no negatives here and the taste is clean and sweet, with orange and berry fruits. The finish is short and the shortfall in oak and spice will right itself with time.

AUSTRALIA

Bakery Hill Classic 46% ABV
www.bakeryhilldistillery.com.au

Single malt

You might assume that Bakery Hill distillery is named after David and Lynne Baker, who run it, but it isn't. The label of the whisky features a miner's pick and shovel, and the name comes from the name of a hill where a miners' rebellion started in 1854. For years there had been growing unrest among miners who were denied the right to vote, had to pay for costly equipment and licences and were forced to use some of their paltry income to buy a small piece of land from which they could keep any gold or valuable stones they found, but invariably yielded nothing. About 10,000 miners gathered at Bakery Hill, and after a few days' stand off between the miners and the authorities the miners set up the Eureka Stockade. The uprising was suppressed brutally three weeks later, with scores of miners killed and many others fleeing to die lonely deaths in the wilderness. But, the rebellion was a watershed because it prompted political reform and the granting of rights to the workers, excluding Aborigines.

This is further proof that the Australians are coming – the fruit and barley are perfectly balanced, there are some nice milk-chocolate notes and the overall taste is pleasant and fruity, with apples and marzipan in the mix.

Bakery Hill Classic Cask Strength
60.1% ABV
www.bakeryhilldistillery.com.au

Single malt

'Born Sandy Devotional' by Australian band The Triffids is one of the finest albums ever made. Released in the 1980s when Australian sporting prowess meant that Australia was soaked in its own cockiness, the album revealed a more sensitive side to the country, and hinted at its insecurities and fears. It captures perfectly a sense of desolation in Australia's vastness. I listened to it again while tasting whiskies from Bakery Hill, and the combination is perfect. Like that album, this whisky is about nuance and detail, almost the opposite of the brash experience you may associate with Down Under. There are some strong citrus notes, clean, fresh apple and pear and a layer of sweet vanilla. Songwriting genius David McComb died from heroin poisoning following a car crash just before his 37th birthday. This one is for him.

Bakery Hill Double Wood
46% ABV
www.bakeryhilldistillery.com.au

Single malt

A mix of bourbon and French-oak wine casks make for a busy and playful malt. Vanilla and coconut mixed with Christmas cake and stewed fruits. Utterly captivating.

Bakery Hill Peated Malt 46% ABV
www.bakeryhilldistillery.com.au

Single malt

Surprisingly refined, with a soft and sweet, vanilla-dominated core and gentle smoke. A touch of pepper and wood are in the mix, but nothing too heavy.

ABOVE Peter Bignell of Belgrove distillery is a farmer and he uses homegrown rye.

BELOW Bill Lark has had a hand in the growth of most Tasmanian distilleries.

AUSTRALIAN DISTILLERIES

Of all the new whisky-making nations, Australia is the brashest, most confident and most ambitious.

It must be something to do with the Aussie character because they approach making whisky the way their cricketers approach knocking over a few Englishman when they get the chance: with a relish, exuberance and enthusiasm that's hard not to admire.

While the Australian distillers love and respect what Scotland has done with malt whisky just as every other whisky producing country does, they are not intimidated or over-awed by the country's many great distilleries. Quite the opposite, in fact. They have confidently gone their own way, created whiskies that are significantly different to those from the old country, and have challenged some of the accepted and unchallenged wisdom, forcing everyone to ask searching questions of whisky made elsewhere in the world.

Australian whisky can be put into one of two groupings: distilleries on Tasmania and distilleries on the mainland. Tasmania makes total sense: its climate is ideal for whisky making, it is blessed with outstanding natural resources, and its landscape is not dissimilar to the Scottish Highlands.

The island's whisky story began in 1992 with Bill Lark, a man whose name crops up time and time again. It was Bill who approached the authorities to set about ending a prohibition that had been introduced decades before to prevent the island's convicts spending their whole existence drunk.

Since that first licence was issued Bill has been generous with his time and has helped a number of other would-be whisky producers to succeed. They include Patrick Maguire, who helped turn the Tasmania Distillery from an ordinary and unimpressive operation to the producer of world beating malts under its Sullivans Cove label.

In Hobart, Casey Overeem established the Old Hobart distillery with Bill's help, before it was

ABOVE Don't give up the day job: Belgrove farm.

merged with Lark distillery. Casey has retired now but his daughter Jane is still in the business.

Peter Bignell went down a different route altogether. The farmer, sand and ice sculptor used his own rye to make a rye whisky called Belgrove in a homemade still, fired by used cooking oil, housed in an old horse cart on his farm.

But, the man putting together the island's boldest, heavy-hitting monsters is Tim Duckett of Heartwood. He also owns some of the oldest Lark stocks and he's not afraid to bottle liquid at more than 70% ABV. He gives his malts names such as Convict Resurrection and Devil In The Detail, too.

The largest distillery on the island is the most removed from the others at Burnie, on the other side of Tasmania to Hobart. It makes a more nuanced

ABOVE Not what the rest of the world thinks.

whisky and is exporting to Europe. Among the new distilleries on the island are Redlands, William McHenry & Sons, Sheen eastate and Fannys Bay.

On the Australian mainland there are three significant distilleries that have exported in the past. Bakery Hill near Melbourne in Victoria, was established by David Baker in 1998 and makes a peated and unpeated whisky. Both are bottled at 46% ABV and at cask strength.

In the city of Melbourne itself is Starward distillery, on the site of the city's original airport (it's actually housed in an old Qantas air hanger). The distillery was set up by David Vitale, another who worked for Bill Lark. Starward was thinking big from the start

and could be found at Europe's principle whisky shows soon after it was first released. The distillery has been picked up by Distill Ventures, the Diageo-owned company set up to invest in fledgling craft whisky makers.

The Great Southern Distilling Company is home to the Limeburners range of single malts. There have been peated and unpeated versions of the whisky, as well as a number of different cask finishes. The company also makes Tiger Snake, an American-style sour-mash whisky made with a mash of corn, rye and malted barley.

With so many distilleries making high-quality whisky, it may seem surprising that it is rarely seen in the Northern Hemisphere. But there are very good reasons for that. After a flurry of activity, favourable reviews and success in the world's biggest awards events, the distillers won over whisky fans in their own country. This, coupled with a shortage of Scotch whisky and a subsequent surge in its price, has meant that the Australians have struggled to meet demand at home, let alone maintain high levels of export sales.

'From where we're standing we can't even see Scotland because it's round the other side of the world,' commented Sullivan Coves' Patrick Maguire. 'In between us and Europe is the rather sizeable region known as Southeast Asia.

'And anyway, why would we go to all the effort to get our whiskies up next to Scotland and Ireland, which are both pretty good at making whisky already?'

Fair point, but what a shame for those of us love the big-hearted Aussie style of single malt.

WELL, FANCY THAT...

The Tasmanian link to whisky doesn't end at the Australian borders. Aussie businessman and former golf pro Greg Ramsay bought up all New Zealand's remaining whisky stocks, recasked much of it to improve it and is bottling it under The New Zealand Whisky Company. And while working as a golf pro in Scotland he met Doug Clement, who was on a mission to bring a distillery to Fife. Greg told him about the Nant distillery project that he had worked on in Tasmania, and suggested it would be the perfect model. That project eventually turned in to Kingsbarns distillery in Fife. The distillery is owned by independent bottler Wemyss Malts.

ABOVE Rolling out the barrel at Sullivans Cove.
BELOW Belgrove is one of the world's most environmentally friendly distilleries.

Bakery Hill Peated Malt
Cask Strength 60% ABV
www.bakeryhilldistillery.com.au

Single malt

A chunky, chewy, classy malt that displays a concentrated mix of lemon and bitter-orange and dusty, smoky peat. Hickory and liquorice are at it's core but then it just melts away, with the softest, finest of peaty endings: extremely impressive.

Belgrove 100% Rye
47% ABV
www.belgrovedistillery.com.au

Rye whisky

Described as bio-diesel powered, this rye is made by Peter Bignell, with 100% rye from his farm and no other grain. He is definitely on to something here, because this is a bold and different rye whisky with a sharp spicy base and a rich, fruity outer shell. The finish is long and warming.

Lark Classic Cask 43% ABV
www.larkdistillery.com.au

Single malt

A sure sign that things are moving swiftly forwards for this wonderful distillery is that Bill Lark's daughter, Kristy, is now in charge of distilling here. You can't see the joins because after some over-young malt in the past, the whisky has continued to move forwards. This is crisp and clean – like the Tasmanian air. Fresh green fruits and cocoa are held together by mouthcoating oils.

Lark Distiller's Selection 46% ABV
www.larkdistillery.com.au

Single malt

Talk to anyone involved with the Australian whisky industry and they'll talk about boutique whiskies and how small-still producers are giving the Scots a run for their money, because most of Scotland is sacrificing quality for quantity. It's not as black and white as all that, but undoubtedly the small distillers from Germany, Belgium, the Netherlands, France and Australia that are getting it right have all brought some small-still qualities to their whisky.

This is a case in point. There are some chunky, oily notes, plus its a little rustic, with sharp, crisp green fruit. Very good indeed.

Lark Single Malt Cask Strength 58% ABV
www.larkdistillery.com.au

Single malt

Melbourne band Wedding Parties Anything were described as the Australian Pogues and one of their best tracks is 'A Tale They Won't Believe', based on a true story from Robert Hughes' excellent history of Australia, *The Fatal Shore*.

It tells of how a group of convicts escaped from prison in Tasmania when Australia was a penal colony, in the hope of finding a boat and sailing back to England. When one prisoner was caught some time later he told how the desperate men had eaten first a prisoner who had died and then the weaker members of the group until finally there was just him left. The authorities didn't believe him, deciding he was using the story to cover up the other prisoners' escape. He was returned to prison only to escape again with one other man. And the authorities started to believe his original story when they recaptured him again – with body parts of his fellow escapee in his pockets...

A few years ago I was good friends with a Tasmanian girl who spoke so affectionately about her homeland that you couldn't help but want to visit. Throw in some stunning scenery and garish history and the island becomes utterly irresistible. After hearing this song the desire became even stronger.

The distillery is yet a further reason for a trip down under one day, as is its top-quality malt whisky. Get past its distinctive linseedy oiliness and you get a big fruity treat, with apples, pears, some chocolate and pepper. A corker of a whisky.

Limeburners Darkest Winter 65.1% ABV
www.distillery.com.au

Single malt

Limeburners has come on leaps and bounds in the last decade. It started out producing sappy and over-young malt. Now it is producing bottles like this. Darkest Winter recently took out the category of best whisky in the southern hemisphere in *Jim Murray's Whisky Bible 2018*. It also won the prestigious international award for best international craft whisky in the world as named by the American Distillers Institute earlier this year.

This whisky uses peat collected by hand and the barley was smoked for an extended period, resulting in a heavier, more intense style of whisky ideally suited for darkest winter. This whisky was matured in an ex-bourbon American oak cask, and exhibits spice and floral aromas when neat, while a splash of water unleashes malted barley and intense, complex, smoky aromas.

Overeem Bourbon Cask Strength 60% ABV
www.overeemwhisky.com

Single malt

A beautifully balanced burst of tropical fruits, vanilla ice cream, toasted oak and kitchen pantry spices. Another whisky that has come a long way from its early days.

Overeem Port Cask 43% ABV

Single malt

It's hard not to make a link between Old Hobart distillery's move to be part of Lark and the increasingly high standards of its Overeem whiskies, but that's probably harsh. Perhaps it's suffice to see that on the combined watch of Casey Overeem's daughter Jane, the distilling team, and the Lark guys, this whisky has continued on an upwards trajectory and has never tasted so good. A lovely taste of nut-and-raisin milk chocolate bar, dipped in cocoa.

Sullivans Cove Bourbon Cask Strength 60% ABV
www.sullivanscove.com

Single malt

If you are wondering what sort of country produces whisky like this, then take a listen to 'So Much Water so Close to Home' by Paul Kelly. Based on a Raymond Carver short story, it tells of a group of friends who go away on a fishing trip. Once there, after a long trek, they discover the body of a young woman in the water. They debate going back to report the find but have looked forward to their trip so decide not to. This whisky is perfect for such a grim scenario: big and gutsy, with plenty of oak, honey and spice battling against the barley.

Sullivans Cove Double Cask
40% ABV
www.sullivanscove.com

Single malt

This is a mix of malts from both bourbon and port casks and it makes for a weird combination, though not unpleasant. The chocolate and honey are still there, but winey intense berry fruits join the mix for an unusual finish.

Sullivans Cove French Oak Cask
47.5% ABV
www.sullivanscove.com

Single malt

Sullivans Cove has played a pioneering role in the story of Australian whisky, and was one of the first to export to Europe. Like so many distilleries across the world, however, its earlier efforts were immature, unbalanced and unpleasant. So good has its whisky become that it has won the title of world's best whisky at the World Whisky Awards. With a number of varying single-cask bottlings, expect a fruit bowl here, with a clean, sweet palate and rich, warming finish.

ABOVE The Alps provide ideal conditions for whisky making.
BELOW Appenzeller is making some of the best whisky, Säntis Malt, in the Alpine region.

ALPINE DISTILLERIES

Switzerland. It's an autumn Sunday morning and the first snow has settled on the mountains. Here in the valley the church bells are ringing, the sun is shining and cows with bells around their necks are grazing peacefully.

And, I don't know it yet, but I'm about to have one of the most surreal mornings of my working life. I'm in the passenger seat of a vintage British car – perhaps a Daimler – and my driver points at a nondescript building surrounded by a barbed wire fence.

'See that building?' he says. 'That's where they print all of Europe's euro notes. My day job is providing it with online security.'

This strikes me as odd, because Switzerland isn't in the European Union and doesn't use the euro. But we drive on into the Alps, high up until the valley floor is far below us. We pull onto a short track that leads to a cave overlooking the valley. This is, I'm told, the world's highest whisky 'warehouse'.

Here, my driver's business partner is waiting.

'He doesn't really speak English,' I am told. In fact his natural language is Romansh, a language spoken by 50,000–70,000 people in this small enclave of

Switzerland. And what's his day job? It seems he turns human ashes into diamonds and then makes jewellery out of them. Yes, you read that right.

'So rather than scatter your loved one's ashes, you get to wear them instead.'

Welcome to Orma, one of a large number of new distilleries that have sprung up in this part of the world, and one with a firm eye on the Asian market. They have thought this through. The distillery's logo is a capricorn goat, a symbol of this part of Switzerland, but with its long curved horns and tail it looks like the number eight – a lucky number in Asia. Orma has an M made up of three lines for the letter M and an inverted V for the final A. Turn the word upside down and the last two letters read VIII – or eight. The strength of their whisky, which they transport to the cave by cable car, is 44% ABV. So, they pour three large cask-strength whiskies and in

ABOVE Casks of Säntis Malt mature at Appenzeller distillery.

the crisp mountain air we look out over the sun-filled valley below, toast each other and drink. And I can't help thinking I have the weirdest job in the world.

These are exciting days for whisky from the Alpine region. We're in the part of Switzerland where it meets Austria and Germany. All three countries are on the brink of bringing top-quality whisky to the new-world whisky party.

New world isn't totally accurate. They have been distilling in these parts for generations. *Genevers*, brandies, fruit liqueurs, schnapps and all sorts of herbal alcohols – which have become fashionable among youngsters as shot drinks – have helped ward off the long winter cold in these parts. Whisky, too. But, not to put too fine a point on it, most of it wasn't very good. Of course, there are notable exceptions, but in most cases, the conversion from schnapps or brandy to malt whisky wasn't a happy one.

There was a very good reason for that. The science behind distilling whisky is different to other spirits – it's all to do with temperatures and spirits cuts. But the region boasts some of the best distillers in the world, and with the support of training organization, Spirituosenakademie, and spirits educator, Arthur Nägele, local distillers have

started to produce some outstanding, though still very young, malt whiskies.

Switzerland seems to be leading the way with three distilleries in particular getting whisky enthusiasts to sit up and take notice. Perhaps the key moment came when a Swiss whisky triumphed in a blind tasting, when it was up against some outstanding Scotch and world whiskies. It was called Langatun Quinta do Zambujeiro, a single malt finished in a Portuguese red wine cask, and its victory showed three things: that the Alpine region really is making world-class whisky; that some distilleries are learning quickly from the Scots on how to pep-up spirits with special wood finishes; and that a region that has traditionally been inward facing is starting to reach out to other countries, both for resources, and as export markets.

Langatun excelled in the competition overall, with its Port Cask and Old Deer cask strength whiskies finishing in the top 20. But Säntis Malt, with its delicate incense-like smoke also did well, while two of Swiss Mountain's whiskies performed strongly.

There are other Alpine whiskies that were absent from the competition, but have turned heads. Austria's Broger has won acclaim in the United States for its peat-bomb malts, and Säntisblick, whose distiller has an adventurous and experimental soul, can be hit and miss but when he gets it right, can produce delightful whiskies. Pfanner, which is a huge company selling fruit juices, has invested in a state-of-the-art micro-distillery and will be making whisky for export in the coming years. Over in Germany both Blaue Maus and Slyrs have made outstanding whiskies.

One of the most exciting aspects of new world whisky is how it will mature. There are very few examples of world whisky aged 18 years or older, and while many distilleries are laying down whisky for the long haul, they do not know how their spirits will hold up against the influence of the cask. However, while countries such as India and Taiwan benefit from accelerated maturation, but are likely to struggle with whisky aged for anything more than a few years, the Alpine region would seem to have the perfect conditions for Scottish-like maturation. And, if they are well made when they are young – as an increasing number of Swiss, Austrian and German whiskies are – chances are they're going to grow up to be extraordinary.

Only time will tell. But it promises to be quite a journey.

ABOVE Testing the spirit: some Swiss whiskies taste good at just four years old.

ABOVE Dramatic landscapes, peaceful valleys and stunning views all contribute to make many Alpine distilleries among the prettiest in the world.

AUSTRIA

Alpenwhisky
Crocodile Charring 55% ABV
www.alpenwhisky.com

Single malt

The Alpine nations have turned a massive corner in recent years and are now starting to make some very fine whisky indeed. Much of it, like this, is still very young and with its best days some years ahead – but give it a decade and the world will be talking about whiskies from this region as we do Swedish and Australian whisky now. This has some sappy notes to iron out, but the combination of soft, sweet apple juice and smoky, burnt barbecue notes are a delight.

Broger Burn Out 50% ABV
www.broger.info

Single malt

Bruno and Eugen Broger are at the forefront of a growing Alpine spirit revolution, and their whiskies are being recognized internationally. This is a gem. It's described as heavily peated – but it is a very different use of peat. Imagine burnt toast with burning rubber over a stick of candy.

Reisetbauer 12-year-old
50% ABV
www.reisetbauer.at

Single malt

The nose on this is a nightmare, stodgy and oily with linseed and paint – a typically off-European nose. The palate is altogether better, I guess we are not in Kentucky any more, but reset the tastebuds and there is plenty to enjoy, including some cereal and straw notes, and what is the oral equivalent of intense church incense.

BELGIUM

Belgian Owl Intense
70.5% ABV
www.belgianwhisky.com

Single malt

Intense is the cask strength version of Passion, and because of the high alcoholic strength it requires water. Funnily enough, it tastes best when it's reduced to somewhere in the mid-40s. Same as Passion. Who knew.

Belgian Owl Passion
46% ABV
www.belgianwhisky.com

Single malt

Passion is a umbrella name for a series of single-cask bottlings, from casks selected by distillery owner and distiller Etienne Bouillion. Each is aged from three to five years in ex-bourbon barrel. Typically, Belgian Owl whisky will be sweet and clean, with banana, tinned pear, tropical fruits and vanilla all to the fore.

DENMARK

Stauning KAOS 51.5% ABV
www.stauningwhisky.com

Grain whisky

Chaotic it is. There's so much going on here, it's exhausting just tasting it. A mix of peated barley, traditional barley and rye, it is matured in ex-bourbon casks and virgin oak casks. The result is sweet and sour, sugar and spice, honey and peat and any number of other permutations. Making tasting sense of it all is like trying to shoot an arrow at a moving target while skiing downhill. Don't bother trying. Just immerse yourself and enjoy the ride.

Stauning Peated 6th Edition 51.5% ABV
www.stauningwhisky.com

Single malt

Stauning is a distillery to watch. It knows exactly what it is doing when it comes to making whisky, and now with a big cash injection from Diageo and access to the technical advice that comes with the cash, the Danish distillery has every opportunity to go global. At the heart of this is a soft, chewy, sugary and malty whisky, and it's all wrapped up in a distinctive barbecued-sausage-style of peat smoke, distinctively different to the peat whiskies of Scotland.

ENGLAND

Cotswolds Single Malt Whisky
46% ABV
www.cotswoldsdistillery.com

Grain whisky

A welcome addition to England's whisky-making family, Cotswolds makes clean and sweet malt, which is both floral and fruity. This is just three years old, so there's not much depth or length to it. But, it's well made, the interplay with orange fruits and sugar candy are a delight.

St George's The English Chapter 15 43% ABV
www.englishwhisky.co.uk

Single malt

How much better the English Whisky Company's malts look in their new livery! Quite possibly the best of the old Chapter series, though Chapter 7 is pretty special, too. This is a big, peated whisky, with growling industrial smoke and barbecued meats dominating. Subtle this is not. That said, there are some lovely citrus notes, pink candy and toasted oak among the smoke.

St George's The English Original 46% ABV
www.englishwhisky.co.uk

Single malt

At the risk of using a bad pun, the first chapter of the English Whisky Company is over, as is the use of chapters to indicate each new bottling. In its place each bottle has smart new packaging and a new name. The Original is unpeated and is a smooth, dapper gentleman of a whisky, It is all sweet barley, milk chocolate and vanilla ice cream. Lots of yellow fruits and honey, too.

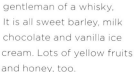

St George's The English Smokey 43% ABV
www.englishwhisky.co.uk

Single malt

A welcoming nose of smoke, spice and fruit, and this theme continues on the palate. Buttered toast, peppery grain and lots of peaty smoke. The finish is smoky, too.

St George's The Norfolk Farmers 45% ABV
www.englishwhisky.co.uk

Grain whisky

The Norfolk is made up of eight different grains, and it is a straight-down-the-line grain whisky, picking up vanilla and cocoa from the ex-bourbon casks it's been matured in. Baked pear and honey are in the mix, too. Some light spices keep it honest, and the finish is medium.

ABOVE One of Stauning's traditional stills. A new distillery opened in late 2018.
BELOW Locally sourced materials contribute to Stauning's unique taste.

STAUNING

Stauningvej 38, 6900 Skjern, Denmark
www.stauningwhisky.com

If you want to make the perfect hot dog, talk to the team at Stauning. Using Danish sausage, dried onions and an assortment of condiments every one of them can assemble the perfect lunchtime treat.

They taste pretty good, too.

Why am I telling you this? Because a Danish hotdog – or at least a Stauning one – tastes distinctly Scandinavian. It's a twist on a classic concoction, and it is at once strikingly familiar, and deliciously alien. It's a hot dog, Johan, but not as we know it. And it's a perfect metaphor for what they're doing with single-malt whisky in Denmark – something recognizably whisky, but with a distinctive and unique twist.

Until now Danish whisky has struggled a little, overshadowed by what has been happening in Sweden. That's because Swedish distillery Mackmyra was not only in the first wave of new-world distilleries, it had international ambitions from its outset, and it grew very fast, opening the door for a number of other new Swedish distilleries. And, with Sweden's passion for whisky – it has more clubs than any other country – Swedish whisky became a big story very quickly.

But, that's starting to change. There is a growing demand for whisky from outside traditional whisky-producing areas, a thirst for unusual and challenging new whiskies, and an acceptance of whisky from countries as varied as Argentina, Iceland and Italy. And Denmark is ideally placed to take advantage, not least because distilleries such as Braunstein and Fary Lochan have form in the country.

And then there's Stauning, a distillery set up by a group of friends who knew nothing about making whisky, but through sheer determination have built up a business that has attracted the interest of drinks giant Diageo and proved successful enough to warrant the building of a new and bigger distillery in 2018. Stauning was founded by friends in 2005 – a group that included engineers, a teacher, a pilot, a baker, a doctor and, crucially, a butcher. Crucially because the distillery was set up in the butcher's old abattoir.

'Money was tight, so the distillery was created with a lot of making-do,' says the group.

'Among other things, this meant using the floor of the old cold store in the abattoir to revive the old Scottish production method of floor malting.

'At the same time, an old mincer was turned into a grain mill, the pickling vat was used for fermentation, and the smoke oven – which still smelt wonderfully of smoked bacon – was fed with grain instead of meat. We got the peat for the smoke oven from the nearby Klosterlund Museum, where they exhibit and work with peat in the same way as people have done in Denmark since the Iron Age.'

The plan was to make a smoky whisky in an Islay style. And the team received the perfect boost when whisky expert Jim Murray tasted Stauning whisky and declared that it reminded him of Ardbeg from the 1970s. Since then Stauning has gone from strength to strength. The group was approached by Distill Ventures, a Diageo owned group which seeks out and invests in world craft-whisky makers, offering support and advice in return for a future opportunity to purchase the business.

That agreement meant that Stauning could think bigger. The company had already left the abattoir behind, purchasing a farm on the end of the under-populated region of West Jutland. In 2018, it completed work on a new distillery on the farm site, and production is now set to be about 900,000 litres (237,755 US gallons) a year.

The whiskies it's making are as distinctive as those hotdogs. The team may have set out to emulate the malts of west Scotland, but the whiskies are distinctive and different, particularly Stauning KAOS, which twists and turns like a hooked salmon. This is a distillery that is leading Denmark out of its neighbour's shadow. Stauning is just one of a number of new distilleries in Denmark. Fary Lochan, Trolden, Nybog Destilleri and Brænderiet Limfjorden are all producing single malts.

There are also new distilleries in Iceland and Finland. Exciting times.

FRANCE

Armorik Dervenn 46% ABV
www.distillerie-warenghem.com

Single malt

What a difference a decade makes. Or can do. One of the most fascinating things about updating this book has been seeing how some distilleries have moved forward and some clearly haven't. Warengem has come on leaps and bounds. With the help of the late Dr Jim Swan, David Ropussier has tweaked his production, experimented a little with flavours and made gems such as this. It's matured in Breton oak barrels made specially for the distillery by the last barrel maker in the region. It is a wonderful sweet treat, with milky malt drink and oaky notes, intense nutmeg, ginger and cinnamon.

Armorik Sherry Cask 46% ABV
www.distillerie-warenghem.com

Single malt

The decision by David Roussier to up the ABV is an inspired one, as is the decision to finish the distillery's standard malt in a sherry cask. It makes for a full, fruity, berry-driven and majestic single malt. Warenghem is now competing with the very best that the New World can offer and if the aim is to give a lot of Scottish distilleries a run for their money David and his team have achieved it.

Eddu Gold 43% ABV
www.distillerie.fr

Buckwheat spirit

Eddu Gold is one of the mainstay range of Distellerie des Menhirs, a family run business in Brittany. This really walks the line. Buckwheat might be called *blé noir* in French (and *eddu* in Breton) but it isn't a grain, it's a pulse, and so you have to

question whether we have whisky at all. But Brittany is a fascinating whisky-producing region and this is no slouch. There are fluffy apples and over-ripe pears on both nose and palate, some slushy melon comes into play, and the finish is spicy. A very pleasant experience.

Eddu Grey Rock 40% ABV
www.distillerie.fr

Blended whisky

Surprisingly assertive and grungy for a blend, with plenty of fruit, but a coastal tang and some smoke. The appley notes mixed with the earthiness give this whisky a distinctly different and attractive character all its own. Impressive.

Eddu Silver 40% ABV
www.distillerie.fr

Buckwheat spirit

There is nothing subtle about this whisky, but that is no bad thing. It is rich in fruit and honey, the oak and spices slap you round the mouth a bit. The finish is pleasant and intense.

Glann Ar Mor 46% ABV
www.glannarmor.com

Single malt

There are many things to get excited about at this distillery in Brittany, not least its judicious use of casks and the way that even its young whiskies are balanced and complete. There are grassy, hay-like notes on the nose, and the salt-and-pepper flavours are not totally in balance with the fruit, but the beautiful big apple and pear flavours and gorgeous rich oak suggest that this distillery is well on the way to producing some whisky classics.

Guillon No 1 46% ABV
www.distillerie-guillon.com

Single malt

Guillon matures in wine casks and this whisky is a revelation. Rich, sweet orange and citrus, sponge and malt in the centre and swirling red fruits late on, with a touch of earthiness, too. A complex and impressive whisky.

GERMANY

Blaue Maus 40% ABV
www.fleischmann-whisky.de

Single malt

There's some off-putting linseed oil on the nose, but past this you will discover the most gentle, honeyed, fudge-like taste and finally a significant, but not harsh, level of spice.

Blaue Maus Fasstarke 58.9% ABV
www.fleischmann-whisky.de

Single malt

Treat this one carefully, it is capable of biting. The nose is oily and pruney, the taste liqueur-like, with intense fruits and a fierce, un-Fleischmann-like wave of pepper. But, it is a pleasant experience, with a malty heart.

Grüner Hund 40% ABV
www.fleischmann-whisky.de

Single malt

This has soft fudge and honey on the nose, with polished wood and beeswax making an appearance. The taste is liquid honey – soft and rounded, beautifully put together and delivered on a palate of very delicate and gentle spice.

Grüner Hund Fasstarke 51% ABV
www.fleischmann-whisky.de

Single malt

The most bizarre whisky in the whole Fleischmann stable, this has lots and lots going on. On the nose there are pistachio nuts, and rich fruit liqueur notes. This takes you out of your comfort zone but ultimately rewards you with a smörgåsbord palate of camp coffee, burnt treacle and a wave of spice.

Slyrs Bavarian Single Malt
43% ABV
www.slyrs.de

Single malt

Both beautifully packaged and beautifully made, with sweet pear and apple, honey and toffee strutting along merrily and being buffeted by the warmest oak and milk chocolate. There's an attractive bitter-sweet thing going on, too. World-class whisky by any standards.

INDIA

Amrut Cask Strength 61.9% ABV
www.amrutdistilleries.com

Single malt

An intense, outstanding roller-coaster ride of a malt. There is lemon and citrus on the nose; on the palate an intense bitter-sweet battle is going on. Astringency from the casks gives an added depth, then there are honeyed, dusty spice notes and a sweet, rich barley core.

ABOVE The still room at Warenghem.

BELOW & OPPOSITE Armorik whisky: the late Dr Jim Swan improved the spirit significantly.

WARENGHEM

Route de Guingamp, Boutill, 22300 Lannion, France
www.distillerie-warenghem.com

France is rightfully famous for its wine and brandy making but Francophiles will know that the French have plenty of other strings to their alcohol-producing bows.

Normandy makes great cider and calvados and the country's beers can match with anything from England, Belgium or Germany.

France produces whisky, too. As with other countries gripped by craft-distillery mania, a number of new and smaller distilleries have sprung up since 2010 and now there are more than 20 in total. But, until relatively recently, the most established ones were spread a cross Brittany – Distilleries des Menhirs, making soft, sweet and fruity whiskies with *blé noir*; Glann ar Mor, which makes rich and enjoyable whiskies under the distillery name, and big, peaty Islay-style monsters under the name Kornog; and Warenghem, which offers the nearest thing that France has to a Speyside whisky.

Distillerie Warenghem can be found on the edge of the town of Lannion, and there has been a distillery bearing the name since the Warenghem family moved to the region from northern France and established a distillery there. The distillery first specialized in the production of fruit and plant liqueurs and creams. One of these was Elixir d'Armorique, a blend of 35 plants, which won awards at the international trade fairs of Brest then Bordeaux before going on to international renown, particularly in the United States. More than 100 years later it is still being marketed and has discovered a new market among younger drinkers.

The company introduced a blended whisky as long ago as 1987, the first French and Breton whisky ever to be released, and a single malt called Armorik followed in 1998. It was aimed at the domestic market and particularly superstores. But while Armorik was a slow-burn success story it's only since 2010 that Armorik has become a fixture on the world whisky stage. Company chief executive David Roussier recruited whisky-troubleshooter and consultant Dr Jim Swan to work on the malts, and his tweaks turned a good whisky in to a great one. We're just starting to see the results of that work now, a fitting tribute to the late Dr Swan.

The distillery isn't big – it makes about 100,000 litres (26,417 US gallons) of pure alcohol every year, but if you can find it it is worth trying.

Armorik has grown in stature in recent years and there has been a series of special bottlings, and experimental finishes, including the excellent Maitre de Chai. In 2015 the distillery also released a limited-edition rye whisky called Roof Rye, a joint collaboration with acclaimed bartender Guillaume Ferroni. It was matured for eight years, partially in Brittany, but also in Marseille.

Warenghem is open to the public and offers free tours and tastings from April to September. It also has a small shop.

Amrut Fusion Single Malt 50% ABV
www.amrutdistilleries.com

Single malt

Fusion was the whisky that announced to the world that Amrut wasn't just making good whisky, it was a world-class distillery with the ability to innovate and diversify. I defy anyone to go from Two Continents to Fusion and not conclude that Amrut is competing in the upper echelons of the premier league, with its intense, wonderful fruit notes, lashings of oak, smoke and dark chocolate.

Amrut Greedy Angels 50% ABV
www.amrutdistilleries.com

Single malt

Up there with the best whiskies I've ever tasted. It's called Greedy Angels because after eight years in the Indian climate, where maturation is on fast forward, the angels have taken 75% of the liquid in the cask. Chances of finding this one are not great, but perhaps the reaction to it will encourage Amrut to repeat the experiment. There are even older versions, but at eight years the malt is nib on perfect – all chewy Starburst and tropical fruits, with a balanced tannin and spice combination. Best of all, there's a menthol/red liquorice taste (similar to what can be found in Scotch whisky older than 25 years), and which may be described as whisky rancio.

Amrut Kadhambam 50% ABV
www.amrutdistilleries.com

Single malt

Kadhambam is matured in three different cask-types: ex-Bangalore Blue Brandy casks, rum casks and oloroso sherry butts. It also has some peated whisky spirit in what is one glorious mix. With berry fruits, sweet spices, honey, liquorice, dark chocolate cocoa powder and coffee, the finish is to die for.

Amrut Peated Cask Strength 50% ABV
www.amrutdistilleries.com

Single malt

There was a time when a new Amrut release was cause for genuine excitement. This was the malt that started it all – there was a genuine buzz when this whisky was unveiled. Not surprising: it's a gem, with peppered smoked fish dancing around the fruit and barley. It seems to have found a niche of its own, while maintaining enough recognizable flavours to win over hardened Scotch fans. Very classy indeed.

Amrut Two Continents 46% ABV
www.amrutdistilleries.com

Single malt

This is extremely hard to find because when the word got out about how good it was, it flew off the shelf. It is an intense flavour experience – almost Ardmore-like savoury peatiness and the most attractive rounded, balanced fruitiness. It gets its name from the fact that it is matured in India and then Europe. If you've any lingering doubts about the world-class quality of this distillery this will well and truly banish them. Wonderful.

Paul John Bold 46% ABV
www.pauljohnwhisky.com

Single malt

John Distilleries has been going up through the gears since it was first launched in 2012, and – as Amrut has focused on specific target markets due to stock limitations – it has not only kept the Indian whisky flame alight, it has ensured that it is shining brighter than ever. The company has a core range comprising of Bold, Brilliance and Edited, and supports them with a series of hard-hitting and excellent single-cask bottlings. Bold is a big, peaty whisky, with the barley dried in Goa with peat from Islay. The sweet smoke weaves its way between honey, malty grain and juicy fruit.

Paul John Brilliance 46% ABV
www.pauljohnwhisky.com

Single malt

Brilliance takes a Speyside line at first and then veers left field somewhat. On the nose and up front on the palate this is a clean, sweet and fruity malt, with a nice mouthfeel and impressive balance. There are honey and vanilla notes, then raisins, almonds and rich malt. Towards the end and in to the finish it takes its own distinct path, with cocoa, cream and rich honey. Very impressive.

Paul John Edited 46% ABV
www.pauljohnwhisky.com

Single malt

Fifteen per cent of this whisky is made up of whisky peated with barley imported from Islay, and the rustic, earthy base the smoke gives this whisky imparts a distinctly Highland character. It's my least favourite of the three whiskies, but it's still pretty good. The peat teases the palate before giving way to chilli chocolate and then Crunchie bar. At times smoky, at times spicy, at times sweet – it's intriguing but it never quite makes up its mind. I am still tempted to taste again though.

Paul John Peated 55.5% ABV
www.pauljohnwhisky.com

Single malt

Paul John comes in to its own with its cask strength bottlings. There have been a series of them and this is the best, proving beyond doubt that John Distilleries has upped its game. This mixes tropical fruit, musty earthiness and lots and lots of tarry smoke.

ITALY

Puni Sole 46% ABV
www.puni.com

Single malt

Traditionally the Italians like young spirits, eg. grappa or 5-year-old Glen Grant (one of their favourite Scottish single malts). So, this 4-year-old is perfect for them. But, Puni will win followers a lot further afield if they continue to make whiskies like this. It is matured for two years in ex-bourbon barrels, then in ex-sherry casks. The result is a soft and nuanced malt, with peach, sweet lemon, honey and a faint sherry note.

THE NETHERLANDS

Millstone 92 Rye Whisky 46% ABV
www.zuidam-distillers.com

Rye whisky

Zuidam used to make an excellent whisky called Millstone 100 Rye: 100 proof (50% ABV), 100 months old, from 100% rye. This is clearly 92 proof, but I'm not sure whether it is 92 months old and made with 92% rye. The rye spice is tangy and firm, followed up by clementine and raspberry and finally a toffee note. The spices dominate the excellent finish.

Millstone 12-year-old Sherry Cask
46% ABV
www.zuidam-distillers.com

Single malt

It seems almost patronizing to say it, but this big-hearted sherry bomb really holds its own with most of what Speyside has to offer. This is classic stuff, beautifully made and rich in plummy notes, berries, oranges and Christmas cake, all rounded off with some tannins and spices. Wonderful.

Key whiskies

Paul John Bold 46% ABV
Paul John Brilliance 46% ABV
Paul John Classic 55.2% ABV
Paul John Edited 46% ABV
Paul John Peated 55.5% ABV

ABOVE Paul John whiskies from John Distilleries are picking up awards across the world.
BELOW & OPPOSITE The still room at John Distilleries.

JOHN DISTILLERIES

No.110, Pantharapalya, Mysore Road, Bangalore 560039, Karnataka, India
www.pauljohnwhisky.com

The Indian whisky market is like no other on earth. It has two distinctive and separate parts: Indian whisky within India itself, and Indian whisky that is exported to other parts of the world.

Within India a small amount of quality whisky is consumed by a growing middle class. India makes some of the world's biggest whisky brands but they are only consumed within the country. Some of the whiskies are made by mixing local spirit with imported whisky. And a large quantity of Indian 'whisky' is made with molasses and therefore not recognized as whisky at all outside India.

But, there are Indian whisky distilleries making single-malt whisky and exporting it to other countries. Not only that, but it is of a very high quality, and it has found willing markets around the world. So much so that pioneering company Amrut became a victim of its own success and had to focus on a limited number of export markets to meet demand.

For Shilton Almeida, regional manager for the Paul John whisky range, consumer knowledge has moved forward noticeably.

'People are very surprised by the fact that India makes single-malt whiskies and impressed at the same time once they try them. Certainly the brand is better known in the market nowadays compared to say 2015 or 2016. Most consumers have moved from "new to Paul John and Indian whiskies" to "new to a particular Paul John expression".

'As long as people have an open mind to try world whiskies, we have a trend setting in. Otherwise, blind tastings are also a way to break in.'

Indian whisky finds itself benefiting from a surge of interest in whiskies from non-traditional territories. Shilton thinks that the consumer definitely understands more about maturation.

'I believe after the Japanese whiskies were out in the market, people became aware of the fact that whisky matures faster in hotter climates,' he says. 'Consumers nowadays are intrigued and want to learn more about world whisky offerings, and how it is different from whiskies from traditional areas. And they really appreciate them once tasted. But, it could be the other way round, too. With the love

for whisky that I have, I personally feel that age is just a number. At the same time I would like to know more about it, and we can always find out a lot more in today's digital world through various social media platforms from the brand and experts.'

The age issue may have helped world whiskies in general. Australian distillers have long argued that an age statement means nothing unless you know the size and type of cask, what it has previously been used for, temperature and climate, and humidity. Then, for reasons of expedience, Scotland started releasing no-age-statement whiskies, at least some of them significantly younger than the 10 or 12 years Scotch whisky drinkers were accustomed to. And Scotland often came off second best in comparison to some world whiskies.

Paul John has a core range of peated, lightly peated and unpeated whiskies and has released cask strength and single-cask whiskies on a regular basis.

Millstone 2010 Peated 54.4% ABV

www.zuidam-distillers.com

Single malt

This is an earthy, peaty treat and couldn't be more different to the thrills and spills of sweet bourbon Millstone 1996. Zuidam says that the warm and dry conditions in which this whisky is matured accounts for its rapid maturation and a large annual evaporation of 4–5%. But, that same maturation has left all the smoky notes in place. This is a third of the age of the Millstone 1996 and is zippy and zesty.

Millstone 1996 American Oak Single Cask 52.3% ABV

www.zuidam-distillers.com

Single malt

Incredibly this was bottled at 20 years old, making it one of the oldest whiskies from a non-traditional-whisky-making area (though some of Germany's whiskies are older). It's an absolute belter: fresh and fruity, with tropical fruits, grapefruit, coconut, menthol and the most delicious wave of spices; the finish is fruity, with hints of aniseed. Only Kavalan's Solist Cask Strength Ex-Bourbon Cask can match this, and it's certainly the best whisky Zuidam has released – that's saying something.

NEW ZEALAND

NZ Whisky Co Diggers & Ditch

45% ABV

www.thenzwhisky.com

Blended malt

Diggers & Ditch honours the troops of Australia and New Zeland, and is made up of Willowbank distillery malt and a malt from a secret Tasmanian location. Not subtle, but tasty, with berries, orange and lingering spices.

NZ Whisky Co High Wheeler

43.3% ABV

www.thenzwhisky.com

Single blend

I've called this a single blend because it is made up of 70% malt whisky and 30% grain whisky made from unmalted barley. That mashbill is effectively what the Irish call pot still whiskey. This has been matured in bourbon casks for 21 years, but you wouldn't know it. It's light, with pear and sweet apple up front, and traces of oak and pepper, particularly on the finish.

NZ Whisky Co Oamaruvian

57.7% ABV

www.thenzwhisky.com

Single grain

www.thenzwhisky.com

In recent years, Australian Greg Ramsay has bought all the remaining stocks of whisky from New Zealand's Willowbank distillery and has been rescuing it by recasking and mixing different blends. The Oamaruvian is one of its best releases. The whisky was aged in ex-bourbon casks for six years and then former red wine casks for a further ten, this is fruity, very fruity. Like alcoholic blackcurrant juice. If you have a sweet tooth you'll love it. Given the age, wood takes quite a back seat.

NZ Whisky Co Otago 30-year-old 51.6% ABV

www.thenzwhisky.com

Single malt

This was bottled as a 24-year-old to mark the All Blacks' world-cup victory in 2011, and with a whisky of 30 years old, New Zealand joins a very select group of nations capable of having anything drinkable at the age. And it is drinkable. Very. In fact the oak is quite shy, and the malt is more defined by grain, honey and vanilla.

SOUTH AFRICA

Bain's 43% ABV
www.distell.co.za

Single grain

Produced at the James Sedgwick distillery in Wellington, this is a captivating and somewhat feisty number for a grain whisky. Indeed, it starts off aggressively, with a distinctive sharp and fiery bite before softening up into a soft and honeyed tipple, with an apricot heart and the gentlest of spices. Grain can be too sweet and soft for my palate, but this is a robust and intriguing dram.

Three Ships 10-year-old Limited Edition 43% ABV
www.distell.co.za

Blended whisky

Time hasn't tamed this feisty and characterful whisky. Better made and more mature than the 5-year-old, but it's still a fruity tree with some earthy, rustic notes to keep it interesting. The company website said that the 5-year-old included Scottish as well as South African peat. These days, Three Ships' parent company has grown a lot, and now owns some Scottish distilleries, so maybe that's still the case here.

Three Ships Bourbon Cask Finish
43% ABV
www.distell.co.za

Blended whisky

This is the latest and best release from the Distell company. Blended from South African malt and grain, then returned to bourbon casks for a further period of maturation, it has the sort of honey and vanilla heart that you only get from real ice-cream-van ice cream.

SWEDEN

Box Dálvve 46% ABV
www.boxwhisky.se

Blended whisky

I'm a big fan of this distillery, and having tasted some of its maturing spirits, I'm convinced that it will produce world-class whiskies. For the time being this will do as a pointer. It's beautifully made, with toasted oak and wispy and somewhat salty smoke on the nose, and over-ripe apples, vanilla and liquorice. The finish is peaty and fruity.

Mackmyra Brukswhisky 41.4% ABV
www.mackmyra.com

Single malt

In a few years' time Swedish whisky will be accepted in the same way as Japanese whisky is now. It will retain an exotic element, but no one will question its validity. The first four distilleries to release whiskies from Sweden have demonstrated their ability to make quality malt, and more will follow.

But, Mackmyra is where it all started, and although like any great success story it has been criticized by some of the more extreme elements within the Swedish whisky community, it has done a remarkable job of leading from the front. The easy option would have been to create a standard portfolio of core malts and market them to death. They haven't done that though – instead they have served up a regular series of unusual, exciting and unpredictable small-batch releases. It's a brave thing to do, but it has ensured that each special release creates a frisson of excitement among the distillery's many fans – and your writer is very much among them.

At times Mackmyra has struggled commercially. It moved in to a state-of-the-art, gravity-driven distillery and perhaps over extended itself, and so some commercial reality was bound to come in to play at some point. And this whisky is an example of just that.

ABOVE The holiday-island distillery of Hven has brought science to whisky making.
BELOW Smögen distillery makes peaty, flavoursome award-winning malts.

THE RISE AND RISE OF SWEDISH WHISKY

It's a quiet afternoon in the Old Kiln Café at Ardbeg distillery on Islay. A few elderly folk are enjoying a cup of tea and a piece of cake.

Suddenly the door flies open and a group of very big men in leather jackets, with long blonde hair and with tattoos and piercings, burst in to the room.

'I honestly think that some of the people in the café thought that they were Vikings coming in to finish what they started all those centuries ago,' smiles Ardbeg visitor-centre manager Jackie Thomson. 'But you should never judge a book by its cover. They were members of the Stockholm Heavy Metal and Malt Society, they all spoke perfect English, were very polite and they asked a lot of very intelligent and in depth questions. They were a delight.'

This captures the relationship Sweden has with whisky to a tee. Swedish whisky drinkers tend to be polite, educated, curious, passionate and respectful of Scottish single malt, particularly peated single malt. But, also just a tad quirky, too. It's in Sweden, for instance, that Mackmyra matures some of its whisky in an old armoury on an island off the coast of Stockholm, and in a huge disused mine. Box is produced in the middle of nowhere in an old sawmill, and to get to it from Stockholm you have to take a road that passes a Chinese fort, and a one-horse town where grown men go to dress up as cowboys and act out shoot outs outside the saloon.

But, when it comes to making whisky, Sweden can be very serious. At any given time there tends to be three levels of whisky production: established distilleries eg. Mackmyra trading home and abroad; those that have recently bottled their first whiskies and are starting out on their whisky journey; and new distilleries producing spirit, but not yet bottling.

Spirit of Hven is in the first category. It is a small distillery on the island of Hven, which is close to the Danish mainland. It is part of a hotel and conference resort that also has a pub and restaurant, and the man behind it is Henrik Molin. He brings a typically Swedish approach to his distilling and his whiskies

ABOVE Box distillery's experiment with wood, barley and peat are creating world-class whiskies.

are outstanding. He has achieved gold medals at the Wizards of Whisky World Whisky Awards every year since he launched his first single-malt whisky in 2012.

Spirit of Hven is a classic example of a rapidly developing and distinctive whisky style. It has an earthy, almost salty base, and a perfect glance of sweet fruit and tangy spice. It's still early days, but it may be that Swedish whiskies are developing some shared taste traits. This may be in at least part due to the peat used to dry the barley, much of which was at some point under the Baltic Sea,

imparting a saltiness that sits well with the Swedish palate because salt is used as a food preservative. Another factor may be the way some Swedish barley is dried over a fire made up of juniper twigs, once again a method common in Swedish cooking.

But, the new distilleries are also creating unique whiskies through their own attention to detail. Box distillery was originally founded by Mats and Per de Vahl and is sited beside the Ångerman River in Ådalen around 100-km (62-miles) north of Sundsvall in northern Sweden. The distillery is in a wood mill that used timber brought down the river to make boxes for Victorian England.

'With its source lying deep in the mountains, the river provides us with almost unlimited access to crystal clear, chilled water – a defining factor in creating a rich, character filled distillation,' says distillery manager Roger Melander. 'For much of the year, the temperature of this water is only a few degrees above freezing. This fresh mountain water is an exclusive resource, which allows us to distil more effectively than in any other location in the world.'

Roger and his team have also focused on the basic ingredients of whisky production, seeking out rarely used barley grains to maximize quality, focusing heavily on cask management, and experimenting with virgin and Hungarian oak, as well as ex-bourbon and ex-sherry wood. The distillery even went as far as to release a box of five different spirits samples to demonstrate toasting under the collective name Advanced Master Class. Box is in no hurry to rush things but its first whiskies, despite being very young, have been critically acclaimed and they sold in hours, restricting the opportunity for anyone outside the country get hold of them.

The most recent Swedish distillery to start exporting is Smögen on the west coast of Sweden. Here Pär Caldenby imports peated barley from Scotland and is seeking to make peated whisky. The first bottling from the distillery was released in 2014 and there have been a series of releases under the umbrella name Sherry Project.

There are a smattering of other distilleries operating in the country and more are planned, though on what scale they will be and whether they will be aimed at the international market is not known yet, but most of them are modest in size, producing just 20,000–40,000 litres (5283–10,567 US gallons) a year.

ABOVE The steam pipes at Spirit of Hven distillery.

ABOVE The copper boiler at Spirit of Hven.
BELOW The distillery, between Denmark and Sweden, can only be accessed by boat.

It's Mackmyra Lite, and it's designed for mainstream consumption. A classic example of an easy-going, vanilla and butterscotch flavoured malt, it is light and easy-drinking, and displays sweet tinned fruits and some mint. The earthiness and spiciness are there, but they are held in check. It is beautifully made, though.

Mackmyra Moment Prestige

46.1% ABV
www.mackmyra.com

Single malt

Moment is a regular series of special-release whiskies, which cover a broad range of maturation processes and finishes. As a result each one is different, but they are never less than exciting. Moment Prestige, released in 2018, is an 11-year-old whisky aged in casks of French oak that previously held wine from the artisanal Champagne producer Philipponnat. The malt has delicious, fresh grapefruit and toasted oak notes.

Mackmyra Svensk Ek 46.1% ABV
www.mackmyra.com

Single malt

There is something altogether oddball about Mackmyra. Although the distillery's owners based their malts on the whiskies of Scotland, they have struck out in a distinctive and unique direction. You're never quite sure what the distillery is going to do next, and it has the capability of releasing safe and sweet confectionery delights, or savoury and smoke-tinged monsters. But, beyond the whisky itself there are all sorts of charming quirks about the distillery's way of making whisky. Mackmyra matures a good proportion of its whisky in an old mine, so large that articulated lorries can drive in to it. It's like something off a James Bond set, with a myriad of mined rock corridors crammed with quarter casks of maturing spirit, many of them

privately owned. Other casks are stored in an ex-military armoury on an island off the coast of Stockholm. More still are matured at the opposite at the country. If you own one you can come and visit it.

Once you know the Mackmyra back story you can't help but smile every time you encounter the whisky. There's no other word for it: it's kooky.

Svensk Ek means Swedish Oak and this malt is matured in barrels made from Swedish oak trees, something of a rarity, because most Swedish oak was used up centuries ago akin battle ships, and there isn't much of it left. This comes from the island of Visingsö. That oak passes on a wave of pepper and ginger spice, but vanilla and toffee still work their through the overall taste.

Mackmyra Svensk Rök 46.1% ABV
www.mackmyra.com

Single malt

It's early days yet, but there are signs that world whiskies are diverging from their Scottish blueprints and are developing distinct flavours unique to their location. There is a growing view that terroir could be a thing in whisky just as it is in wine, and a growing number of distillers, particularly in the United States, are bigging up their unique barley strains. More directly, different woods are making a difference to whisky production. Unlike Scotland, world distillers are not restricted to maturing their spirit in oak, and all sorts of experimentation is going on. And even with oak, regional influences are coming to the fore, with Hungarian and East European oaks offering a more influential effect on whisky.

The most dramatic effect on whisky, though, is the way the barley is dried at the start of the production process. In Sweden, it is common to preserve food in salt, and to smoke food over juniper twigs. Much of the peat in Sweden has spent time under the Baltic Sea, so it has a natural saltiness. Some barley is dried over juniper twigs, and is influenced in the same way that food is smoked. Here, you get both Swedish influences, distinctly different to a Scottish peated whisky, with the spices, fruit notes and menthol smoke combining to form a volcano of a malt whisky. More please!

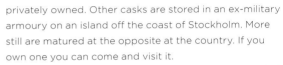

Smögen 6-year-old 59.2% ABV
www.smogenwhisky.se

Single malt

Biff, bash, bosh. This is a power-pack whisky, with the earthy, slightly salty, peaty heart that we're coming to expect from Swedish whisky, coupled with big fruity notes. Grape, peach and some citrus all contribute to a very nice whisky indeed.

Smögen Sherry Project
55.7% ABV
www.smogenwhisky.se

Single malt

I tasted this while listening to Michael Monroe, who is Finnish rather than Swedish. He plays pinky, colourful, anthemic and energetic rock and roll, and I think this whisky might just be the ideal partner. Sweet plums and grapes bounce off each other, smoke slips in and out and the core malt provides a pumping rhythm section. Ace.

Spirit of Hven Organic Seven Stars Mizar 45% ABV
www.hven.com

Single malt

For year after year now this distillery, sited on a holiday island off the coast of Denmark, has produced excellent whisky. In fact, every bottling it has done has won gold in the Wizards of Whisky World Whisky Awards. This is another perfectly crafted Swedish malt. There's a distinctive tanginess and the odd maritime note, but this is all about green fruits and soft toffee. Excellent.

Spirit of Hven Tycho's Star 45% ABV
www.hven.com

Single malt

Liquid curry spirit, with all sorts of spices under a glorious rustic, peated malt. Milk chocolate, tangerine and pink candy all make a contribution, too. Malty, and full-bodied, with a smoky finish.

SWITZERLAND

Langatun Old Deer Cask Strength 58.5% ABV
www.langatun.ch

Single malt

Old Deer is made with unpeated whisky, it is triple distilled and then matured in a mixture of cask types, including sherry and Chardonnay. The result is a huge-hearted, balanced and malty whisky, with the most delightful savoury and forest-floor notes. Some liquorice arrives late on. Old Deer's sister, Old Bear, is also worth seeking out – made with peated barley.

Langatun Port Cask 58.5% ABV
www.langatun.ch

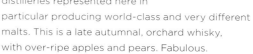

Single malt

I won't lie. A decade ago I could barely stomach Swiss whisky. I thought it was so bad I wouldn't have given it to a Nottingham Forest soccer fan (though I might have considered giving it to a fan from Derby or Spurs). But, what a ten years the Alpine countries have had. And, amazingly, Switzerland is leading the way with the three distilleries represented here in particular producing world-class and very different malts. This is a late autumnal, orchard whisky, with over-ripe apples and pears. Fabulous.

Key whiskies

Mackmyra Brukswhisky 41.4% ABV
Mackmyra Moment Prestige 46.1% ABV
Mackmyra Reserve 46.1% ABV
Mackmyra Svensk Ek 46.1% ABV
Mackmyra Svensk Rök 46.1% ABV

ABOVE Inspecting Mackmyra casks: These are stored underground in a disused mine.

BELOW The new gravity-driven distillery at Mackmyra.

MACKMYRA

Bruksgatan 4, 818 32 Valbo, Sweden
www.mackmyra.com

Trust the Swedish to give the world its most democratic whisky distillery, and while we are about it, one of its most unusual.

Mackmyra was set up by a group of friends who had hired a chalet for a skiing holiday. Each was asked to bring a bottle of something to furnish the bar, and each brought a bottle of Scotch. Which got them to thinking, several whiskies later, why Sweden had not got its own distillery and whether they might provide one.

As with most late-night, whisky-fuelled ideas, this one went to bed when most of the party did. But two of the group got up next day and continued dreaming the dream. Now Mackmyra is a dynamic and thriving business with some of the most attractive whiskies outside the traditional regions.

So how did the dream become reality? The distillery's master distiller, Angela D'Orazio, takes up the story.

'This was at the time of the dot.com boom so no serious investor was going to look at this project,' she says. 'So the group agreed to give up their next holiday or a new car and put the money into distilling one batch of whisky to see how it went. If it worked they could try making some more, if not, well they would each have some Swedish whisky of their own.'

Then, someone hit on the idea of advertising the project on the internet and offering shares in it, and the right to have a say in how the whisky was made in return for a small amount of investment. This struck a chord with the Swedish public, attracting scores of investors and establishing a bond that has meant that queues form at the state-owned liquor store every time Mackmyra releases a new whisky.

The whisky is distinctively Swedish. The barley is Swedish and, where possible, Swedish oak is used, plus a unique peat, which is salty from years under the Baltic Sea, has helped contribute to a distinctive flavour. Juniper twigs, used as a smoking agent in traditional Swedish cooking, have been used for drying malt. Since the distillery hit its stride it has taken a two-probe approach to whisky making. On the one hand are the core malts, such as Brukswhisky and Svensk Ek, sweet and easy-drinking

whiskies. Svensk Rök is smoky and a little more challenging. But, it's the distillery's special releases where everything gets more interesting. Angela is nothing if not imaginative and the special releases, which tend to fly off the shelf, vary massively, depending on the time of the year, or, you suspect, the mood the whisky maker is in. Over the years there have been honeycomb, vanilla and sweet citrus delights, with the merest hints of the trademarks salty notes, or fiery, gurney, swampy monsters, single malt's equivalent of impenetrable dark forests.

Mackmyra is one of the biggest and most successful distilleries representing the New World, but the journey hasn't always been a straightforward one. The company moved to a bigger site and has at times struggled to keep it in large production. But, the whiskies are well worth seeking out.

ABOVE Flaming the casks is crucial to developing Mackmyra's unusual and challenging flavours.

Langatun Quinta do Zambujeiro 49.12% ABV
www.langatun.ch

Single malt

Only five years old and matured in a Portuguese wine barrel, this was the overall winner in an Alpine whisky competition I attended, in which all other nine of the top-ten places went to Scottish or world whiskies. This malt is fresh, sparkling and clean, with apple on the nose and palate. And lots of it. There's also toasted oak, dark coffee and an appealing bitter note that stops the whisky becoming cloying.

Säntis Malt Edition Dreifaltigkeit 52% ABV
www.santismalt.ch

Single malt

The whisky equivalent of one of those big European smoked cheeses. This is like barbecuing peppered trout over charcoal embers. There is some oiliness here, but it is robust, well-balanced and thoroughly enjoyable. Brauerei Locher mostly produces beer at its Appenzeller distillery, but this is another most pleasant new discovery made during the course of this book.

Säntisblick Peat Fire 48% ABV
www.saentisblick-destillerie.ch

Single malt

You know what to expect from the name, but this isn't all about peat and smoke. It's actually very nice, with pureed fruits and honey at its core. The smoke is a mix of charcoal and wood fire.

Säntisblick Portwein Fass ausgereift 43% ABV
www.saentisblick-destillerie.ch

Single malt

I think it's fair to say that whisky-maker Bruno Eschmann isn't afraid to experiment, and his whiskies can be hit or miss affairs. When they're good, as this one is, they are really quite special. This has a delicate, winey and floral nose, and a light and fruity taste, surprisingly delicate with rosehip, rose water and blackcurrant cordial.

TAIWAN

Kavalan Solist Cask Strength Ex-Bourbon Cask 57.3% ABV
www.kavalanwhisky.com

Single malt

When Kavalan was launched, it produced one of whisky's greatest surprises. A decade later no one blinks when Taiwan produces yet another great whisky. This is its best of all, a monster tropical fruit and vanilla charge that makes desserts redundant. Very sweet, very chewy and very more-ish.

Kavalan Solist Cask Strength Port Cask 59.4% ABV
www.kavalanwhisky.com

Single malt

Here, making an unholy trinity, is the bad boy, taking no prisoners and pouring wave after wave of dark cherry, berry and citrus fruits and feisty spices. Not much point in drinking anything else after a glass of this. The taste just keeps on giving.

Kavalan Solist Cask Strength Sherry Cask 57.3% ABV
www.kavalanwhisky.com

Single malt

If the bourbon sample was all bright summer and sunlight, this is all winter and night-time, with a huge blast of sherry, some distinctive winey notes and a mix of toasted raisins and dates that suggests several years ageing. Maybe there is a clue to the whisky's youthfulness in the upfront flavours and lack of great depth, but the flavours and remarkable spicy undernotes make for a very enjoyable ride.

Penderyn Sherrywood 46% ABV
www.welsh-whisky.co.uk

Single malt

This is the whisky equivalent of removing your elegant throwing quarterback from the game, and replacing him with a running quarterback. Not better or worse – just a different way of playing. The Madeira influence is much reduced, and a grittier, spicier alternative appears in its place. The busier, more fruity and nutty characteristics are closer to a single malt.

WALES

Penderyn Madeira 46% ABV
www.welsh-whisky.co.uk

Single malt

Penderyn's owners set out to make a unique-tasting malt whisky and they have succeeded. Each batch of Penderyn varies, but there are some consistent threads. There is a sweet, almost liqueur-like wine flavour to this, which is probably the result of the high proportion of madeira casks used in maturation. There is plenty of sweet raisins and some spice, but no peat or oak at all.

Penderyn Peated 46% ABV
www.welsh-whisky.co.uk

Single malt

A very small amount of Penderyn has peat in it. The story goes that this expression was discovered by accident, when some casks sent to Penderyn from Scotland were not peat-free as ordered. In other words, the peatiness comes from the wood and not from the barley. The plus here is that the peat adds more depth. The downside is that grizzly peat and sweet grape are not the best match.

ABOVE European stills can be markedly different to those used in Scotland.

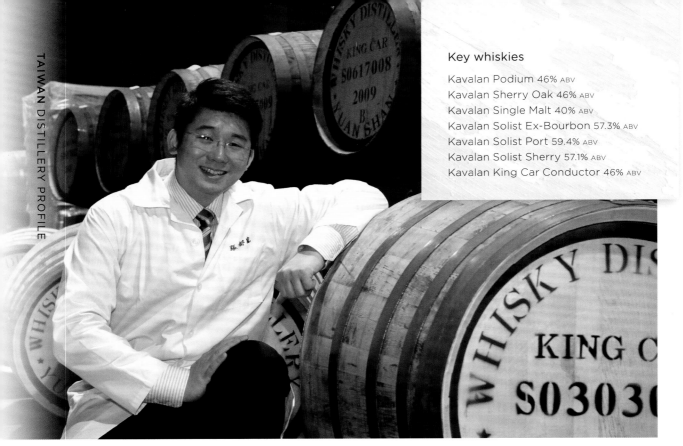

Key whiskies

Kavalan Podium 46% ABV
Kavalan Sherry Oak 46% ABV
Kavalan Single Malt 40% ABV
Kavalan Solist Ex-Bourbon 57.3% ABV
Kavalan Solist Port 59.4% ABV
Kavalan Solist Sherry 57.1% ABV
Kavalan King Car Conductor 46% ABV

ABOVE Under the guidance of Ian Chang, Kavalan has earned plaudits across the world.
BELOW Kavalan: a large distillery owned by food-and-drink producer King Car.

KAVALAN

No.326, S.2, Yuanshan Road Yuanshan Township, Yilan County, Taiwan
www.kavalanwhisky.com

It's hard to believe that Kavalan only made its first tentative steps in to the world of whisky in 2009. To describe its rise as meteoric is to sell it well short. It all started with two samples entered in to the World Whisky Awards.

One was golden-yellow, the other deep-chestnut, and both were marked 'China'. They were stunning. Soon after that a Scottish newspaper tried to trick some Scottish experts by getting them to taste some very young whiskies. The hope was that the experts would choose the English sample. They didn't – they chose the Taiwanese one.

Kavalan takes the old name of Yilan county where the distillery is located in northeastern Taiwan, in a region rich in pure water. It is no micro-distillery. It is part of a large family-owned business called King Car, which makes soft drinks and sells bottled waters, and it has had a fortune invested in it, being designed as a state-of-the-art, highly automated distillery. It's unique, too. Master-distiller Ian Chang worked with the late whisky troubleshooter Dr Jim Swan to find a way to distill in a country that can be very hot and humid and where cooling water is a challenge. Dr Swan became something of a fixture at the distillery, enthusiastically chasing up the best casks and providing ongoing advice.

The whisky itself has been revelation, though there remains some scepticism as to whether the malts are mere replicas of what happens in Scotland. I have no such doubts – those first two samples, one from an ex-bourbon cask and the other from ex-sherry were the real deal, exquisitely made and of the finest quality.

Since then there has been a steady stream of wonderful bottlings, many of them as part of the company's Solist range. Bottled at cask strength, malts have been matured in a range of different casks. The Ex-Bourbon Cask bottling is up there as one of the world's very best whiskies.

Kavalan knew it would face natural opposition, so it set out to change hearts and minds show by show, and critic by critic. With such great whiskies it didn't take long. But Kavalan had a couple of things going for it. One was that Suntory and Nikka in Japan and Amrut in India had already done the groundwork for the concept of Eastern whisky. Furthermore, all three of them had run into distribution and supply problems, with demand far exceeding supply. Indeed, they had not just made Eastern whisky, they had proved that it could match pretty much anything else in the world, picking up countless awards. But, they had become victims of their own success. Kavalan was well placed to step in to the gap and is now widely accepted as one of the great distilleries of world whisky, and other distillers are starting to export from the country. Taiwanese whisky is now increasingly found across the world. Nobody's sure what will come next but it's highly likely that Kavalan will grow and grow. Who would have thought it when those first samples arrived?

ABOVE The huge still room at Kavalan.

INDEPENDENT BOTTLERS

Wander into a whisky shop anywhere in the world and you will find on the shelves a whole range of bottles that are listed not only by distillery name. These bottlings are ranged under banners such as Connoisseurs' Choice, Old Malt Cask or The Vintage Collection, and contain malts of different ages and from different distilleries. Many of the bottles are limited in number, and contain whisky from just one cask. When they're gone, they are gone forever, but there will always be new ones on the way. This is an evolving, dynamic end of the whisky market that really excites enthusiasts.

The bottles are marketed by companies known as independent bottlers. They buy up stocks of surplus malt, often a single cask or a handful of casks, they might mix them or mature them further, and then bottle them. Some independents are fastidious about what they do, and go in search of quality whisky, bottling only what they consider to be of the highest standard. The world of the independent bottler is a hit-and-miss affair, and the bottlers tend to enjoy a love-hate relationship with the rest of the whisky industry. That said, though, they can be outstanding, and hunting them and finding them is to whisky lovers what finding a nugget of gold is to prospectors.

Listed here (right) are a few of the better ones.

ADELPHI SELECTION, SCOTLAND
www.adelphiselection.com

Breath of Speyside 10-year-old 57.7% ABV
Big-hitting, fruity delight.

AD RATTRAY, SCOTLAND
www.adrattray.com

Stronachie 18-year-old 46% ABV
Appealing mix of honey, berries and spice.

BERRY BROS & RUDD, ENGLAND
www.bbr.com

Ardmore 8-year-old 2008 54.5% ABV
Sweet and savoury, peat and fruit.
Islay Reserve Blend 46% ABV
Smoke and citrus treat.
Miltonduff 20-year-old 1995 46% ABV
Vanilla, pine, spice and oak.

DOUGLAS LAING & CO, SCOTLAND
www.douglaslaing.com

**Old Particular Bunnahabhain 15-year-old
2001** 48.4% ABV Savoury spice, fruitcake, vanilla.
**Old Particular Consortium of Cards
Laphroaig 18-year-old** 50% ABV
Rich, thick charcoal peat.
**Old Particular Consortium Of Cards
Mortlach 13-year-old 2003** 50% ABV
Oily, dates, brandy-filled chocolates.

DUNCAN TAYLOR, SCOTLAND
www.duncantaylor.com

Aultmore 8-year-old The Octave 49.8% ABV
Cornflakes, tinned fruits, cinnamon.
Black Bull 12-year-old 50% ABV
Superb, big-tasting blended whisky.
Invergordon 10-year-old 2007 53.7% ABV
Sweet apple, honeycomb, sharp spice.

IAN MACLEOD DISTILLERS, SCOTLAND
www.ianmacleod.com

As We Get It Highland Malt 64% ABV
Orange, red and green fruit bowl.
As We Get It Islay Malt 61.3% ABV
Big, bold and peaty.
Chieftain's Aberfeldy 14-year-old 2003 43% ABV
Creamy with red berries, honey and orange.

MACKILLOP'S CHOICE, SCOTLAND
Tamdhu 28-year-old 48.1% ABV
Fruity beauty from underrated distillery.

MASTER OF MALT, ENGLAND
www.masterofmalt.com

Millstone 6-year-old 48.9% ABV
Orange, cinnamon, berry fruits.
Redbreast 16-year-old 2001 60.2% ABV
Caramel, fudge, chocolate and nuts.
**Tobermory Heavily Peated
19-year-old** 59.5% ABV
Peat, chilli, green fruits, mint.

SPECIALITY DRINKS, ENGLAND
www.specialitydrinks.com

Elements of Islay Ar8 54.3% ABV
Peat, dark chocolate, ginger, 23-year-old.
Port Askaig 100 Proof 57.1% ABV
Sweet fruit, peat, seaside.

WEMYSS MALTS, SCOTLAND
www.wemyssmalts.com

Gingerbread House 2017 46% ABV
Apple Danish, ginger.
Tutty Fruity Zing 23-year-old 1993 46% ABV
The name says it all.

WM CADENHEAD & CO, SCOTLAND
www.cadenhead.scot

**Linkwood 24-year-old 1992
Small Batch** 50.9% ABV
Lots of fruit, chocolate and citrus.
**Old Pulteney 11-year-old 2006
Small Batch** 55.8% ABV
Citrus, spring meadow, wood shavings.
Strathmill 24-year-old 1993 50.3% ABV
Cream, trifle, kitchen parlour.

OPPOSITE Berry Bros & Rudd in Mayfair, London, England:
Exceptionally good whisky.

WHISKY DIRECTORY

HOW TO FIND OUT MORE ABOUT WHISKY

You can talk and write about whisky all you like, but the only proper way to experience it is of course to drink it. So how can you go about trying a number of different whiskies without taking out a mortgage? The most obvious way is to go and visit a distillery or two. Whisky tourism is big business these days and a growing number of distilleries not only offer a visitor experience, but have invested heavily in interactive centres, cafés, restaurants and exhibitions. Some distilleries do not offer formal tours, but will show you around if you ring in advance. There are also many whisky festivals and tasting events held across the world. Events come and go, and they vary significantly in size. Check carefully in advance if you're thinking of going to one because many have sprung up in recent years to make a quick buck from the booming whisky market. But, there are now a number of well-established shows, and the key ones are listed here.

WHISKY FESTIVALS

Feis Ile
www.theislayfestival.co.uk
The Islay Festival is a celebration of music and whisky held on the island over the second May bank holiday weekend. Events are held at all eight distilleries and on Jura.

Kentucky Bourbon Festival
www.kybourbonfestival.com
Normally held in the third week of September in and around Bardstown, this week of events celebrates bourbon. It includes a cigar and bourbon evening, events at individual distilleries and the prestigious black-tie gala on the final Saturday night.

Spirit of Speyside Whisky Festival
www.spiritofspeyside.com
An annual celebration of the distilleries of Speyside. This takes place over the first bank holiday weekend at the end of April/beginning of May.

The Whisky Fair, Limburg, Germany
www.festival.whiskyfair.com
Held each April this is now one of the world's most popular whisky events. It takes place in April and was first launched in 2001 – a veteran compared to many upstart whisky festivals.

The Whisky Show
www.thewhiskyshow.com
First launched in 2009 at the Guildhall in London, this is now a highly successful whisky event held over three days – a two day weekend event for consumers, and a third trade day. It started as a luxury whisky-tasting event focused on premium whisky brands and aimed at the connoisseur. But it is now a broad and sizeable consumer show, and a premium spin off show is held separately in Scotland.

Whiskies of the World
www.whiskiesoftheworld.com
Originally held in San Francisco each March, this expo has now been rolled out to other destinations including Houston, Dallas, Atlanta and San Jose. Each show features whisky, bourbon and a range of other craft spirit products. In 2018, the San Francisco event was held on the huge paddleboat entertainment centre The San Francisco Belle.

WhiskyFest
www.maltadvocate.com/docs/whiskyfest
Organized by top American whisky magazine *Malt Advocate*, this is a whisky show held in three American cities: Chicago *March*, San Francisco *October*, New York *November*. Featuring more than 200 whiskies, gourmet buffets and seminars by distillery managers and master blenders.

Whisky Fringe
www.royalmilewhiskies.com
Whisky Fringe held around the time of the Edinburgh Festival in August, and is organized by Royal Mile Whiskies, featuring more than 200 whiskies.

Whisky Live
www.whiskylive.com
Owned by *Whisky Magazine* in the United Kingdom, this is franchised out by the magazine to cities across the world. The number now staged has grown significantly in recent years, reflecting the huge interest in whisky. The events vary from territory to territory but in essence they offer whisky drinkers the chance to try different whiskies, to meet the people who made them and to attend masterclasses. Some of the events are now major attractions, with celebrated distillers and blenders attending.

WHISKY MAGAZINES

Irish Whiskey Magazine
www.irishwhiskeymagazine.com
With Irish whiskey booming, this magazine is the perfect vehicle to keep readers bang up to date with country's best whiskey releases and the ever growing number of new distilleries.

Malt Advocate
www.maltadvocate.com
American-based magazine, published quarterly, covering whiskies from all over the world. Also hosts an Internet forum and publishes a strong blog.

Scotchwhisky.com
www.scotchwhisky.com/magazine
It's a fine line between a website, blog and online mag, but, with its heavyweight writing team paid to dedicate time to it, and well-researched and informative news and features, this is not just a magazine, it's a journal. Top stuff.

Unfiltered
www.smws.com/unfiltered-magazine
The magazine of the Scotch Malt Whisky Society, sent to all its members. Impressive fresh angles on all sorts of whisky stories.

Whiskeria
www.whiskyshop.com
Published by The Whisky Shop in the United Kingdom, this is aimed at entry-level whisky enthusiasts and has a circulation of 30,000. Also digital.

Whisky Magazine
www.whiskymag.com
The English edition of *Whisky Magazine* is published eight times a year. Its website hosts a forum and an adapted version of the magazine is also published in French and Japanese.

WHISKY BOOKS

1001 Whiskies You Must Try Before You Die
Edited by Dominic Roskrow
Background and tasting notes, tasted by 25 different writers, enthusiasts and bloggers. An updated version of the book was published in 2017.

Jim Murray's Whisky Bible
Frank, funny, direct, occasionally offensive, notes to hundreds of world whiskies from the industry's answer to Jerry Sadowitz. Updated annually.

Malt Whisky Yearbook
Edited by Ingvar Ronde
Updated every year with new features written by the whisky world's leading writers – an essential annual purchase. Information and history on every Scottish distillery, there is a growing world section, but it still treats non-Scottish distilleries as less important to those in the motherland. But the statistics sections and the meticulous recording of new releases makes it an unmissable annual highlight.

Michael Jackson's Malt Whisky Companion
Updated by D Roskrow, G Smith, W Meyers (2010)
This is the sixth edition of the world's best-selling whisky book. There are 550 tasting notes and new chapters on Japanese, world and blended malts.

Peat Smoke and Spirit
Andrew Jefford
A few years old now, but this guide to the people, distilleries and whiskies of Islay is beautifully written. Insightful as any book on the subject of whisky.

Spirit of Place: Whisky Distilleries of Scotland
C MacLean, L Platman, A MacDonald
A new handbook-sized editon, this is a lovingly created and highly evocative portrait of Scotland's distilleries.

Whiskey America
Dominic Roskrow
Published in Autumn 2018, this is the follow up to *Whisky Japan*, taking a detailed and wide-ranging look at the American craft-distilling phenomenon, plotting its rise from the turn of the millennium, telling the stories of the new distillers, seeking out the best whiskies from the micro-distilling boom and featuring dozens of bars where you can taste some of them.

Whiskies, The Definitive Guide
Michael Jackson
The late-great Michael Jackson first wrote this guide in 2005. Fully updated by G Smith and myself in 2017, it is totally redesigned with several new sections, including a detailed section on new world producers.

Whisky Japan
Dominic Roskrow
Features Japan's principal distilleries, the whiskies they produce and the bars and restaurants where you can drink them. It also has interviews with the key people who witnessed and contributed to the rise and rise of Japanese whisky in the early part of the millennium.

Whisky Rising: The Definitive Guide to the Finest Whiskies and Distillers of Japan
Stefan Van Eycken
An excellent book covering the distilleries and whiskies of Japan. Van Eycken spent years gaining the trust of naturally suspicious Japanese whisky folk, and his conversations with them are a revelation.

WHISKY WEBSITES & BLOGS
There are lots of websites and blogs and they continue to grow by the day. Here are a few that I enjoy.

A Whisky Lover's Whisky Blog
www.blog.thewhiskyexchange.com
This is the live blogging arm of The Whisky Exchange.

Billy's Booze Blog
www.spiritedmatters.com
Billy Abbott works for Whisky Exchange and is one of the most knowledgeable and enthusiastic whisky guys in the business. This is his site.

Edinburgh Whisky Blog
www.edinburghwhiskyblog.com
I like this site. Written by 20-something year-old students – and done extremely well. Nice and irreverent. It says there are four of them but deceptively quiet man Chris Hoban seems to do the lion's share of this dynamic website and blog.

I Love Whisky
www.ilovewhisky.blog
I love this site! Run by Smiley Smoggy, this is the home of a woman who is documenting her whisky journey while running a business selling whisky-flavoured fudge – which takes her to whisky shows where she meets folk and learns even more. Brilliant.

Malt Review
www.malt-review.com
A site that does much more than just review malt. Its good that it takes the moral high-ground with a statement of intent about independence, criticizing whisky magazines for linking editorial to advertising. But, Mark Newton then states he has worked for *Whisky Magazine* and *Whisky Quarterly* – the two worst offenders. Great site though.

Master of Malt Whisky Blog
www.masterofmalt.com/blog
Anything they can do... A positive guide to what's happening out there.

Nonjatta
www.nonjatta.com
If Japanese whisky is your interest then this site is totally indispensable. Stefan Van Eyckan publishes here and it would be great if he did so a bit more often.

Ralfy
www.ralfy.com
This is an irreverent, down-to-earth man of the people site. To the point.

The Amateur Drammer
www.amateurdrammer.com
One of the better websites, run by Andy Flatt, with his musings and reviews. He covers both whisky and cigars, and the site also contains his guide to the best online whisky shops.

The Scotch Noob
www.scotchnoob.com
As in 'newbie'. A modest, unpretentious, highly informative journey through whisky with someone who is clearly not that much of a noob any more.

The Whisky Lady
www.thewhiskylady.net
The new Whisky Queen! Well-written reviews, well-told stories and a refreshing and engaging text from a young female perspective.

To Do Whisky
www.todowhisky.es
The Spanish website of Emma Briones, who describes herself as 'old-fashioned with a twist. Geek in progress.' Reviews and background on selected distilleries.

Whisky for Everyone
www.whiskyforeveryone.blogspot.co.uk
A straightforward, plain-and-simple guide to all things whisky. A bit over-reliant on press releases, but a useful summary of what's going on.

Whiskyfun
www.whiskyfun.com
My type of site. A bit rock and roll, kooky and undoubtedly written with authority by Malt Maniac Serge Valentin.

Whisky Israel
www.whiskyisrael.co.il
Highly professional and informative site from enthusiast Gal Granov and friends.

Whisky Notes
www.whiskynotes.be
A straightforward, easy-to-follow reviews site.

Whisky Wednesday
www.youtube.com/user/WhiskyWednesday
YouTube blog reviewing whiskies since 2012. Well-made, imaginatively thought out video of whisky comparisons, and series on hard to find whisky.

WHISKY INDEX

100 Pipers, Chivas/Pernod Ricard, Scotland 130–1

A

Aberfeldy 12-year-old, Dewars, Scotland 50
Aberfeldy 16-year-old Single Cask, Dewars, Scotland 50
Aberfeldy 21-year-old, Dewars, Scotland 50
Aberlour 10-year-old, Pernod Ricard, Scotland ...51
Aberlour 12-year-old Double Cask Matured, Pernod Ricard, Scotland 51
Aberlour 15-year-old Select Cask Reserve, Pernod Ricard, Scotland 51
Aberlour 16-year-old, Double Cask Matured, Pernod Ricard, Scotland 51
Aberlour 18-year-old, Sherry Wood Matured, Pernod Ricard, Scotland 51
Aberlour a'bunadh ("The Origin"), Pernod Ricard, Scotland 51
Akashi Red, Eigashima, Japan 233
Alberta Premium, Beam Suntory, Calgary, Canada 202
Alberta Springs 10-year-old, Beam Suntory, Calgary, Canada 202
Alpenwhisky Crocodile Charring, Alpenwhisky, Austria 252
Amrut Cask Strength, Amrut, India 257
Amrut Fusion Single Malt, Amrut, India 260
Amrut Greedy Angels, Amrut, India 260
Amrut Kadhambam, Amrut, India 260
Amrut Peated Cask Strength, Amrut, India 260
Amrut Two Continents, Amrut, India 260
AnCnoc 12-year-old, Knockdhu, Inver House, Scotland 107
AnCnoc 16-year-old, Knockdhu, Inver House, Scotland 107
AnCnoc 1975, Knockdhu, Inver House, Scotland 107
AnCnoc 1993, Knockdhu, Inver House, Scotland 107
AnCnoc 1994, Knockdhu, Inver House, Scotland 107
Ancient Age 10-year-old, Buffalo Trace, Kentucky, USA 157
Angel's Envy Bourbon Finished in Port Casks, Angel's Envy, Kentucky, USA 198
Angel's Nectar, William Grant, Scotland 145
The Antiquary 12-year-old, Tomatin, Scotland ...131
The Antiquary 21-year-old, Tomatin, Scotland ...131
The Antiquary 30-year-old, Tomatin, Scotland .131
Ardbeg 10-year-old, Glenmorangie, Scotland 54
Ardbeg 17-year-old, Glenmorangie, Scotland 54
Ardbeg Auriverdes, Glenmorangie, Scotland 54
Ardbeg Blasda, Glenmorangie, Scotland 54
Ardbeg Corryvreckan, Glenmorangie, Scotland 54, 57
Ardbeg Kelpie, Glenmorangie, Scotland 55
Ardbeg Perpetuum, Glenmorangie, Scotland 55
Ardbeg Supernova, Glenmorangie, Scotland 55
Ardbeg Uigeadail, Glenmorangie, Scotland 55
Ardmore 8-year-old 2008, Berry Bros & Rudd, England 279
Ardmore Legacy, Beam Global, Scotland 55
Ardmore Traditional Cask, Beam Global, Scotland 55
Armorik Dervenn, Distillerie Warenghem, France 256
Armorik Sherry Cask, Distillerie Warenghem, France 256
The Arran Malt 100 Proof, Isle of Arran Distillers, Scotland 58
The Arran Malt 8-year-old Madeira Finish, Isle of Arran Distillers, Scotland 58
The Arran Malt 10-year-old, Isle of Arran Distillers, Scotland 58
The Arran Malt 12-year-old, Isle of Arran Distillers, Scotland 59
The Arran Malt 14-year-old, Isle of Arran Distillers, Scotland 59
The Arran Malt Fontallaro Finish, Isle of Arran Distillers, Scotland 58
The Arran Moscatel Finish, Isle of Arran Distillers, Scotland 58
As We Get It Highland Malt, Ian MacLeod Distillers, Scotland 279
As We Get It Islay Malt, Ian MacLeod Distillers, Scotland 279
Auchentoshan 12-year-old, Beam Suntory, Scotland 59
Auchentoshan 18-year-old, Beam Suntory, Scotland 59
Auchentoshan 21-year-old, Beam Suntory, Scotland 59
Auchentoshan Select, Beam Suntory, Scotland 60
Auchentoshan Three Wood, Beam Suntory, Scotland 60
Auchroisk 10-year-old, Auchroisk, Scotland 60
Aultmore 8-year-old The Octave, Duncan Taylor, Scotland 279

B

Bailie Nicol Jarvie, Glenmorangie, Scotland 131
Bains, James Sedgwick Distillery, South Africa 265
Baker's Aged 7 years, Jim Beam, Kentucky, USA 157
Bakery Hill Classic, Bakery Hill, Australia 241
Bakery Hill Classic Cask Strength Malt, Bakery Hill, Australia 241
Bakery Hill Double Wood, Bakery Hill, Australia 241
Bakery Hill Peated Malt, Bakery Hill, Australia ...241
Bakery Hill Peated Malt Cask Strength, Bakery Hill, Australia 246
Balblair 1990, Inver House, Scotland 61
Balblair 1997, Inver House, Scotland 60
Balblair 2004, Inver House, Scotland 60
Balblair 2005, Inver House, Scotland 60
Balcones Baby Blue, Balcones, Texas, USA 194
Balcones Blue Corn Bourbon, Balcones, Texas USA 157
Balcones Brimstone, Balcones, Texas, USA....... 194
Balcones Texas Single Malt, Balcones, Texas, USA 196
Ballantine's 12-year-old, Glenburgie, Scotland ...131
Ballantine's 17-year-old, Glenburgie, Scotland ...131
Ballantine's 21-year-old, Glenburgie, Scotland ...131
Ballantine's 30-year-old, Glenburgie, Scotland 132
The Balvenie DoubleWood 12-year-old, William Grant, Scotland 61
The Balvenie DoubleWood 17-year-old, William Grant, Scotland 61
The Balvenie PortWood Finish 21-year-old, William Grant, Scotland 61
The Balvenie Rum Cask, 17-year-old, William Grant, Scotland 61
The Balvenie Signature 12-year-old, William Grant, Scotland 61
The Balvenie Single Barrel 15-year-old, William Grant, Scotland 61
The Balvenie Tun 1509 Batch 4, William Grant, Scotland 61
Barrogill, Inver House, Scotland 145
Barry Crockett Legacy, Irish Distillers Pernod Ricard, Ireland 218
Basil Hayden's 8-year-old, Jim Beam, Kentucky, USA 160
Belgian Owl Intense, The Belgian Owl Distillery, Belgium 252
Belgian Owl Passion, The Belgian Owl Distillery, Belgium 252
Belgrove 100% Rye, Belgrove, Australia 246
Bell's Original, Teacher's, Scotland 132
Ben Nevis 10-year-old, Nikka, Scotland 62
Ben Nevis Blended At Birth 40-year-old, Nikka, Scotland 132
Benchmark Old No. 8, Buffalo Trace, Kentucky, USA 160
BenRiach 10-year-old, BenRiach, Scotland 62
BenRiach 16-year-old, BenRiach, Scotland 62
BenRiach 20-year-old, BenRiach, Scotland 62
BenRiach 35-year-old, BenRiach, Scotland 62
BenRiach Aromaticus Fumosus, 12-year-old, BenRiach, Scotland 63
BenRiach Authenticus 21-year-old, BenRiach, Scotland 63
BenRiach Curiositas, BenRiach, Scotland 63
BenRiach Dark Rum Wood Finish 15-year-old, BenRiach, Scotland 63
BenRiach Heart of Speyside, BenRiach, Scotland 63
BenRiach Heredotus Fumosus, 12-year-old, BenRiach, Scotland 63
BenRiach Importanticus Fumosus, 12-year-old, BenRiach, Scotland 63
BenRiach Maderensis Fumosus 13-year-old, BenRiach, Scotland 63
BenRiach Moscatel Finish 22-year-old, BenRiach, Scotland 64
BenRiach Pedro Ximénez Finish, 17-year-old, BenRiach, Scotland 64
BenRiach Sauternes Wood Finish, 16-year-old, BenRiach, Scotland 64
BenRiach Tawny Port Wood Finish, 15-year-old, BenRiach, Scotland 64
Benromach 10-year-old, Gordon & MacPhail, Scotland 64
Benromach 15-year-old, Gordon & MacPhail, Scotland 64
Benromach 35-year-old, Gordon & MacPhail, Scotland 64
Benromach 1955, Gordon & MacPhail, Scotland 65
Benromach 1976, Gordon & MacPhail, Scotland 65
Benromach Château Cissac Wood Finish, Gordon & MacPhail, Scotland 65
Benromach Hermitage, Gordon & MacPhail, Scotland 65
Benromach Organic, Gordon & MacPhail, Scotland 65
Benromach Origins 2010, Gordon & MacPhail, Scotland 65
Benromach Peat Smoke Batch 2007, Gordon & MacPhail, Scotland 65
Benromach Triple Distilled, Gordon & MacPhail, Scotland 65
Bernheim Original, Heaven Hill, Kentucky, USA 195
Big Peat, Douglas Laing, Scotland 145
The Big Smoke, Duncan Taylor, Scotland 145
Black & White, Diageo, Scotland 132
Black Bottle, Burn Stewart, Scotland 132
Black Bull 12-year-old, Duncan Taylor, Scotland 132, 279
Black Bull 40-year-old, Duncan Taylor, Scotland 132
Blair Athol 12-year-old Flora and Fauna, Diageo, Scotland 66
Blanton's Single Barrel No. 209, Buffalo Trace, Kentucky, USA 160
Blaue Maus, Blaue Maus, Germany 257
Blaue Maus Fasstarke, Blaue Maus, Germany ...257
Blue Hanger 30-year-old, Berry Bros and Rudd, Scotland 133
Booker's 6-year-old, Jim Beam, Kentucky, USA 160
Bowmore 12-year-old, Bowmore, Scotland 66
Bowmore 15-year-old Darkest, Bowmore, Scotland 66
Bowmore 18-year-old, Bowmore, Scotland 66
Bowmore 25-year-old, Bowmore, Scotland 67
Bowmore Legend, Bowmore, Scotland 67
Box Dalvve, Box Whisky, Sweden 265
Breath of Speyside 10-year-old, Adelphi, Scotland 279
Broger Burn Out, Broger, Austria 252
Bruichladdich 12-year-old, Bruichladdich, Scotland 67
Bruichladdich 15-year-old Links, Bruichladdich, Scotland 67

Bruichladdich 16-year-old Bourbon,
Bruichladdich, Scotland 67
Bruichladdich 18-year-old, Bruichladdich,
Scotland 67
Bruichladdich 20-year-old, Bruichladdich,
Scotland 67
Bruichladdich 21-year-old, Bruichladdich,
Scotland 68
Bruichladdich Black Art, Bruichladdich,
Scotland 68
Bruichladdich Blacker Still, Bruichladdich,
Scotland 68
Bruichladdich The Classic Laddie Scottish Barley,
Bruichladdich, Scotland..................68
Bruichladdich Infinity, Bruichladdich, Scotland .68
Bruichladdich Islay Barley, Bruichladdich,
Scotland 68
Bruichladdich Octomore, Bruichladdich,
Scotland 68
Bruichladdich Organic Scottish Barley,
Bruichladdich, Scotland 68
Bruichladdich PC11, Bruichladdich, Scotland 69
Bruichladdich PC12, Bruichladdich, Scotland 69
Bruichladdich Port Charlotte Heavily Peated,
Bruichladdich, Scotland..................69
Bruichladdich Redder Still, Bruichladdich,
Scotland 69
Buchanan's 12-year-old, Diageo, Scotland 133
Buffalo Trace, Buffalo Trace, Kentucky, USA 161
Bulleit, Four Roses, Kentucky, USA 161
Bunnahabhain 12-year-old, Bunnahabhain,
Scotland 69
Bunnahabhain 18-year-old, Bunnahabhain,
Scotland 69
Bunnahabhain 25-year-old, Bunnahabhain,
Scotland 72
Bunnahabhain Ceòbanach, Bunnahabhain,
Scotland 72
Bunnahabhain Stiùireadair, Bunnahabhain,
Scotland 72
Bushmills 10-year-old, Bushmills, Ireland 208
Bushmills 16-year-old, Bushmills, Ireland 208
Bushmills Black Bush, Bushmills, Ireland 212
Bushmills Original, Bushmills, Ireland 212

C

Canadian Club 6-year-old,
Hiram Walker and Sons, Ontario, Canada 202
Canadian Club Chairman's Select,
Hiram Walker and Sons, Ontario, Canada 202
Canadian Club Classic,
Hiram Walker and Sons, Ontario, Canada 202
Canadian Mist, Brown-Forman, Canada 202
Caol Ila 12-year-old, Diageo, Scotland 72
Caol Ila 18-year-old, Diageo, Scotland 72
Caol Ila 25-year-old, Diageo, Scotland 73
Caol Ila Moch, Diageo, Scotland 73
Cardhu 12-year-old, Diageo, Scotland 73
Cardhu 15-year-old, Diageo, Scotland 73
Cardhu Amber Rock, Diageo, Scotland 74
Catdaddy, Piedmont Distillers,
North Carolina, USA 198
Catto's 12-year-old, Chivas/Pernod Ricard,
Scotland 133
Catto's 25-year-old, Chivas/Pernod Ricard,
Scotland 133
Catto's Rare Old Scottish, Chivas/Pernod Ricard,
Scotland 133
Charbay Hop Flavoured Whisky, Charbay,
USA 198
Chichibu IPA Cask Finish, Chichibu, Japan 225
Chichibu On The Way, Chichibu, Japan 225
Chichibu The Peated, Chichibu, Japan 228
Chieftan's Aberfeldy 14-year-old 2003,
Ian MacLeod Distillers, Scotland 279
Chivas Regal 12-year-old, Chivas/Pernod Ricard,
Scotland 133
Chivas Regal 18-year-old, Chivas/Pernod Ricard,
Scotland 133
Chivas Regal 25-year-old, Chivas/Pernod Ricard,
Scotland 133
Clan Campbell, Chivas/Pernod Ricard,
Scotland 133

Clan Denny Islay, Douglas Laing, Scotland 145
Clan Denny Speyside, Douglas Laing,
Scotland 146
The Claymore, Whyte & Mackay, Scotland 133
Clynelish 14-year-old, Clynelish, Scotland 74
Clynelish Distiller's Edition, Clynelish, Scotland ..74
Compass Box Aylsa Marriage, Compass Box,
Scotland 134
Compass Box Flaming Heart 15th Anniversary
Edition, Compass Box, Scotland 146
Compass Box Hedonism, Compass Box,
Scotland 151
Compass Box Oak Cross, Compass Box,
Scotland 146
Compass Box Optimism, Compass Box,
Scotland 146
Compass Box The Spice Tree, Compass Box,
Scotland 146
Compass Box The Peat Monster, Compass Box,
Scotland 146
Connemara, Cooley, Ireland 208
Connemara 10-year-old Sherry Finish,
Cooley, Ireland 208
Copper Dog, Diageo, Scotland 147
Corsair Ryemaggeddon, Corsair Distillery,
Kentucky, USA 188
Corsair Triple Smoke, Corsair Distillery,
Tennessee, USA 196
Cotswolds Single Malt Whisky, Cotswolds
Distillery, England 253
Cragganmore 12-year-old, Diageo, Scotland 74
Crawford's, Whyte & Mackay, Scotland 134
Crown Royal, Crown Royal Distillery,
Manitoba, Canada 202
Crown Royal Special Reserve, Crown Royal
Distillery, Manitoba, Canada 203
Cutty Sark, Edrington, Scotland 134
Cutty Sark 12-year-old, Edrington, Scotland 134
Cutty Sark 15-year-old, Edrington, Scotland 134
Cutty Sark 18-year-old, Edrington, Scotland 134
Cutty Sark 25-year-old, Edrington, Scotland 134

D

The Dalmore 12-year-old, Whyte & Mackay,
Scotland 75
The Dalmore 15-year-old, Whyte & Mackay,
Scotland 75
The Dalmore 18-year-old, Whyte & Mackay,
Scotland 75
The Dalmore 40-year-old, Whyte & Mackay,
Scotland 75
The Dalmore 1263 King Alexander III, Whyte &
Mackay, Scotland 75
The Dalmore Cigar Malt, Whyte & Mackay,
Scotland 76
The Dalmore Dominium, Whyte & Mackay,
Scotland 76
Dalwhinnie 15-year-old, Diageo, Scotland 76
Dalwhinnie Distiller's Edition, Diageo,
Scotland 76
Deanston 12-year-old, Burn Stewart Distillers,
Scotland 77
Devils Bit, McMenamin's, Oregon, USA 188
Dewar's 12-year-old, Dewar's, Scotland 135
Dewar's 18-year-old, Dewar's, Scotland 135
Dewar's Signature, Dewar's, Scotland 135
Dimple 12-year-old, Diageo, Scotland 135
Dimple 15-year-old, Diageo, Scotland 135
Dixie Dew, Heaven Hill, Kentucky, USA 194

E

Eagle Rare 17-year-old, Buffalo Trace,
Kentucky, USA 161
Eagle Rare Single Barrel 10-year-old,
Buffalo Trace, Kentucky, USA 161
Early Times, Brown Forman, Kentucky, USA 198
Eddu Gold, Distillerie des Menhirs, France 256
Eddu Grey Rock, Distillerie des Menhirs,
France 256
Eddu Silver, Distillerie des Menhirs, France 256
Edgefield Hogshead, McMenamins, Oregon,
USA 198
Elements of Islay Ar8, Speciality Drinks, England ..
..................279

Elijah Craig 12-year-old, Heaven Hill, Kentucky,
USA 164
Elijah Craig 18-year-old, Heaven Hill, Kentucky,
USA 164
Elmer T Lee, Buffalo Trace, Kentucky, USA 164
Evan Williams, Heaven Hill, Kentucky, USA 164
Evan Williams 12-year-old, Heaven Hill,
Kentucky, USA 164
Evan Williams 23-year-old, Heaven Hill,
Kentucky, USA 165

F

The Famous Grouse, Edrington, Scotland 135
The Famous Grouse 10-year-old, Edrington,
Scotland 147
The Famous Grouse The Black Grouse,
Edrington, Scotland 135
The Famous Grouse Gold Reserve 12-year-old,
Edrington, Scotland 136
The Famous Grouse Scottish Oak Finish,
Edrington, Scotland 136
The Famous Grouse The Snow Grouse,
Edrington, Scotland 151
Fettercairn 24-year-old, Fettercairn, Scotland ...77
Fettercairn 30-year-old, Fettercairn, Scotland ...77
Fettercairn 40-year-old, Fettercairn, Scotland ...77
FEW Bourbon, FEW, Illinois USA 165
Forty Creek Barrel Select, Kittling Ridge,
Ontario, Canada 203
Forty Creek Confederation Oak, Kittling Ridge,
Ontario, Canada 203
Forty Creek Double Barrel Reserve, Kittling Ridge,
Ontario, Canada 203
Four Roses, Four Roses, Kentucky, USA 165
Four Roses Small Batch, Four Roses,
Kentucky, USA 165
Four Roses Mariage, Four Roses, Kentucky,
USA 165
Four Roses Single Barrel, Four Roses, Kentucky,
USA 165
Fuji Gotemba 15-year-old, Kirin, Japan 228

G

Garrison Brothers Straight Bourbon, Garrison
Brothers, Texas, USA 166
George Dickel No 8, Diageo, Tennessee, USA ...185
George Dickel Superior No 12, Diageo,
Tennessee, USA 185
George T Stagg, Buffalo Trace, Kentucky,
USA 166
Georgia Moon, Heaven Hill, Kentucky, USA 194
Gingerbread House 2017, Wemyss Malts,
Scotland 279
Glann Ar Mor, Glan Ar Mor, France 256
Glen Breton 10-year-old, Glenora, Nova Scotia,
Canada 201
Glen Elgin 12-year-old, Diageo, Scotland 79
Glen Elgin 1998, Diageo, Scotland 79
Glen Garioch Founder's Reserve, Morrison
Bowmore, Scotland 88
Glen Garioch Virgin Oak, Morrison Bowmore,
Scotland 88
Glen Grant 10-year-old, Campari, Scotland 92
Glen Moray 12-year-old, Glen Moray, Scotland 97
Glen Spey 12-year-old, Diageo, Scotland 102
Glencadam 10-year-old, Glencadam, Scotland ...78
Glencadam 15-year-old, Glencadam, Scotland ...78
Glencadam 25-year-old, Glencadam, Scotland ...78
The GlenDronach 8-year-old The Hielan,
GlenDronach, Scotland 78
The GlenDronach 12-year-old, GlenDronach,
Scotland 78
The GlenDronach 15-year-old, GlenDronach,
Scotland 79
The GlenDronach 18-year-old, GlenDronach,
Scotland 79
The GlenDronach Peated, GlenDronach,
Scotland 79
Glenfarclas 10-year-old, Glenfarclas, Scotland ...80
Glenfarclas 12-year-old, Glenfarclas, Scotland ...80
Glenfarclas 15-year-old, Glenfarclas, Scotland ...80
Glenfarclas 21-year-old, Glenfarclas, Scotland ...80
Glenfarclas 25-year-old, Glenfarclas, Scotland ...80
Glenfarclas 30-year-old, Glenfarclas, Scotland .80

Glenfarclas 40-year-old, Glenfarclas, Scotland .80
Glenfarclas 105, Glenfarclas, Scotland 80
Glenfarclas Family Cask 1952 ED2 Cask 2115, Glenfarclas, Scotland 81
Glenfarclas Family Cask 1954 Cask 444, Glenfarclas, Scotland 81
Glenfarclas Family Cask 1957 Release III Cask 2, Glenfarclas, Scotland 81
Glenfarclas Family Cask 1959 Release III Cask 3227, Glenfarclas, Scotland 81
Glenfarclas Family Cask 1962 Cask 2647, Glenfarclas, Scotland 81
Glenfarclas Family Cask 1969 Cask 3188, Glenfarclas, Scotland 81
Glenfarclas Family Cask 1972 Cask 3546, Glenfarclas, Scotland 81
Glenfarclas Family Cask 1975 Cask 5038, Glenfarclas, Scotland 81
Glenfarclas Family Cask 1976 Cask 3111, Glenfarclas, Scotland 81
Glenfarclas Family Cask 1978 Cask 587, Glenfarclas, Scotland 81
Glenfarclas Family Cask 1979 Cask 146, Glenfarclas, Scotland 81
Glenfarclas Family Cask 1981 Cask 29, Glenfarclas, Scotland 81
Glenfarclas Family Cask 1988 Cask 7033, Glenfarclas, Scotland 81
Glenfarclas Family Cask 1989 Cask 11721, Glenfarclas, Scotland 81
Glenfarclas Family Cask 1991 Cask 5623, Glenfarclas, Scotland 81
Glenfarclas Family Cask 1993 Cask 11, Glenfarclas, Scotland 81
Glenfiddich 12-year-old, William Grant & Sons, Scotland 84
Glenfiddich 15-year-old Solera Reserve, William Grant & Sons, Scotland 84
Glenfiddich 18-year-old, William Grant & Sons, Scotland 84
Glenfiddich 21-year-old, William Grant & Sons, Scotland 85
Glenfiddich 50-year-old, William Grant & Sons, Scotland 85
Glenfiddich 125th Anniversary Edition, William Grant & Sons, Scotland 85
Glenfiddich Age of Discovery Bourbon 19-year-old, William Grant & Sons, Scotland ...85
Glenfiddich Age of Discovery Madeira 19-year-old, William Grant & Sons, Scotland ...85
Glenfiddich Rare Collection 40-year-old, William Grant & Sons, Scotland 85
Glenglassaugh 21-year-old, Glenglassaugh, Scotland 88
Glenglassaugh 30-year-old, Glenglassaugh, Scotland 88
Glenglassaugh 40-year-old, Glenglassaugh, Scotland 88
Glengoyne 10-year-old, Ian MacLeod, Scotland 89
Glengoyne 12-year-old, Ian MacLeod, Scotland .89
Glengoyne 15-year-old, Ian MacLeod, Scotland 89
Glengoyne 18-year-old, Ian MacLeod, Scotland 89
Glengoyne 21-year-old Sherry, Ian MacLeod, Scotland 89
Glengoyne Cask Strength Batch 4, Ian MacLeod, Scotland 89
Glenkinchie 12-year-old, Diageo, Scotland 92
The Glenlivet 12-year-old, Glenlivet, Scotland 92
The Glenlivet 15-year-old French Oak Reserve, Glenlivet, Scotland 92
The Glenlivet 18-year-old, Glenlivet, Scotland 93
The Glenlivet 21-year-old, Glenlivet, Scotland 93
The Glenlivet XXV, Glenlivet, Scotland 93
The Glenlivet Nadurra 16-year-old, Glenlivet, Scotland 93
Glenmorangie 18-year-old, Glenmorangie, Scotland 93
Glenmorangie Astar, Glenmorangie, Scotland ...96
Glenmorangie Milsean, Glenmorangie, Scotland 96
Glenmorangie Nectar d'Or, Glenmorangie, Scotland 96
Glenmorangie Original, Glenmorangie, Scotland 96
Glenmorangie Quinta Ruban, Glenmorangie, Scotland 96
Glenmorangie Signet, Glenmorangie, Scotland .96
Glenmorangie Tusail, Glenmorangie, Scotland ..96
The Glenrothes 25-year-old, Berry Bros, Scotland 100
The Glenrothes 30-year-old, Berry Bros, Scotland 100
The Glenrothes 1972, Berry Bros, Scotland 101
The Glenrothes 1978, Berry Bros, Scotland 101
The Glenrothes 1981, Berry Bros, Scotland 101
The Glenrothes 1984, Berry Bros, Scotland 101
The Glenrothes 1985, Berry Bros, Scotland 101
The Glenrothes 1987, Berry Bros, Scotland 101
The Glenrothes 1991, Berry Bros, Scotland 101
The Glenrothes 1992, Berry Bros, Scotland 101
The Glenrothes 1994, Berry Bros, Scotland 100
The Glenrothes Robur Reserve, Berry Bros, Scotland 100
The Glenrothes Select Reserve, Berry Bros, Scotland 100
Glenturret 10-year-old, Famous Grouse, Scotland 102
Grand Macnish, Macduff International, Scotland 136
Green Spot, Irish Distillers Pernod Ricard, Ireland 218
Greenore 15-year-old, Cooley, Ireland 219
Grüner Hund, Blaue Maus, Germany 257
Grüner Hund Fasstarke, Blaue Maus, Germany 257
Guillon No 1, Guillon, France 257

H

Haig Gold, Diageo, Scotland 136
The Hakushu 10-year-old, Hakushu Distillery, Japan 228
The Hakushu 12-year-old, Hakushu Distillery, Japan 228
The Hakushu 18-year-old, Hakushu Distillery, Japan 228
The Hakushu 25-year-old, Hakushu Distillery, Japan 228
The Hakushu Distiller's Reserve, Hakushu Distillery, Japan 228
Hankey Bannister, Hankey Bannister, Scotland .136
Hankey Bannister 12-year-old, Hankey Bannister, Scotland 136
Hankey Bannister 21-year-old, Hankey Bannister, Scotland 136
Hankey Bannister 25- year-old, Hankey Bannister, Scotland 136
Hankey Bannister 40-year-old, Hankey Bannister, Scotland 136
Hanyu 1988, Hanyu Distillery, Japan 229
Hanyu Single Cask 1991, Hanyu Distillery, Japan 229
Hazelburn 8-year-old, Springbank, Scotland 102
Heaven Hill, Heaven Hill, Kentucky, USA 166
Henry McKenna Single Barrel 10-year-old, Heaven Hill, Kentucky, USA 166
Hibiki 12-year-old, Suntory Distillery, Japan 236
Hibiki 17-year-old, Suntory Distillery, Japan 236
Hibiki 21-year-old, Suntory Distillery, Japan 236
Hibiki Harmony, Suntory Distillery, Japan 236
High West American Prairie Reserve, High West, Utah, USA 166
High West Campfire, High West, Utah, USA 199
Highland Park 12-year-old, Highland Park, Scotland 102
Highland Park 15-year-old, Highland Park, Scotland 102
Highland Park 16-year-old, Highland Park, Scotland 102
Highland Park 18-year-old, Highland Park, Scotland 103
Highland Park 21-year-old, Highland Park, Scotland 103
Highland Park 25-year-old, Highland Park, Scotland 103
Highland Park 30-year-old, Highland Park, Scotland 103
Highland Park 40-year-old, Highland Park, Scotland 103
Highland Park Dark Origins, Highland Park, Scotland 103
Highland Park Einar, Highland Park, Scotland 103
Highland Park Valkyrie, Highland Park, Scotland 103
Hokuto 12-year-old, Suntory Distillery, Japan ...229
Hudson Baby Bourbon, Tuthilltown, New York, USA 166
Hudson Four Grain Bourbon, Tuthilltown, New York, USA 167
Hudson Manhattan Rye, Tuthilltown, New York, USA 188
Hudson New York Corn, Tuthilltown, New York, USA 195

I

Ichiro Malt Eight of Hearts, Hanyu Distillery, Japan 229
Ichiro's Malt and Grain, Hanyu Distillery, Japan 236
Invergordon 10-year-old 2007, Duncan Taylor, Scotland 279
The Irishman Founder's Reserve, Walsh Whiskey, Ireland 212
The Irishman Single Malt, Walsh Whiskey, Ireland 208
The Irishman Single Malt 12-year-old, Walsh Whiskey, Ireland 208
Ironroot Hubris, Ironroot Republic, Texas, USA 195
Islay Mist 12-year-old, Macduff International, Scotland 137
Islay Reserve Blend, Berry Bros & Rudd, England 279
Isle of Arran Robert Burns, Isle of Arran Distillers, Scotland 59
Isle of Skye 21-year-old, Ian Macleod, Scotland 137
IW Harper, Four Roses, Kentucky, USA 167

J

J&B Jet, Diageo, Scotland 137
J&B Rare, Diageo, Scotland 137
Jack Daniel's Gentleman Jack, Jack Daniels, Tennessee, USA 185
Jack Daniel's Old No 7, Jack Daniels, Tennessee, USA 185
Jack Daniel's Single Barrel Select, Jack Daniels, Tennessee, USA 185
Jack Daniel's Single Barrel Rye, Jack Daniels, Tennessee, USA 185
Jameson, Irish Distillers Pernod Ricard, Ireland 212
Jameson 12-year-old Special Reserve, Irish Distillers Pernod Ricard, Ireland 212
Jameson 18-year-old Gold Reserve, Irish Distillers Pernod Ricard, Ireland 213
Jameson Crested, Irish Distillers Pernod Ricard, Ireland 212
Jameson Rarest Vintage Reserve, Irish Distillers Pernod Ricard, Ireland 213
Jameson Select Reserve Black Barrel, Irish Distillers Pernod Ricard, Ireland 213
Jefferson's 8-year-old, McLain and Kyne, New York, USA 167
Jim Beam, Jim Beam, Kentucky, USA 167
Jim Beam Black 8-year-old, Jim Beam, Kentucky, USA 167
Jim Beam Devil's Cut, Jim Beam, Kentucky, USA 167
Jim Beam Rye, Jim Beam, Kentucky, USA 189
John Barr, Whyte & Mackay, Scotland 137
John J Bowman Virginia Straight Bourbon, A Smith Bowman, Virginia, USA 172
Johnnie Walker Black Label, Diageo, Scotland .137
Johnnie Walker Blue Label, Diageo, Scotland 137–8
Johnnie Walker Gold Label, Diageo, Scotland ..138
Johnnie Walker Green Label 15-year-old, Diageo, Scotland 147
Johnnie Walker Island Green, Diageo, Scotland 147
Johnnie Walker Red Label, Diageo, Scotland 138
Johnny Drum, Kentucky Bourbon Distillers, Kentucky, USA 172

Johnny Drum Private Stock, Kentucky Bourbon
    Distillers, Kentucky, USA 172
Jura 10-year-old, Whyte & Mackay, Scotland 106
Jura 12-year-old, Whyte & Mackay, Scotland 106
Jura 18-year-old, Whyte & Mackay, Scotland 106
Jura Journey, Whyte & Mackay, Scotland 106
Jura Seven Wood, Whyte & Mackay, Scotland .106
JW Corn, Heaven Hill, Kentucky, USA 195

K
Karuizawa 17-year-old, Mercian, Japan 229
Karuizawa 1985 Single Cask, Karuizawa Distillery,
    Japan 229
Karuizawa 1986 Single Cask, Karuizawa Distillery,
    Japan 229
Kavalan Solist Cask Strength Ex-Bourbon Cask,
    Kavalan, Taiwan 274
Kavalan Solist Cask Strength Port Cask, Kavalan,
    Taiwan 275
Kavalan Solist Cask Strength Sherry Cask,
    Kavalan, Taiwan 274
Kentucky Gentleman Straight Bourbon, Heaven
    Hill, Kentucky, USA 172
Kentucky Peerless Rye, Kentucky Peerless,
    Louisville, USA 189
Kentucky Tavern, Barton, Kentucky, USA 172
Kilbeggan, Cooley, Ireland 213
Kilbeggan 15-year-old, Cooley, Ireland 213–14
Kilchoman Machir Bay, Kilchoman, Scotland 107
Knob Creek 9-year-old, Kentucky, USA 172
Knockando 12-year-old, Diageo, Scotland 107

L
La Alazana Sherry Cask, La Alazana Whisky,
    Argentina 241
Lagavulin 12-Year-old Cask Strength, Diageo,
    Scotland 110
Lagavulin 16-year-old, Diageo, Scotland 110
Lagavulin Distiller's Edition, Diageo, Scotland 110
Lambay Small Batch Blend, Lambay, Ireland 214
Langatun Old Deer Cask Strength, Langatun,
    Switzerland 271
Langatun Port Cask, Langatun, Switzerland 271
Langatun Quinta do Zambujeiro, Langatun,
    Switzerland 274
Laphroaig 10-year-old, Diageo, Scotland 110
Laphroaig 10-year-old Cask Strength, Diageo,
    Scotland 110
Laphroaig 18-year-old, Diageo, Scotland 111
Laphroaig 25-year-old, Diageo, Scotland 111
Laphroaig 30-year-old, Diageo, Scotland 111
Laphroaig Quarter Cask, Diageo, Scotland 111
Lark Classic Cask, Lark, Australia 246
Lark Distiller's Selection, Lark, Australia 246
Lark Single Malt Cask Strength, Lark,
    Australia 246
The Last Drop, Last Drop Distillers, Scotland 138
Lauder's, Macduff, Scotland 139
Limeburners Darkest Winter, Great Southern
    Distilling Company, Australia 247
Linkwood 12-year-old, Diageo, Scotland 111
Linkwood 24-year-old 1992 Small Batch,
    WM Cadenhead & Co, Scotland 279
Locke's 8-year-old, Cooley, Ireland 214
Longmorn 15-year-old, Pernod Ricard,
    Scotland 114
Longmorn 16-year-old, Pernod Ricard,
    Scotland 114
Longmorn 17-year-old Cask Strength, Pernod
    Ricard, Scotland 114
Longrow 10-year-old, Springbank, Scotland 114
Longrow 10-year-old 100 Proof, Springbank,
    Scotland 114
Longrow 14-year-old, Springbank, Scotland 114
Longrow CV, Springbank, Scotland 114
Longrow Gaja Barolo, Springbank, Scotland 114

M
The Macallan 10-year-old, The Macallan,
    Scotland 115
The Macallan 12-year-old, The Macallan,
    Scotland 115
The Macallan 18-year-old, The Macallan,
    Scotland 115
The Macallan 25-year-old, The Macallan,
    Scotland 115

The Macallan 30-year-old, The Macallan,
    Scotland 115
The Macallan Fine Oak 10-year-old,
    The Macallan, Scotland 116
The Macallan Fine Oak 12-year-old,
    The Macallan, Scotland 116
The Macallan Fine Oak 15-year-old,
    The Macallan, Scotland 116
The Macallan Fine Oak 18-year-old,
    The Macallan, Scotland 116
The Macallan Fine Oak 21-year-old,
    The Macallan, Scotland 116
The Macallan Fine Oak 25-year-old,
    The Macallan, Scotland 116
The Macallan Fine Oak 1824 Series Amber,
    The Macallan, Scotland 116
The Macallan Fine Oak 1824 Series Gold,
    The Macallan, Scotland 117
The Macallan Fine Oak 1824 Series Ruby,
    The Macallan, Scotland 117
The Macallan Fine Oak 1824 Series Sienna,
    The Macallan, Scotland 117
McCarthy's Oregon Single Malt, Clear Creek,
    Oregon, USA 196
Machrie Moor Batch 7, Isle of Arran Distillers,
    Scotland 59
Mackmyra Brukswhisky, Mackmyra,
    Sweden 265, 270
Mackmyra Moment Prestige, Mackmyra, Sweden ..270
Mackmyra Svensk Ek, Mackmyra, Sweden 270
Mackmyra Svensk Rök, Mackmyra, Sweden 270
Maker's Mark, Maker's Mark, Kentucky, USA ..172–3
Mellow Corn, Heaven Hill, Kentucky, USA 195
Method and Madness Pot Still,
    Method and Madness, Ireland 218
Michter's US *1 Small Batch, Buffalo Trace,
    Kentucky, USA 173
Millstone 6-year-old, Master of Malt, England ..279
Millstone 12-year-old Sherry Cask, Zuidam
    Distillers, The Netherlands 261
Millstone 92 Rye Whisky, Zuidam Distillers,
    The Netherlands 261
Millstone 1996 American Oak Single Cask,
    Zuidam Distillers, The Netherlands 264
Millstone 2010 Peated, Zuidam Distillers,
    The Netherlands 264
Miltonduff 15-year-old, Miltonduff, Scotland 117
Miltonduff 20-year-old 1995, Berry Bros & Rudd,
    England 279
Miyagikyo 10-year-old, Nikka Distillery, Japan ..229
Miyagikyo 12-year-old, Nikka Distillery, Japan ..229
Miyagikyo 15-year-old, Nikka Distillery, Japan ..232
Miyagikyo Single Cask 1989, Nikka Distillery,
    Japan 232
Miyagikyo Single Malt, Nikka Distillery, Japan ..232
Monkey Shoulder, William Grant, Scotland 150
Mortlach 16-year-old, Diageo, Scotland 117
Mortlach 18-year-old, Diageo, Scotland 117
Mortlach 25-year-old, Diageo, Scotland 117
Mortlach Rare Old, Diageo, Scotland 118

N
New Holland Beer Barrel Bourbon, High West,
    Utah, USA 199
Nikka Pure Black, Nikka Distillery, Japan 237
Nikka Pure Malt 12-year-old, Nikka Distillery,
    Japan 237
Nikka Pure Malt 17-year-old, Nikka Distillery,
    Japan 237
Nikka Pure Malt 21-year-old, Nikka Distillery,
    Japan 237
Nikka Pure Red, Nikka Distillery, Japan 237
Nikka Pure White, Nikka Distillery, Japan 237
Nikka Rare Old Super, Nikka Distillery, Japan ..236
Nikka Single Cask Malt 1991, Nikka Distillery,
    Japan 232
Noah's Mill, Willet, Kentucky, USA 173
NZ Whisky Co Diggers & Ditch,
    Diggers & Ditch, New Zealand 264
NZ Whisky Co High Wheeler,
    Diggers & Ditch, New Zealand 264
NZ Whisky Co Oamaruvian,
    Diggers & Ditch, New Zealand 264

NZ Whisky Co Otago 30-year-old,
    Diggers & Ditch, New Zealand 264

O
Oban 14-year-old, Diageo, Scotland 118
Oban The Distiller's Edition, Diageo, Scotland 118
Old Crow, Jim Beam, Kentucky, USA 173
Old Fitzgerald Prime, Buffalo Trace, Kentucky,
    USA 173
Old Forester, Brown Forman, Kentucky, USA 176
Old Forester Signature, Brown Forman, Kentucky,
    USA 176
Old Parr 12-year old, Diageo, Scotland 139
Old Parr Superior, Diageo, Scotland 139
Old Particular Bunnahabhain 15-year-old 2001,
    Douglas Laing & Co, Scotland 279
Old Particular Consortium of Cards Laphroaig
    18-year-old, Douglas Laing & Co, Scotland 279
Old Particular Consortium of Cards Mortlach
    13-year-old 2003, Douglas Laing & Co,
    Scotland 279
Old Pogue, Old Pogue, Kentucky, USA 176
Old Potrero 18th-Century-Style Whiskey,
    Anchor Brewery, California, USA 189
Old Potrero Hotaling's Single Malt Whiskey,
    Anchor Brewery, California, USA 189
Old Potrero Single Malt Straight Rye Whiskey,
    Anchor Brewery, California, USA 189
Old Pulteney 12-year-old, Pulteney, Scotland 118
Old Pulteney 17-year-old, Pulteney, Scotland 118
Old Pulteney 21-year-old, Pulteney, Scotland 119
Old Pulteney 30-year-old, Pulteney, Scotland 119
Old Rip Van Winkle 10 years,
    Old Rip Van Winkle, Kentucky, USA 176
Old Taylor, Jim Beam, Kentucky, USA 176
Overeem Bourbon Cask Strength, Overeem,
    Australia 247
Overeem Port Cask, Overeem, Australia 247

P
Paddy Old Irish, Irish Distillers Pernod Ricard,
    Ireland 214
Paul John Bold, John Distilleries, India 260
Paul John Brilliance, John Distilleries, India 261
Paul John Edited, John Distilleries, India 261
Paul John Peated, John Distilleries, India 261
Penderyn Madeira, Penderyn, Wales 275
Penderyn Peated, Penderyn, Wales 275
Pendryn Sherrywood, Penderyn, Wales 275
Pig's Nose, Whyte & Mackay, Scotland 139
Pikesville Supreme, Heaven Hill, Kentucky,
    USA 192
Port Askaig 100 Proof, Speciality Drinks,
    England 279
Powers 12-year-old, Irish Distillers
    Pernod Ricard, Ireland 214
Powers Gold Label, Irish Distillers
    Pernod Ricard, Ireland 214
Pulteney 11-year-old 2006 Small Batch,
    WM Cadenhead & Co, Scotland 279
Puni Sole, Puni, Italy 261

R
Rebel Yell Small Batch, Rebel Yell, Kentucky,
    USA 177
Redbreast 12-year-old, Irish Distillers Pernod
    Ricard, Ireland 218
Redbreast 12-year-old Cask Strength, Irish
    Distillers Pernod Ricard, Ireland 218
Redbreast 15-year-old, Irish Distillers Pernod
    Ricard, Ireland 218
Redbreast 16-year-old 2001, Master of Malt,
    England 279
Redbreast 21-year-old, Irish Distillers Pernod
    Ricard, Ireland 219
Redbreast Lustau, Irish Distillers Pernod Ricard,
    Ireland 218
Reisetbauer 12-year-old, Reisetbauer, Austria ..252
Ridgemont Reserve 1792, Barton, Kentucky,
    USA 177
Rittenhouse 23-year-old, Heaven Hill, Kentucky,
    USA 192
Rittenhouse 100 Proof Bottled-in-Bond,
    Heaven Hill, Kentucky, USA 192
Rittenhouse Rye, Heaven Hill, Kentucky, USA ..192
Rock Oyster, Douglas Laing, Scotland 150

Roe & Co, Diageo, Ireland 215
Rogue Dead Guy, Rogue, Oregon, USA 199
Royal Brackla 10-year-old, John Dewar & Sons, Scotland 119
Royal Lochnagar 12-year-old, Diageo, Scotland 119
Royal Lochnagar Selected Reserve, Diageo, Scotland 119
Royal Salute 21-year-old, Pernod Ricard, Scotland 139
Royal Salute Hundred Cask Selection, Pernod Ricard, Scotland 139

S

St George, St George, California, USA 199
St George's The English Chapter 15, St George's, England 253
St George's The English Original, St George's, England 253
St George's The English Smokey, St George's, England 253
St George's The Norfolk Farmers, St George's, England 253
Säntis Malt Edition Dreifaltigkeit, Santis Malt, Switzerland 274
Säntisblick Peat Fire, Säntisblick, Switzerland ..274
Säntisblick Portwein Fass ausgereift, Säntisblick, Switzerland 274
Sazerac 6-year-old Rye, Buffalo Trace, Kentucky, USA 192
Sazerac 18-year-old Rye, Buffalo Trace, Kentucky, USA 192
Scallywag, Douglas Laing, Scotland 150
Scapa Glansa, Scapa, Scotland 120
Scapa Skiren, Scapa, Scotland 120
Scottish Leader 12-year-old, Burn Stewart, Scotland 140
Seagram's 83, Seagrams, Canada 203
Sheep Dip, Sheep Dip, Scotland 150
Singleton of Dufftown, Diageo, Scotland 77
The Singleton 12-year-old, Diageo, Scotland 97
The Singleton 15-year-old, Diageo, Scotland 97
The Singleton 18-year-old, Diageo, Scotland 97
The Singleton 28-year-old, Diageo, Scotland 97
The Six Isles, Ian MacLeod, Scotland 150
Slyrs Bavarian single malt, Slyrs, Germany 257
Smögen 6-year-old, Smögen Whiskey, Sweden 271
Smögen Sherry Project, Smögen Whiskey, Sweden 271
Something Special, Chivas/Pernod Ricard, Scotland 140
Speyburn 25-year-old, Inver House, Scotland ...120
Spirit of Hven Organic Seven Stars Mizar, Spirit of Hven, Sweden 271
Spirit of Hven Tycho's Star, Spirit of Hven, Sweden 271
Springbank 10-year-old, Springbank, Scotland .121
Springbank 15-year-old, Springbank, Scotland ..121
Springbank 16-year-old Rum Wood, Springbank, Scotland 121
Springbank 18-year-old, Springbank, Scotland .121
Springbank 100 Proof, Springbank, Scotland 120
Springbank Vintage 1997, Springbank, Scotland 121
Stagg Junior, Buffalo Trace, Kentucky, USA 177
Stauning KAOS, Stauning, Denmark 252
Stauning Peated 6th Edition, Stauning, Denmark 252
Stewarts Cream of the Barley, Stewarts of Dundee, Scotland 140
Stranahan's Colorado Whiskey, Stranahan's, Colorado, USA 197
Strathisla 12-year-old, Chivas Regal, Scotland 121
Strathmill 24-year-old 1993, WM Cadenhead & Co, Scotland 279
Stronachie 18-year-old, AD Rattray, Scotland ..279
Sullivans Cove Bourbon Cask Strength, Tasmania Distillery, Australia 247
Sullivans Cove Double Cask, Tasmania Distillery, Australia 247
Sullivans Cove French Oak Cask, Tasmania Distillery, Australia 247
Suntory Kakubin White Label, Suntory, Japan 236

T

Talisker 10-year-old, Diageo, Scotland 122
Talisker 18-year-old, Diageo, Scotland 122
Talisker 25-year-old, Diageo, Scotland 122
Talisker 30-year-old, Diageo, Scotland 122
Talisker 57 North, Diageo, Scotland 122
Talisker Dark Storm, Diageo, Scotland 122
Talisker The Distiller's Edition, Diageo, Scotland 122
Talisker Storm, Diageo, Scotland 123
Tamdhu, Edrington, Scotland 123
Tamdhu 25-year-old, Edrington, Scotland 123
Tamdhu 28-year-old, MacKillop's Choice, Scotland 279
Tamnavulin 12-year-old, Whyte & Mackay, Scotland 123
Té Bheag Connoisseurs Blend, Praban na Linne, Scotland 140
Teacher's Highland Cream, Beam Global, Scotland 140
Teacher's Origin, Beam Global, Scotland 140
Teeling The Revival, Teeling Whiskey, Ireland ..209
Teeling Single Grain, Teeling Whiskey, Ireland 219
Teeling Single Malt, Teeling Whiskey, Ireland ...209
Teeling Small Batch, Teeling Whiskey, Ireland ...215
Templeton Rye, Templeton, Iowa, USA 193
Ten High, Barton, Kentucky, USA 177
Thomas H Handy Sazerac Rye 2017, Buffalo Trace, Kentucky, USA 193
Three Ships 10-year-old Limited Edition, James Sedgwick Distillery, South Africa 265
Three Ships Bourbon Cask Finish, James Sedgwick Distillery, South Africa 265
Timorous Beastie, Douglas Laing, Scotland 151
Tobermory 10-year-old, Tobermoray, Scotland 123
Tobermory 15-year-old, Tobermoray, Scotland 123
Tobermory Heavily Peated 19-year-old, Master of Malt, England 279
Tomatin 12-year-old, Tomatin, Scotland 128
Tomatin 14-year-old, Tomatin, Scotland 128
Tomatin 18-year-old, Tomatin, Scotland 128
Tomatin 25-year-old, Tomatin, Scotland 128
Tomatin 30-year-old, Tomatin, Scotland 128
Tomatin Cask Strength, Tomatin, Scotland 128
Tomatin Legacy, Tomatin, Scotland 128
Tomintoul 10-year-old, Tomintoul, Scotland 129
Tomintoul 16-year-old, Tomintoul, Scotland 129
Tomintoul 27-year-old, Tomintoul, Scotland 129
Tomintoul Peaty Tang, Tomintoul, Scotland 129
Tormore 12-year-old, Tormore, Scotland 129
Triple Eight Notch, Triple Eight Distillery, Massachusetts, USA 199
Tullamore Dew 10-year-old, Midleton, Ireland ...215
Tullibardine 1993, Tullibardine, Scotland 129
Tutty Fruity Zing 23-year-old 1993, Wemyss Malts, Scotland 279
The Tyrconnell 10-year-old Madeira Cask, Cooley, Ireland 209
The Tyrconnell 10-year-old Port Cask, Cooley, Ireland 209
The Tyrconnell 10-year-old Sherry Cask, Cooley, Ireland 209
The Tyrconnell 15-year-old Single Cask 957/92, Cooley, Ireland 209
The Tyrconnell 15-year-old Single Cask 1850/52, Cooley, Ireland 209

V

Van Winkle Special Reserve 12-year-old, Old Rip Van Winkle, Kentucky, USA 178
VAT 69, Diageo, Scotland 140
Very Old Barton 6-year-old, Kentucky, USA 178

W

Wasmund's Rappahannock Single Malt, Copper Fox, Virginia, USA 197
Weller Antique, Buffalo Trace, Kentucky, USA ..178
Wemyss Malts The Hive 12-year-old, Wemyss, Scotland 151
Wemyss Malts Peat Chimney 12-year-old, Wemyss, Scotland 151
Wemyss Malts The Spice King 12-year-old, Wemyss, Scotland 151
Westland American Oak, Westland Distillery, Washington, USA 197
Westland Peated, Westland Distillery, Washington, USA 197
Westland Sherry Wood, Westland Distillery, Washington, USA 197
WhistlePig 12-year-old Old World Cask Finish, WhistlePig Whiskey, Vermont, USA 193
WhistlePig The Boss Hogg IV, WhistlePig Whiskey, Vermont, USA 199
White Horse, Diageo, Scotland 141
Whyte & Mackay 30-year-old, Whyte and Mackay, Scotland 141
Whyte & Mackay 40-year-old, Whyte and Mackay, Scotland 141
Whyte & Mackay Special, Whyte and Mackay, Scotland 141
Whyte & Mackay The Thirteen, Whyte and Mackay, Scotland 141
The Wild Geese Fourth Centennial, Cooley, Ireland 215
The Wild Geese Rare Irish, Cooley, Ireland 215
The Wild Geese Single Malt, Cooley, Ireland 209
Wild Turkey, Wild Turkey, Kentucky, USA 179
Wild Turkey 101, Wild Turkey, Kentucky, USA 179
Wild Turkey 101 Rye, Wild Turkey, Kentucky, USA 193
Wild Turkey American Spirit 15 year-old, Wild Turkey, Kentucky, USA 179
Wild Turkey Kentucky Spirit, Wild Turkey, Kentucky, USA 179
Wild Turkey Rare Breed, Wild Turkey, Kentucky, USA 184
Wild Turkey Russell's Reserve Bourbon, Wild Turkey, Kentucky, USA 184
Wild Turkey Russell's Reserve Rye, Wild Turkey, Kentucky, USA 193
William Grant 12-year-old, William Grant, Scotland 144
William Grant 15-year-old, William Grant, Scotland 144
William Grant 25-year-old, William Grant, Scotland 144
William Grant Ale Cask, William Grant, Scotland 144
William Larue Weller, Buffalo Trace, Kentucky, USA 179
Wiser's Deluxe, Hiram Walker and Sons, Ontario, Canada 203
WL Weller 7-year-old Special Reserve, Buffalo Trace, Kentucky, USA 178
Woodford Reserve Distiller's Select, Brown-Forman, Kentucky, USA 184
Wood's High Mountain Tenderfoot Whiskey, Wood's, Colorado, USA 197
Writers' Tears Cask Strength, Walsh Whiskey, Ireland 215
Writers' Tears Copper Pot, Walsh Whiskey, Ireland 215

Y

The Yamazaki 10-year-old, Suntory Distillery, Japan 232
The Yamazaki 12-year-old, Suntory Distillery, Japan 232
The Yamazaki 18-year-old, Suntory Distillery, Japan 232
The Yamazaki 25-year-old, Suntory Distillery, Japan 232
The Yamazaki Distiller's Reserve, Suntory Distillery, Japan 233
Yellow Spot, Spot Whiskeys, Ireland 219
Yoichi, Nikka Distillery, Japan 233
Yoichi 10-year-old, Nikka Distillery, Japan 233
Yoichi 12-year-old, Nikka Distillery, Japan 233

GENERAL INDEX

Page numbers in *italics* refer to illustrations

A
Aberlour 52–3
Akutu, Ichiro 227
alcohol by volume (ABV) 16, 25, 30
alcoholic content 16, 21, 25
Alexander III, King 75
Almeida, Shilton 263
American Distillers Institute 247
American single malt 196–7
Ardbeg 54–5, 56–7, 99, 113, 145, 255, 267
Argentina 11, 241
Arkwright, Richard 76
Australia 11, 241–7, 263
Austria 250, 252
B
backset 20
bacteria 16, 20
Baker, David 241, 244
Balcones 157, 158–9, 194, 196
Baring, Alexander 214
barley 12, 13, *13*, 16, 20, 30
Barrie, Rachel *126*, 127
Beam, Baker 157
Beam, Bettye Jo 178
Beam, Craig 164, 169
Beam, James 'Jim' 157, 169, 171
Beam, Johannes 'Jacob' 10
Beam, Parker 164, 169, 181
Belgium 252
BenRiach Distillery Co 62–4, 127
Berry Green, Christopher 100
Bhakta, Raj Peter 193
Bignell, Peter *242*, 244, 246
Blanton, Colonel Albert 160, 163
blended malt whisky 19, 30, 130
  Japan 237
  New Zealand 264
  Scotland 144–51
blended whisk(e)y 30
  Canada 202–3
  France 256
  how to make 18–19
  Ireland 212–15
  Japan 224, 233
  Scotland 130–44
  South Africa 265
bottles 44
Bouillion, Etienne 252
bourbon 31, 157–84, 191, 198
  how to make 20–1
  straight bourbon 21, 31, 157, 191
Brenne 183
Bridges, Jeff 176
Broger, Bruno and Eugen 252
Bronfman, Sam 143, 202
Brosnan, Pierce 121
Brown, George 176
Bruce, Rob 141
Bruichladdich 67–9, 70–1
buckwheat spirit 256
Buffalo Trace 161, 162–3, 179
Bulleit, Tom 161
Burke, James Lee 143
Bush, George HW 100, 159
Bushmills 10, 206, 208, 210–11, 212
C
Calenby, Pär 268
Camus, Cyril 214
Canada 11, 200–3
  blended whiskey 202–3
  rye whiskey 188
  single malt 201
Capone, Al 178, 193, 202
casks 14–15, 17, 18, 21
Chang, Ian *276*, 277
Charles, Prince of Wales 113, 145
Charlie, Bonnie Prince 125, 130–1
Chasko, Alex 217
Chichibu 225–8
Churchill, Winston 105
Clement, Doug 244
Cockram, Michael 55
cocktails 32–7
Coffey, Aeneas 11
Collina, Pierlugi 137–8
column (continuous or Coffey) still 19, 20–1, 130
corn 20, 30, 31, 194
corn whiskey 31, 194–5
Corsair 188, 190–1, 196
Coughlin, Simon 71
Cowdery, Charles 178
Cox, Ronnie 100, 132, *142*, 143
Craig, Elijah 164
Crow, James 173, 187
Cumming, John Fleetwood 73
Cummings, Elizabeth 73
Cummings, Helen 73
Cummings, John 73
the cut 16–17
D
Daniel, Jack 10
Davis, Greg 177
Dench, Judi 121
Denmark 252–3, 254–5
Dewar, Tommy 135
Dickel, George 163
distillation, malt 16–17
D'Orazio, Angela 273
doubler 21
Duckett, Tim 244
E
Edward of Woodstock 199
England 253
Eschmann, Bruno 274
F
feints 17
fermentation 16, 20, 30
Ferroni, Guillaume 259
flavour categories 26–7
Fleming, Ian 121–2
foreshots 16
France 256–7, 258–9
Frank, Stephen 157
G
Germany 250, 257
Gladstone, William 77
Glaser, John 134, 146, *148*, 149
glasses 24, 27, *28–9*
Glemorangie 93, 96, 98–9
Glen Garioch 88, 90–1, 127, 151
Glenfarclas 80–3
Glenfiddich 84–7
The Glenlivet 92–3, 94–5
Gordon, Peter 84
grain whisk(e)y 19, 30, 130, 151
  Denmark 252
  England 253
  Ireland 219
Grant, George 80, *81*, 83
Grant, John 80, *81*, 83
Grant, Major 92
grist 16, 31
H
Handy, Thomas H 163, 193
Hayden, Basil 160
heads 16
Heaven Hill 166, 168–9, 195
Henderson, Lincoln 181
Henry VIII 10
Heydon, Richard 160
Hicks, Robert 55
Highland Park 102–5
history of whisk(e)y 10–11
Houston, Sam 159
Hunter, Ian 113
I
Inatomi, Dr 235
independent bottlers 278–9
India 250, 257, 260–1, 262–3
Ireland 10, 11, 28, 204–21
  blended whiskey 30, 212–15
  grain whiskey 219
  pot still whiskey 30, 218–19
  single malt 208–9
Irish Whiskey Association (IWA) 218
Italy 261
Izzard, Eddie 203
J
Jackson, Michael 149, 200
James Bond 121–2
Japan 11, 222–37
  blended malt 237
  blended whisky 224, 233
  single malt 224, 225–33
Jim Beam 21, 167, 170–1, 175
John Distilleries 260, 262–3
Johnson, Freddie 163
Johnson, Jimmy 163
Johnson, Pussyfoot 143
Johnston, Donald and Alexander 113
Jones, Owen 143
K
Kamiguchi, Naofumi 231
Kass, Larry 169
Kavalan 274, 276–7
L
labels 44
Lagavulin 108–10, 113
Laphroaig 110–11, 112–13, 140
Lark, Bill *242*, 243, 244, 246
Lark, Kirsty 246
Larue, William 177
Lee, Elmer T 160, 164, 181
Lincoln, Abraham 172
Lincoln County process 31, 184
low wine 17
Lumsden, Dr Bill 57, 93, 96, 99, 127
M
McAfee Brothers 160
MacAskill, Hugh and Kenneth 125
McCarthy, Thomas 181
McClements, George 199
McCoy, William S 134
Mackmyra 265, 267, 270, 272–3
MacLean, Charles 141
Maguire, Patrick 243, 244
Maker's Mark *21*, 171, 172–3, 174–5, 195
malt distillation 16–17
malt tax 10
mash tun 16
mashbill 20
mashing 16, 20, 30
master blenders 19
maturation 17, 21
Maytag, Fritz 189
Melander, Rogers 268
Michalek, Joseph 198
mizuwari-style 231
Molin, Henrik 267–8
moonshine 194
Moore, Chris *32–3*
Morgan, Nicholas 141
Morgan, Piers 137–8
Morris, Chris 187
Murray, Jim 255
N
Nägele, Arthur 250
Napoleon III, Emperor 143
The Netherlands 261, 264
'new make' spirit 17
New Zealand 264
Nikka 224, 225, 230–1, 232, 237
Noe, Booker 160, 171, 181
Noe, Fred 160
nosing 24, 27
Nouet, Martine 114
O
oak, role of 14
Orma 249
Overeem, Casey 243–4, 247
Overeem, Jane 244, 247
P
packaging 44
Parc, Allison *182*, 183
Parr, Thomas 139
Paterson, Richard 75, 139
peat 14, 16
Penn, William 192
Pepper, Elijah and Oscar 187
Peychaud, Antoine 193
Pickerell, Dave 193
pot stills 16, *17*, 21
Q
quaich 28, *28*
R
Ramsay, Greg 244, 264
Ransom, Robert 145
Raymond, Paul 73
Reavey, Carl 71
Reynier, Mark 71
Roussier, David 256, 259
Royal Society for the Protection of Birds 135
Russell, Jimmy 179, *180*, 181, 184, 193
Rutledge, Jim 181
Ryan, John 213
rye 20, 30, 31, 188
rye whisk(e)y
  Canada 31, 188
  The Netherlands 261
  USA 31, 188–93
S
Samuels, Bill 173, 195
Samuels, Rob 173
Samuels, William 172, 173
Scotch Whisky Association (SWA) 130, 144, 146, 147, 149
Scotland 10–11, 20, 21, 46–151, 263
  blended malt 144–51
  blended whisky 48, 130–44
  grain whisky 151
  single malt 30, 48, 50–129, 130
  styles of whisky 18, 19
  whisky drinking 28
single blend 264
single grain 264, 265
single malt whiskies 18, 19, 20, 21, 30
  American single malt 196–7
  Argentina 241
  Australia 241, 246
  Austria 252
  Belgium 252
  Canada 201
  Denmark 253
  England 253
  France 256–7
  Germany 257
  how to make 16–17
  India 257, 260–1
  Ireland 208–9
  Italy 261
  Japan 224, 225–33
  The Netherlands 261, 264
  New Zealand 264
  Scotland 48, 50–129, 130
  Sweden 270–1
  Switzerland 271, 274
  Taiwan 274–5
  Wales 275
Smith, Dr Ashbel 159
Smögen *266*, 268, 271
sour mash process 20–1
South Africa 265
Spirit of Hven *266*, 267–8, *268*, *269*, 271
Stagg, George T 163, 164, 187
Stauning 254–5
Stein, Robert 10
stillage 20
Suntory 224, 225, 234–5
Swan, Dr Jim 127, 256, 259, 277
Sweden 255, 265–71, 272–3
Switzerland 248–51, 271, 274
T
tails 17
Taiwan 11, 250, 274–5, 276–7
Taketsuru, Masataka 231, 235
Talisker 121–3, 124–5
Tasmania 240, 243
tasting symbols 43
tasting whisky 24–5
Tate, Chip 159
Taylor, Colonel Edmund 187
Teeling 215, 216–17, 219
Teeling, Jack and Stephen 206, 217
Teeling, John 206, 217
Tennessee whiskey 31, 184–5
Thomson, Jackie 267
three-step process 20
Torii, Shinjiro 235
U
USA 11, 20, 21, 152–99
  American single malt 196–7
  bourbon 157–84, 191, 198
  corn whiskey 194–5
  other American whiskies 198–9
  rye whiskey 188–93
  Tennessee whiskey 31, 184–5
  wheat whiskey 195
V
Vahl, Mats and Per de 268
Van Winkle, Julian 181
Van Winkle, Pappy 172, 178
Van Winkle, Rip 176
Van Winkle, Sally 173
Vitale, David 244
W
Wales 275
Walker, Billy 62, 127
Walsh 220–1
Walsh, Bernard and Rosemary 206, 221
Warenghem 258–9
washback 16
Wasmund, Rick 197
water
  adding to drinks 24, 25
  in whisky making 12–13
Weller, Keith 178
Weller, William Larue 163, 178–9
wheat 20, 30, 31, 195
wheat whiskey 31, 195
Whisky Magazine 36, 95, 121, 141, 172, 235
white dog 21
Wild Turkey 179–81
Willard, Frances Elizabeth 165
Williams, Evan 10, 164
Williamson, Bessie 113
Winchester, Alan 95
Wizards of Whisky World Whisky Awards 221, 268, 271
Woodford Reserve 186–7
World Whisky Awards 102, 145, 219, 236, 247
wort 16
Y
yeast 12, 13, 16
Z
Zdobylak, Mark and Dustin 166

ACKNOWLEDGEMENTS

AUTHOR'S ACKNOWLEDGEMENTS

It's more than ten years since the first edition of the book, and when it comes to writing acknowledgements it sinks in just how quickly time has flown by, and how much has changed. The first edition was the first book I wrote reflecting my take on this wonderful world of which I'm a part. I wrote two pages of acknowledgements and a lot of it was emotional and sentimental guff. This time around it will be nowhere near as long-winded, but it may well be just as emotional.

I want to start by thanking Jacqui Small for giving me the chance to write both this and the first book, and for pretty much leaving me to get on with it. A big thank you, too, to the incredible Robin Rout, whose design made the first book so wonderful and who has excelled himself on this one. Jacqui has threatened to retire after this book and I doubt I'll work with Robin again, so a huge thank you to both. It's been an absolute honour.

Thank you, too, to my long suffering editors, Jo Copestick, and latterly, Joe Hallsworth, who must have wondered what had hit him when he inherited not one but two huge book projects of mine. Thank you, too, to Hilary Lumsden, who has pored over every word in this book and gone way beyond the call of duty to make me look and sound much, much better than I have any right to.

I'd also like to thank Krzysztof, Ronnie and the whole team at my new employees, Stilnovisti. It's early days, and who knows where we will end up, but believing in me and giving me the chance to edit again means everything to me.

I'd like to thank the many distillers, blenders, warehouse workers, ambassadors, retailers, and public relations folk, who have always worked so hard to make my job as easy as possible in so many different ways. They are far too many to mention by name, but I am proud that I shared drams with wonderful people right across the world, and that they have all made me feel that I am part of a huge and wonderful family. It never ceases to amaze me how humble the world of whisky is, and I am almost embarrassed by the attention we receive in the media, while the real whisky heroes go mostly unsung. My greatest respect to all of them.

I once described the world of whisky as like a conveyor belt which has been moving for hundreds of years, and will move forward for hundreds of years more. Everyone involved with it steps on to the conveyor belt for some years - decades if they're lucky - and then they step or fall off somewhere down the line, and on it moves. Inevitably, then, over a period of ten years, some people have left the conveyor belt.

I want to mention just three of the less celebrated members of the whisky profession who are no longer with us. The first is Henry Besant, who died very prematurely in 2013. He had a huge influence on me, and nurtured my love of bourbon, and his death was a huge shock. I will never forget him.

At the start of 2018, I heard that Carl Reavey had died. He worked at Bruichladdich distillery and his passion and love for Islay and his distillery was infectious. He was full of ideas, was bursting with enthusiasm and was generous with his time. He will be sadly missed.

As I write I have just heard of the passing of John Ryan, the man who introduced me to Irish whiskey in general, and Jameson in particular, long before I started writing about whisky for a living. John was a wonderful advocate for Irish whiskey and a proud Irishman. It's appropriate that in 2018 Jameson released a cask strength version of its 18-year-old, because in the first edition of this book I wrote about John and one of my favourite whiskey stories under the entry for Jameson 18-year-old Reserve, and I have retained it for this edition.

As many people know, I became severely ill in 2013 and I have battled ever since with my health. I have pretty much won that battle, but it has been very tough. If you're reading this and you're struggling, please, please, please talk to someone about it. It might save your life.

I would like to thank those people who looked out for me during those dark days: in particular, my very good friend Tony Bagnall, Andrew Naylor Higgins, Chris Rodden, Doug McIvor, Ronnie Cox, Richard Paterson and Mark Gillespie.

A special thank you to Joanna Seymour, and to my amazing and long-suffering wife Sally and my fantastic children Julian, Louie and Madeleine. I am proud of you all.

Finally, since the last edition of the book, my beloved Leicester City have won the English Premier League and reached the quarter finals of the UEFA Champions League, and my beloved All Blacks have won the Rugby World Cup. Twice. Miracles can happen.

This book is dedicated to the memory of my dad.

May 2018

PUBLISHER'S ACKNOWLEDGEMENTS

The publisher would also like to thank the following people who helped in the production of this book:
Chris Maybin, Liz Lock and Alex Huskinson of The Whisky Exchange;
Riedel for the loan of glassware for photography;
Chris Moore for the cocktail recipes and the use of his bar, Coupette, as the shoot location.

PICTURE CREDITS

The publisher wishes to thank the many distilleries from around the world that kindly provided the images of their whiskies and distillery facilities reproduced here.

Special photography by Simon Murrell:

Front & back cover, 7, 9, 13 top right, 15 (glasses), 17 top right, 19 top left, 21 top left, 22-29, 32-37, 43-46, 152, 204, 222, 238

All other images are credited to their respective distilleries excluding the following:

48 Alan King Engraving/Alamy Stock Photo; 59 Auchentoshan 18YO, 21YO © The Whisky Exchange; 60 Auchentoshan Select © The Whisky Exchange; 62 BenRiach 10YO © The Whisky Exchange; 64 Benromach 15YO © The Whisky Exchange; 65 Benromach Chateau Cissac Finish, 1976 © The Whisky Exchange; 77 Deanston 12YO © The Whisky Exchange; 93 The Glenlivet Nadurra © The Whisky Exchange; 100 Glenrothes 1994 © The Whisky Exchange; 101 Glenrothes 1978, 1972 © The Whisky Exchange; 102 Glenturret 10YO © The Whisky Exchange; 103 Highland Park 30YO, Dark Origins, Einar © The Whisky Exchange; 107 Kilchoman Machir Bay © The Whisky Exchange; 107 AnCnoc 1994, 1975 © The Whisky Exchange; 112 above Cath Harries; 113 Cath Harries; 116 The Macallan Fine Oak 12YO, 1824 Series Amber © The Whisky Exchange; 117 The Macallan 1824 Series Gold, Ruby, Sienna © The Whisky Exchange; 119 Royal Lochnager Selected Reserve © The Whisky Exchange; 122 Talisker 57 North © The Whisky Exchange; 123 Tamdhu 25YO © The Whisky Exchange; 134 Cutty Sark 12YO, 25YO © The Whisky Exchange; 135 Famous Grouse, Famous Grouse Black Grouse © The Whisky Exchange; 136 Famous Grouse Gold Reserve, Famous Grouse Scottish Oak Finish © The Whisky Exchange; 136 J&B Rare © The Whisky Exchange; 146 Compass Box Flaming Heart © The Whisky Exchange; 150 The Six Isles © The Whisky Exchange; 151 Wemyss Peat Chimney 12YO © The Whisky Exchange; 154 Antiqua Print Gallery/Alamy Stock Photo; 166 High West American Prairie Reserve © The Whisky Exchange; 177 Rebel Yell Small Batch © The Whisky Exchange; 192 Rittenhouse 100 Proof © The Whisky Exchange; 194 Image Source/Alamy Stock Photo; 195 RTimages/Alamy Stock Photo; 197 Stranahan's Colorado Whiskey © The Whisky Exchange; 200 NPC Collectiom/Alamy Stock Photo; 206 Antiqua Print Gallery/Alamy Stock Photo; 213 Kilbeggan © The Whisky Exchange; 214 Locke's, Paddy © The Whisky Exchange; 214 Roe & Co © The Whisky Exchange; 224 NPC Collectiom/Alamy Stock Photo; 233 Yoichi, Akashi Red © The Whisky Exchange; 236 Hibiki 12YO, Nikka Rare Old Super © The Whisky Exchange; 240 Tetra Images/Alamy Stock Photo